NAOKI URASAWA'S

MONSTER

volume 5

Naoki Urasawa's
Monster
Volume 5

VIZ Signature Edition

STORY AND ART BY NAOKI URASAWA

English Adaptation/Agnes Yoshida
Translation/Hirotaka Kakiya
Touch-up Art & Lettering/Steve Dutro
Cover & Interior Design/Courtney Utt
Editor/Andy Nakatani

Managing Editor/Annette Roman
Editorial Director/Elizabeth Kawasaki
Editor in Chief/Alvin Lu
Sr. Director of Acquisitions/Rika Inouye
Sr. VP of Marketing/Liza Coppola
Exec. VP of Sales & Marketing/John Easum
Publisher/Hyoe Narita

Published by VIZ Media, LLC
P.O. Box 77010
San Francisco, CA 94107

VIZ Signature Edition
10 9 8 7 6 5 4 3 2 1
First printing, October 2006

www.viz.com
store.viz.com

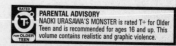

Naoki Urasawa's
Monster
Volume 5
After the Carnival

Story and Art by Naoki Urasawa

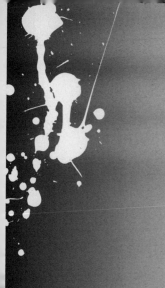

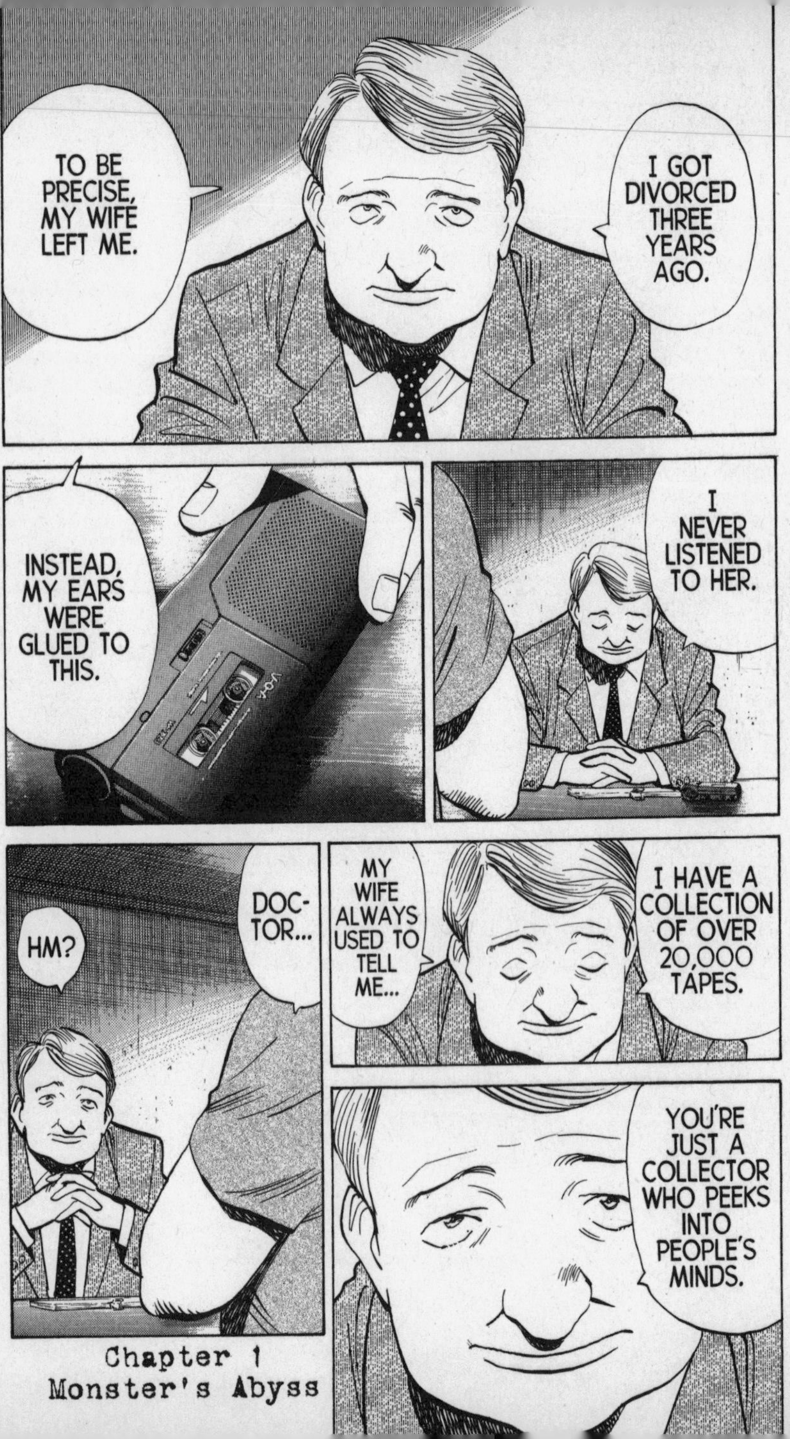
I GOT DIVORCED THREE YEARS AGO.
TO BE PRECISE, MY WIFE LEFT ME.
I NEVER LISTENED TO HER.
INSTEAD, MY EARS WERE GLUED TO THIS.
I HAVE A COLLECTION OF OVER 20,000 TAPES.
MY WIFE ALWAYS USED TO TELL ME...
YOU'RE JUST A COLLECTOR WHO PEEKS INTO PEOPLE'S MINDS.
DOC-TOR...
HM?

Chapter 1
Monster's Abyss

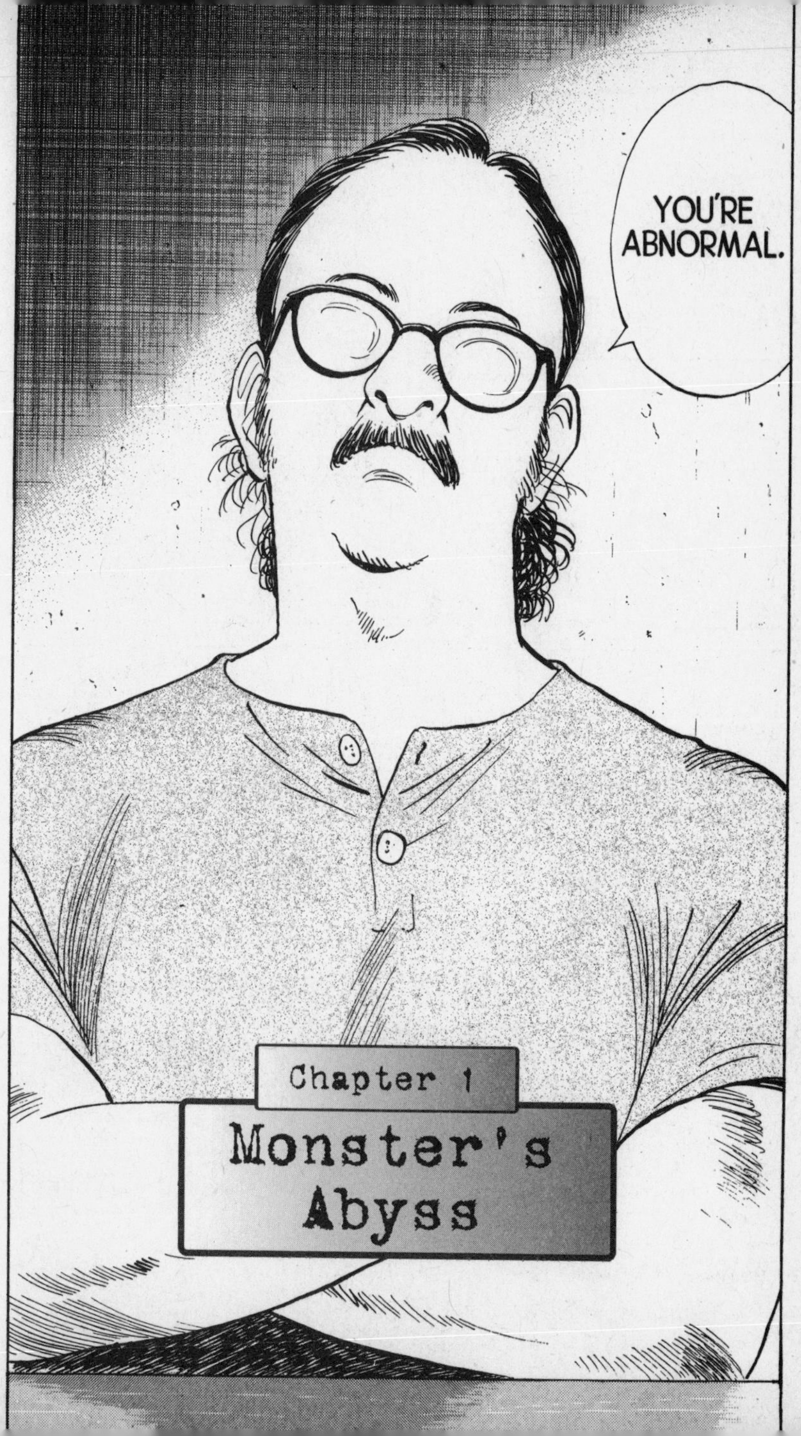
YOU'RE ABNORMAL.
Chapter 1
Monster's Abyss

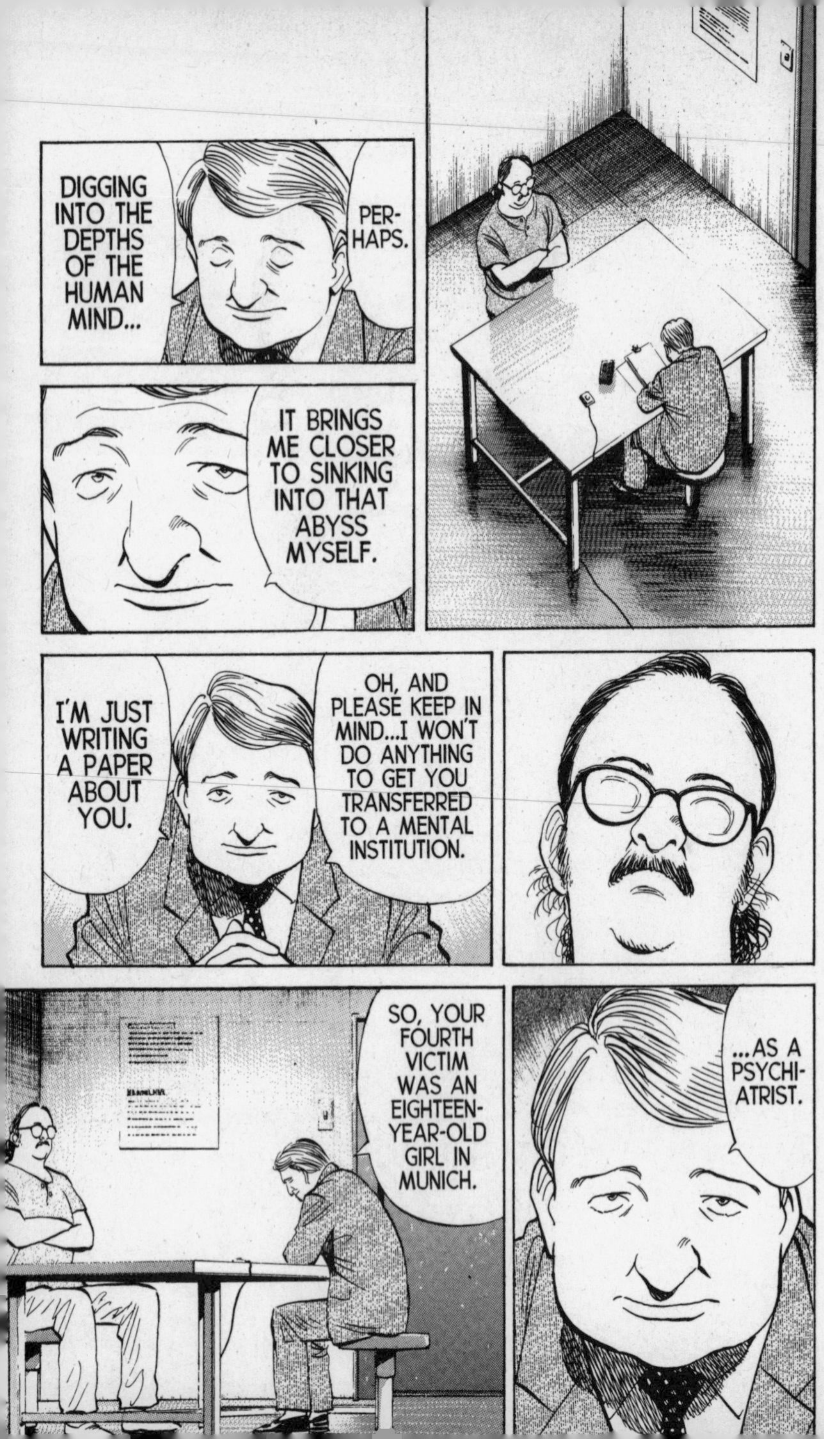
PER-HAPS.
DIGGING INTO THE DEPTHS OF THE HUMAN MIND...
IT BRINGS ME CLOSER TO SINKING INTO THAT ABYSS MYSELF.
OH, AND PLEASE KEEP IN MIND...I WON'T DO ANYTHING TO GET YOU TRANSFERRED TO A MENTAL INSTITUTION.
I'M JUST WRITING A PAPER ABOUT YOU.
...AS A PSYCHI-ATRIST.
SO, YOUR FOURTH VICTIM WAS AN EIGHTEEN-YEAR-OLD GIRL IN MUNICH.

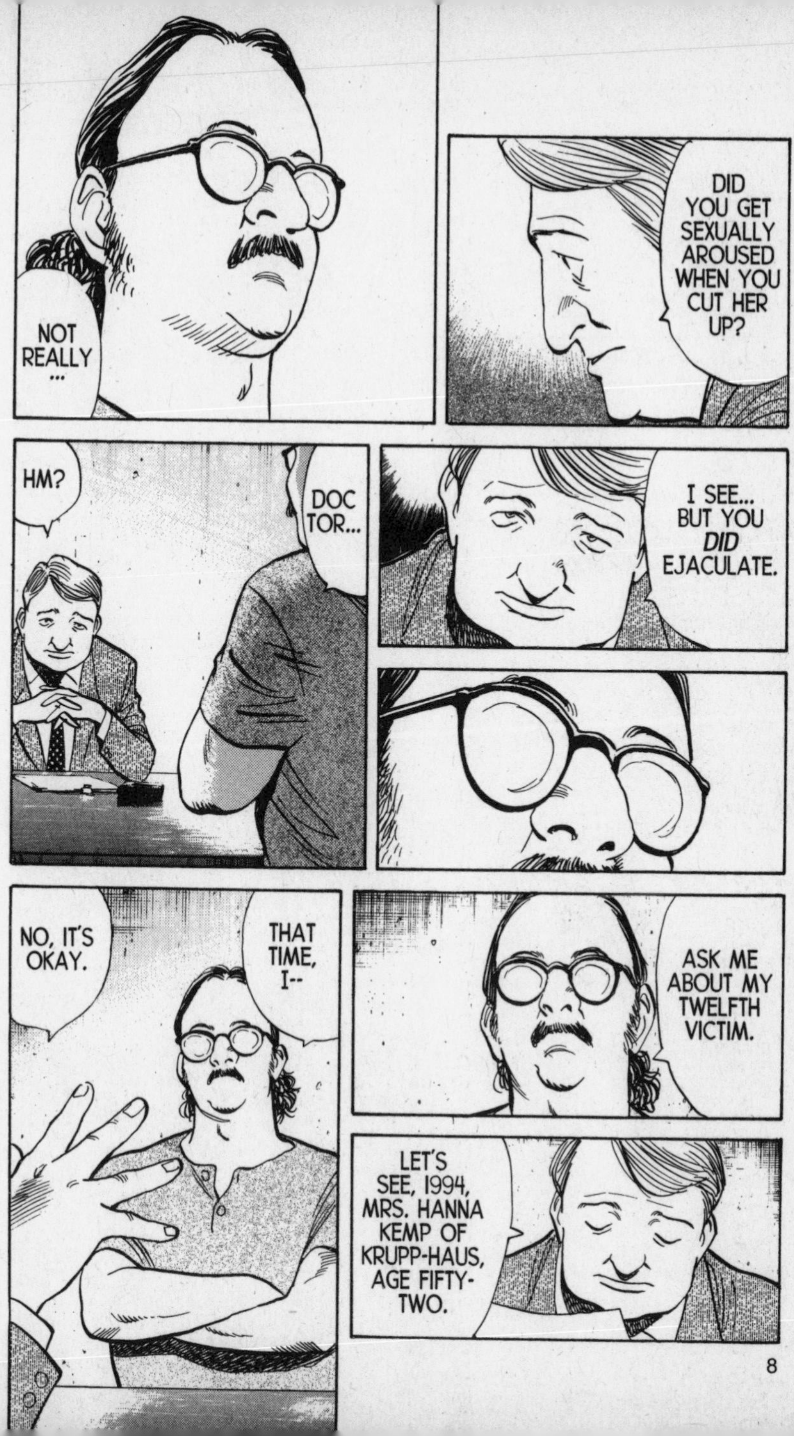
DID YOU GET SEXUALLY AROUSED WHEN YOU CUT HER UP?
NOT REALLY ...
I SEE... BUT YOU *DID* EJACULATE.
DOCTOR...
HM?
ASK ME ABOUT MY TWELFTH VICTIM.
LET'S SEE, 1994, MRS. HANNA KEMP OF KRUPP-HAUS, AGE FIFTY-TWO.
THAT TIME, I--
NO, IT'S OKAY.

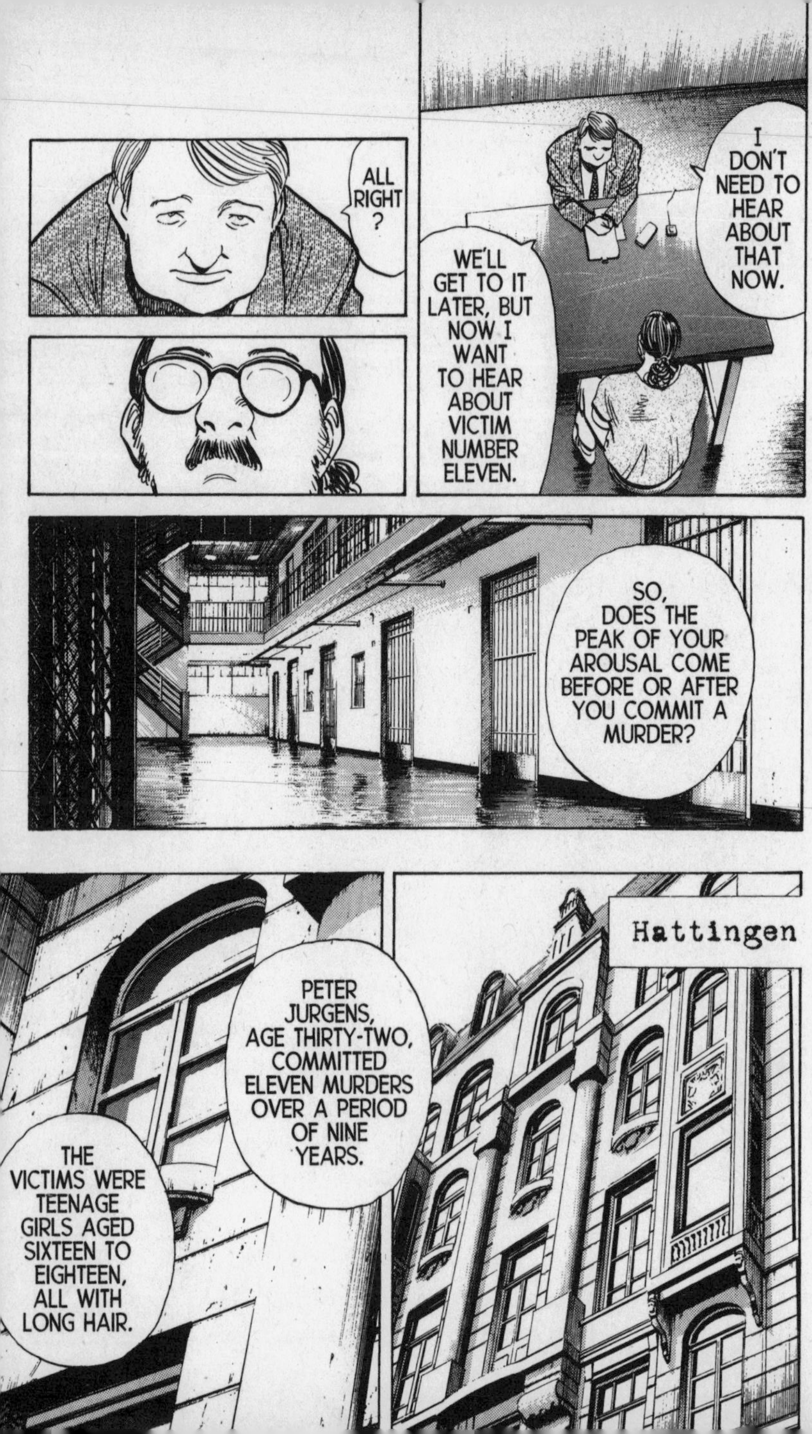
I DON'T NEED TO HEAR ABOUT THAT NOW.
WE'LL GET TO IT LATER, BUT NOW I WANT TO HEAR ABOUT VICTIM NUMBER ELEVEN.
ALL RIGHT?
SO, DOES THE PEAK OF YOUR AROUSAL COME BEFORE OR AFTER YOU COMMIT A MURDER?
Hattingen
PETER JURGENS, AGE THIRTY-TWO, COMMITTED ELEVEN MURDERS OVER A PERIOD OF NINE YEARS.
THE VICTIMS WERE TEENAGE GIRLS AGED SIXTEEN TO EIGHTEEN, ALL WITH LONG HAIR.

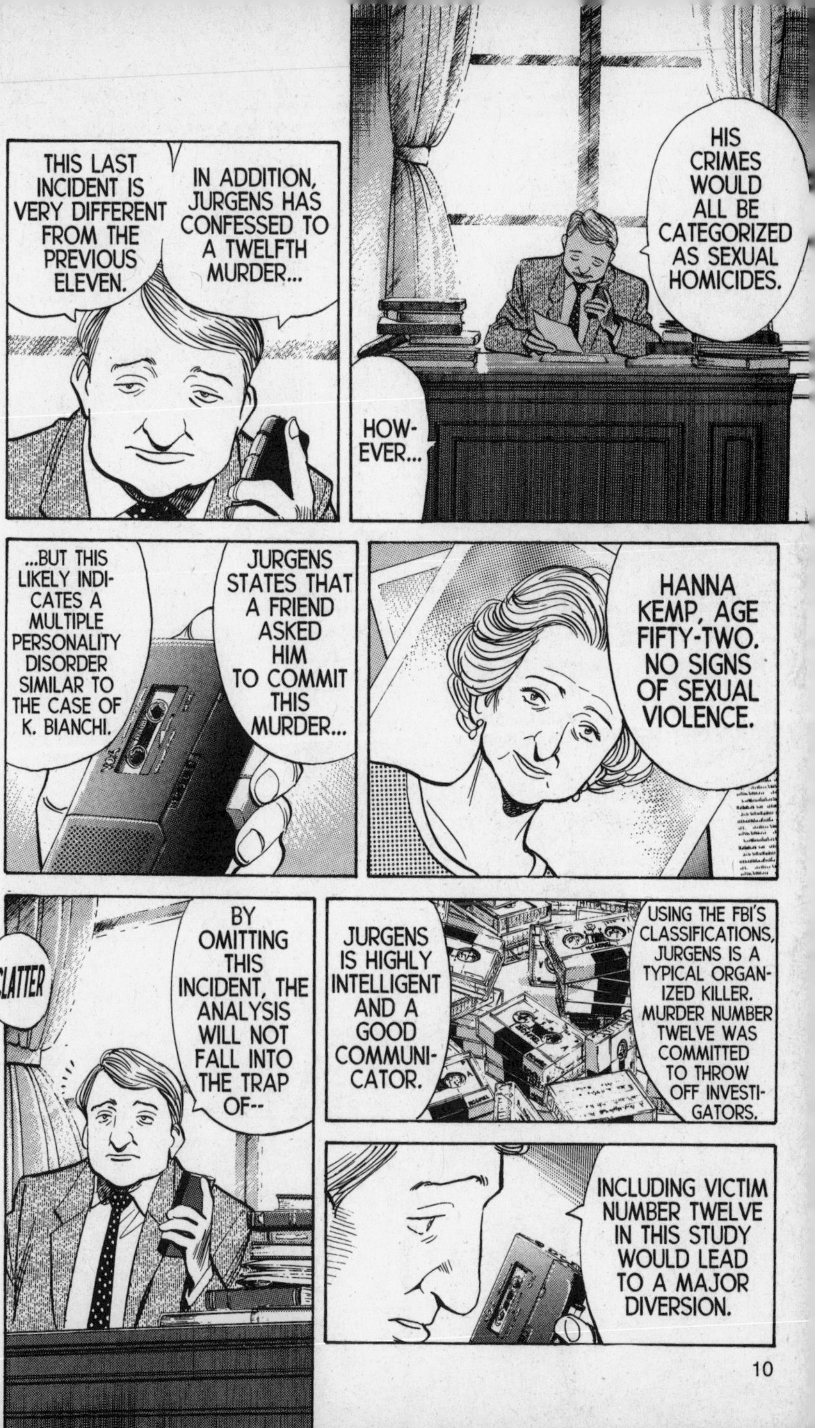
HIS CRIMES WOULD ALL BE CATEGORIZED AS SEXUAL HOMICIDES.
HOW-EVER...
IN ADDITION, JURGENS HAS CONFESSED TO A TWELFTH MURDER...
THIS LAST INCIDENT IS VERY DIFFERENT FROM THE PREVIOUS ELEVEN.
HANNA KEMP, AGE FIFTY-TWO. NO SIGNS OF SEXUAL VIOLENCE.
JURGENS STATES THAT A FRIEND ASKED HIM TO COMMIT THIS MURDER...
...BUT THIS LIKELY INDICATES A MULTIPLE PERSONALITY DISORDER SIMILAR TO THE CASE OF K. BIANCHI.
USING THE FBI'S CLASSIFICATIONS, JURGENS IS A TYPICAL ORGANIZED KILLER. MURDER NUMBER TWELVE WAS COMMITTED TO THROW OFF INVESTIGATORS.
JURGENS IS HIGHLY INTELLIGENT AND A GOOD COMMUNICATOR.
INCLUDING VICTIM NUMBER TWELVE IN THIS STUDY WOULD LEAD TO A MAJOR DIVERSION.
BY OMITTING THIS INCIDENT, THE ANALYSIS WILL NOT FALL INTO THE TRAP OF--
CLATTER

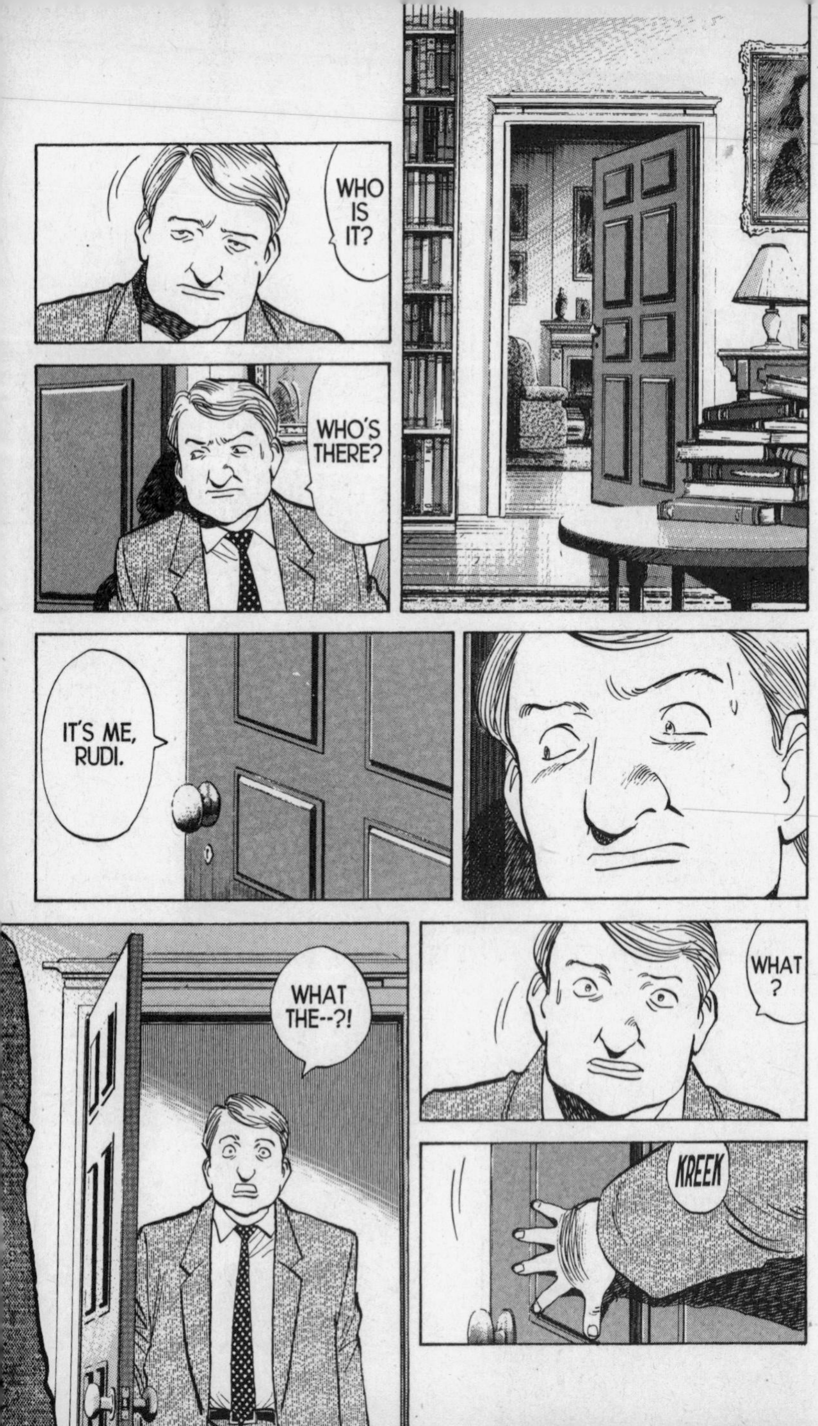
WHO IS IT?
WHO'S THERE?
IT'S ME, RUDI.
WHAT ?
KREEK
WHAT THE--?!

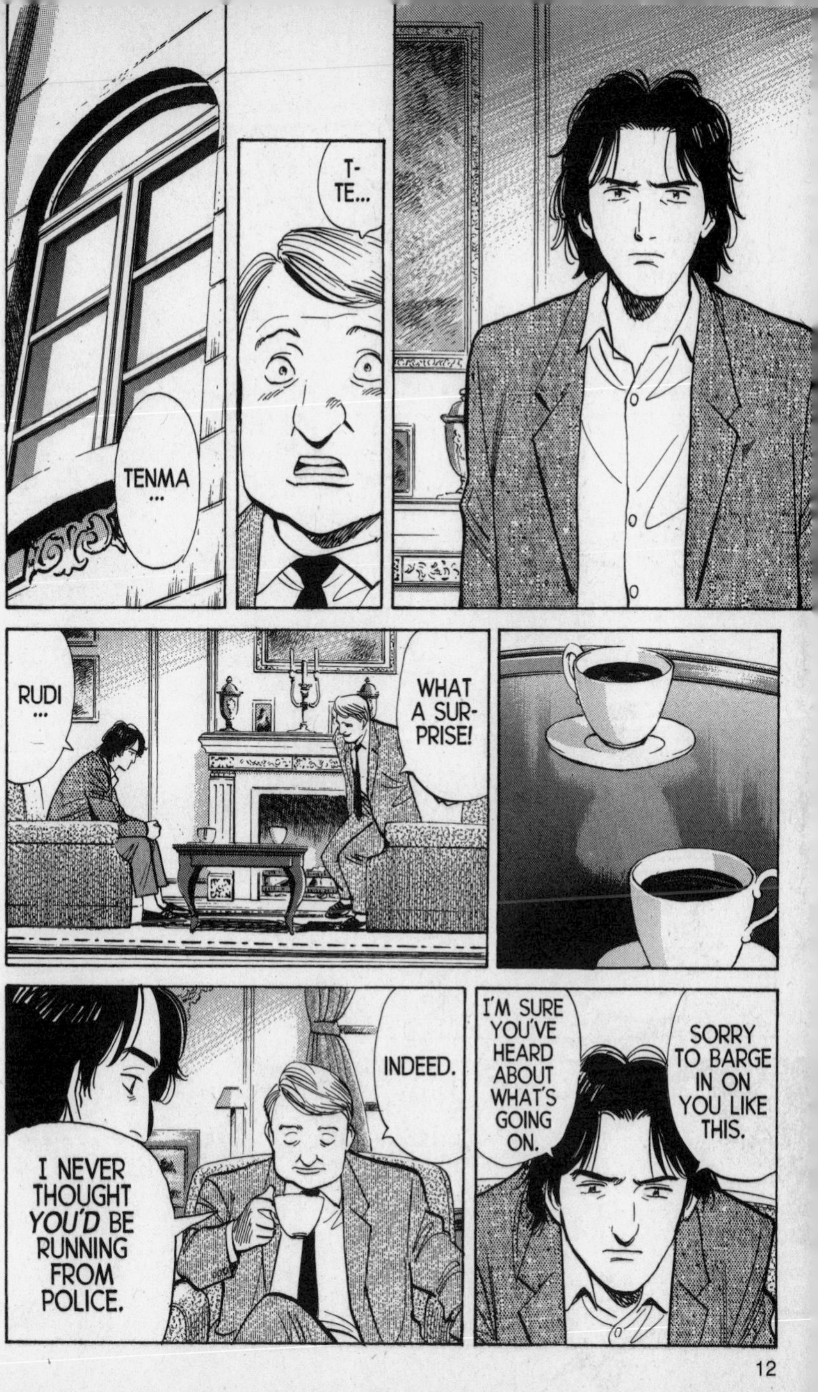
T-TE...
TENMA ...
WHAT A SURPRISE!
RUDI ...
SORRY TO BARGE IN ON YOU LIKE THIS.
I'M SURE YOU'VE HEARD ABOUT WHAT'S GOING ON.
INDEED.
I NEVER THOUGHT *YOU'D* BE RUNNING FROM POLICE.

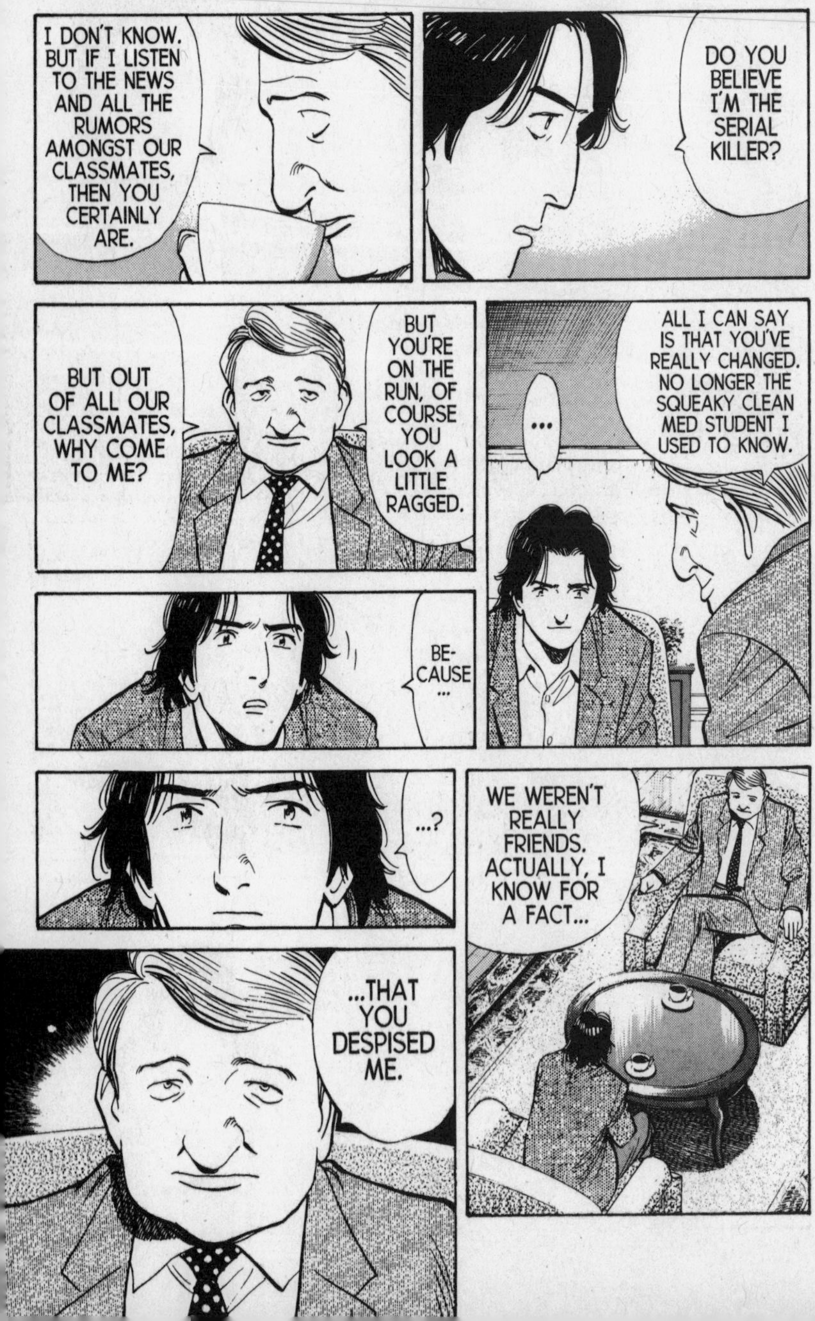
DO YOU BELIEVE I'M THE SERIAL KILLER?
I DON'T KNOW. BUT IF I LISTEN TO THE NEWS AND ALL THE RUMORS AMONGST OUR CLASSMATES, THEN YOU CERTAINLY ARE.
ALL I CAN SAY IS THAT YOU'VE REALLY CHANGED. NO LONGER THE SQUEAKY CLEAN MED STUDENT I USED TO KNOW.
...
BUT YOU'RE ON THE RUN, OF COURSE YOU LOOK A LITTLE RAGGED.
BUT OUT OF ALL OUR CLASSMATES, WHY COME TO ME?
BE-CAUSE...
WE WEREN'T REALLY FRIENDS. ACTUALLY, I KNOW FOR A FACT...
...?
...THAT YOU DESPISED ME.

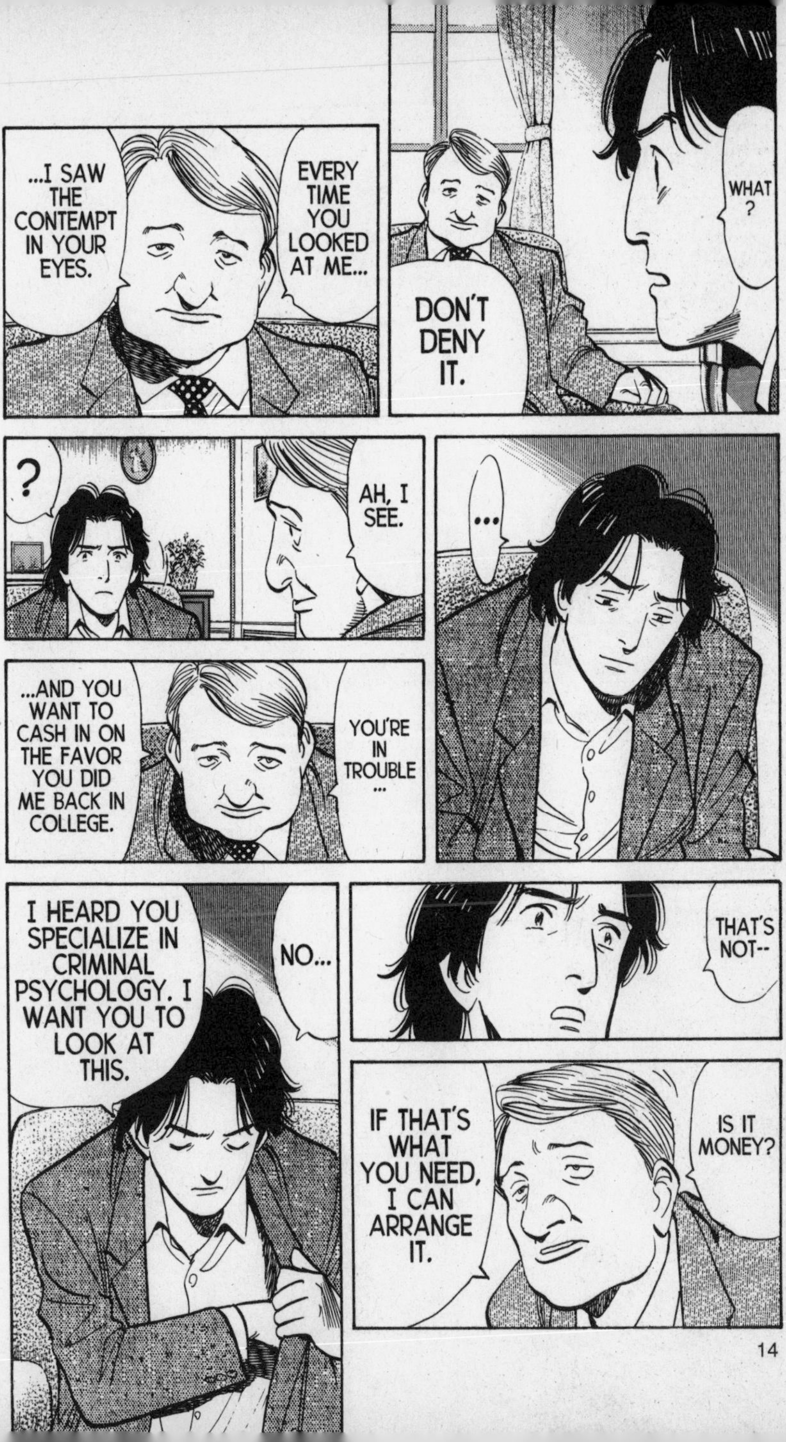
WHAT ?
DON'T DENY IT.
EVERY TIME YOU LOOKED AT ME...
...I SAW THE CONTEMPT IN YOUR EYES.
...
AH, I SEE.
?
YOU'RE IN TROUBLE...
...AND YOU WANT TO CASH IN ON THE FAVOR YOU DID ME BACK IN COLLEGE.
THAT'S NOT--
IS IT MONEY?
IF THAT'S WHAT YOU NEED, I CAN ARRANGE IT.
NO...
I HEARD YOU SPECIALIZE IN CRIMINAL PSYCHOLOGY. I WANT YOU TO LOOK AT THIS.

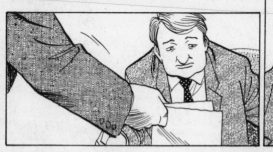

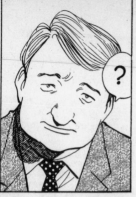

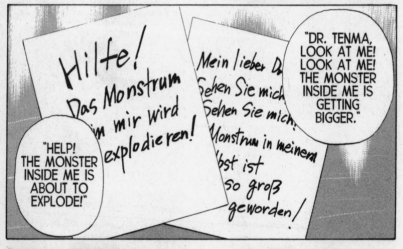

"HELP! THE MONSTER INSIDE ME IS ABOUT TO EXPLODE!"

"DR. TENMA, LOOK AT ME! LOOK AT ME! THE MONSTER INSIDE ME IS GETTING BIGGER."

Hilfe!
Das Monstrum
im mir wird
explodieren!

Mein lieber D...
Sehen Sie mich...
Sehen Sie mich...
Monstrum in meinem
...bst ist
so groß
geworden!

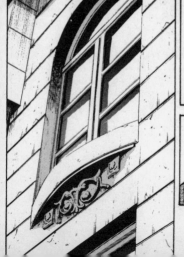

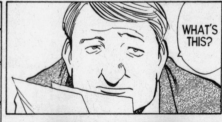

WHAT'S THIS?

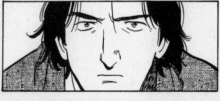

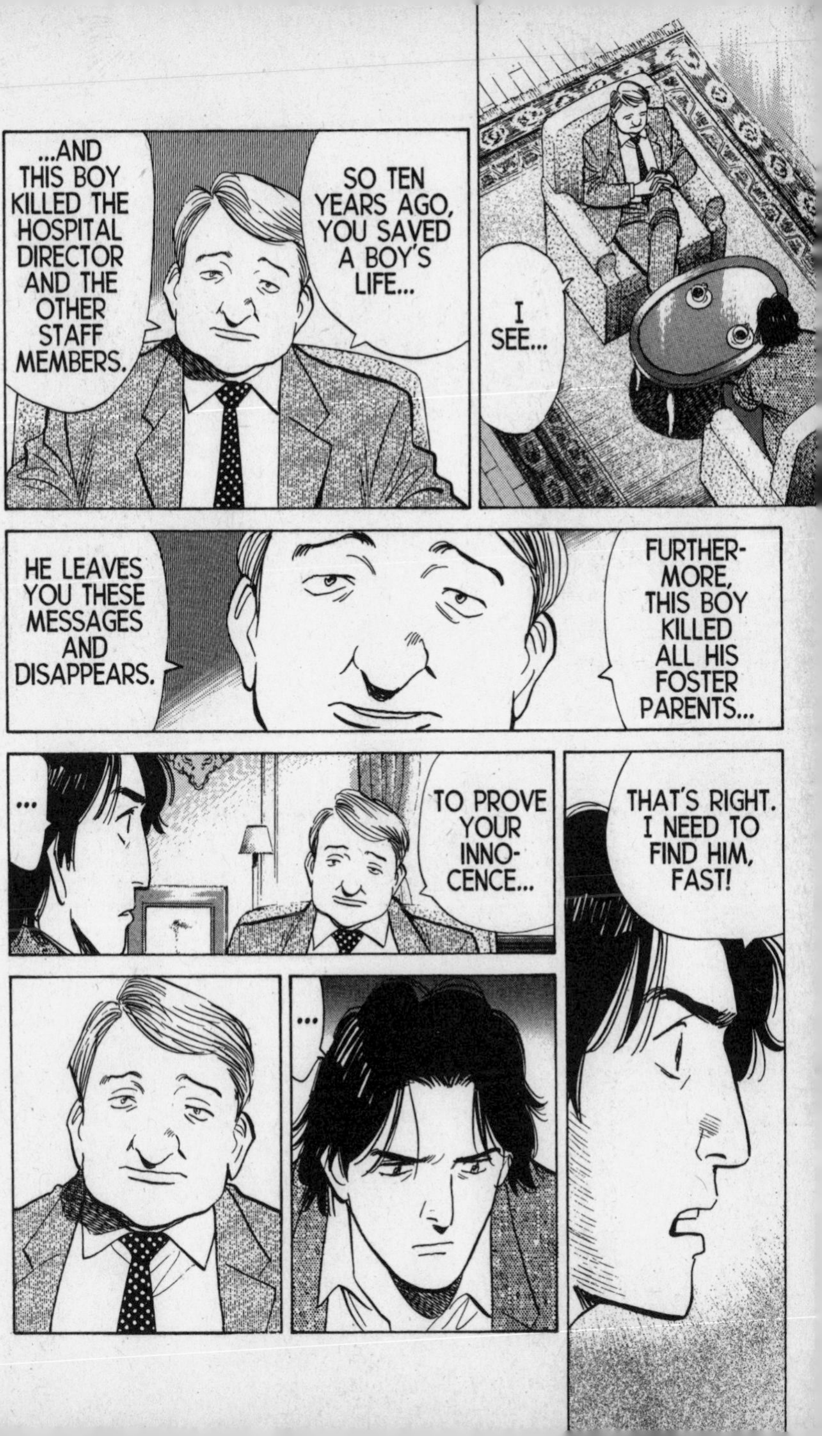
I SEE...
SO TEN YEARS AGO, YOU SAVED A BOY'S LIFE...
...AND THIS BOY KILLED THE HOSPITAL DIRECTOR AND THE OTHER STAFF MEMBERS.
FURTHER-MORE, THIS BOY KILLED ALL HIS FOSTER PARENTS...
HE LEAVES YOU THESE MESSAGES AND DISAPPEARS.
THAT'S RIGHT. I NEED TO FIND HIM, FAST!
TO PROVE YOUR INNO-CENCE...
...
...

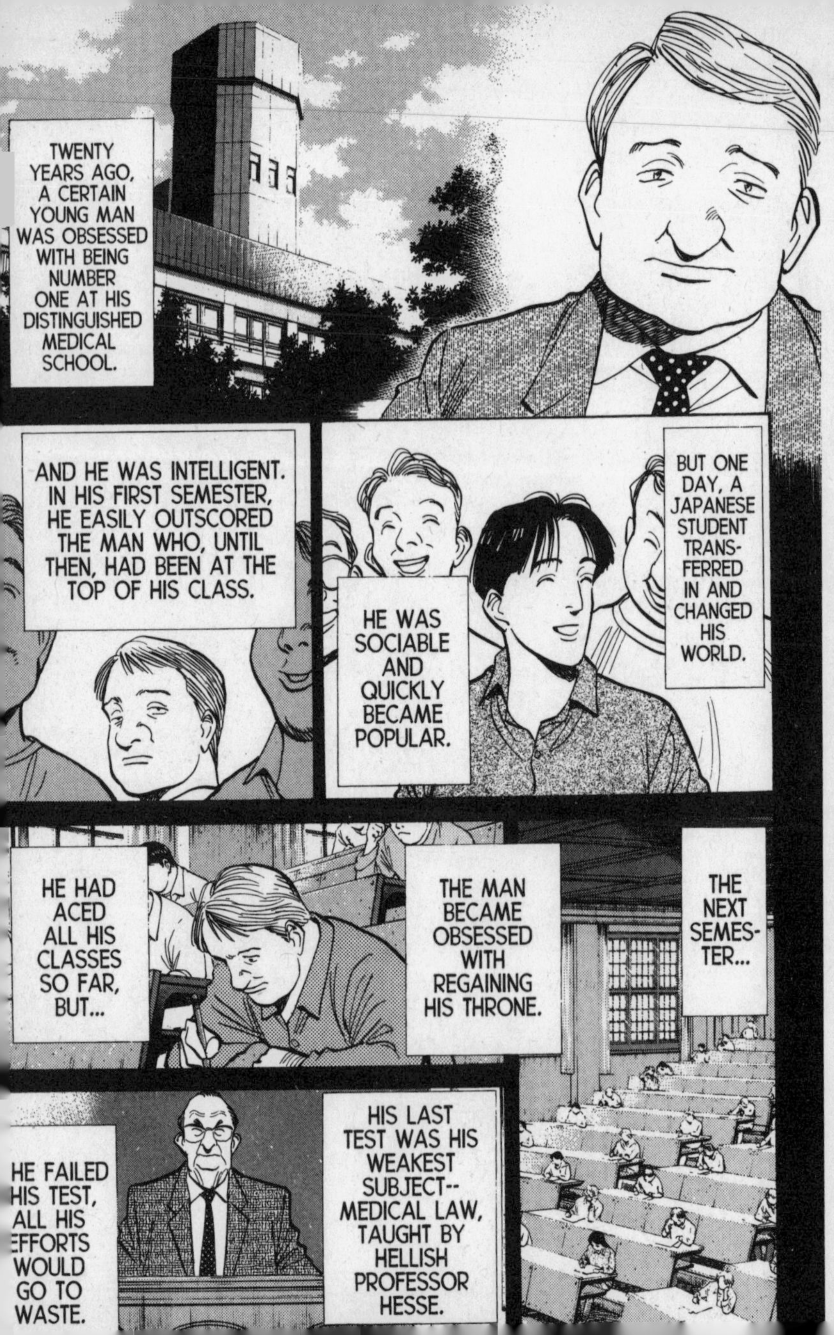
TWENTY YEARS AGO, A CERTAIN YOUNG MAN WAS OBSESSED WITH BEING NUMBER ONE AT HIS DISTINGUISHED MEDICAL SCHOOL.
BUT ONE DAY, A JAPANESE STUDENT TRANS-FERRED IN AND CHANGED HIS WORLD.
HE WAS SOCIABLE AND QUICKLY BECAME POPULAR.
AND HE WAS INTELLIGENT. IN HIS FIRST SEMESTER, HE EASILY OUTSCORED THE MAN WHO, UNTIL THEN, HAD BEEN AT THE TOP OF HIS CLASS.
THE NEXT SEMES-TER...
THE MAN BECAME OBSESSED WITH REGAINING HIS THRONE.
HE HAD ACED ALL HIS CLASSES SO FAR, BUT...
HIS LAST TEST WAS HIS WEAKEST SUBJECT-- MEDICAL LAW, TAUGHT BY HELLISH PROFESSOR HESSE.
HE FAILED HIS TEST, ALL HIS EFFORTS WOULD GO TO WASTE.

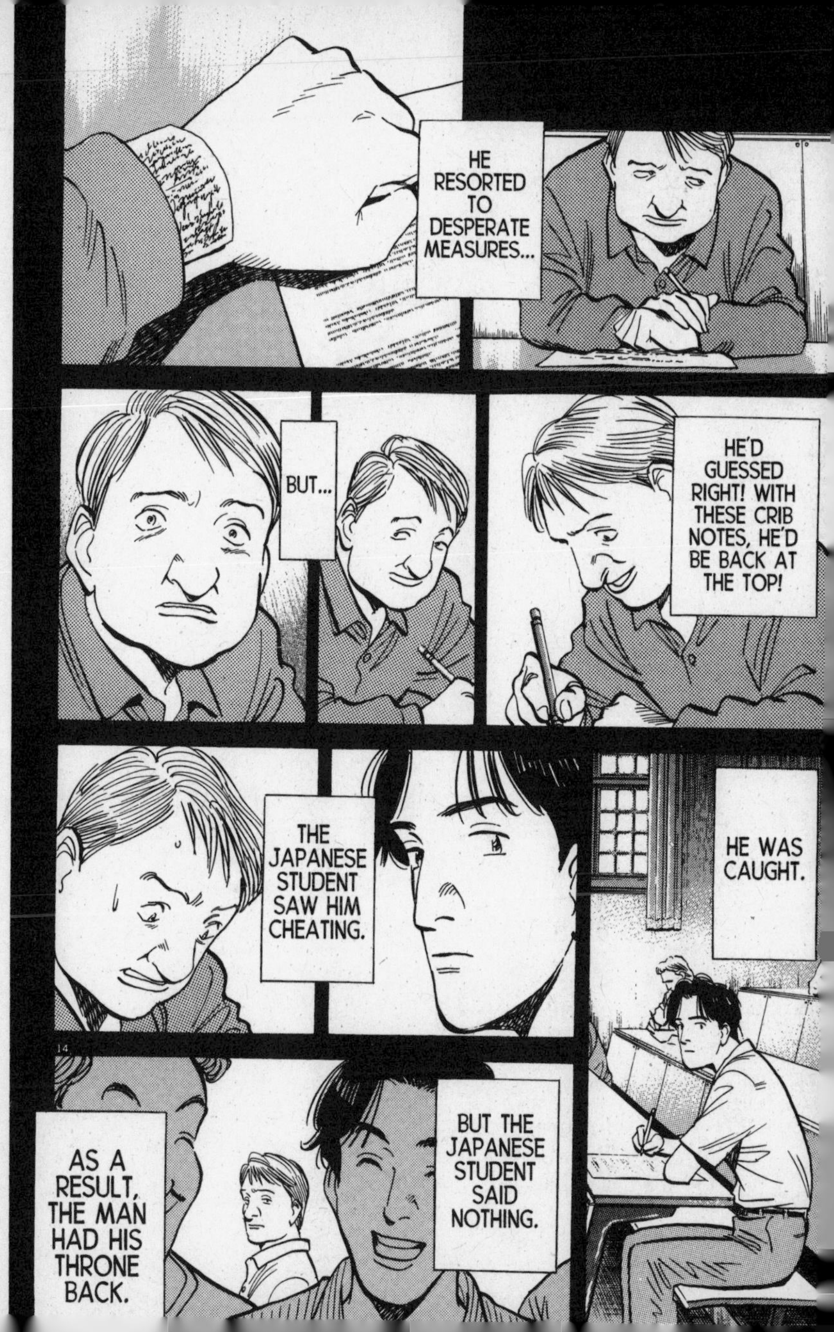
HE RESORTED TO DESPERATE MEASURES...
HE'D GUESSED RIGHT! WITH THESE CRIB NOTES, HE'D BE BACK AT THE TOP!
BUT...
HE WAS CAUGHT.
THE JAPANESE STUDENT SAW HIM CHEATING.
BUT THE JAPANESE STUDENT SAID NOTHING.
AS A RESULT, THE MAN HAD HIS THRONE BACK.

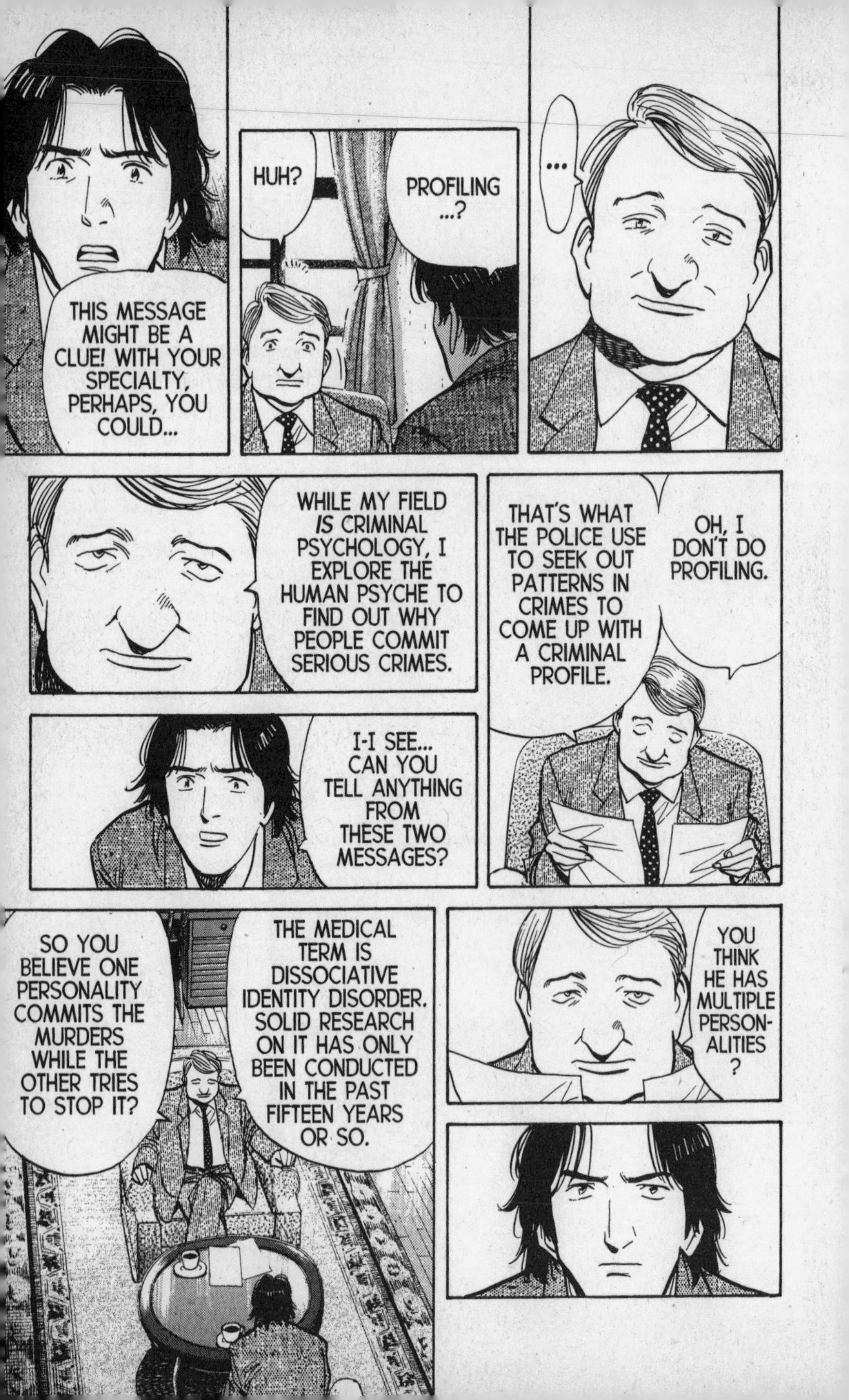

...
PROFILING ...?
HUH?
THIS MESSAGE MIGHT BE A CLUE! WITH YOUR SPECIALTY, PERHAPS, YOU COULD...
OH, I DON'T DO PROFILING.
THAT'S WHAT THE POLICE USE TO SEEK OUT PATTERNS IN CRIMES TO COME UP WITH A CRIMINAL PROFILE.
WHILE MY FIELD *IS* CRIMINAL PSYCHOLOGY, I EXPLORE THE HUMAN PSYCHE TO FIND OUT WHY PEOPLE COMMIT SERIOUS CRIMES.
I-I SEE... CAN YOU TELL ANYTHING FROM THESE TWO MESSAGES?
YOU THINK HE HAS MULTIPLE PERSON-ALITIES ?
THE MEDICAL TERM IS DISSOCIATIVE IDENTITY DISORDER. SOLID RESEARCH ON IT HAS ONLY BEEN CONDUCTED IN THE PAST FIFTEEN YEARS OR SO.
SO YOU BELIEVE ONE PERSONALITY COMMITS THE MURDERS WHILE THE OTHER TRIES TO STOP IT?

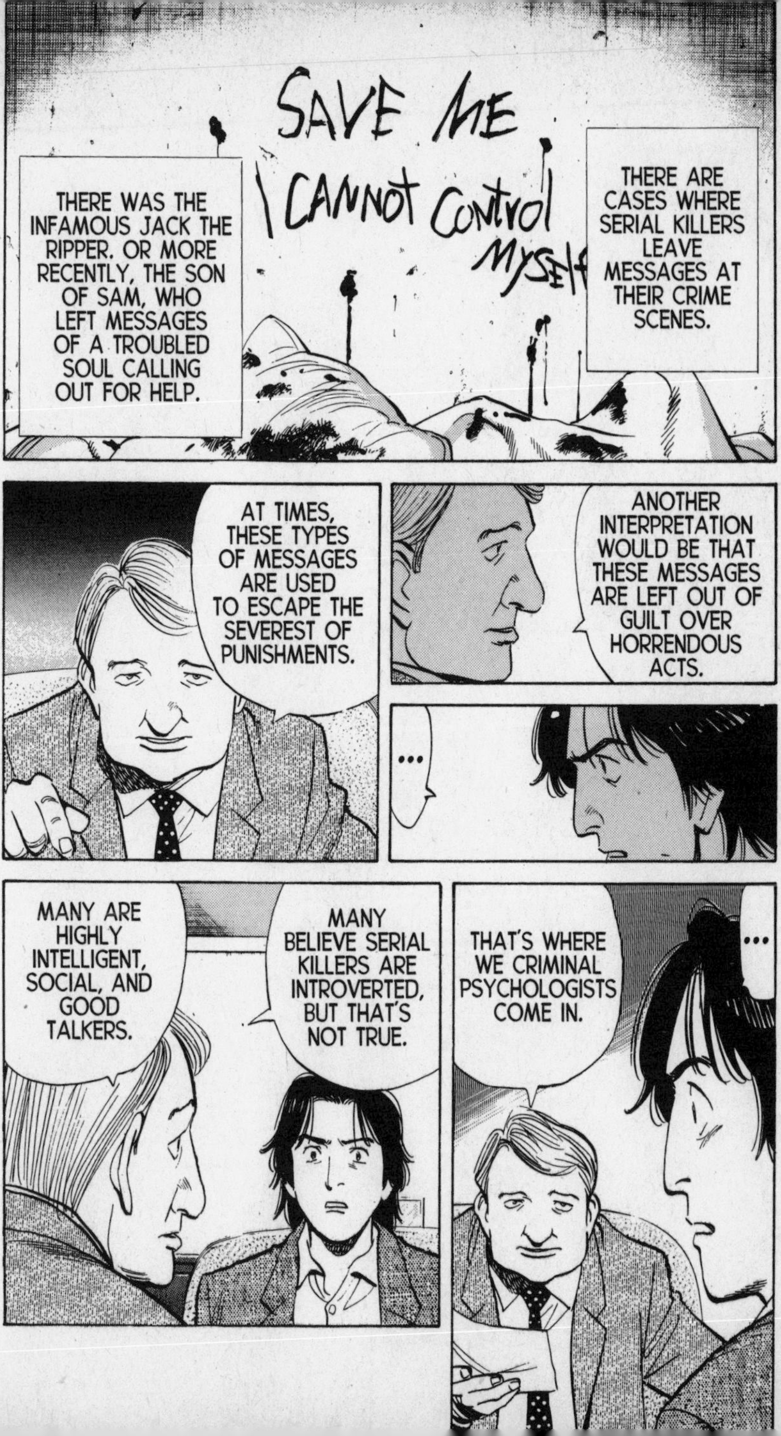
THERE ARE CASES WHERE SERIAL KILLERS LEAVE MESSAGES AT THEIR CRIME SCENES.
SAVE ME
I CANNOT Control
MYSElf
THERE WAS THE INFAMOUS JACK THE RIPPER. OR MORE RECENTLY, THE SON OF SAM, WHO LEFT MESSAGES OF A TROUBLED SOUL CALLING OUT FOR HELP.
ANOTHER INTERPRETATION WOULD BE THAT THESE MESSAGES ARE LEFT OUT OF GUILT OVER HORRENDOUS ACTS.
...
AT TIMES, THESE TYPES OF MESSAGES ARE USED TO ESCAPE THE SEVEREST OF PUNISHMENTS.
...
THAT'S WHERE WE CRIMINAL PSYCHOLOGISTS COME IN.
MANY BELIEVE SERIAL KILLERS ARE INTROVERTED, BUT THAT'S NOT TRUE.
MANY ARE HIGHLY INTELLIGENT, SOCIAL, AND GOOD TALKERS.

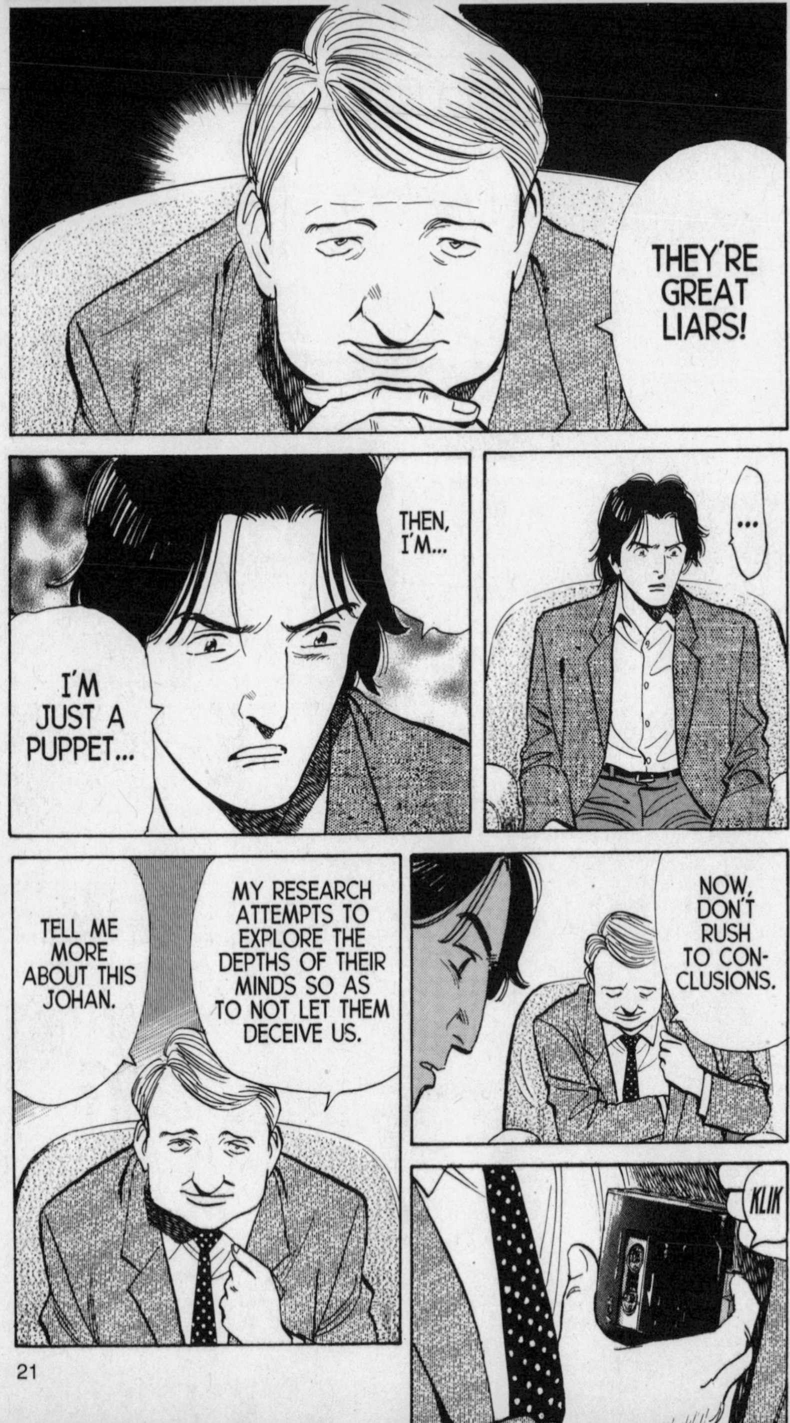
THEY'RE GREAT LIARS!
...
THEN, I'M...
I'M JUST A PUPPET...
NOW, DON'T RUSH TO CON- CLUSIONS.
KLIK
MY RESEARCH ATTEMPTS TO EXPLORE THE DEPTHS OF THEIR MINDS SO AS TO NOT LET THEM DECEIVE US.
TELL ME MORE ABOUT THIS JOHAN.

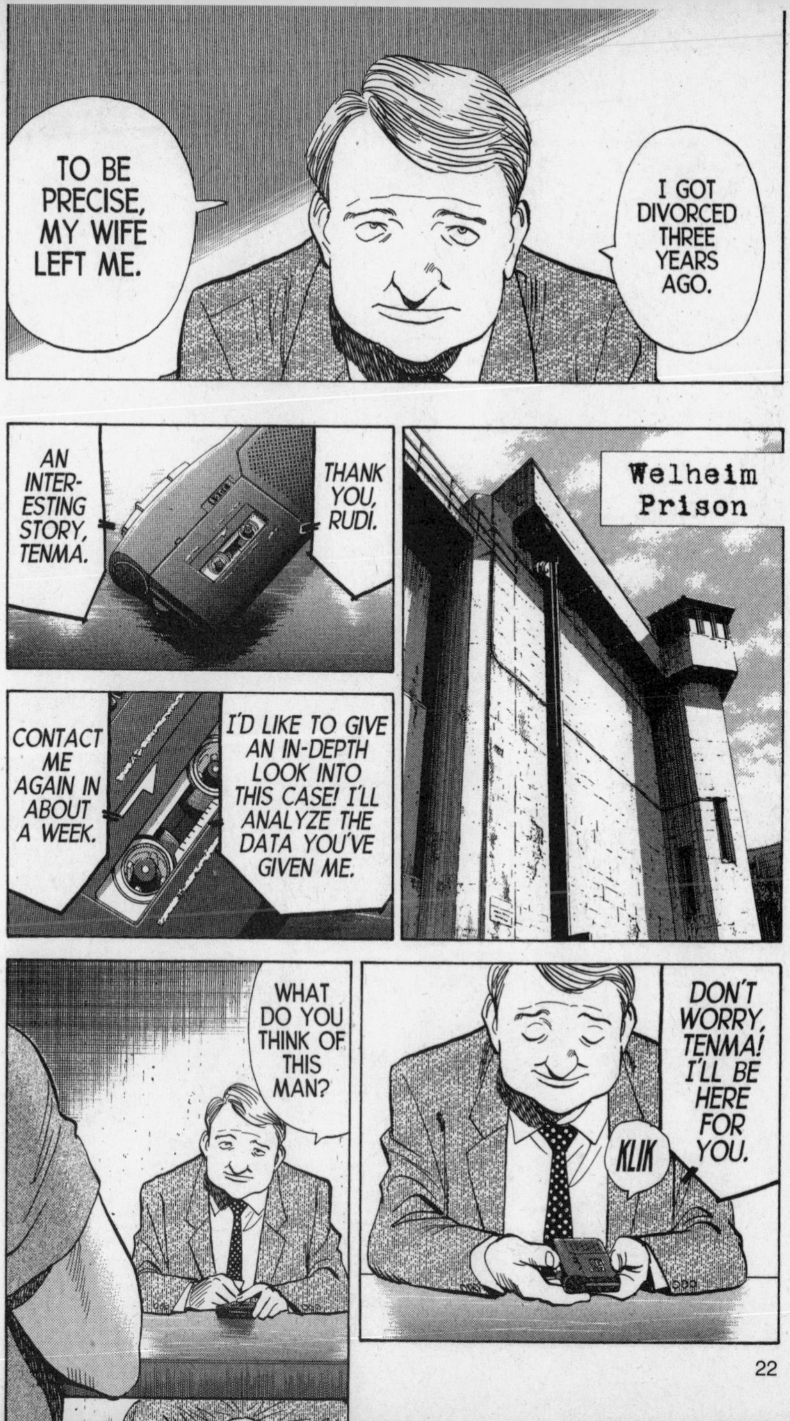
I GOT DIVORCED THREE YEARS AGO.
TO BE PRECISE, MY WIFE LEFT ME.
Welheim Prison
THANK YOU, RUDI.
AN INTERESTING STORY, TENMA.
I'D LIKE TO GIVE AN IN-DEPTH LOOK INTO THIS CASE! I'LL ANALYZE THE DATA YOU'VE GIVEN ME.
CONTACT ME AGAIN IN ABOUT A WEEK.
DON'T WORRY, TENMA! I'LL BE HERE FOR YOU.
KLIK
WHAT DO YOU THINK OF THIS MAN?

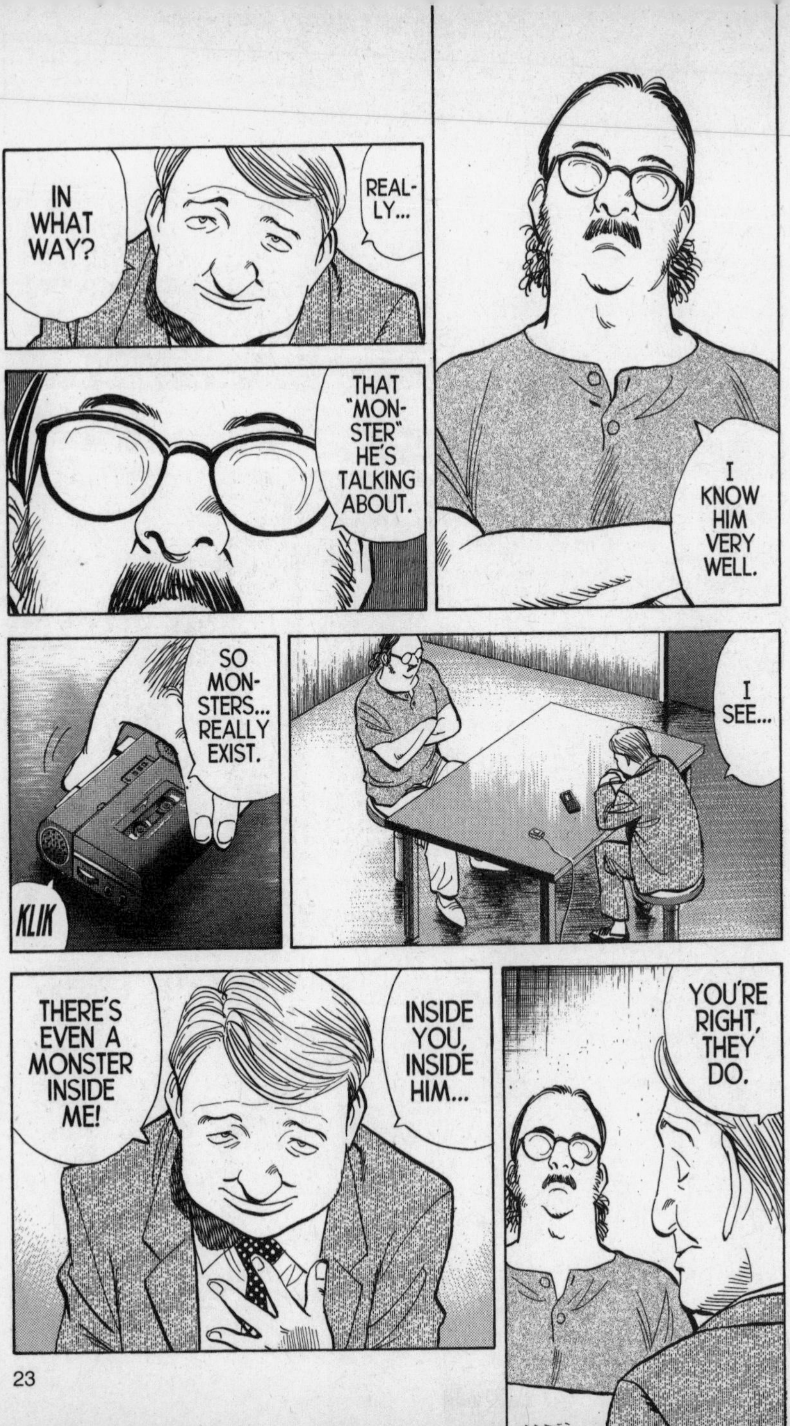
I KNOW HIM VERY WELL.
REAL-LY...
IN WHAT WAY?
THAT "MON-STER" HE'S TALKING ABOUT.
I SEE...
SO MON-STERS... REALLY EXIST.
KLIK
YOU'RE RIGHT, THEY DO.
INSIDE YOU, INSIDE HIM...
THERE'S EVEN A MONSTER INSIDE ME!

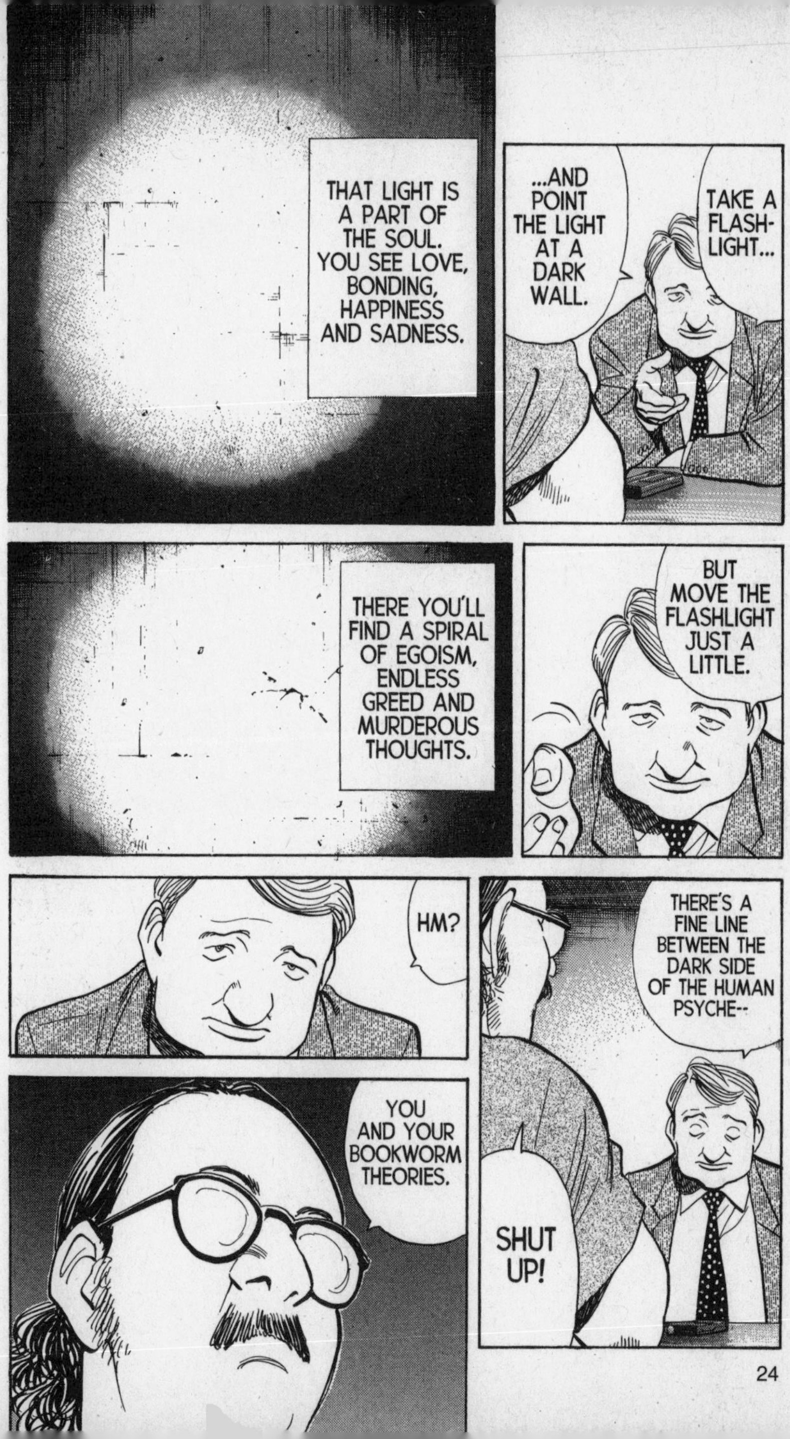
TAKE A FLASH-LIGHT...
...AND POINT THE LIGHT AT A DARK WALL.
THAT LIGHT IS A PART OF THE SOUL. YOU SEE LOVE, BONDING, HAPPINESS AND SADNESS.
BUT MOVE THE FLASHLIGHT JUST A LITTLE.
THERE YOU'LL FIND A SPIRAL OF EGOISM, ENDLESS GREED AND MURDEROUS THOUGHTS.
THERE'S A FINE LINE BETWEEN THE DARK SIDE OF THE HUMAN PSYCHE--
SHUT UP!
HM?
YOU AND YOUR BOOKWORM THEORIES.

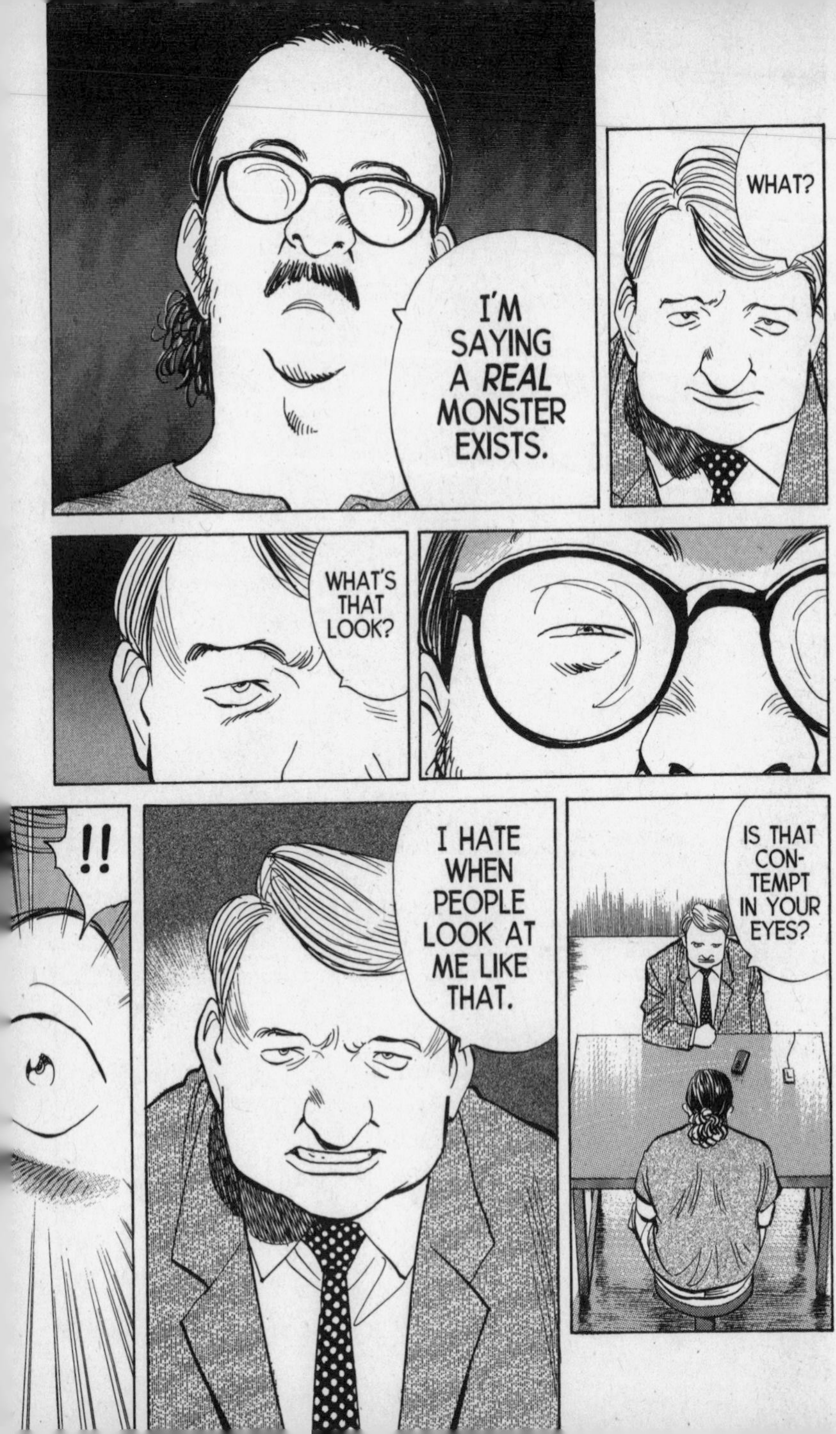
WHAT?
I'M SAYING A REAL MONSTER EXISTS.
WHAT'S THAT LOOK?
IS THAT CON-TEMPT IN YOUR EYES?
I HATE WHEN PEOPLE LOOK AT ME LIKE THAT.
!!

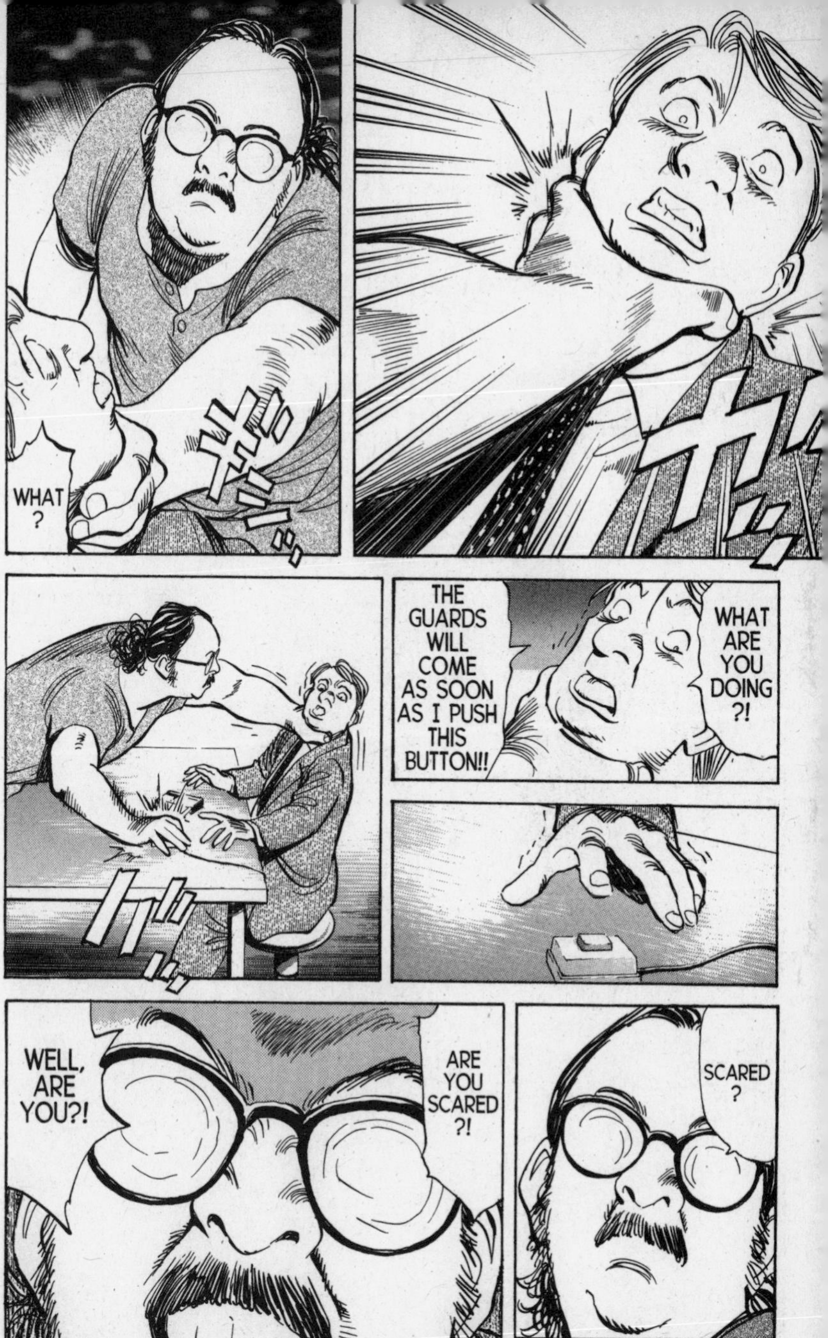
WHAT ?
WHAT ARE YOU DOING ?!
THE GUARDS WILL COME AS SOON AS I PUSH THIS BUTTON!!
SCARED ?
ARE YOU SCARED ?!
WELL, ARE YOU?!

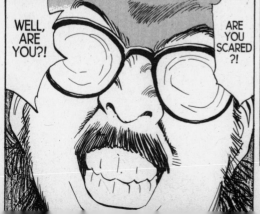

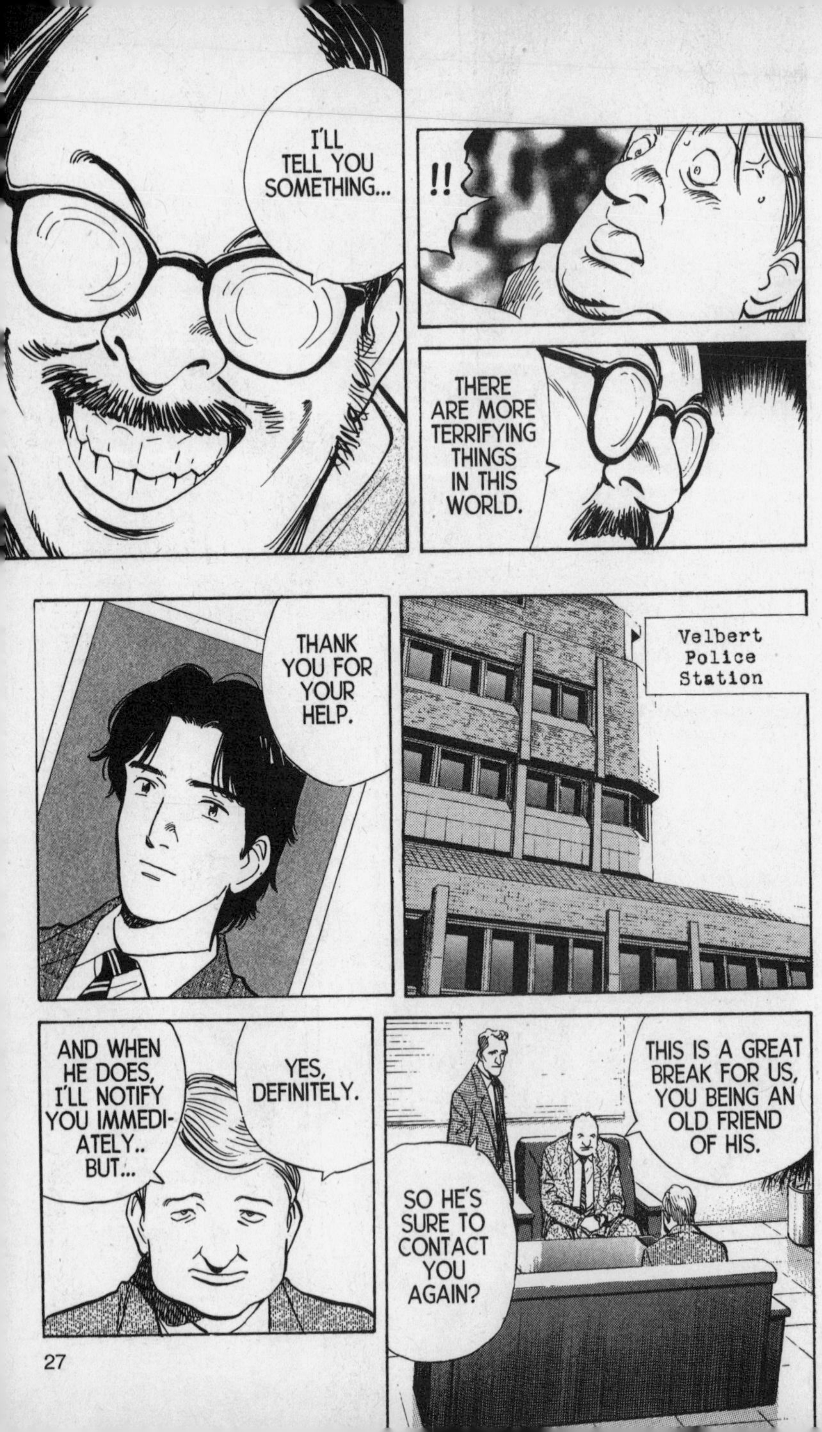
!!
THERE ARE MORE TERRIFYING THINGS IN THIS WORLD.
I'LL TELL YOU SOMETHING...
Velbert Police Station
THANK YOU FOR YOUR HELP.
THIS IS A GREAT BREAK FOR US, YOU BEING AN OLD FRIEND OF HIS.
SO HE'S SURE TO CONTACT YOU AGAIN?
YES, DEFINITELY.
AND WHEN HE DOES, I'LL NOTIFY YOU IMMEDI-ATELY.. BUT...

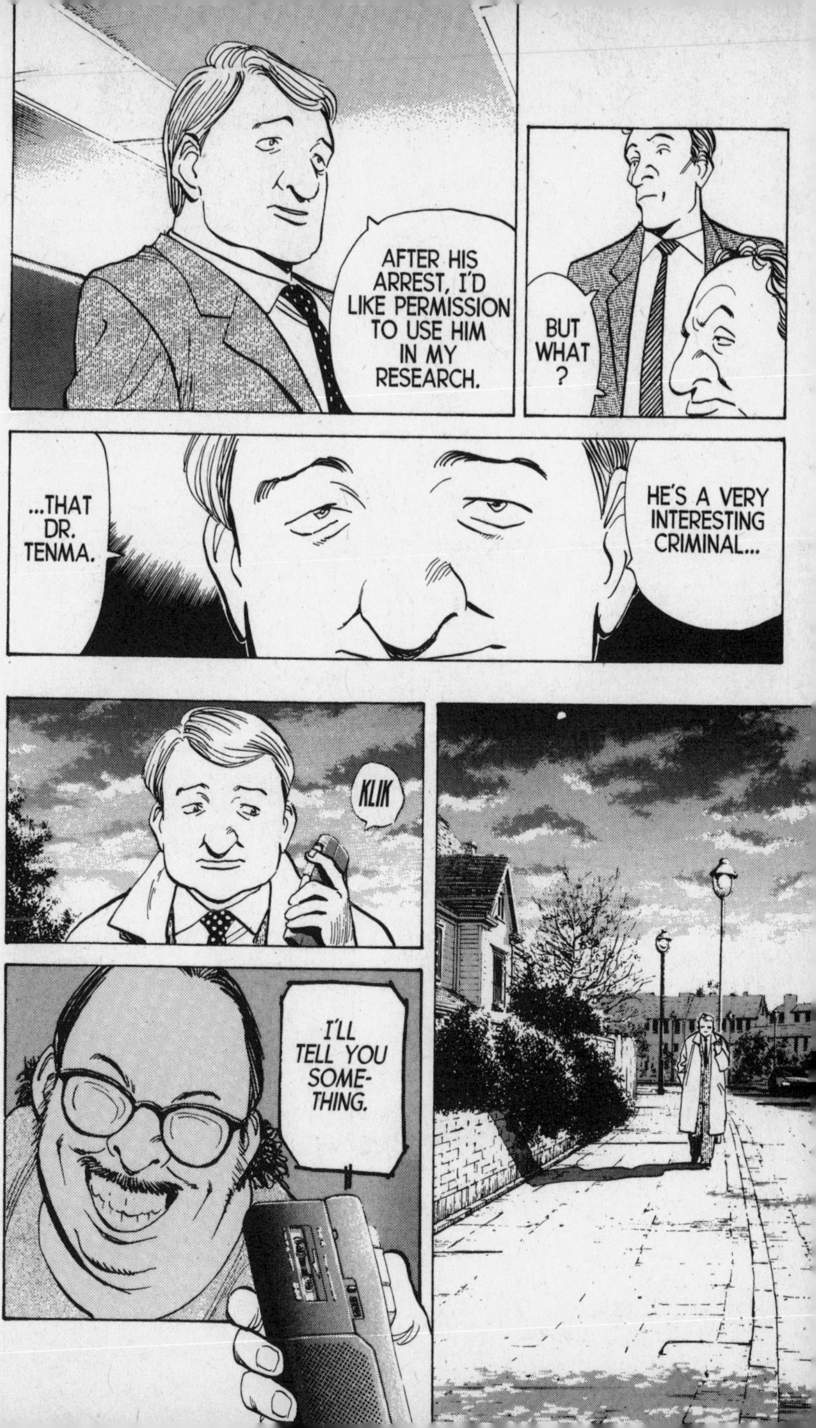
BUT WHAT?
AFTER HIS ARREST, I'D LIKE PERMISSION TO USE HIM IN MY RESEARCH.
HE'S A VERY INTERESTING CRIMINAL...
...THAT DR. TENMA.
KLIK
I'LL TELL YOU SOME-THING.

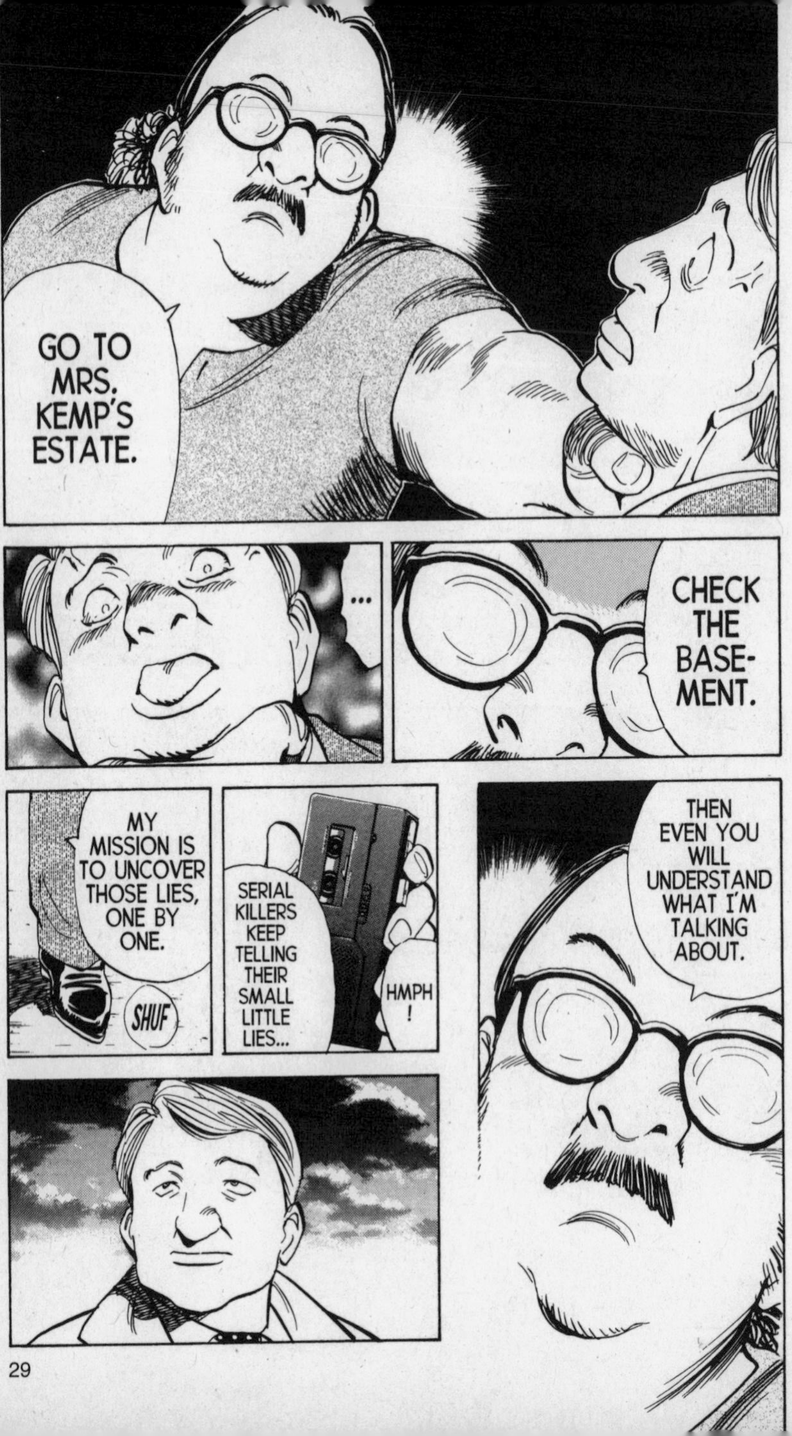
GO TO MRS. KEMP'S ESTATE.
CHECK THE BASEMENT.
...
THEN EVEN YOU WILL UNDERSTAND WHAT I'M TALKING ABOUT.
SERIAL KILLERS KEEP TELLING THEIR SMALL LITTLE LIES...
HMPH!
MY MISSION IS TO UNCOVER THOSE LIES, ONE BY ONE.
SHUF

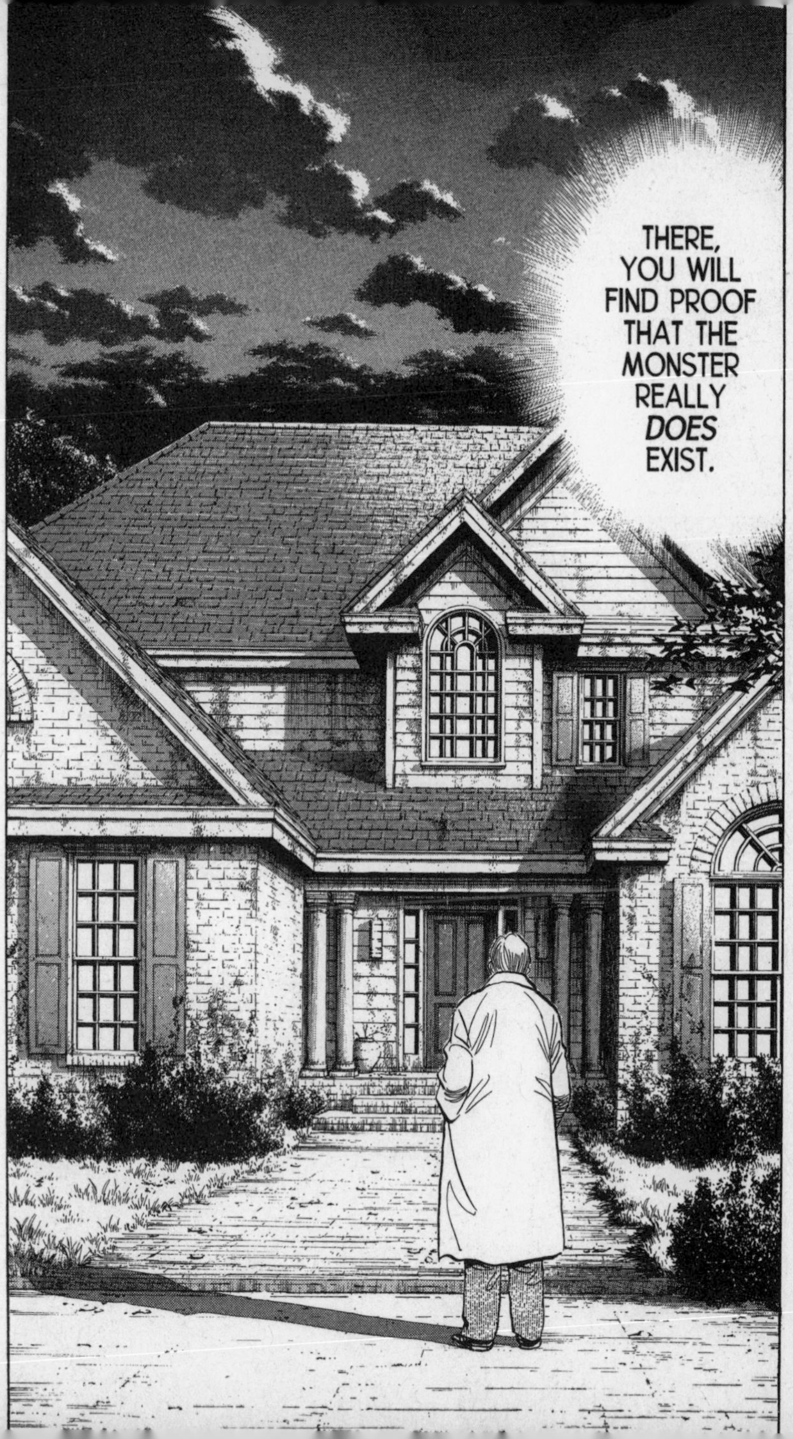
THERE, YOU WILL FIND PROOF THAT THE MONSTER REALLY *DOES* EXIST.

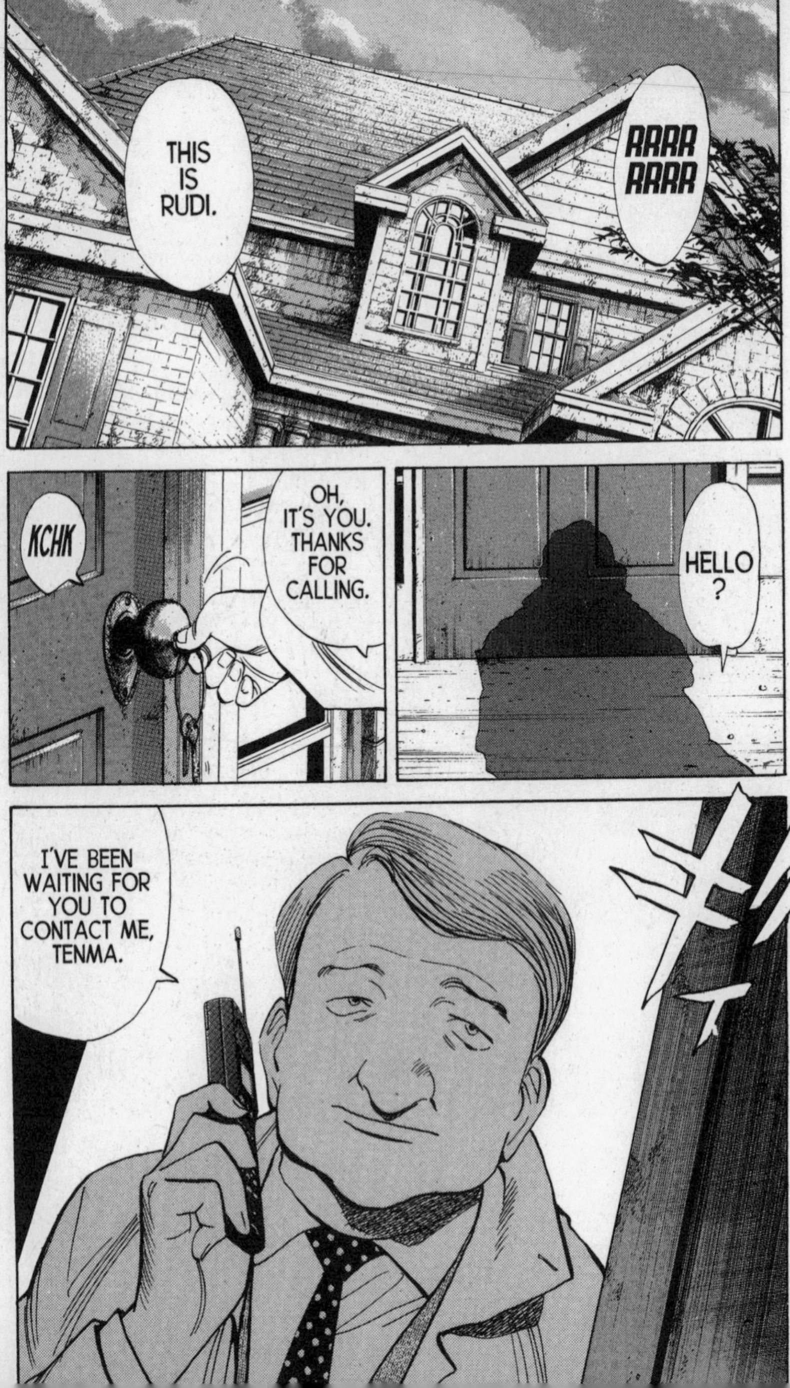
RRRR RRRR
THIS IS RUDI.
HELLO?
OH, IT'S YOU. THANKS FOR CALLING.
KCHK
I'VE BEEN WAITING FOR YOU TO CONTACT ME, TENMA.

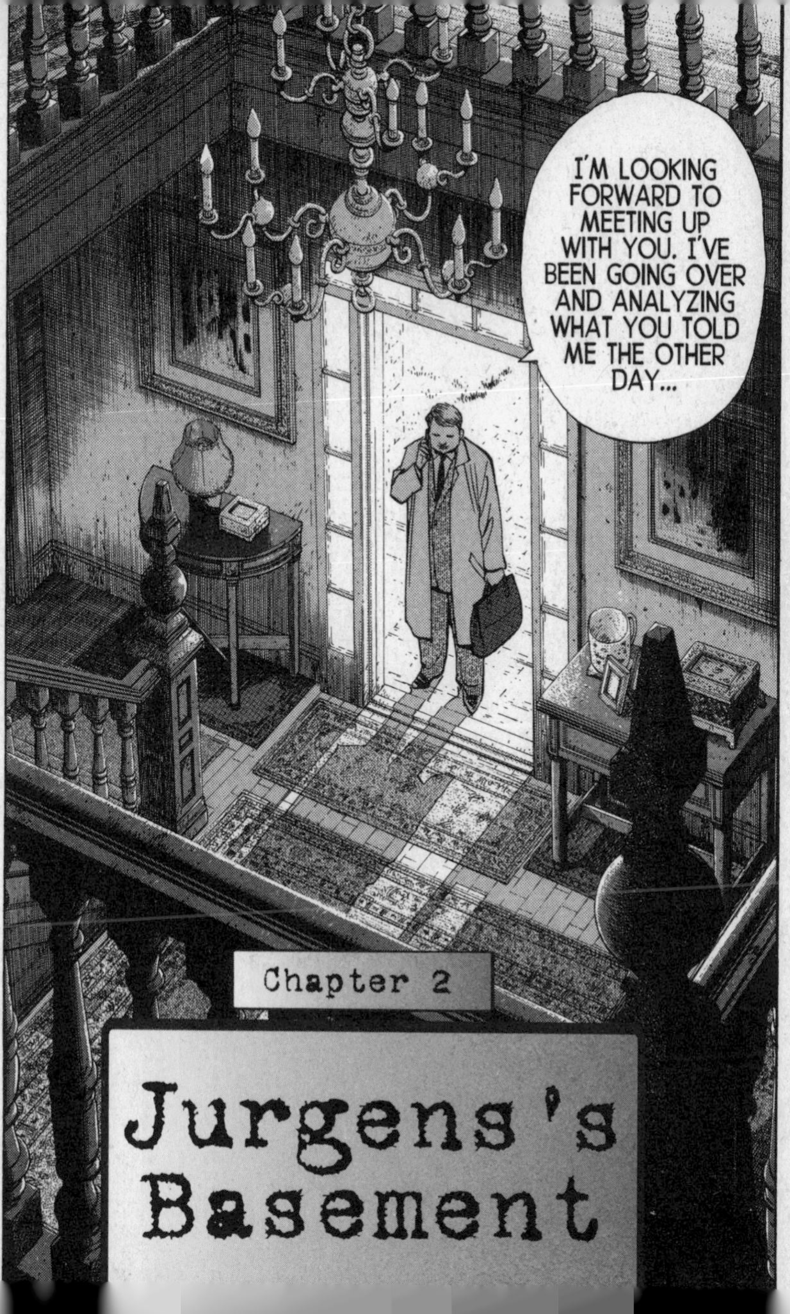
I'M LOOKING FORWARD TO MEETING UP WITH YOU. I'VE BEEN GOING OVER AND ANALYZING WHAT YOU TOLD ME THE OTHER DAY...
Chapter 2
Jurgens's Basement

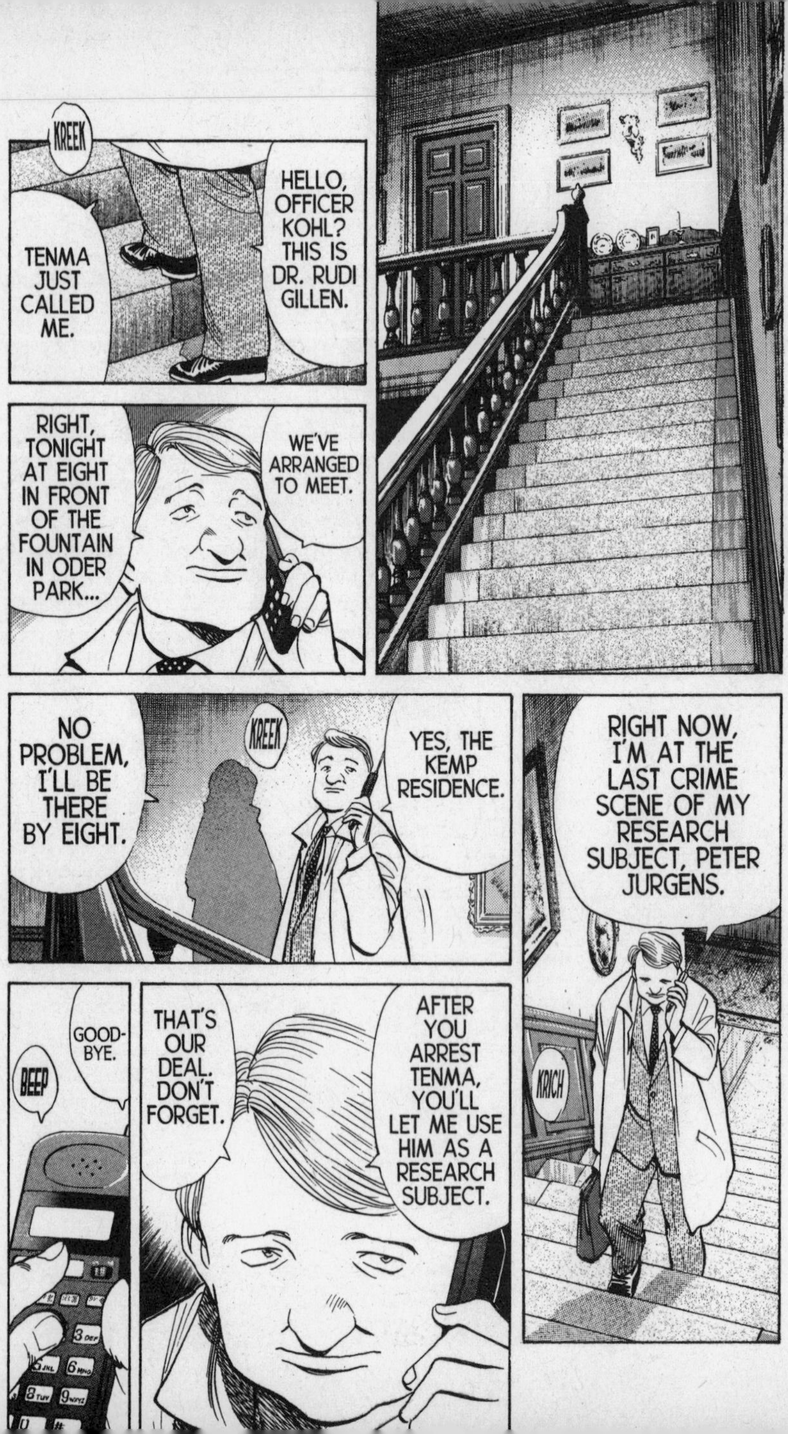
KREEK
HELLO, OFFICER KOHL? THIS IS DR. RUDI GILLEN.
TENMA JUST CALLED ME.
WE'VE ARRANGED TO MEET.
RIGHT, TONIGHT AT EIGHT IN FRONT OF THE FOUNTAIN IN ODER PARK...
RIGHT NOW, I'M AT THE LAST CRIME SCENE OF MY RESEARCH SUBJECT, PETER JURGENS.
KRICH
YES, THE KEMP RESIDENCE.
KREEK
NO PROBLEM, I'LL BE THERE BY EIGHT.
AFTER YOU ARREST TENMA, YOU'LL LET ME USE HIM AS A RESEARCH SUBJECT.
THAT'S OUR DEAL. DON'T FORGET.
GOOD-BYE.
BEEP

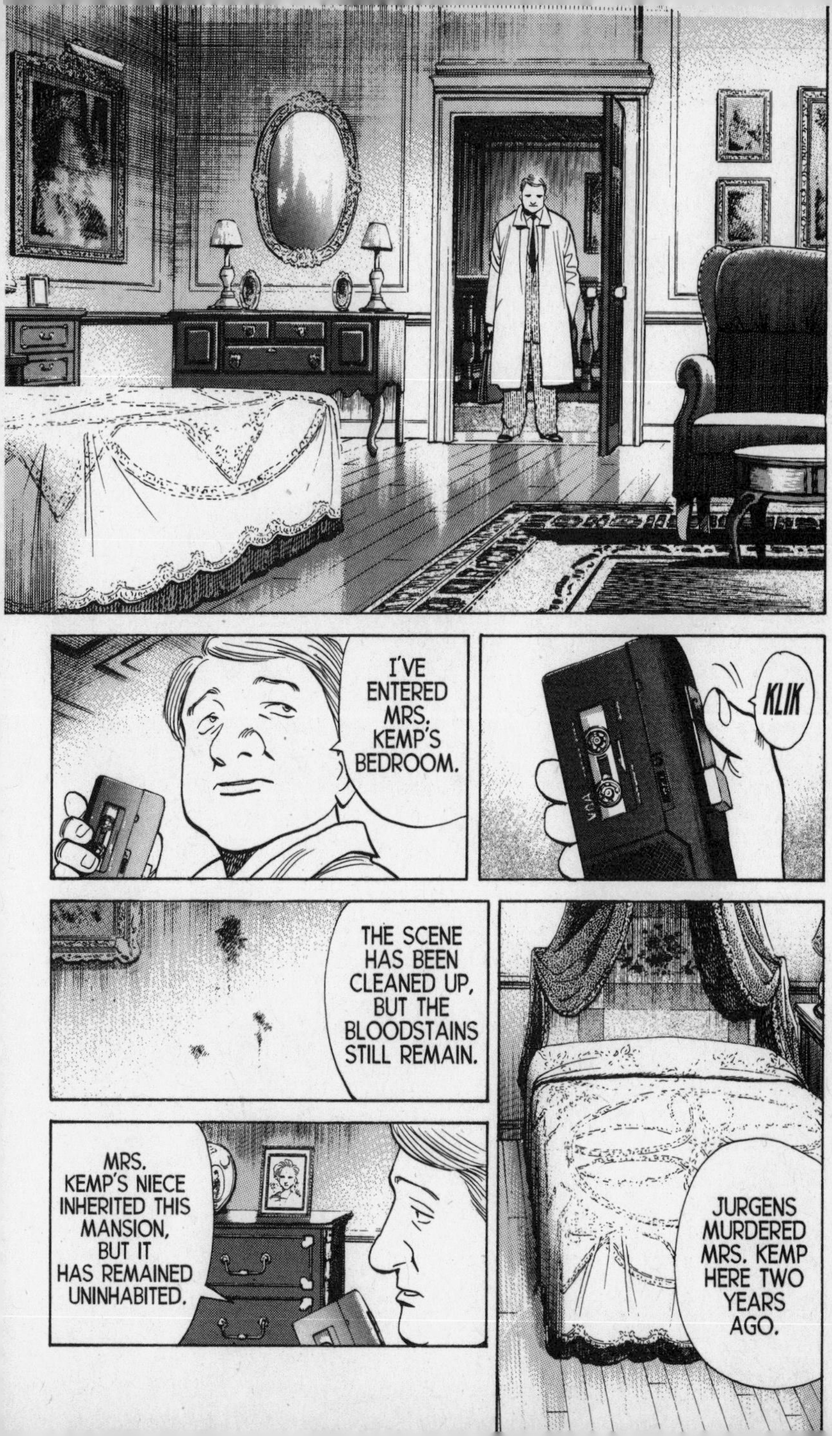
KLIK
I'VE ENTERED MRS. KEMP'S BEDROOM.
JURGENS MURDERED MRS. KEMP HERE TWO YEARS AGO.
THE SCENE HAS BEEN CLEANED UP, BUT THE BLOODSTAINS STILL REMAIN.
MRS. KEMP'S NIECE INHERITED THIS MANSION, BUT IT HAS REMAINED UNINHABITED.

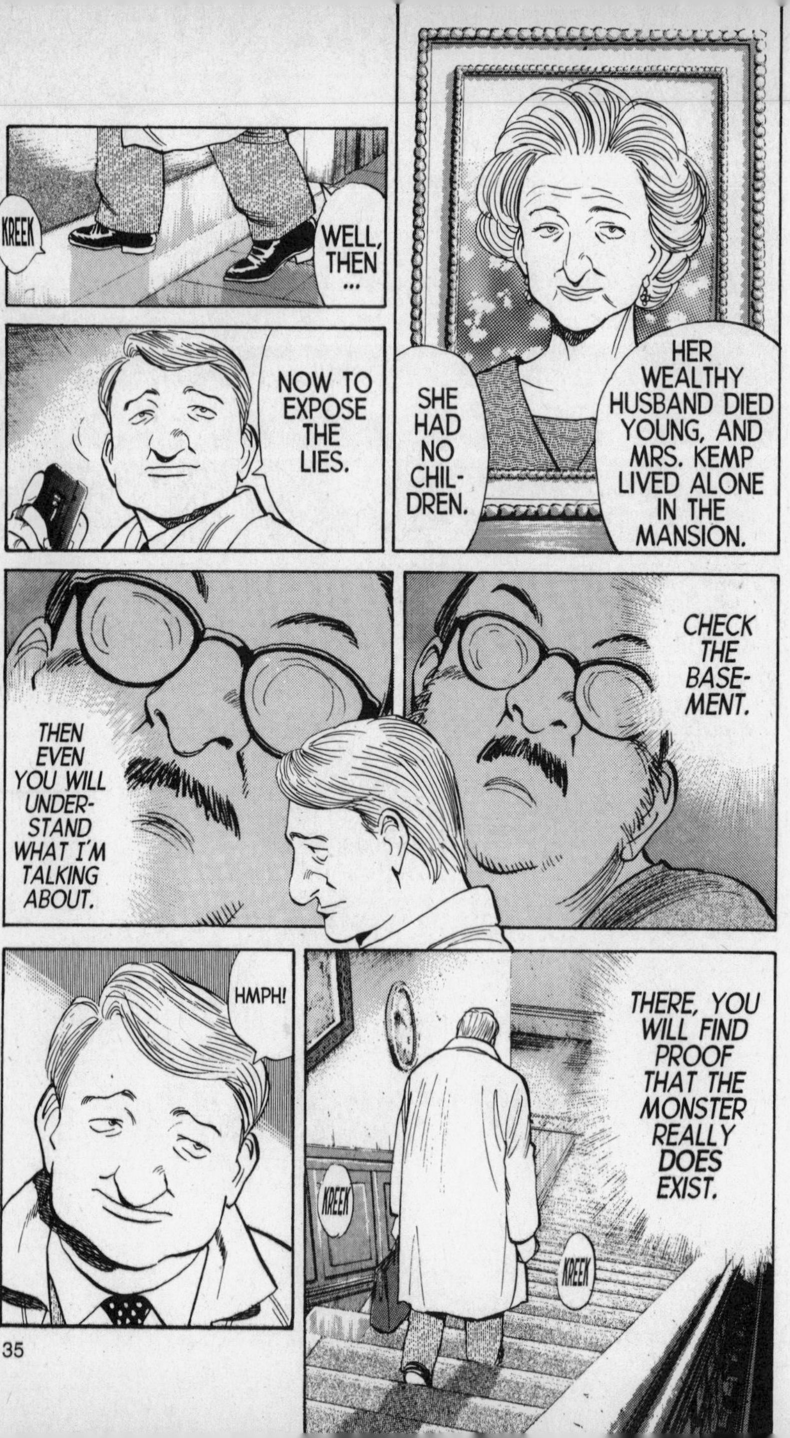
HER WEALTHY HUSBAND DIED YOUNG, AND MRS. KEMP LIVED ALONE IN THE MANSION.
SHE HAD NO CHIL-DREN.
WELL, THEN ...
KREEK
NOW TO EXPOSE THE LIES.
CHECK THE BASE-MENT.
THEN EVEN YOU WILL UNDER-STAND WHAT I'M TALKING ABOUT.
THERE, YOU WILL FIND PROOF THAT THE MONSTER REALLY DOES EXIST.
KREEK
KREEK
HMPH!

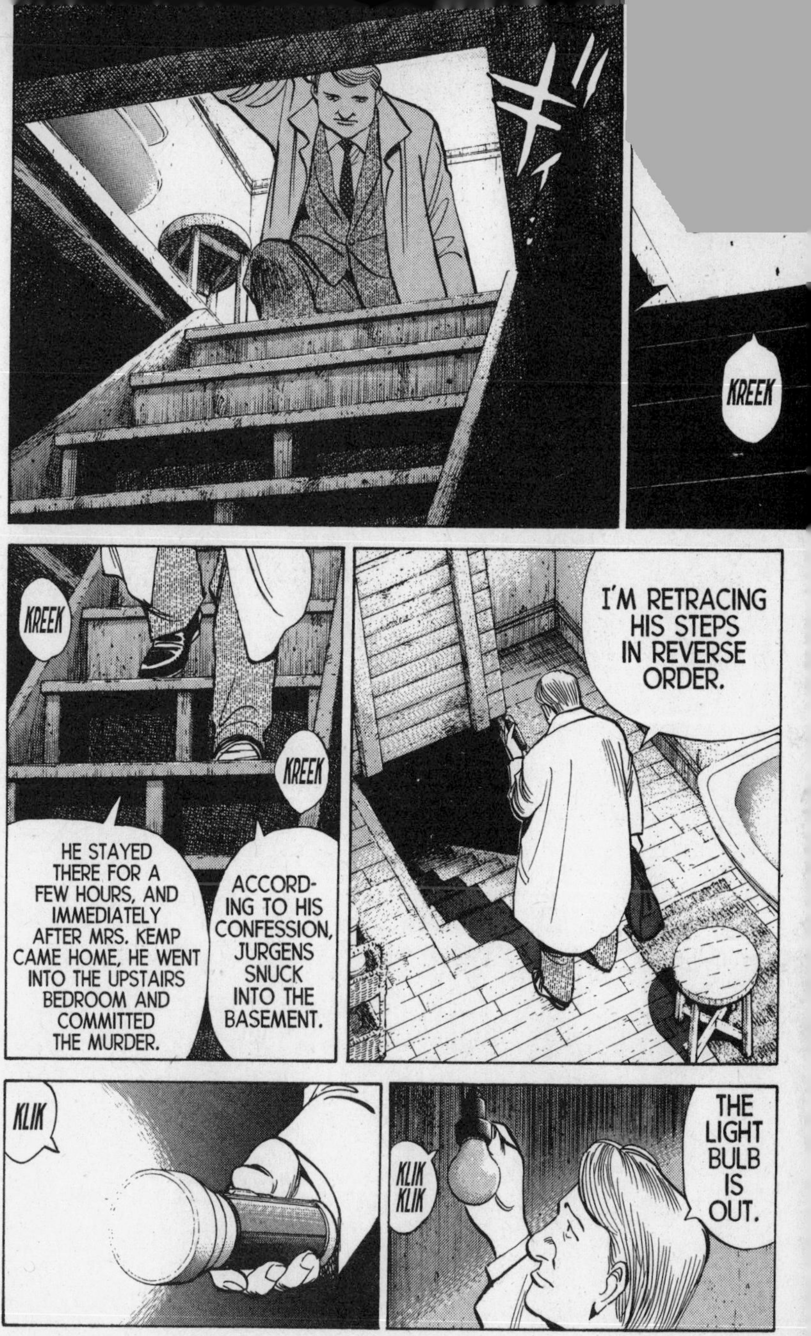
KREEK
I'M RETRACING HIS STEPS IN REVERSE ORDER.
KREEK
KREEK
ACCORDING TO HIS CONFESSION, JURGENS SNUCK INTO THE BASEMENT.
HE STAYED THERE FOR A FEW HOURS, AND IMMEDIATELY AFTER MRS. KEMP CAME HOME, HE WENT INTO THE UPSTAIRS BEDROOM AND COMMITTED THE MURDER.
THE LIGHT BULB IS OUT.
KLIK KLIK
KLIK

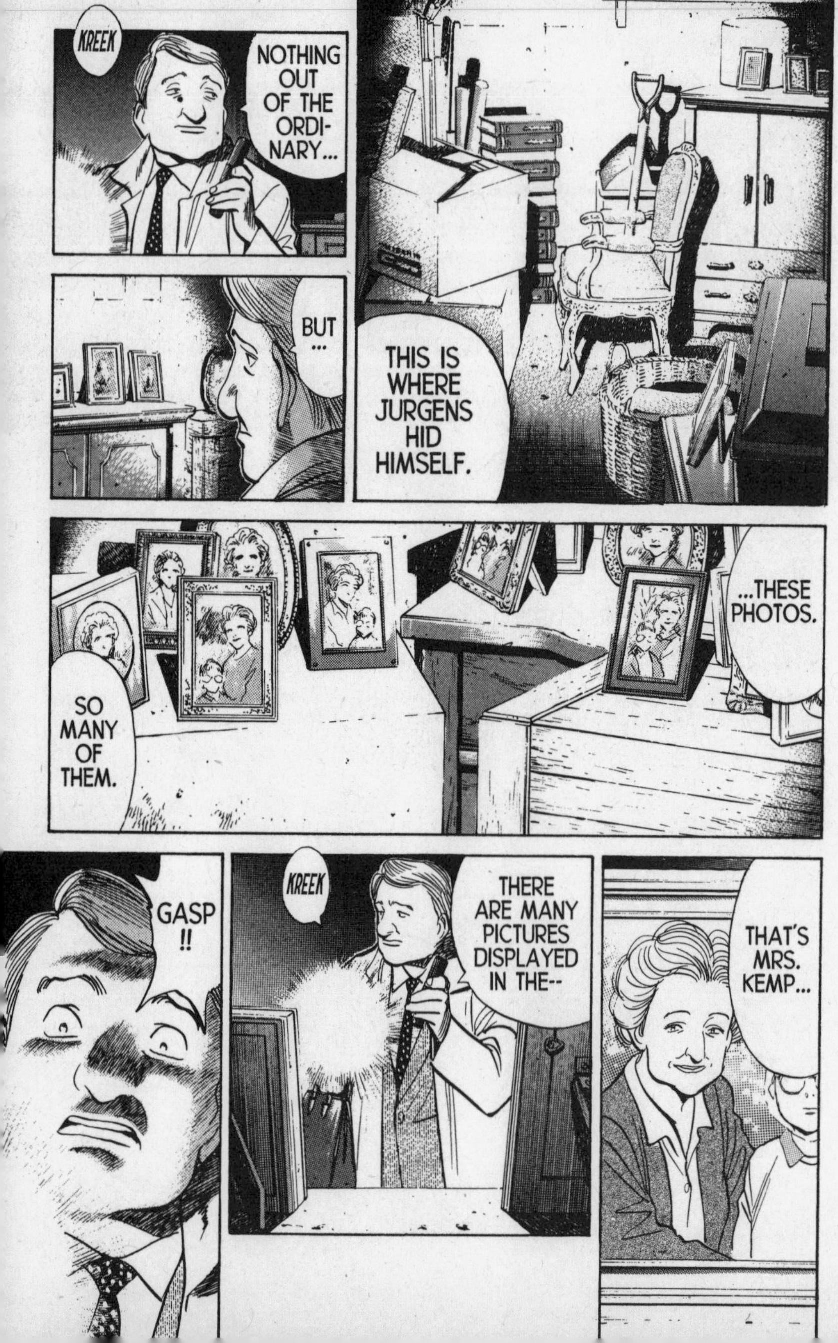
THIS IS WHERE JURGENS HID HIMSELF.
KREEK
NOTHING OUT OF THE ORDINARY...
BUT...
...THESE PHOTOS.
SO MANY OF THEM.
THAT'S MRS. KEMP...
KREEK
THERE ARE MANY PICTURES DISPLAYED IN THE--
GASP !!

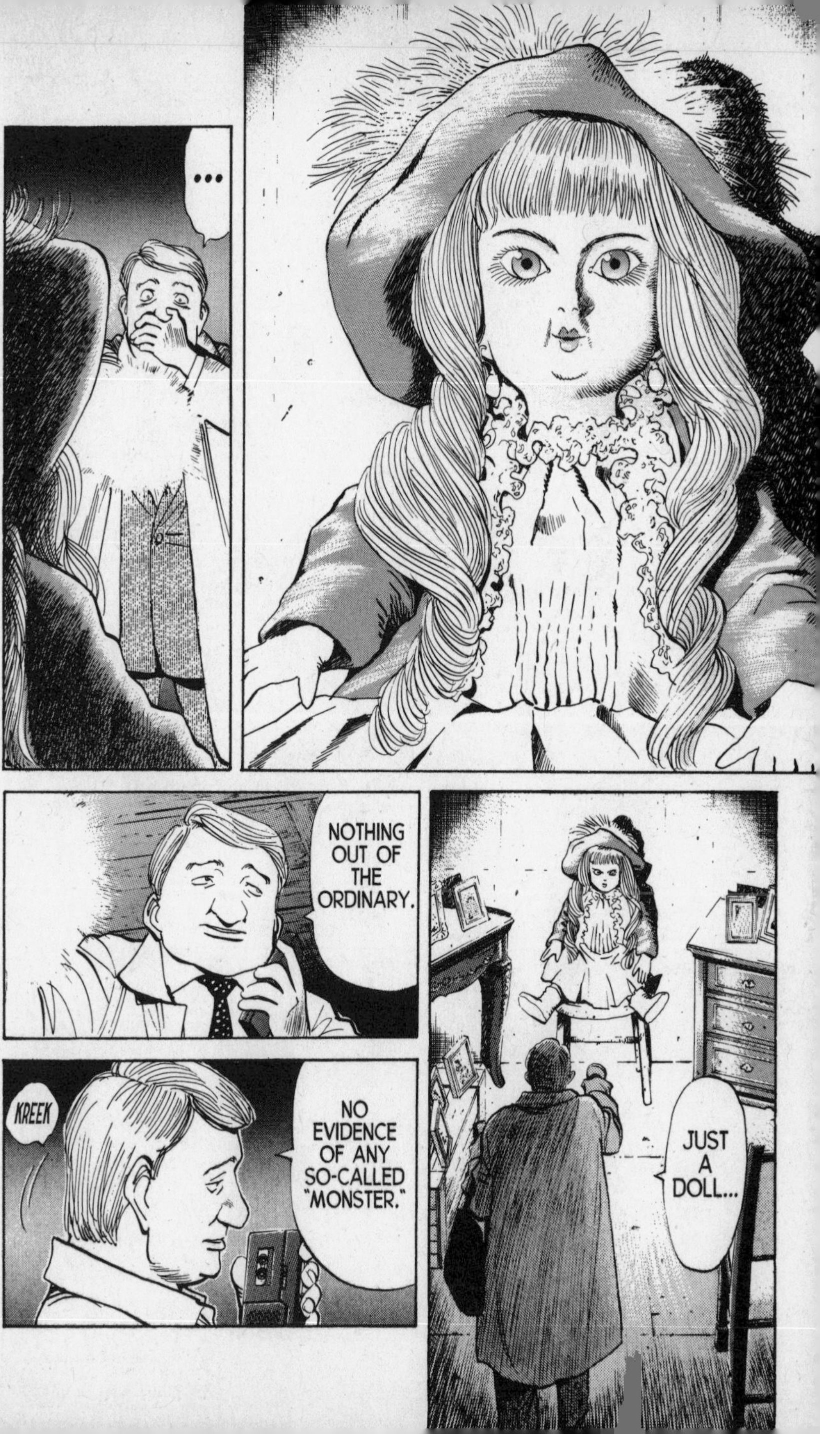
...
JUST A DOLL...
NOTHING OUT OF THE ORDINARY.
KREEK
NO EVIDENCE OF ANY SO-CALLED "MONSTER."

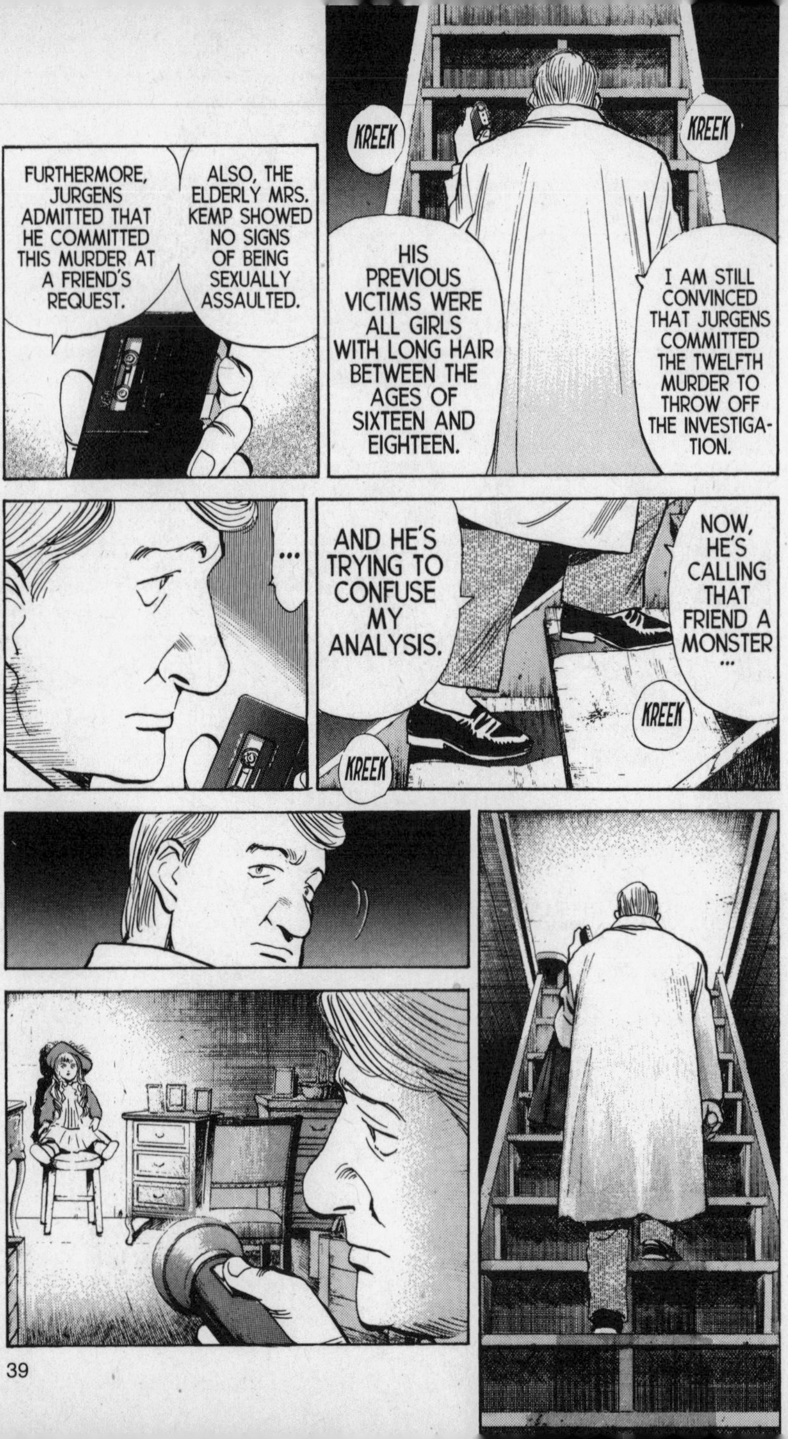

KREEK
KREEK
I AM STILL CONVINCED THAT JURGENS COMMITTED THE TWELFTH MURDER TO THROW OFF THE INVESTIGATION.
HIS PREVIOUS VICTIMS WERE ALL GIRLS WITH LONG HAIR BETWEEN THE AGES OF SIXTEEN AND EIGHTEEN.
ALSO, THE ELDERLY MRS. KEMP SHOWED NO SIGNS OF BEING SEXUALLY ASSAULTED.
FURTHERMORE, JURGENS ADMITTED THAT HE COMMITTED THIS MURDER AT A FRIEND'S REQUEST.
NOW, HE'S CALLING THAT FRIEND A MONSTER...
KREEK
AND HE'S TRYING TO CONFUSE MY ANALYSIS.
KREEK
...

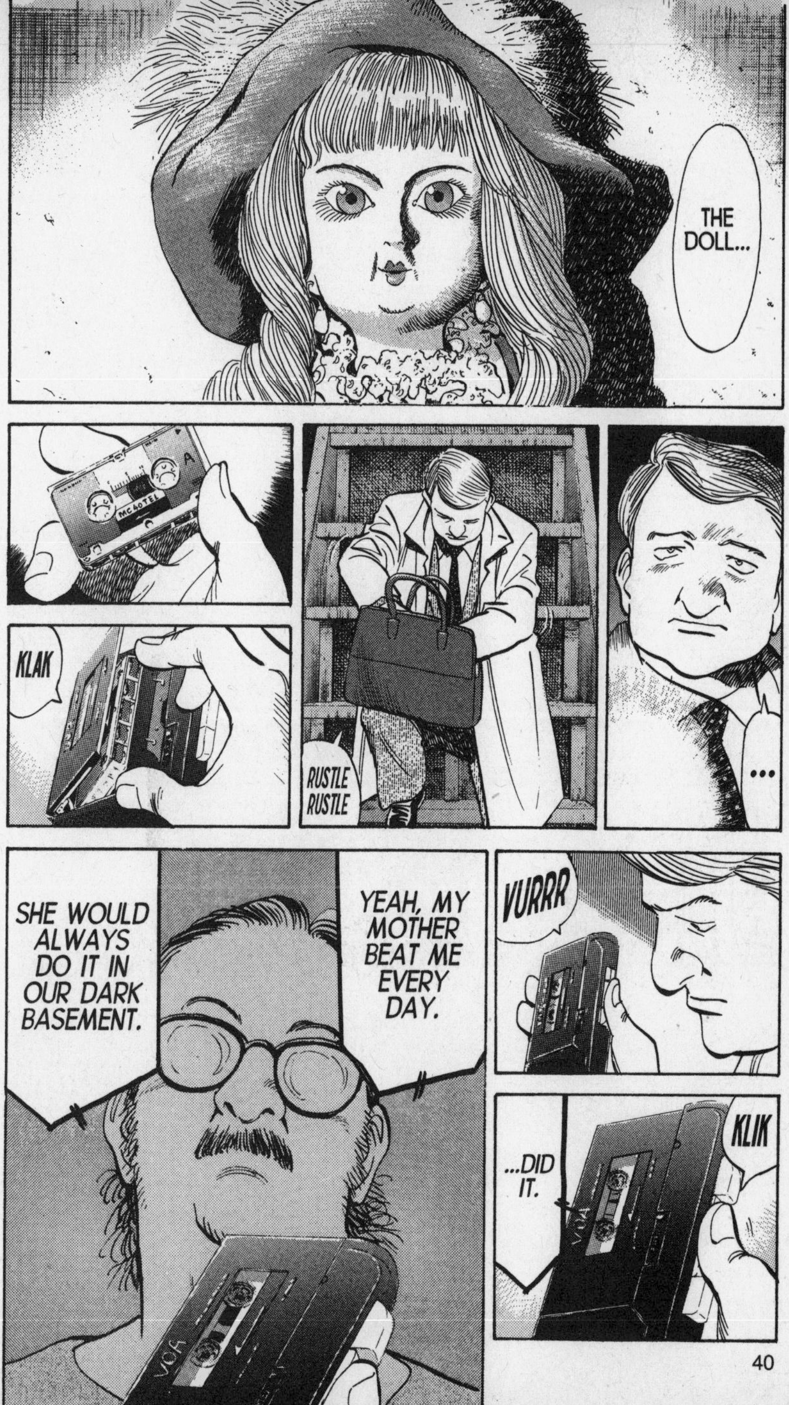
THE DOLL...
...
RUSTLE RUSTLE
KLAK
VURRR
KLIK
...DID IT.
YEAH, MY MOTHER BEAT ME EVERY DAY.
SHE WOULD ALWAYS DO IT IN OUR DARK BASEMENT.

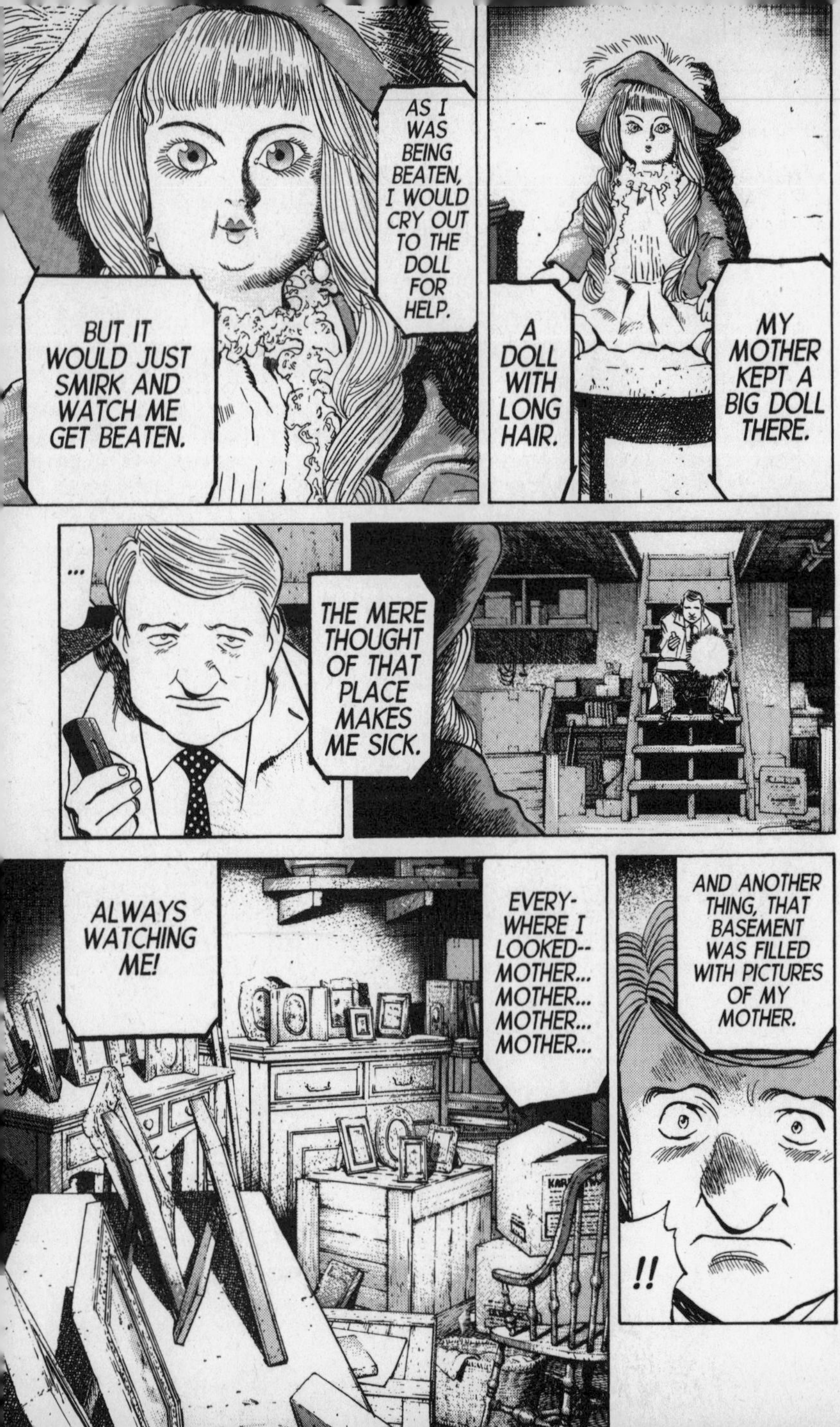
MY MOTHER KEPT A BIG DOLL THERE.
A DOLL WITH LONG HAIR.
AS I WAS BEING BEATEN, I WOULD CRY OUT TO THE DOLL FOR HELP.
BUT IT WOULD JUST SMIRK AND WATCH ME GET BEATEN.
THE MERE THOUGHT OF THAT PLACE MAKES ME SICK.
...
AND ANOTHER THING, THAT BASEMENT WAS FILLED WITH PICTURES OF MY MOTHER.
!!
EVERY-WHERE I LOOKED-- MOTHER... MOTHER... MOTHER... MOTHER...
ALWAYS WATCHING ME!

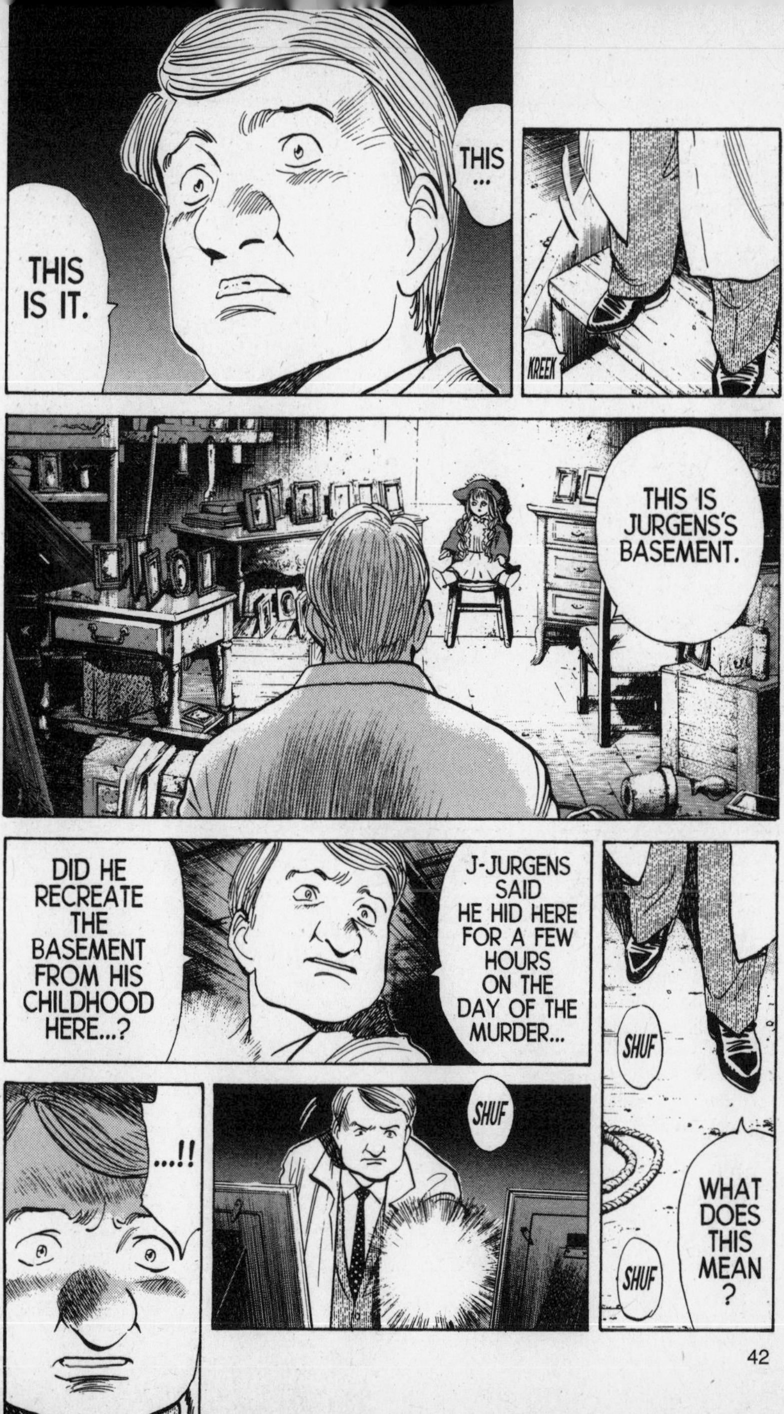
KREEK
THIS ...
THIS IS IT.
THIS IS JURGENS'S BASEMENT.
SHUF
WHAT DOES THIS MEAN?
SHUF
J-JURGENS SAID HE HID HERE FOR A FEW HOURS ON THE DAY OF THE MURDER...
DID HE RECREATE THE BASEMENT FROM HIS CHILDHOOD HERE...?
SHUF
...!!

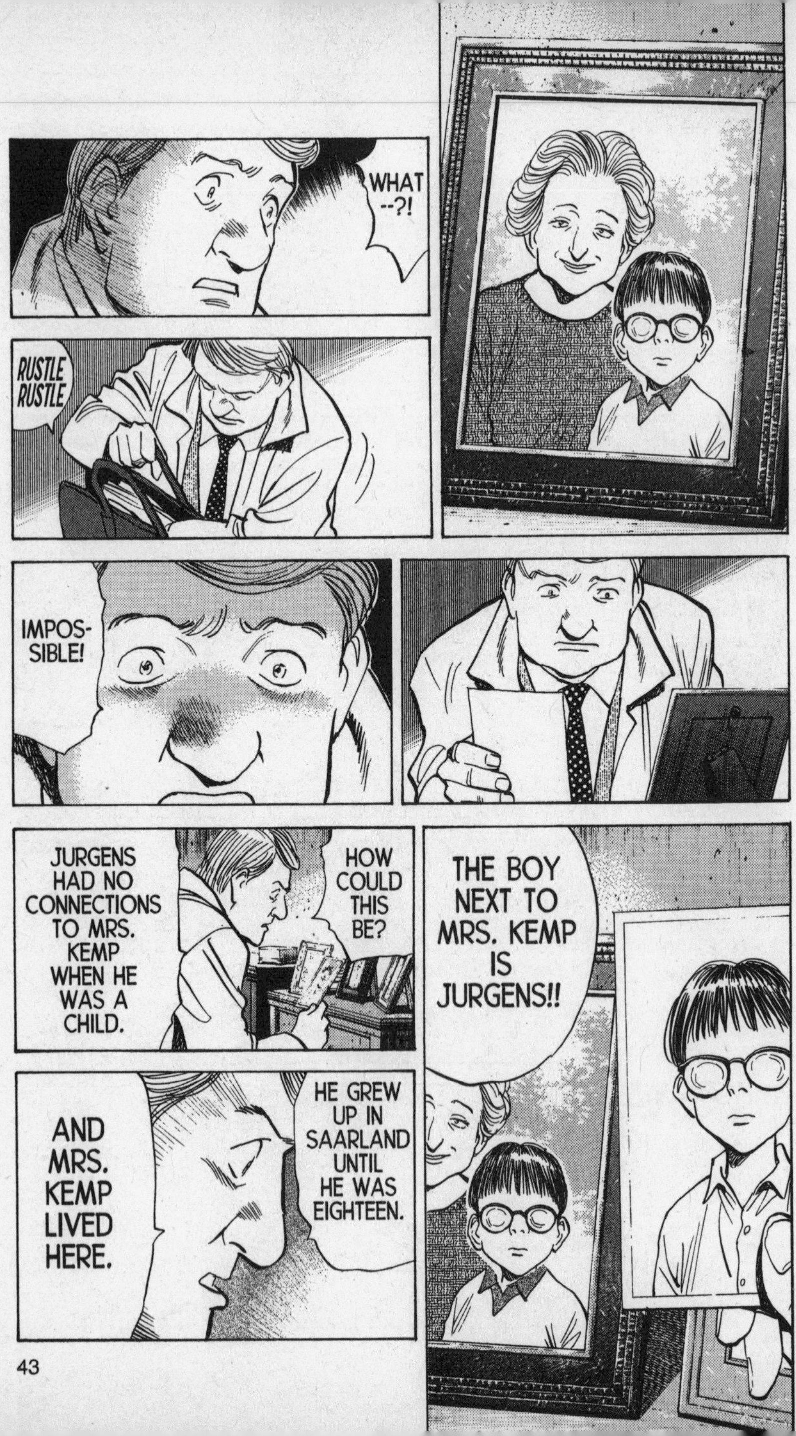
WHAT --?!
RUSTLE RUSTLE
IMPOSSIBLE!
THE BOY NEXT TO MRS. KEMP IS JURGENS!!
HOW COULD THIS BE?
JURGENS HAD NO CONNECTIONS TO MRS. KEMP WHEN HE WAS A CHILD.
HE GREW UP IN SAARLAND UNTIL HE WAS EIGHTEEN.
AND MRS. KEMP LIVED HERE.

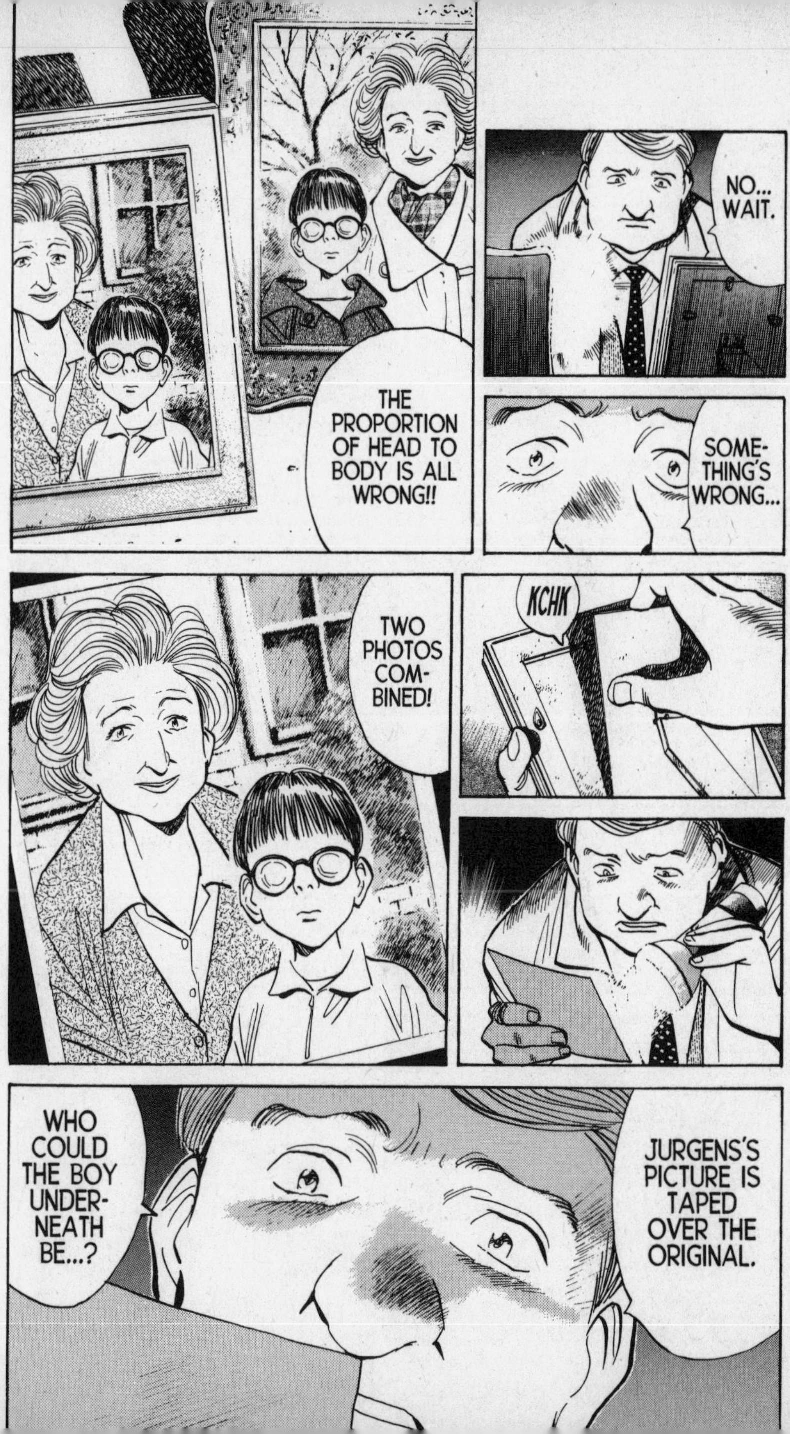
NO... WAIT.
SOME-THING'S WRONG...
THE PROPORTION OF HEAD TO BODY IS ALL WRONG!!
KCHK
TWO PHOTOS COM-BINED!
JURGENS'S PICTURE IS TAPED OVER THE ORIGINAL.
WHO COULD THE BOY UNDER-NEATH BE...?

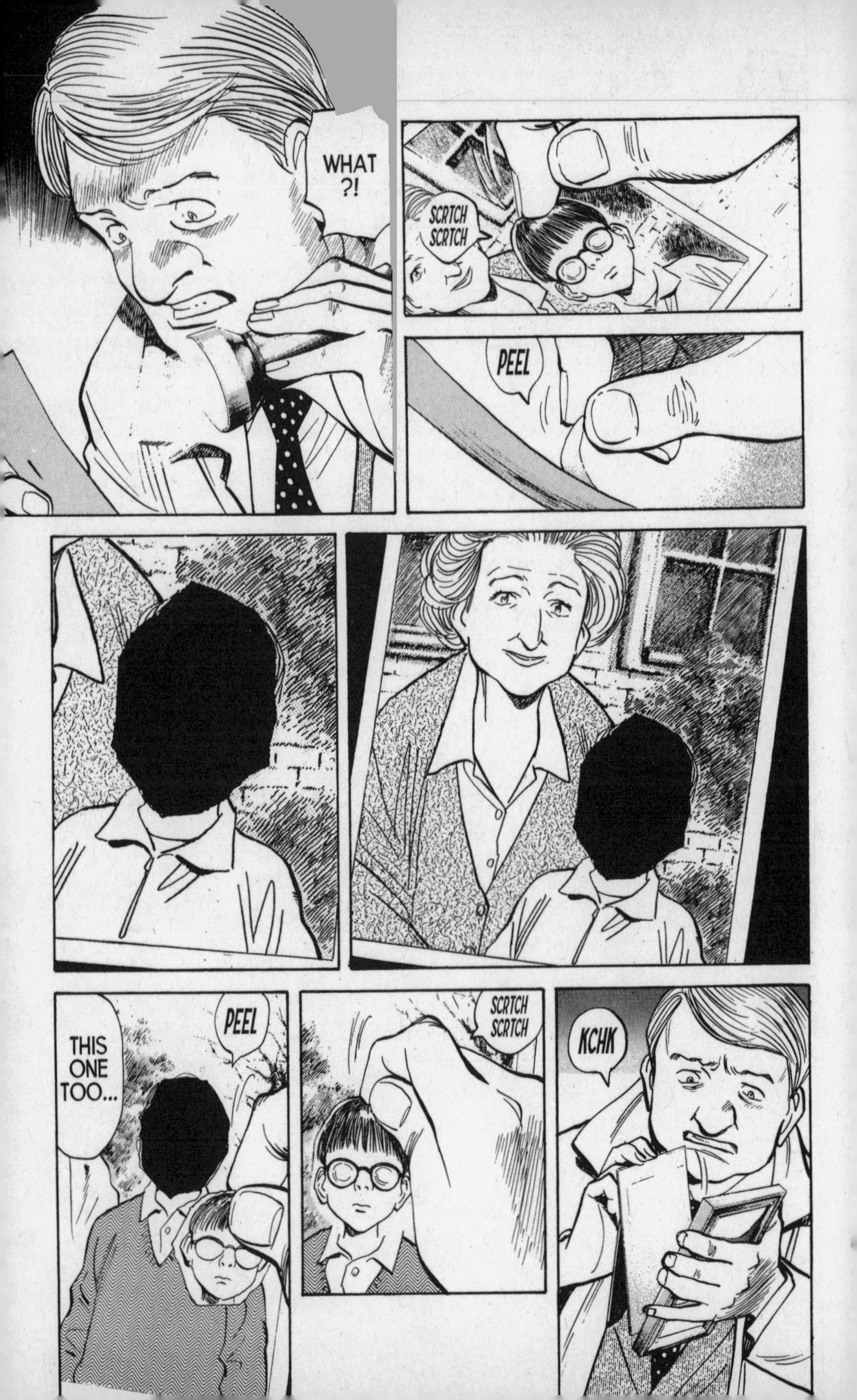
SCRTCH SCRTCH
PEEL
WHAT ?!
KCHK
SCRTCH SCRTCH
PEEL
THIS ONE TOO...

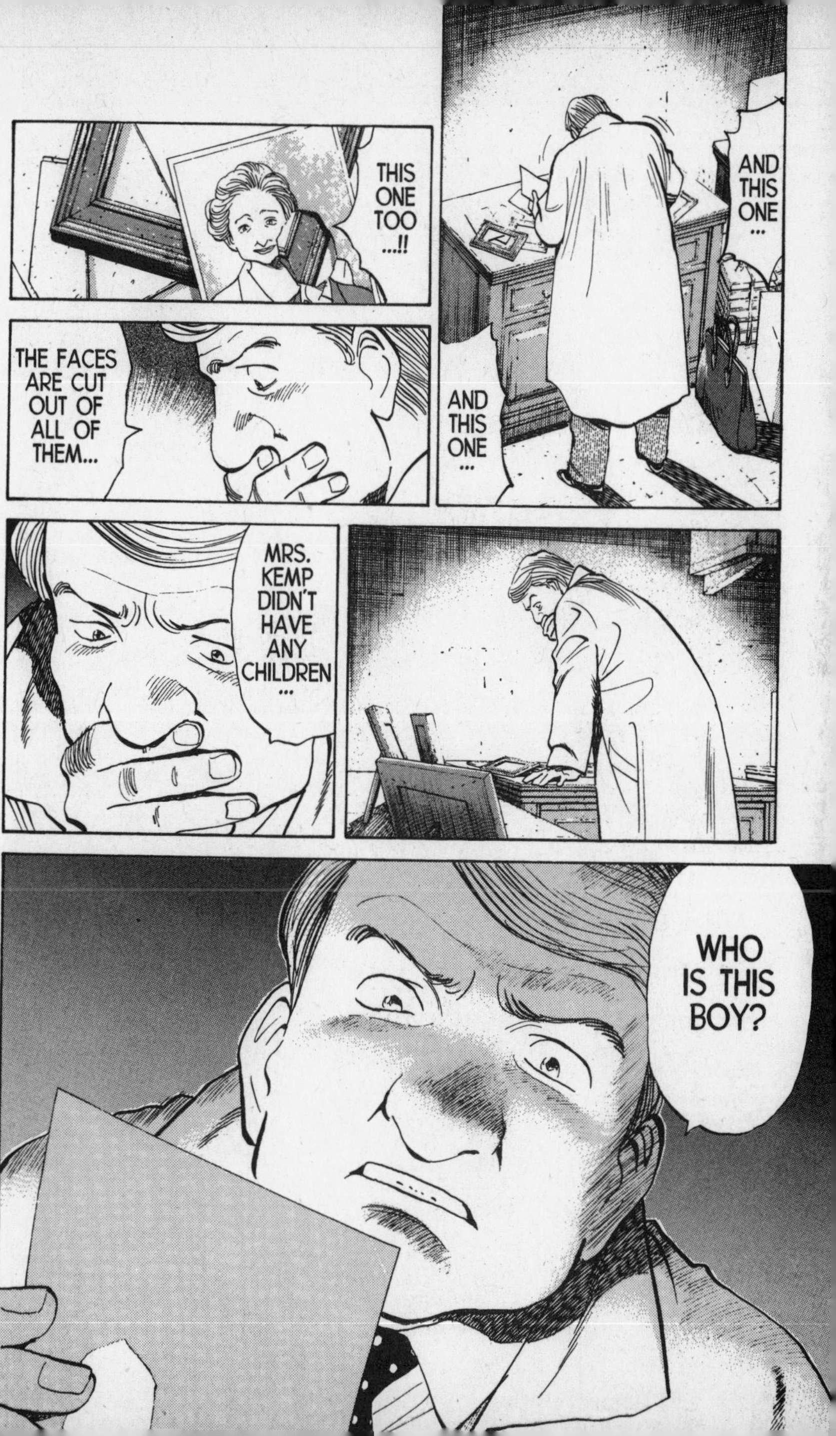
AND THIS ONE ...
AND THIS ONE ...
THIS ONE TOO ...!!
THE FACES ARE CUT OUT OF ALL OF THEM...
MRS. KEMP DIDN'T HAVE ANY CHILDREN ...
WHO IS THIS BOY?

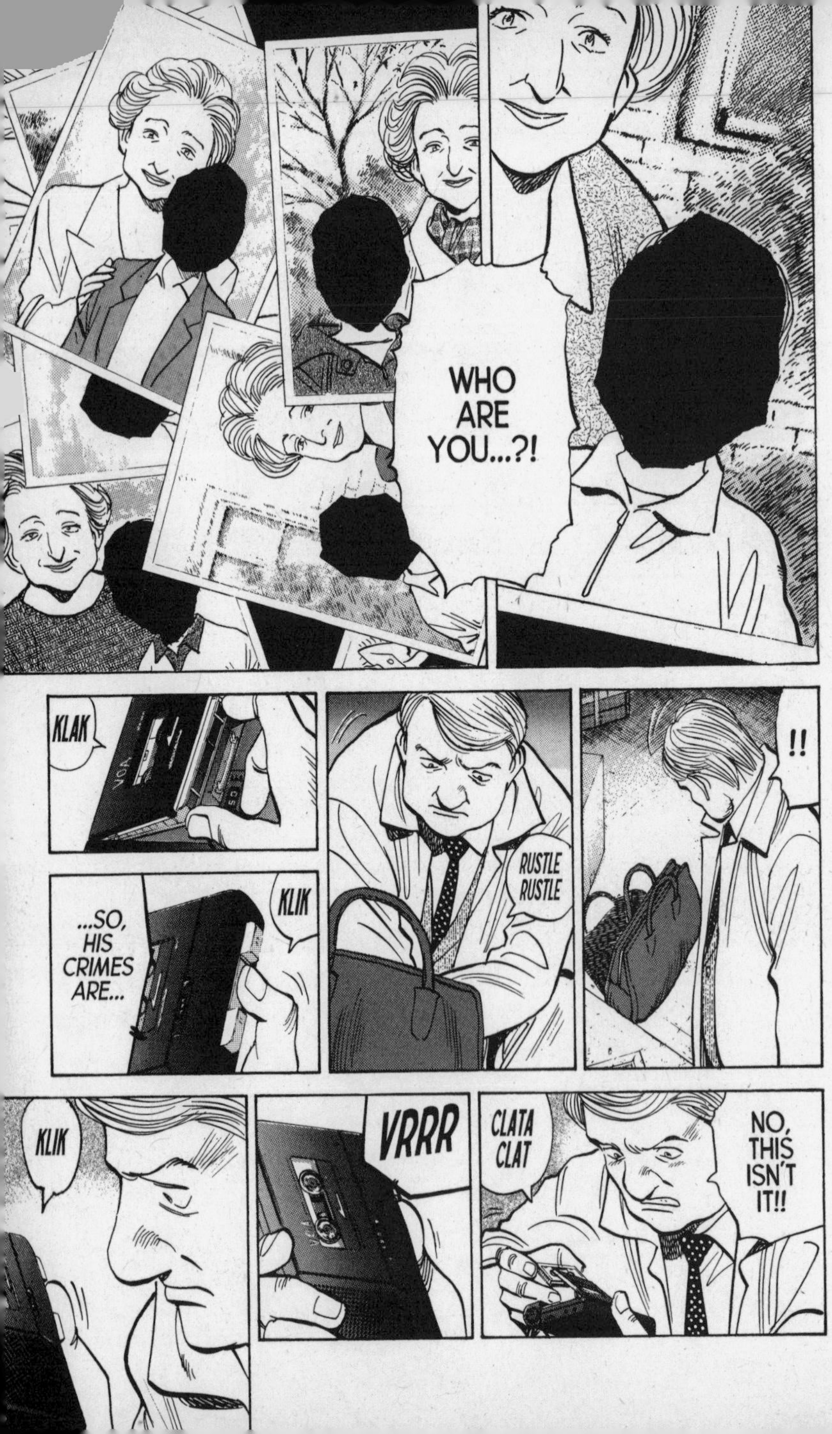
WHO ARE YOU...?!
!!
RUSTLE RUSTLE
KLAK
KLIK
...SO, HIS CRIMES ARE...
NO, THIS ISN'T IT!!
CLATA CLAT
VRRR
KLIK

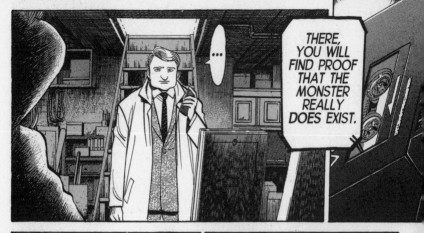

THERE, YOU WILL FIND PROOF THAT THE MONSTER REALLY DOES EXIST.

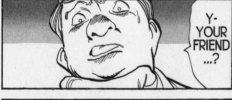

I HID THERE FOR A FEW HOURS...

Y-YOUR FRIEND...?

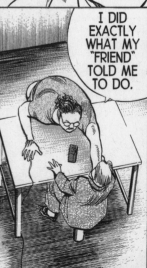

I DID EXACTLY WHAT MY "FRIEND" TOLD ME TO DO.

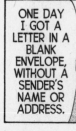

ONE DAY I GOT A LETTER IN A BLANK ENVELOPE, WITHOUT A SENDER'S NAME OR ADDRESS.

YEAH...

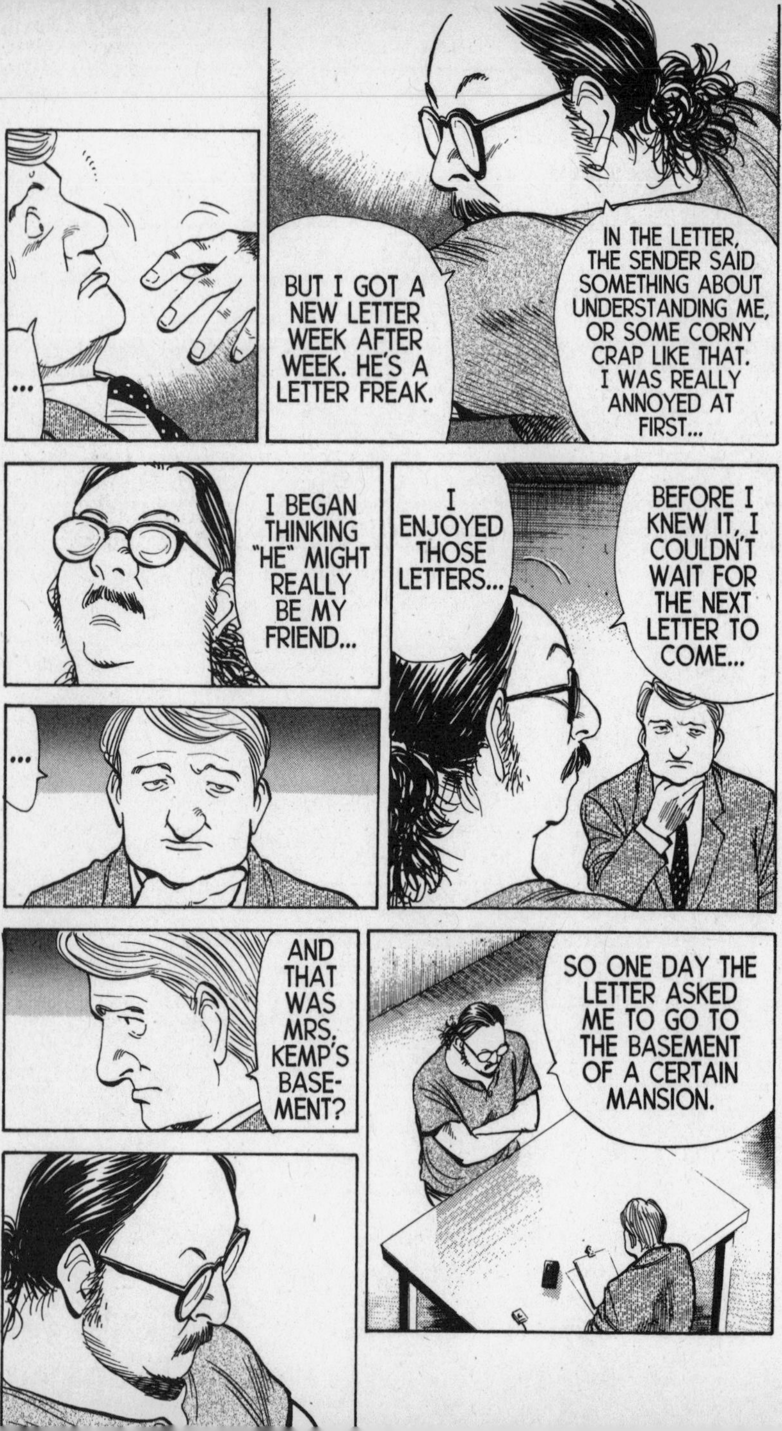
IN THE LETTER, THE SENDER SAID SOMETHING ABOUT UNDERSTANDING ME, OR SOME CORNY CRAP LIKE THAT. I WAS REALLY ANNOYED AT FIRST...
BUT I GOT A NEW LETTER WEEK AFTER WEEK. HE'S A LETTER FREAK.
...
BEFORE I KNEW IT, I COULDN'T WAIT FOR THE NEXT LETTER TO COME...
I ENJOYED THOSE LETTERS...
I BEGAN THINKING "HE" MIGHT REALLY BE MY FRIEND...
...
SO ONE DAY THE LETTER ASKED ME TO GO TO THE BASEMENT OF A CERTAIN MANSION.
AND THAT WAS MRS. KEMP'S BASE-MENT?

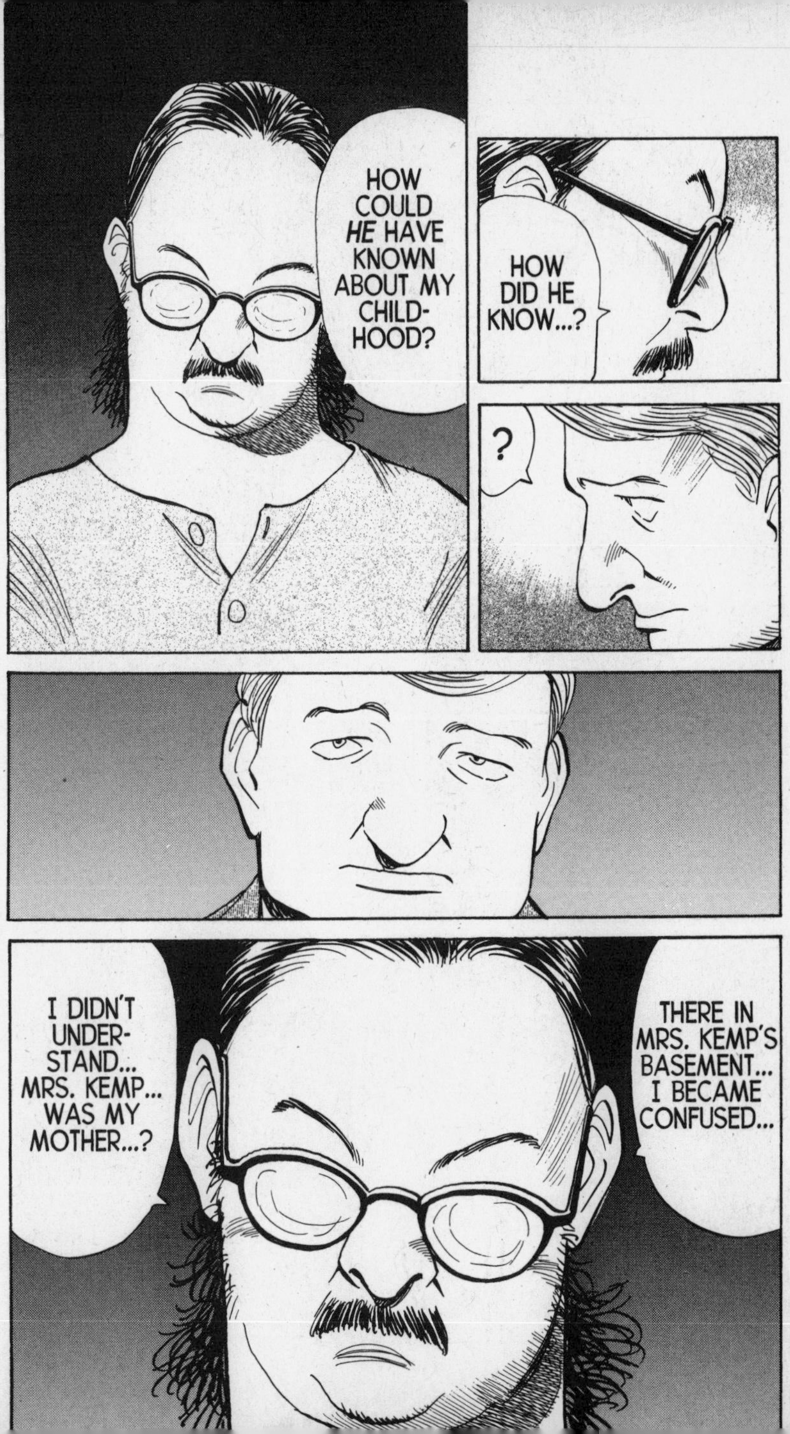
HOW DID HE KNOW...?
?
HOW COULD *HE* HAVE KNOWN ABOUT MY CHILDHOOD?
THERE IN MRS. KEMP'S BASEMENT... I BECAME CONFUSED...
I DIDN'T UNDERSTAND... MRS. KEMP... WAS MY MOTHER...?

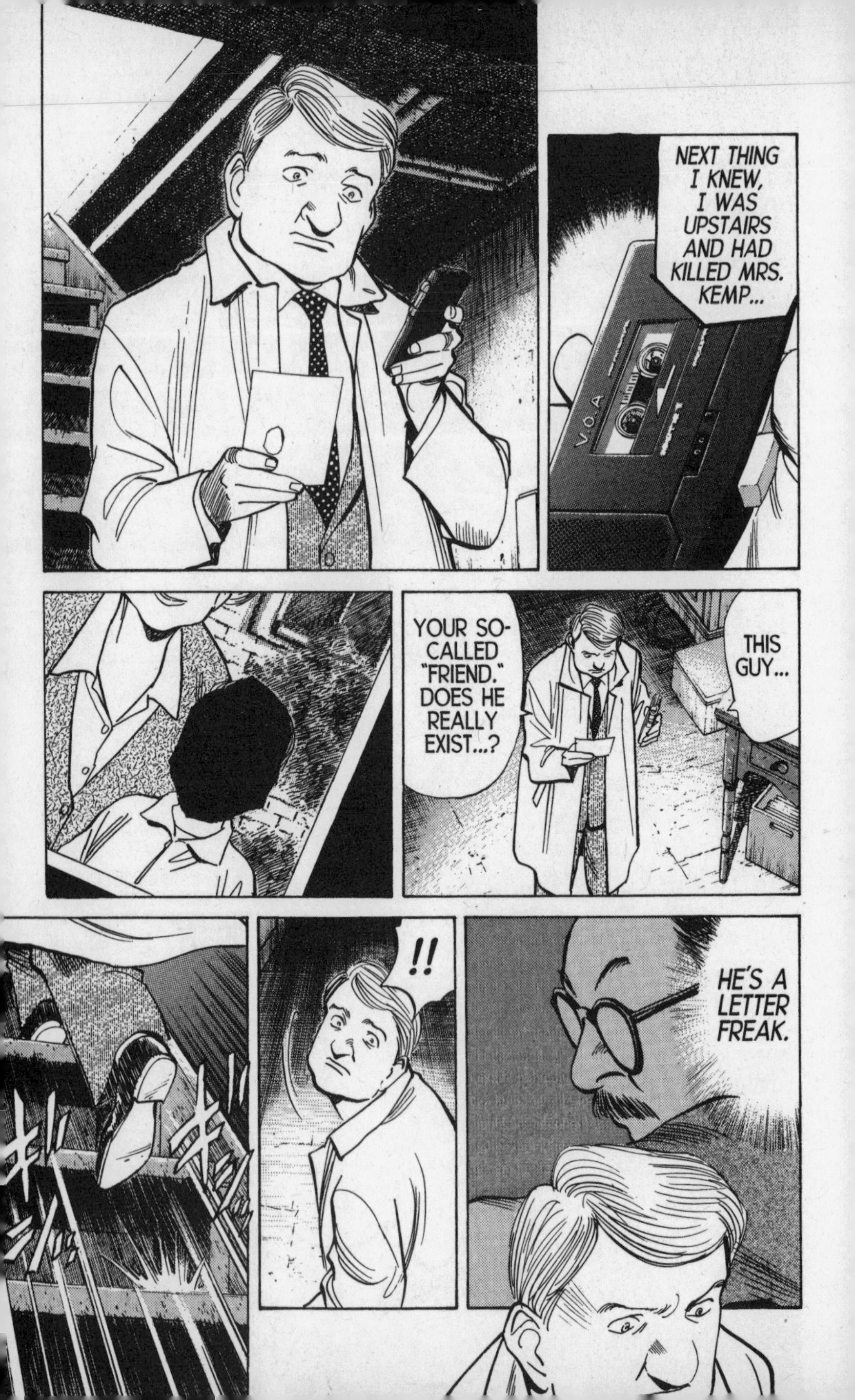
NEXT THING I KNEW, I WAS UPSTAIRS AND HAD KILLED MRS. KEMP...
THIS GUY...
YOUR SO-CALLED "FRIEND." DOES HE REALLY EXIST...?
HE'S A LETTER FREAK.
!!

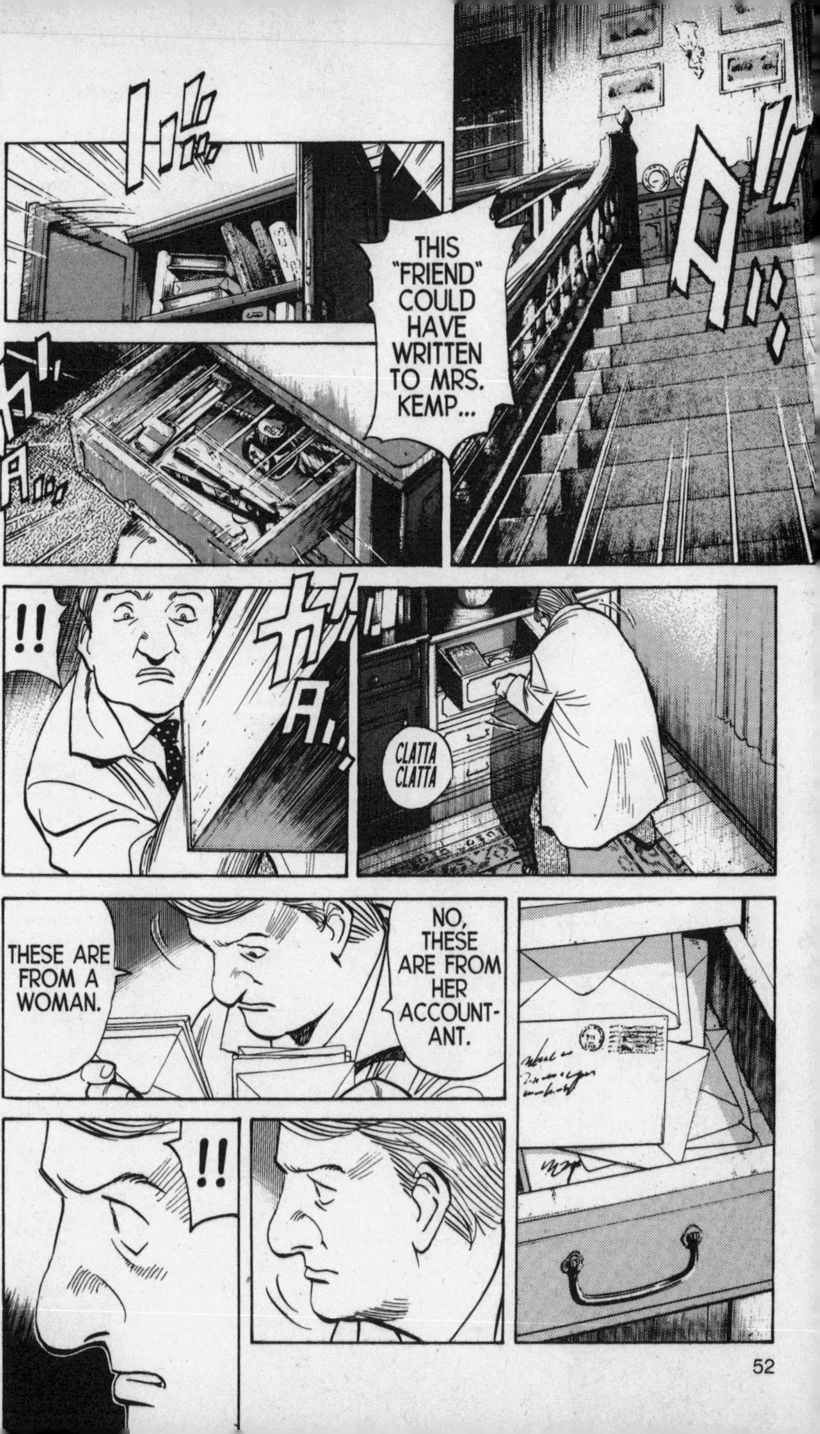
THIS "FRIEND" COULD HAVE WRITTEN TO MRS. KEMP...
!!
CLATTA CLATTA
THESE ARE FROM A WOMAN.
NO, THESE ARE FROM HER ACCOUNTANT.
!!

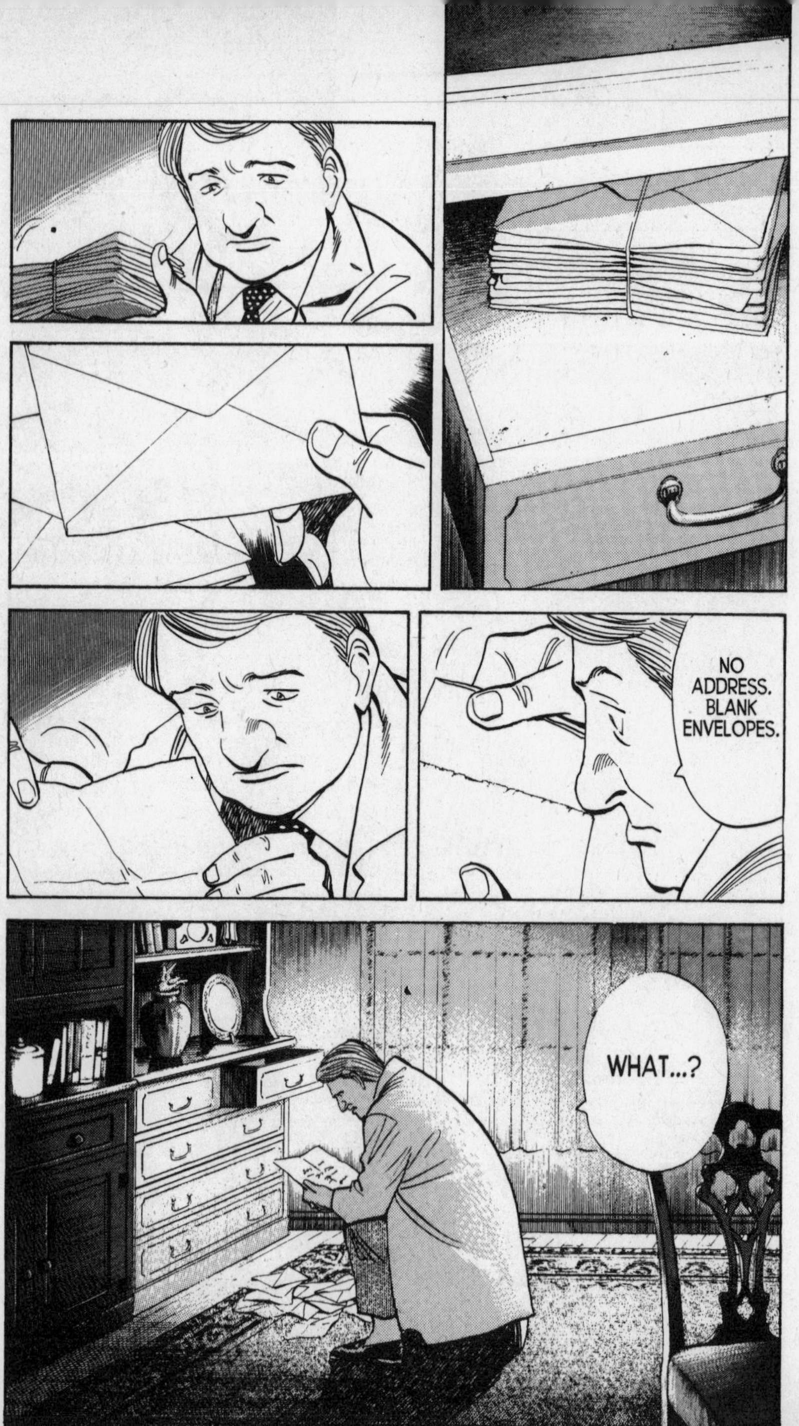
NO ADDRESS. BLANK ENVELOPES.
WHAT...?

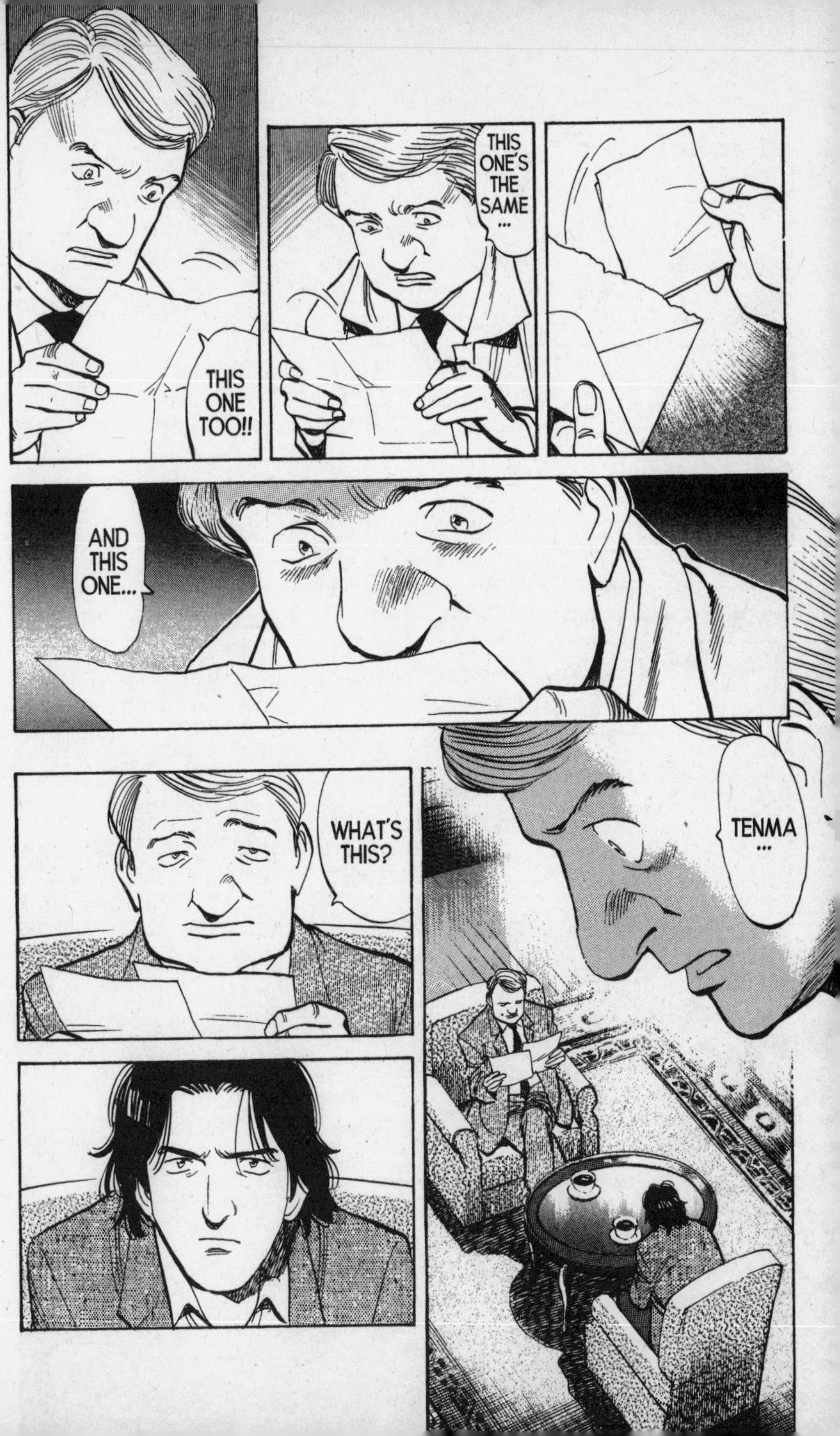
THIS ONE'S THE SAME...
THIS ONE TOO!!
AND THIS ONE...
TENMA...
WHAT'S THIS?

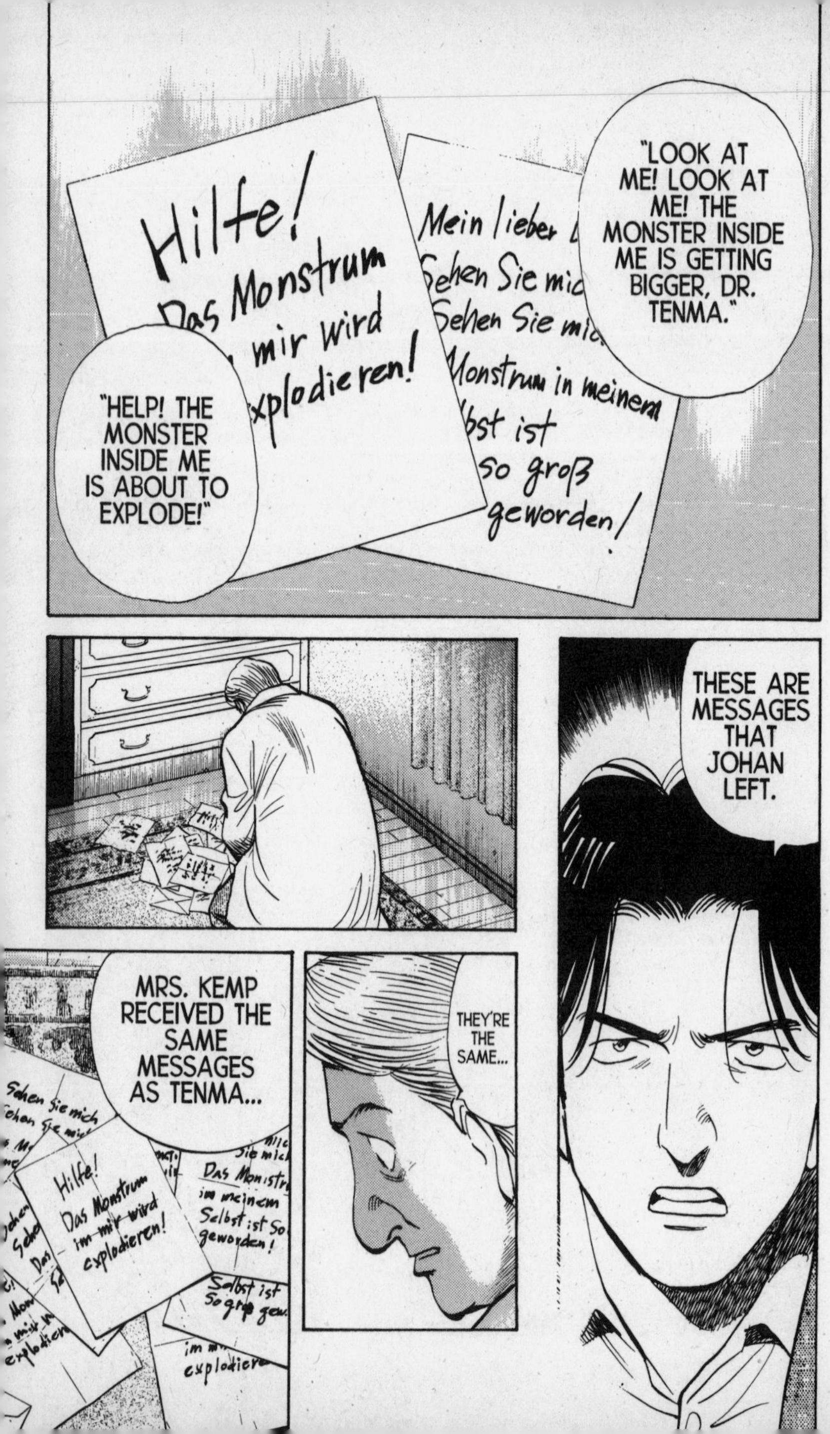
"LOOK AT ME! LOOK AT ME! THE MONSTER INSIDE ME IS GETTING BIGGER, DR. TENMA."
Mein lieber
Monstrum in meinem
so groß
geworden!
Hilfe!
Das Monstrum
mir wird
explodieren!
"HELP! THE MONSTER INSIDE ME IS ABOUT TO EXPLODE!"
THESE ARE MESSAGES THAT JOHAN LEFT.
THEY'RE THE SAME...
MRS. KEMP RECEIVED THE SAME MESSAGES AS TENMA...
Hilfe!
Das Monstrum im mir wird explodieren!
Das Monstrum im meinem Selbst ist So geworden!

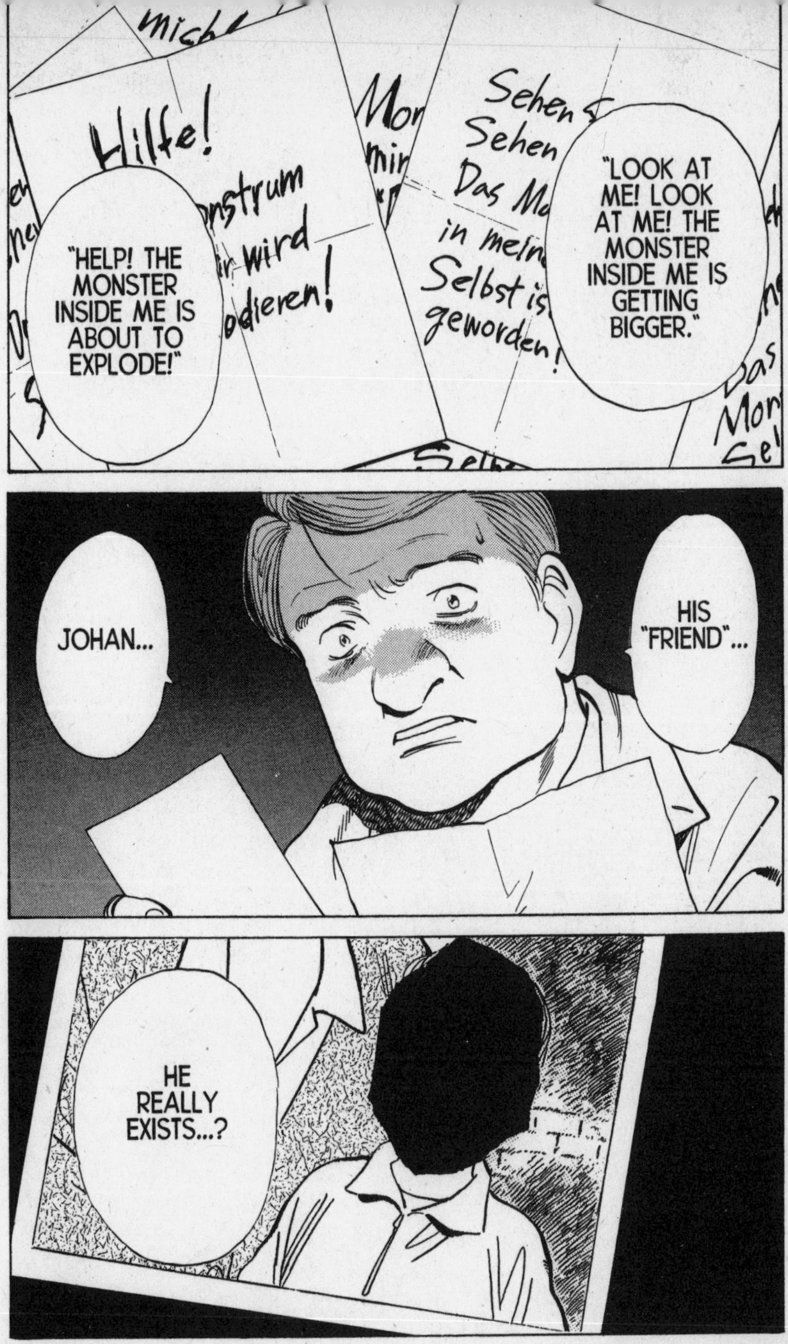
"LOOK AT ME! LOOK AT ME! THE MONSTER INSIDE ME IS GETTING BIGGER."
Hilfe!
"HELP! THE MONSTER INSIDE ME IS ABOUT TO EXPLODE!"
HIS "FRIEND"...
JOHAN...
HE REALLY EXISTS...?

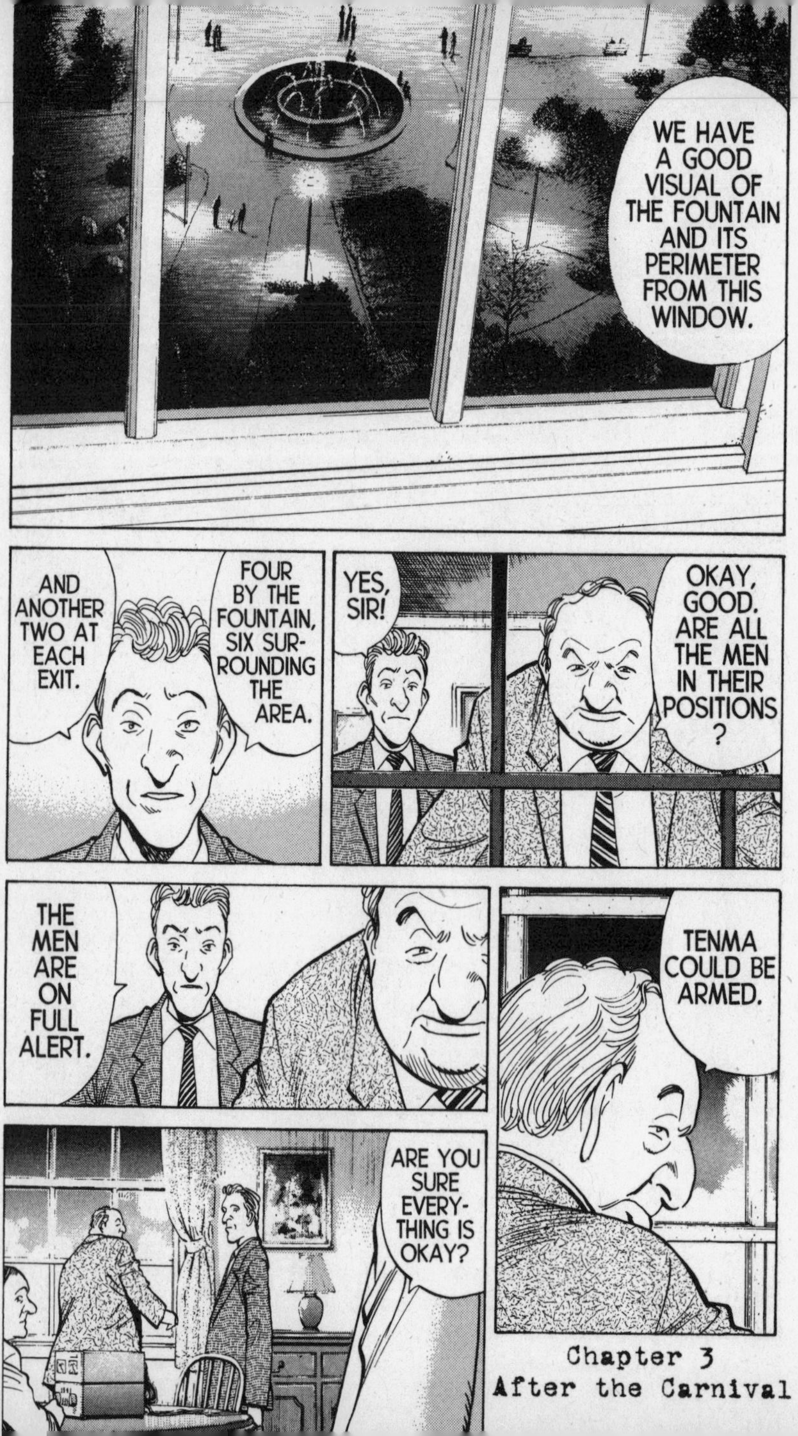
WE HAVE A GOOD VISUAL OF THE FOUNTAIN AND ITS PERIMETER FROM THIS WINDOW.
OKAY, GOOD. ARE ALL THE MEN IN THEIR POSITIONS?
YES, SIR!
FOUR BY THE FOUNTAIN, SIX SUR-ROUNDING THE AREA.
AND ANOTHER TWO AT EACH EXIT.
TENMA COULD BE ARMED.
THE MEN ARE ON FULL ALERT.
ARE YOU SURE EVERY-THING IS OKAY?

Chapter 3
After the Carnival

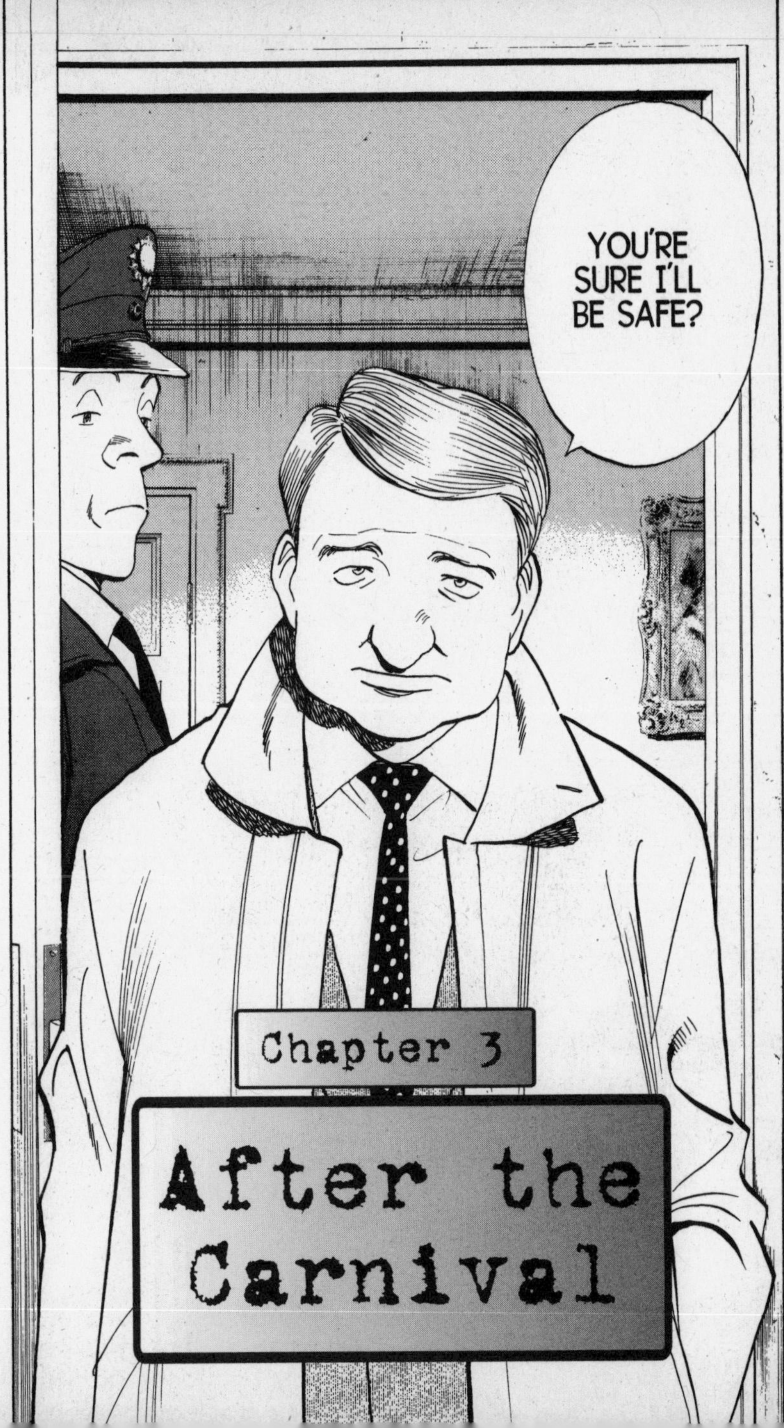
YOU'RE SURE I'LL BE SAFE?
Chapter 3
After the Carnival

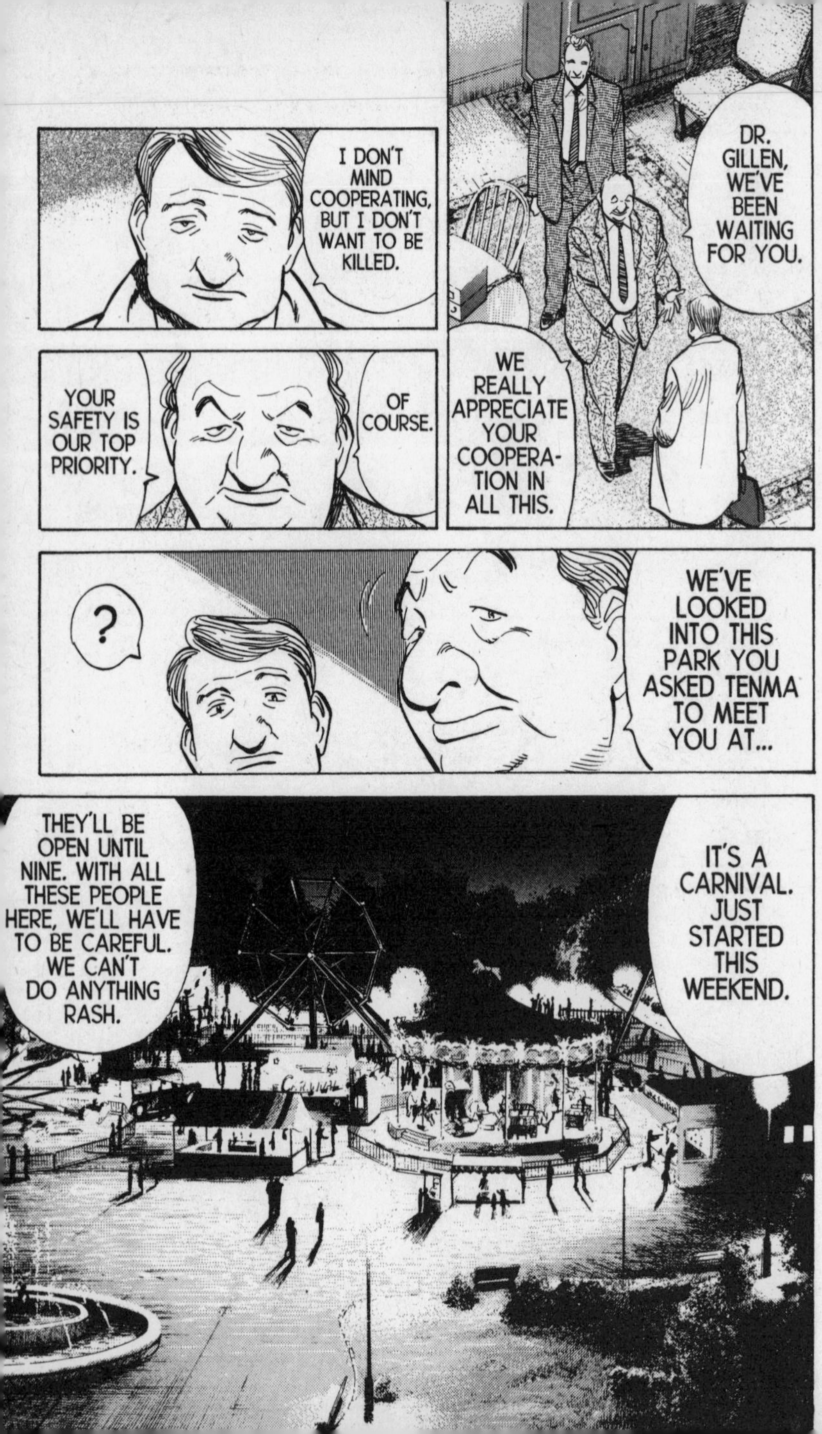
DR. GILLEN, WE'VE BEEN WAITING FOR YOU.
WE REALLY APPRECIATE YOUR COOPERATION IN ALL THIS.
I DON'T MIND COOPERATING, BUT I DON'T WANT TO BE KILLED.
OF COURSE.
YOUR SAFETY IS OUR TOP PRIORITY.
WE'VE LOOKED INTO THIS PARK YOU ASKED TENMA TO MEET YOU AT...
?
IT'S A CARNIVAL. JUST STARTED THIS WEEKEND.
THEY'LL BE OPEN UNTIL NINE. WITH ALL THESE PEOPLE HERE, WE'LL HAVE TO BE CAREFUL. WE CAN'T DO ANYTHING RASH.

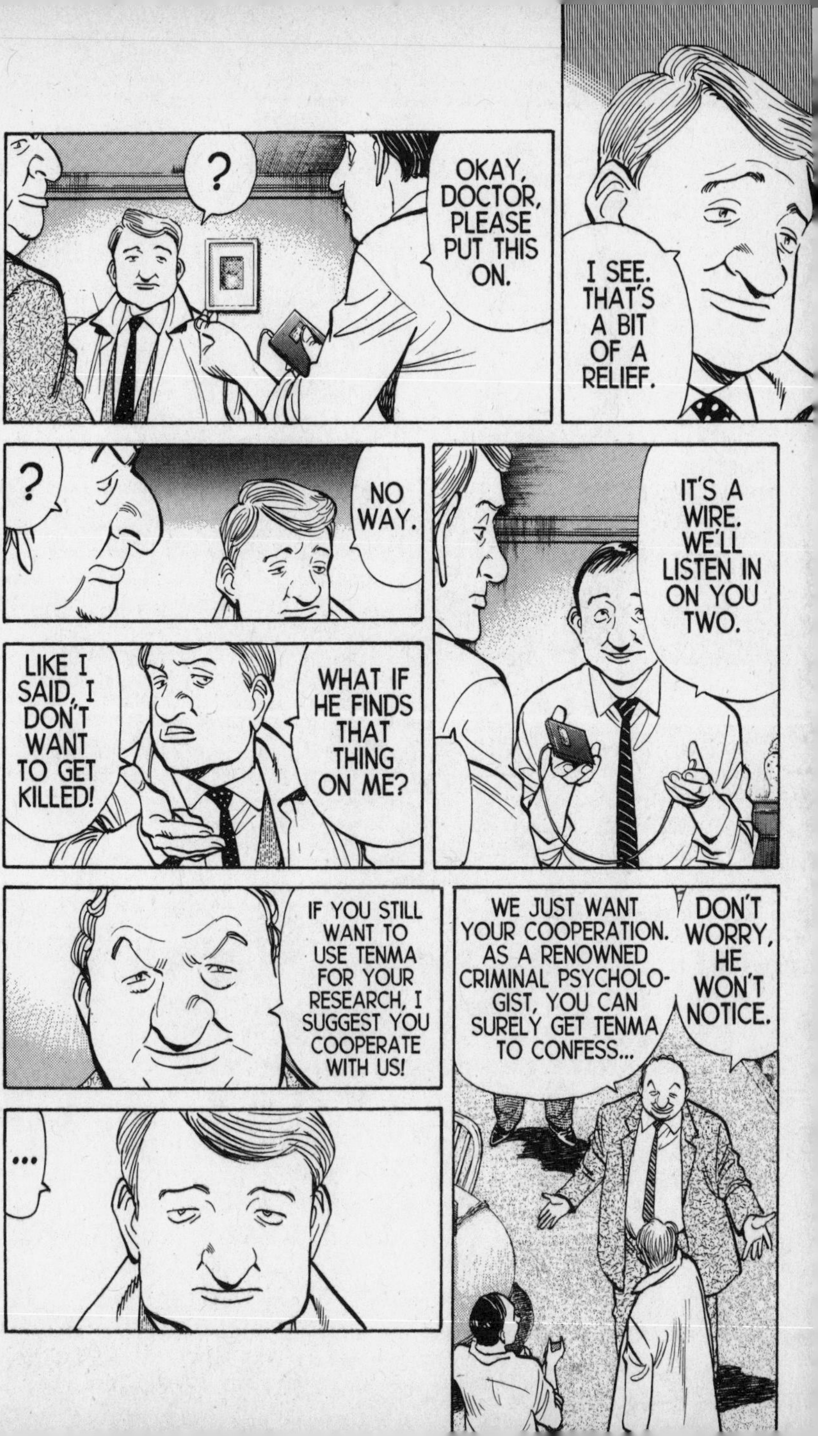
I SEE. THAT'S A BIT OF A RELIEF.
OKAY, DOCTOR, PLEASE PUT THIS ON.
?
IT'S A WIRE. WE'LL LISTEN IN ON YOU TWO.
NO WAY.
?
WHAT IF HE FINDS THAT THING ON ME?
LIKE I SAID, I DON'T WANT TO GET KILLED!
DON'T WORRY, HE WON'T NOTICE.
WE JUST WANT YOUR COOPERATION. AS A RENOWNED CRIMINAL PSYCHOLO-GIST, YOU CAN SURELY GET TENMA TO CONFESS...
IF YOU STILL WANT TO USE TENMA FOR YOUR RESEARCH, I SUGGEST YOU COOPERATE WITH US!
...

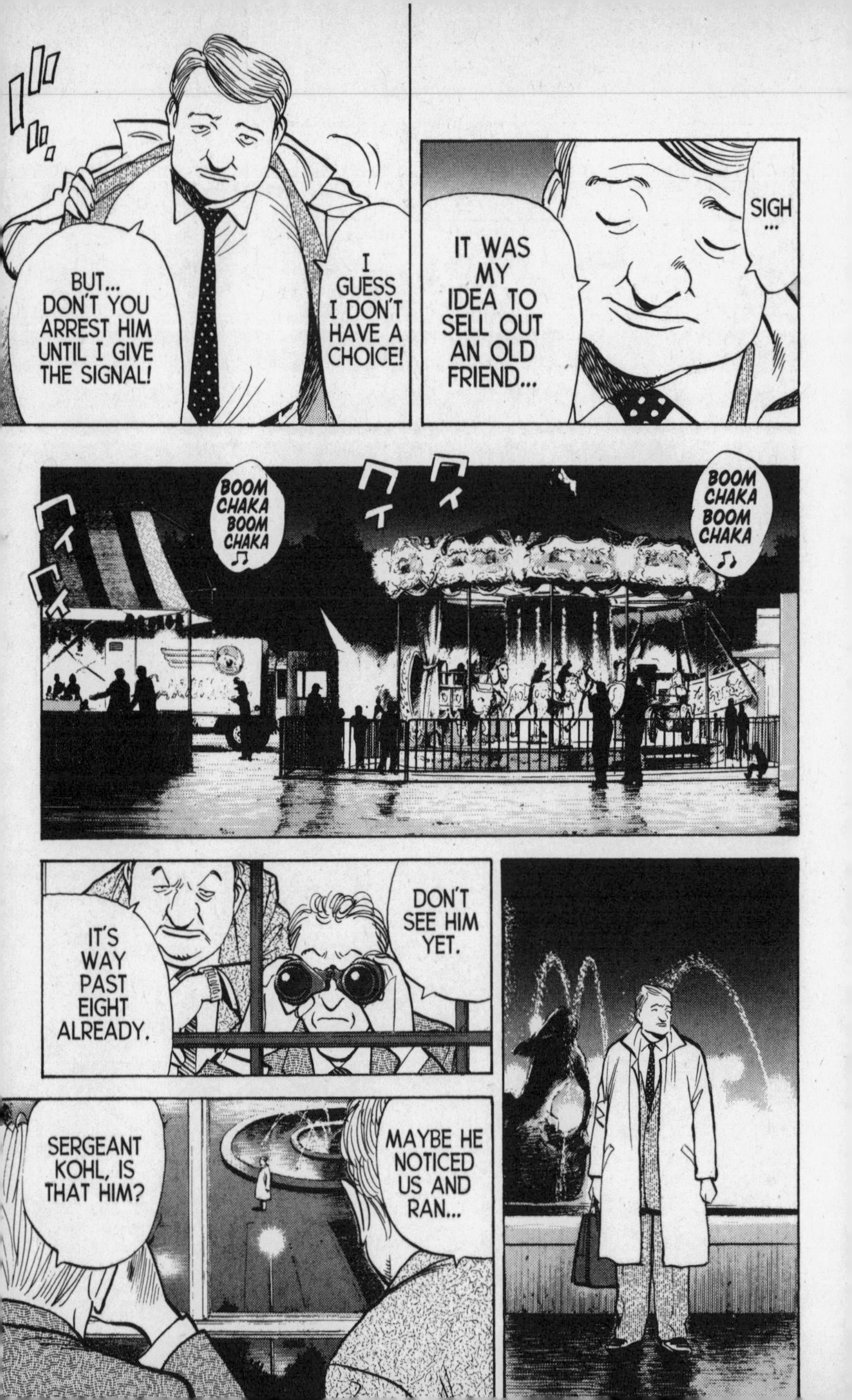
SIGH...
IT WAS MY IDEA TO SELL OUT AN OLD FRIEND...
I GUESS I DON'T HAVE A CHOICE!
BUT... DON'T YOU ARREST HIM UNTIL I GIVE THE SIGNAL!
BOOM CHAKA BOOM CHAKA ♫
BOOM CHAKA BOOM CHAKA ♫
DON'T SEE HIM YET.
IT'S WAY PAST EIGHT ALREADY.
MAYBE HE NOTICED US AND RAN...
SERGEANT KOHL, IS THAT HIM?

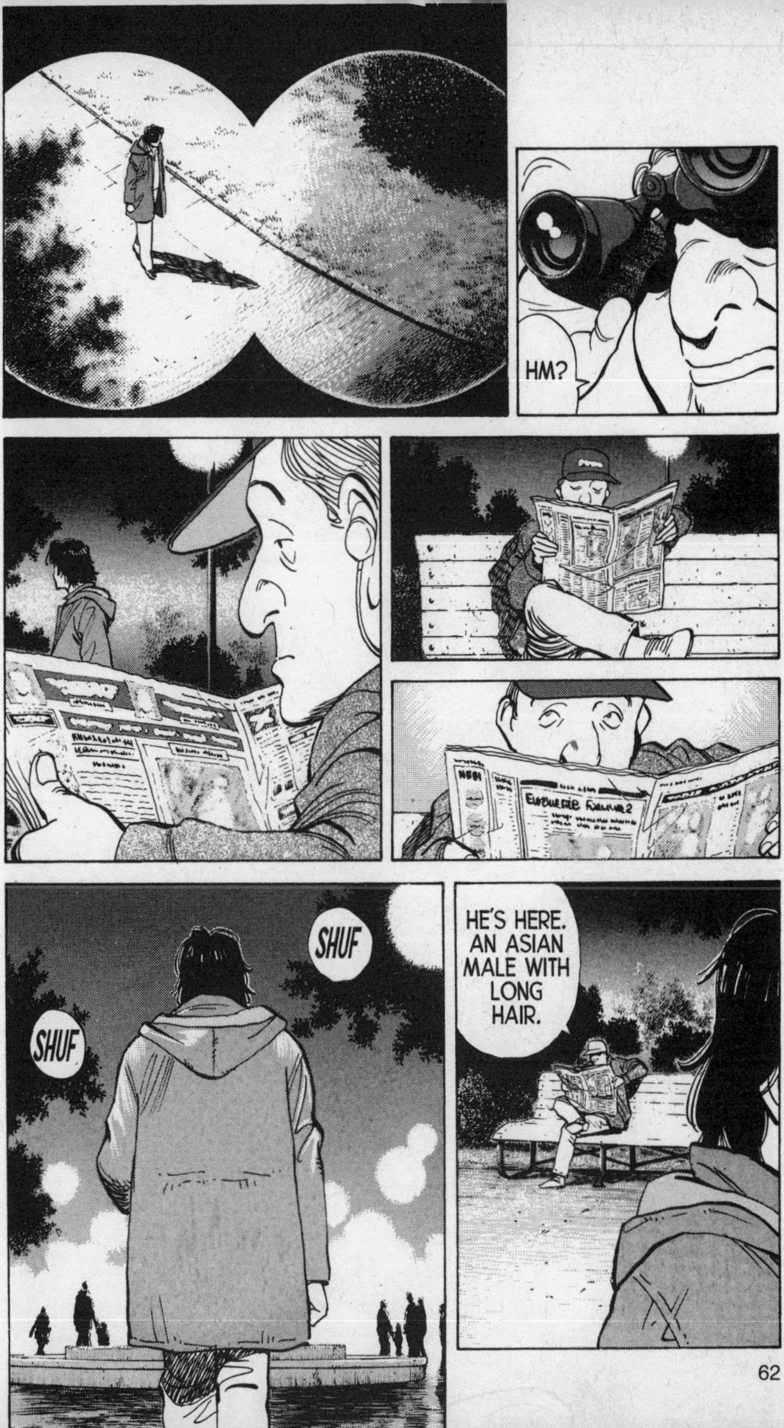
HM?
HE'S HERE. AN ASIAN MALE WITH LONG HAIR.
SHUF
SHUF

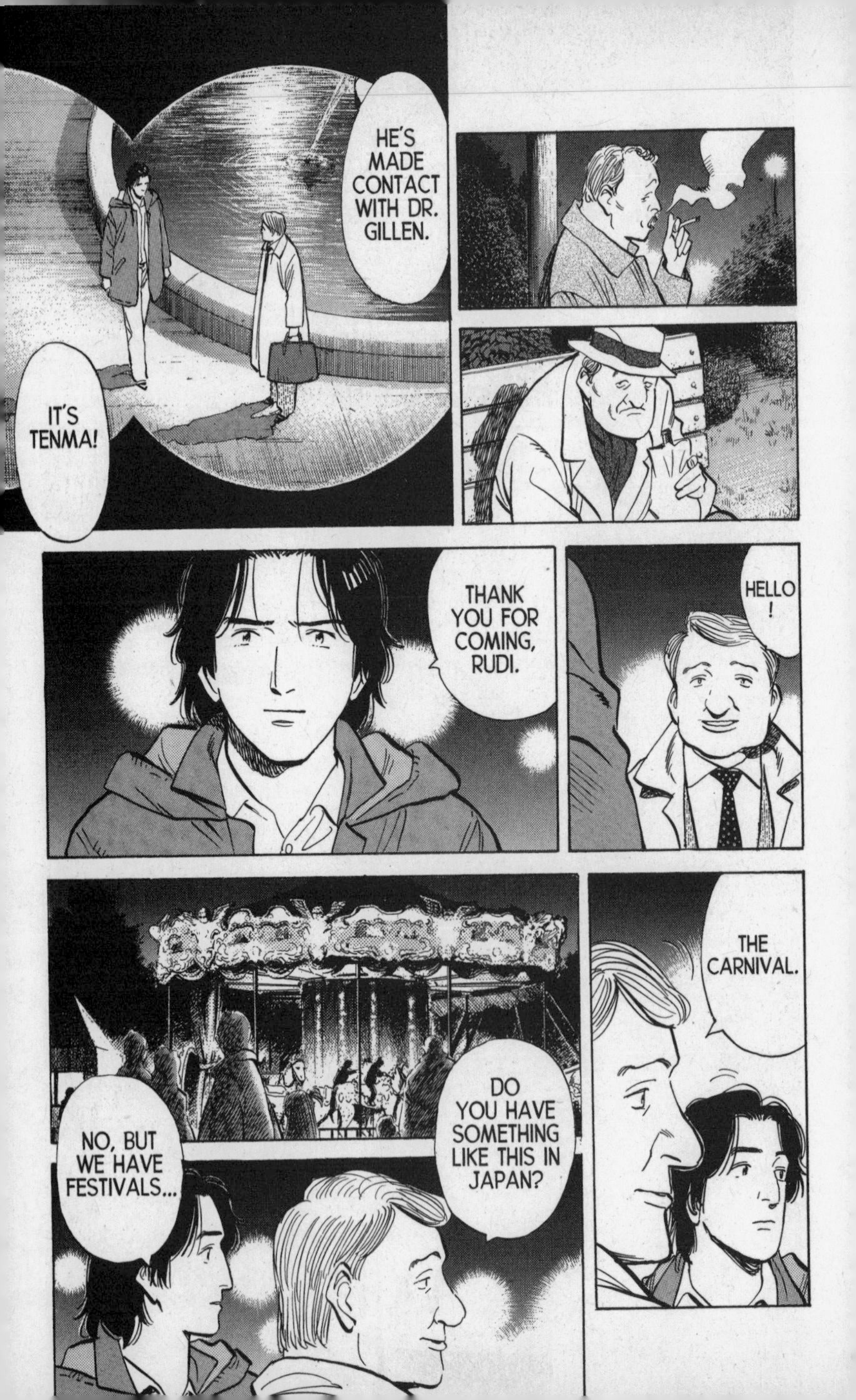
HE'S MADE CONTACT WITH DR. GILLEN.
IT'S TENMA!
HELLO!
THANK YOU FOR COMING, RUDI.
THE CARNIVAL.
DO YOU HAVE SOMETHING LIKE THIS IN JAPAN?
NO, BUT WE HAVE FESTIVALS...

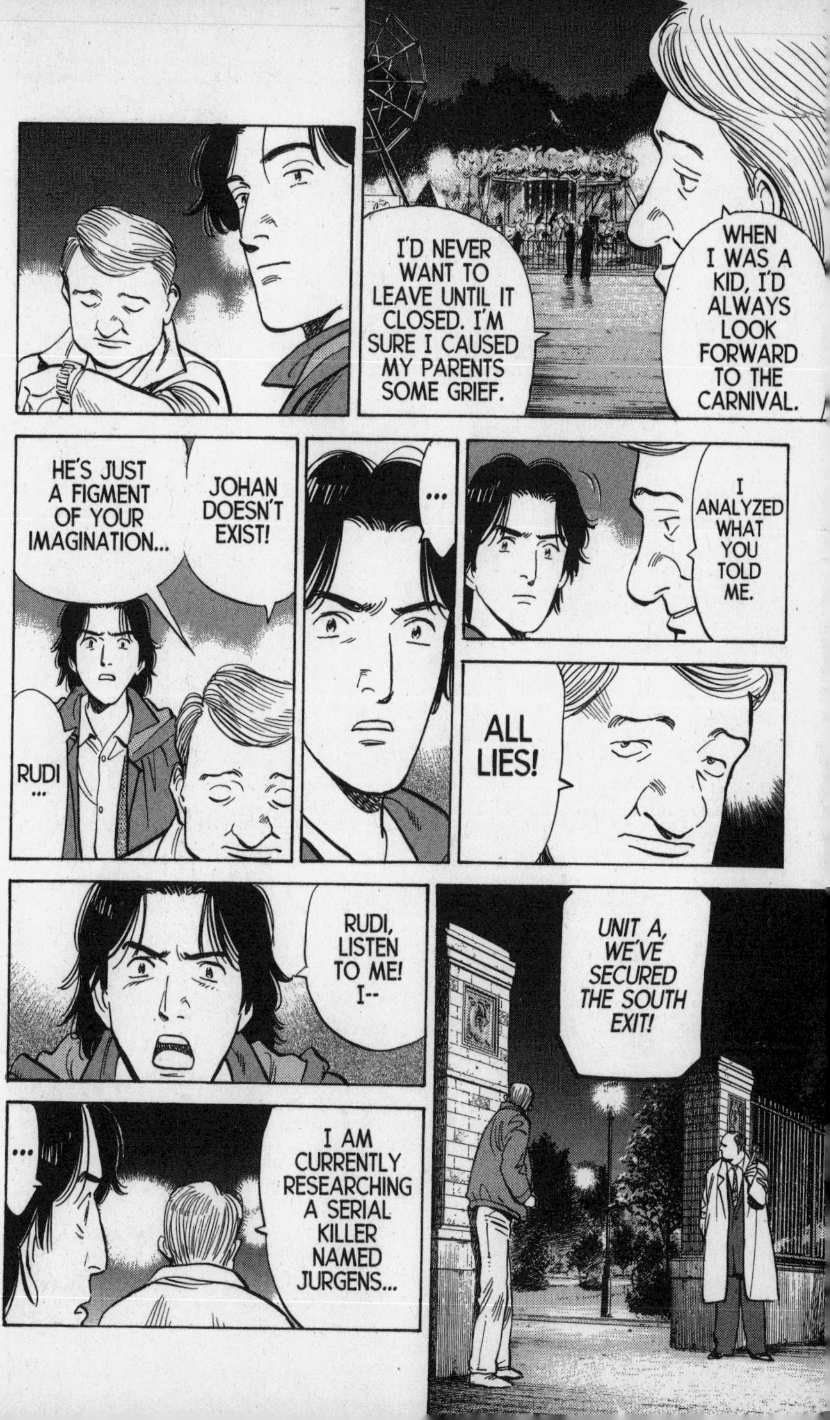
WHEN I WAS A KID, I'D ALWAYS LOOK FORWARD TO THE CARNIVAL.
I'D NEVER WANT TO LEAVE UNTIL IT CLOSED. I'M SURE I CAUSED MY PARENTS SOME GRIEF.
I ANALYZED WHAT YOU TOLD ME.
ALL LIES!
...
JOHAN DOESN'T EXIST!
HE'S JUST A FIGMENT OF YOUR IMAGINATION...
RUDI ...
UNIT A, WE'VE SECURED THE SOUTH EXIT!
RUDI, LISTEN TO ME! I--
I AM CURRENTLY RESEARCHING A SERIAL KILLER NAMED JURGENS...
...

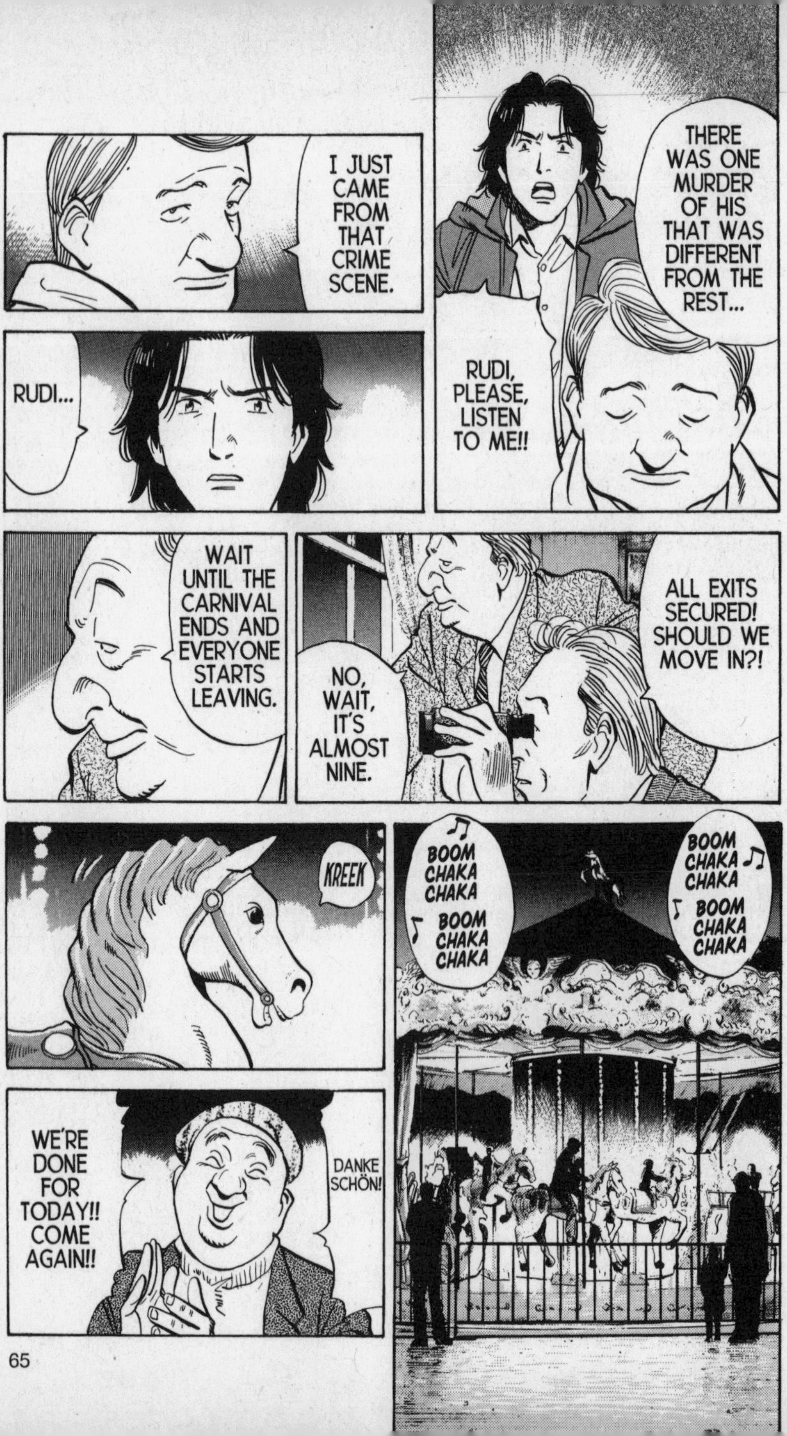
THERE WAS ONE MURDER OF HIS THAT WAS DIFFERENT FROM THE REST...
RUDI, PLEASE, LISTEN TO ME!!
I JUST CAME FROM THAT CRIME SCENE.
RUDI...
ALL EXITS SECURED! SHOULD WE MOVE IN?!
NO, WAIT, IT'S ALMOST NINE.
WAIT UNTIL THE CARNIVAL ENDS AND EVERYONE STARTS LEAVING.
BOOM CHAKA CHAKA
BOOM CHAKA CHAKA
BOOM CHAKA CHAKA
BOOM CHAKA CHAKA
KREEK
DANKE SCHÖN!
WE'RE DONE FOR TODAY!! COME AGAIN!!

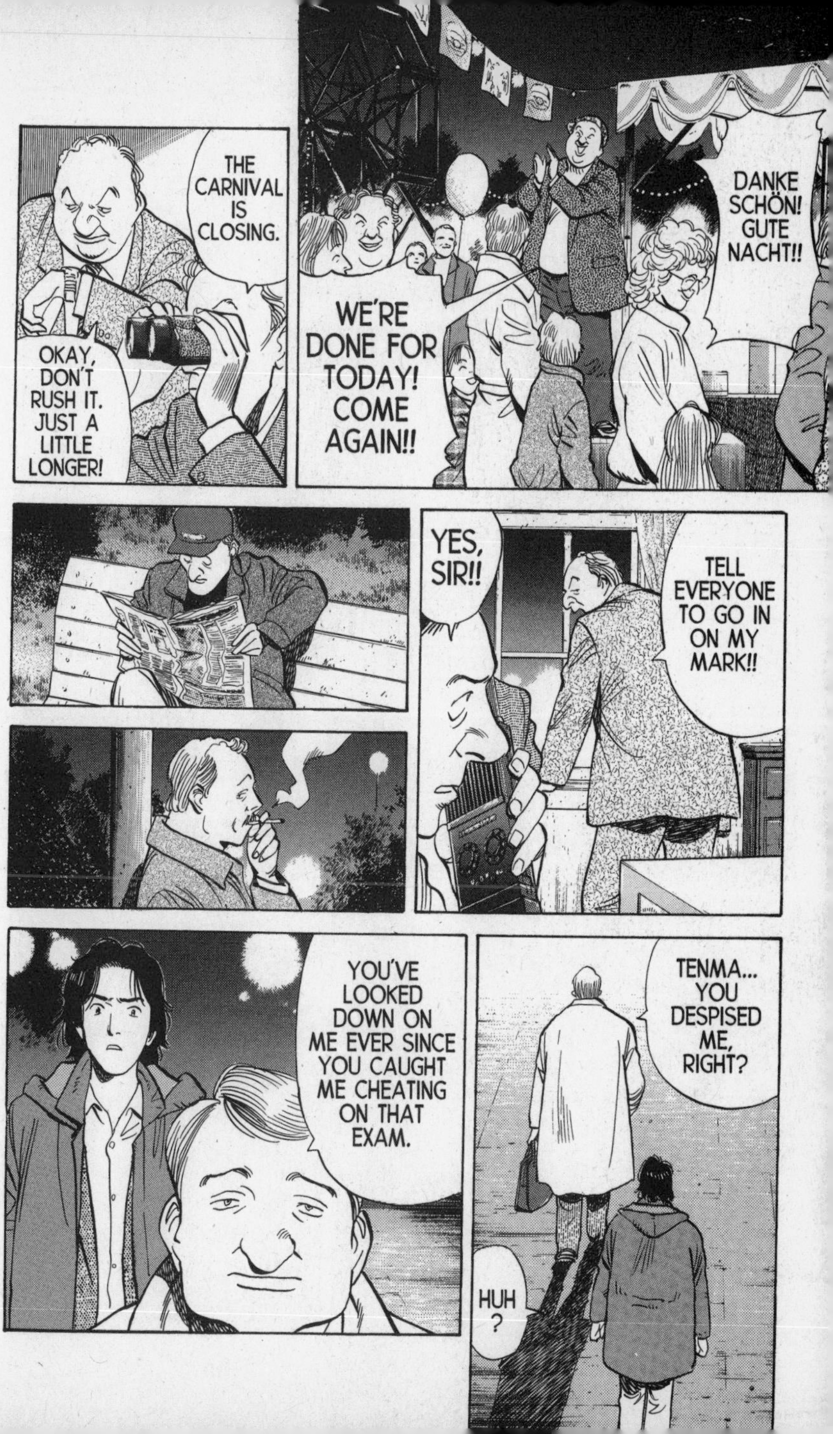
DANKE SCHÖN! GUTE NACHT!!
WE'RE DONE FOR TODAY! COME AGAIN!!
THE CARNIVAL IS CLOSING.
OKAY, DON'T RUSH IT. JUST A LITTLE LONGER!
TELL EVERYONE TO GO IN ON MY MARK!!
YES, SIR!!
TENMA... YOU DESPISED ME, RIGHT?
HUH?
YOU'VE LOOKED DOWN ON ME EVER SINCE YOU CAUGHT ME CHEATING ON THAT EXAM.

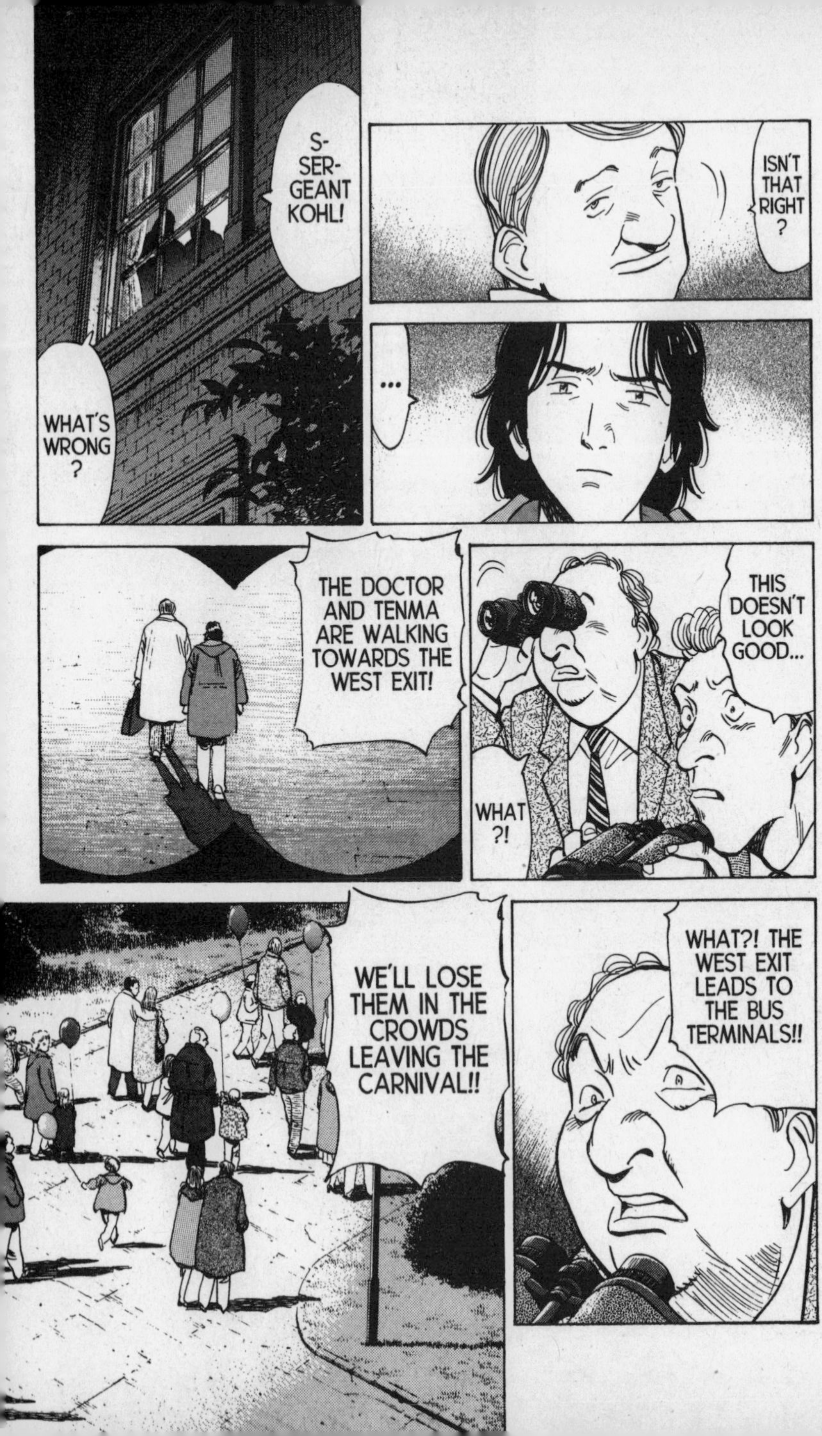
ISN'T THAT RIGHT?
...
S-SER-GEANT KOHL!
WHAT'S WRONG?
THIS DOESN'T LOOK GOOD...
WHAT?!
THE DOCTOR AND TENMA ARE WALKING TOWARDS THE WEST EXIT!
WHAT?! THE WEST EXIT LEADS TO THE BUS TERMINALS!!
WE'LL LOSE THEM IN THE CROWDS LEAVING THE CARNIVAL!!

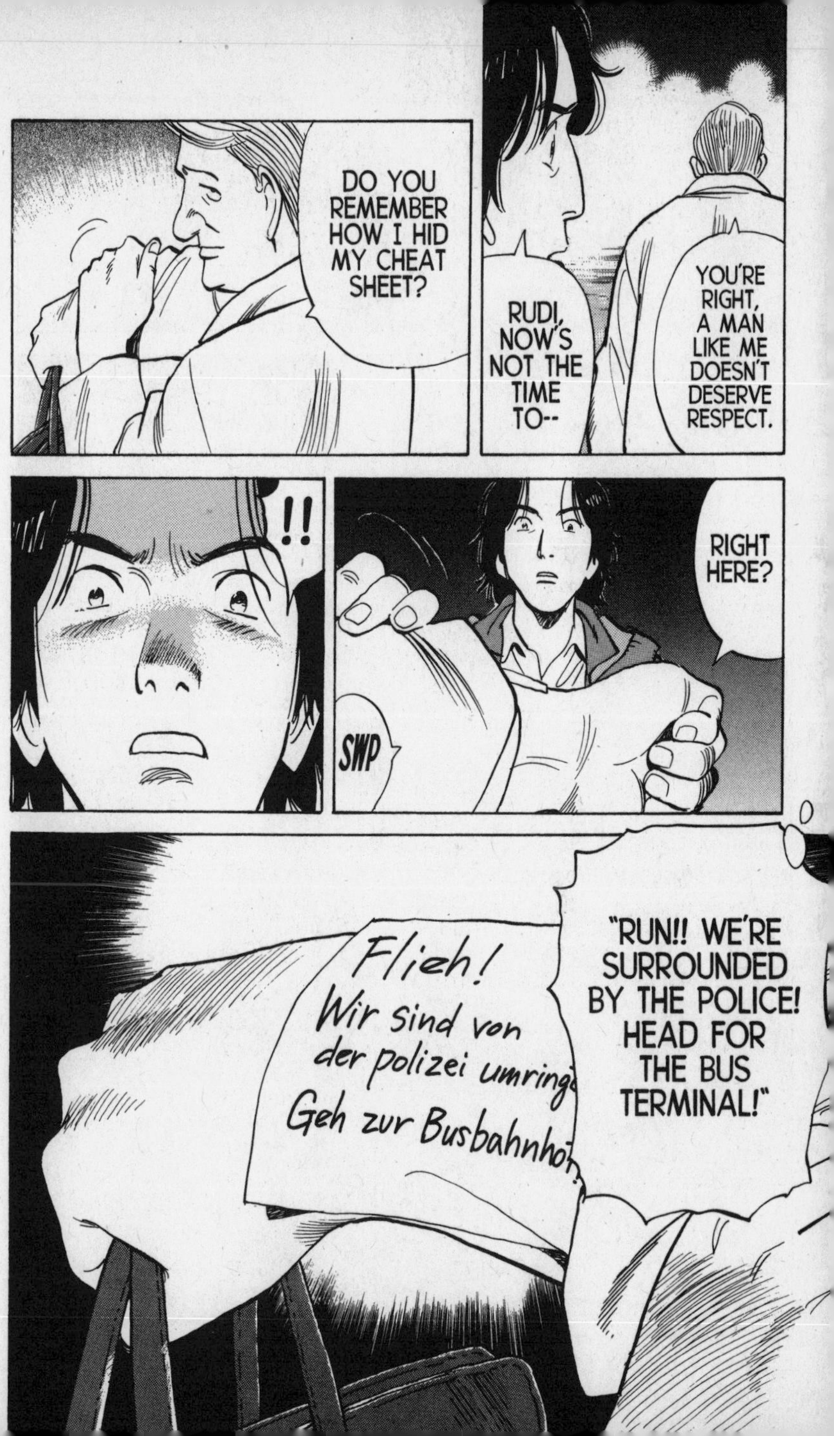
YOU'RE RIGHT, A MAN LIKE ME DOESN'T DESERVE RESPECT.
RUDI, NOW'S NOT THE TIME TO--
DO YOU REMEMBER HOW I HID MY CHEAT SHEET?
RIGHT HERE?
SWP
!!
"RUN!! WE'RE SURROUNDED BY THE POLICE! HEAD FOR THE BUS TERMINAL!"
Flieh!
Wir sind von der polizei umring
Geh zur Busbahnho

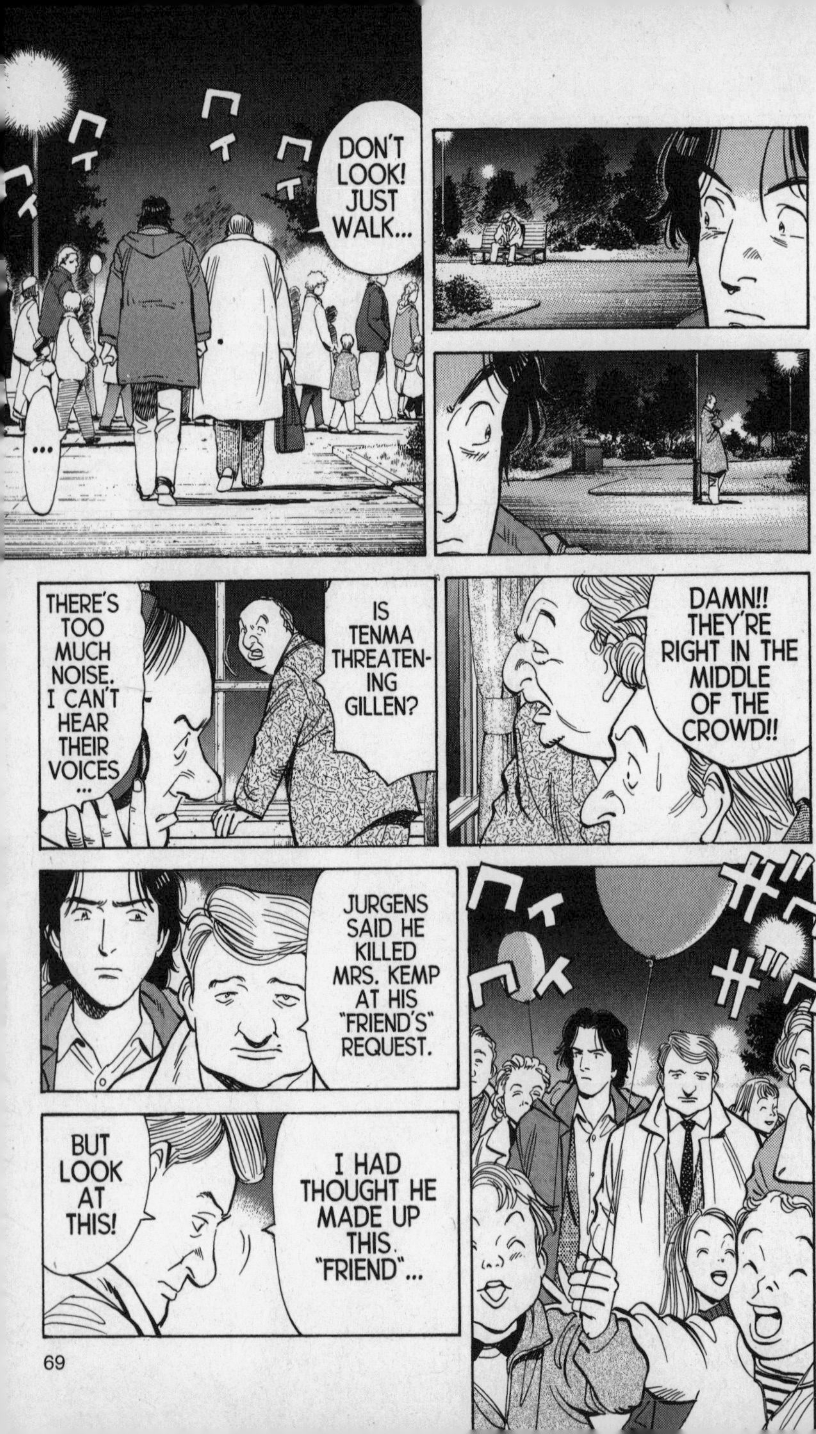
DON'T LOOK! JUST WALK...
...
DAMN!! THEY'RE RIGHT IN THE MIDDLE OF THE CROWD!!
IS TENMA THREATEN-ING GILLEN?
THERE'S TOO MUCH NOISE. I CAN'T HEAR THEIR VOICES...
JURGENS SAID HE KILLED MRS. KEMP AT HIS "FRIEND'S" REQUEST.
I HAD THOUGHT HE MADE UP THIS "FRIEND"...
BUT LOOK AT THIS!

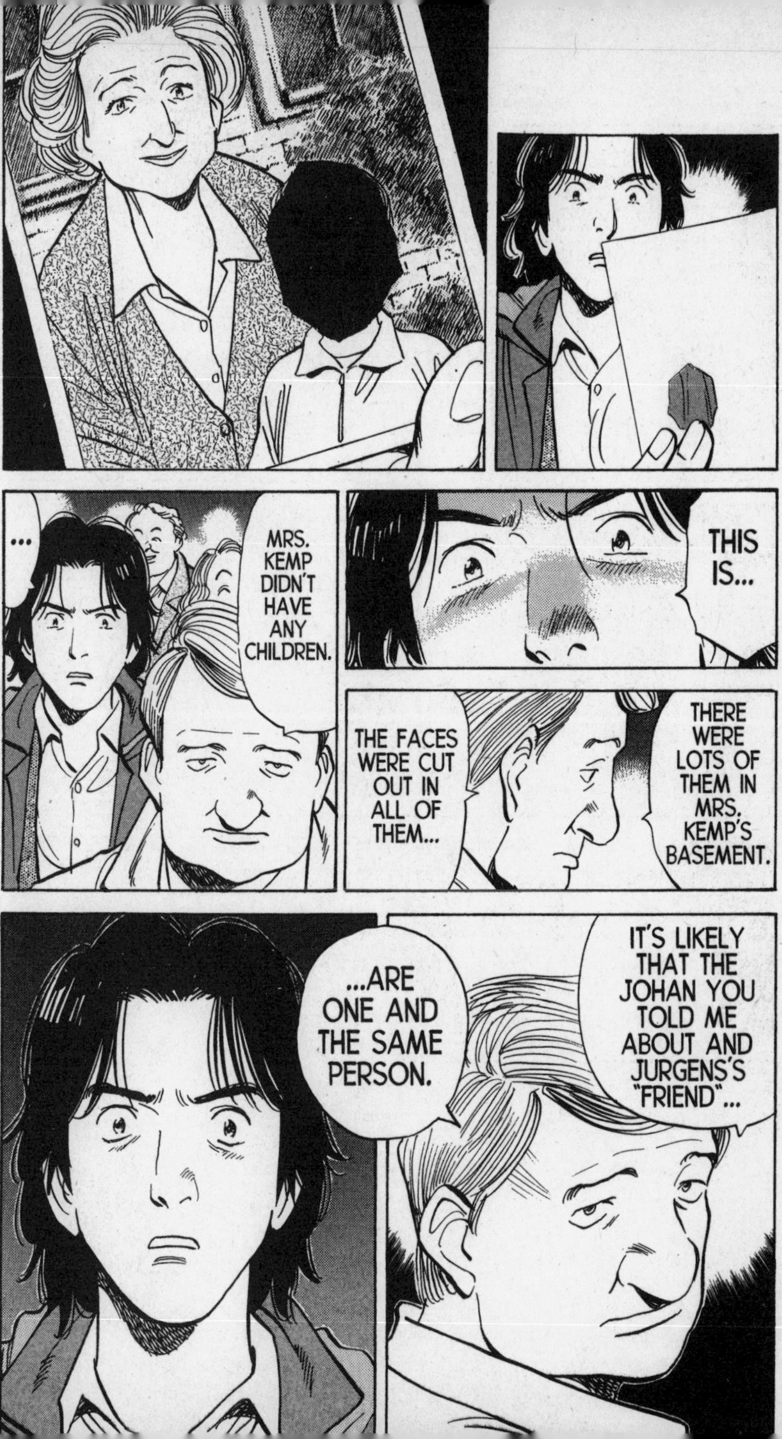
THIS IS...
THERE WERE LOTS OF THEM IN MRS. KEMP'S BASEMENT.
THE FACES WERE CUT OUT IN ALL OF THEM...
MRS. KEMP DIDN'T HAVE ANY CHILDREN.
...
IT'S LIKELY THAT THE JOHAN YOU TOLD ME ABOUT AND JURGENS'S "FRIEND"...
...ARE ONE AND THE SAME PERSON.

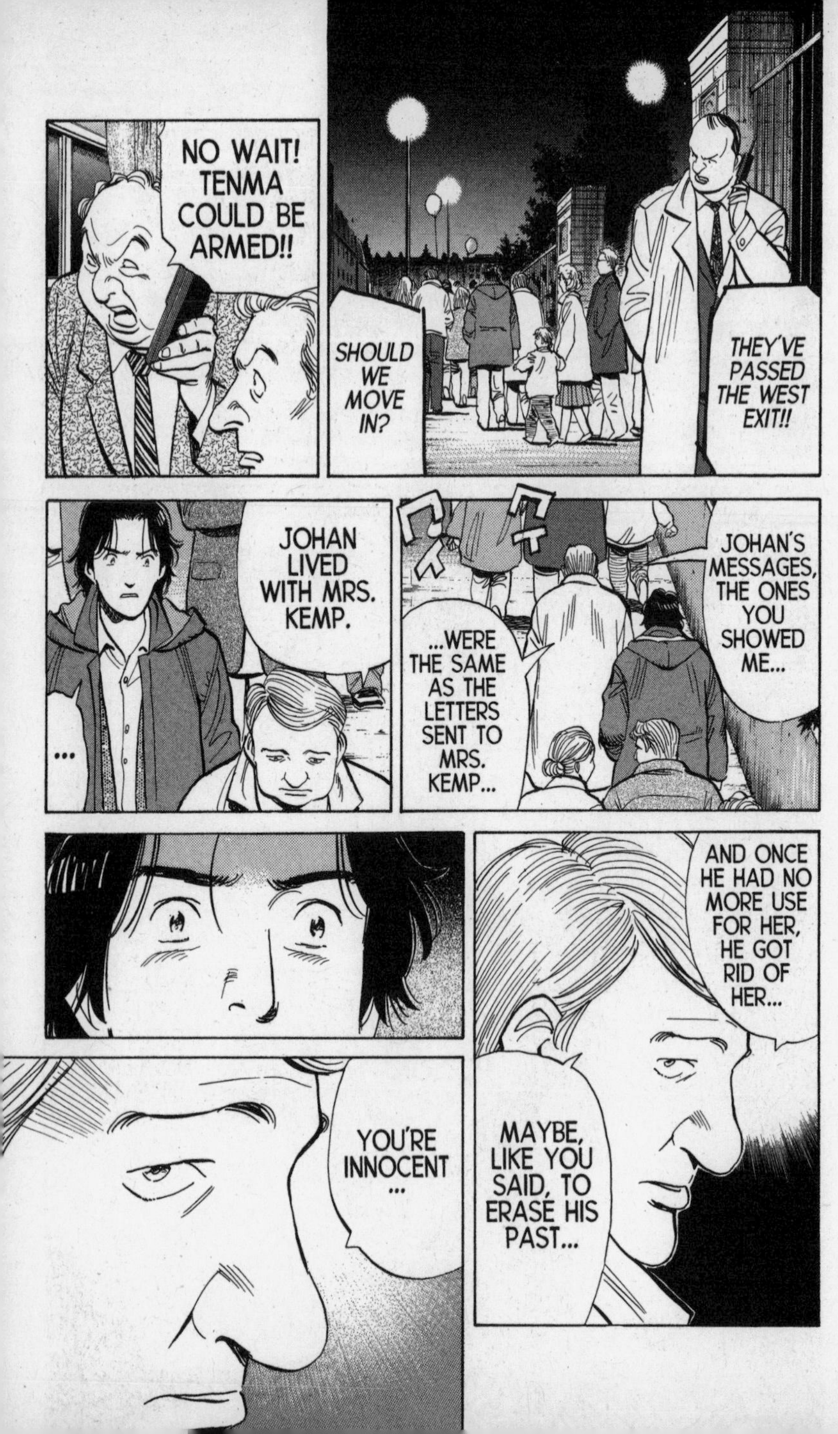
THEY'VE PASSED THE WEST EXIT!!
SHOULD WE MOVE IN?
NO WAIT! TENMA COULD BE ARMED!!
JOHAN'S MESSAGES, THE ONES YOU SHOWED ME...
...WERE THE SAME AS THE LETTERS SENT TO MRS. KEMP...
JOHAN LIVED WITH MRS. KEMP.
...
AND ONCE HE HAD NO MORE USE FOR HER, HE GOT RID OF HER...
MAYBE, LIKE YOU SAID, TO ERASE HIS PAST...
YOU'RE INNOCENT ...

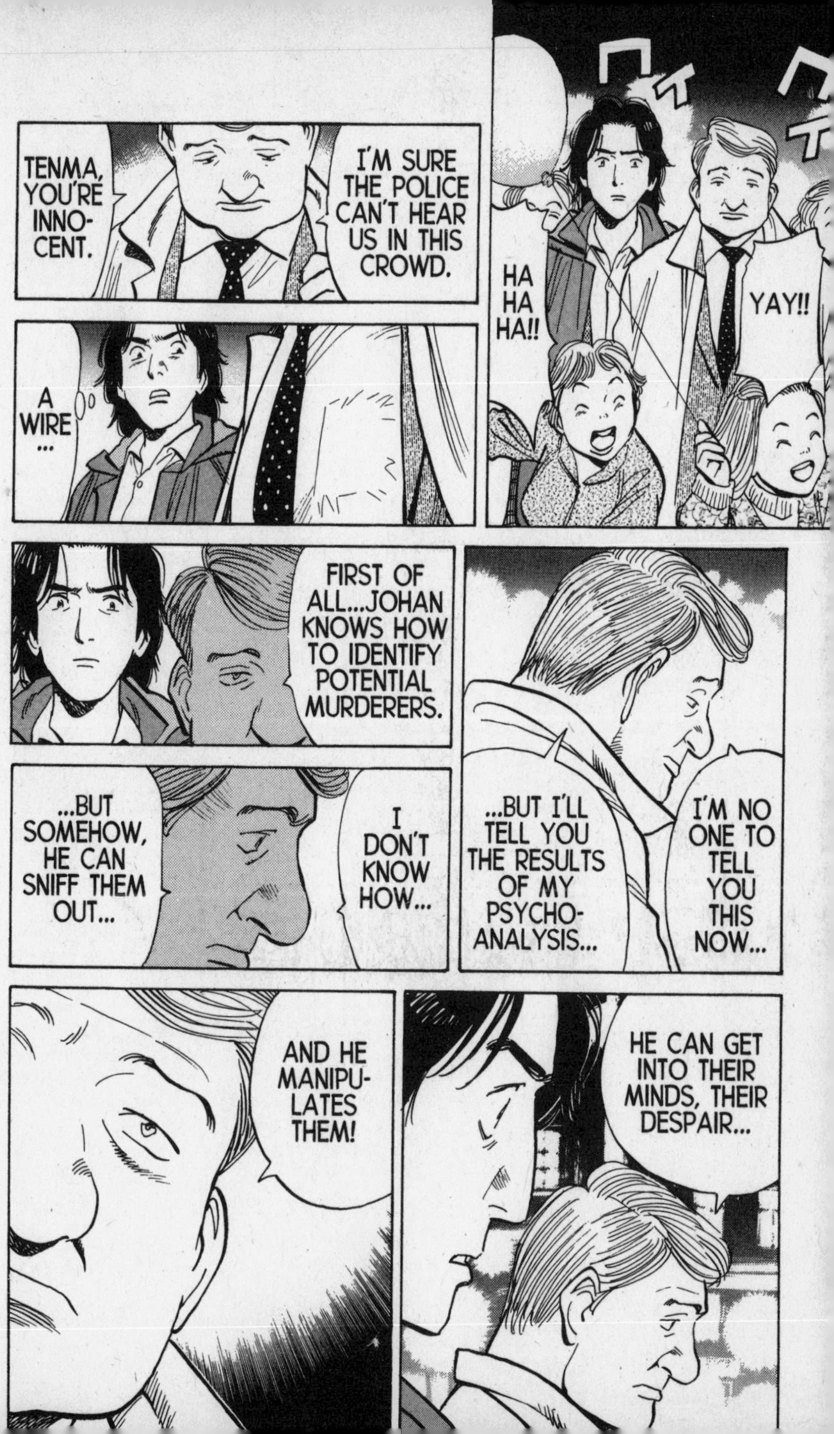
YAY!!
HA HA HA!!
I'M SURE THE POLICE CAN'T HEAR US IN THIS CROWD.
TENMA, YOU'RE INNO-CENT.
A WIRE...
I'M NO ONE TO TELL YOU THIS NOW...
...BUT I'LL TELL YOU THE RESULTS OF MY PSYCHO-ANALYSIS...
FIRST OF ALL...JOHAN KNOWS HOW TO IDENTIFY POTENTIAL MURDERERS.
I DON'T KNOW HOW...
...BUT SOMEHOW, HE CAN SNIFF THEM OUT...
HE CAN GET INTO THEIR MINDS, THEIR DESPAIR...
AND HE MANIPULATES THEM!

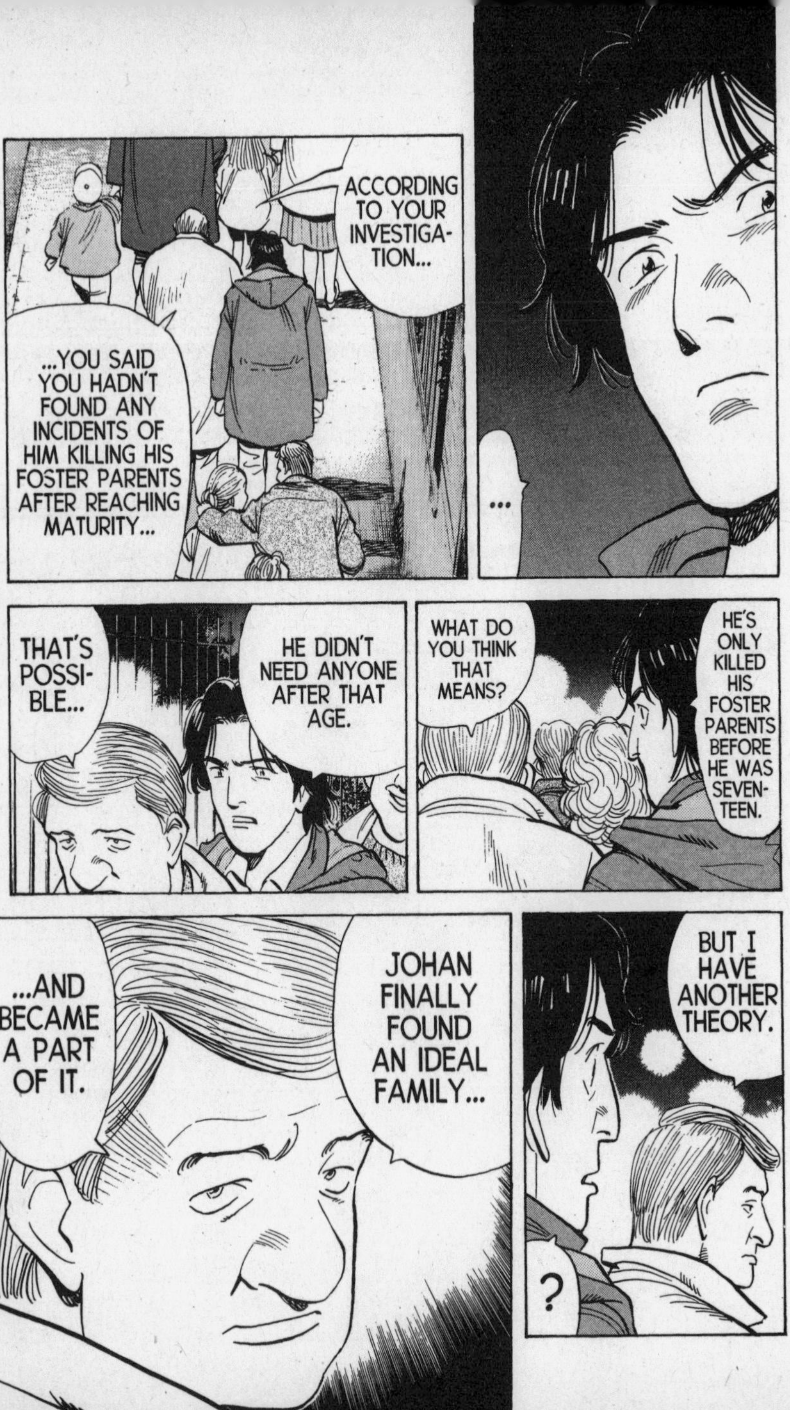
...
ACCORDING TO YOUR INVESTIGATION...
...YOU SAID YOU HADN'T FOUND ANY INCIDENTS OF HIM KILLING HIS FOSTER PARENTS AFTER REACHING MATURITY...
HE'S ONLY KILLED HIS FOSTER PARENTS BEFORE HE WAS SEVENTEEN.
WHAT DO YOU THINK THAT MEANS?
HE DIDN'T NEED ANYONE AFTER THAT AGE.
THAT'S POSSIBLE...
BUT I HAVE ANOTHER THEORY.
?
JOHAN FINALLY FOUND AN IDEAL FAMILY...
...AND BECAME A PART OF IT.

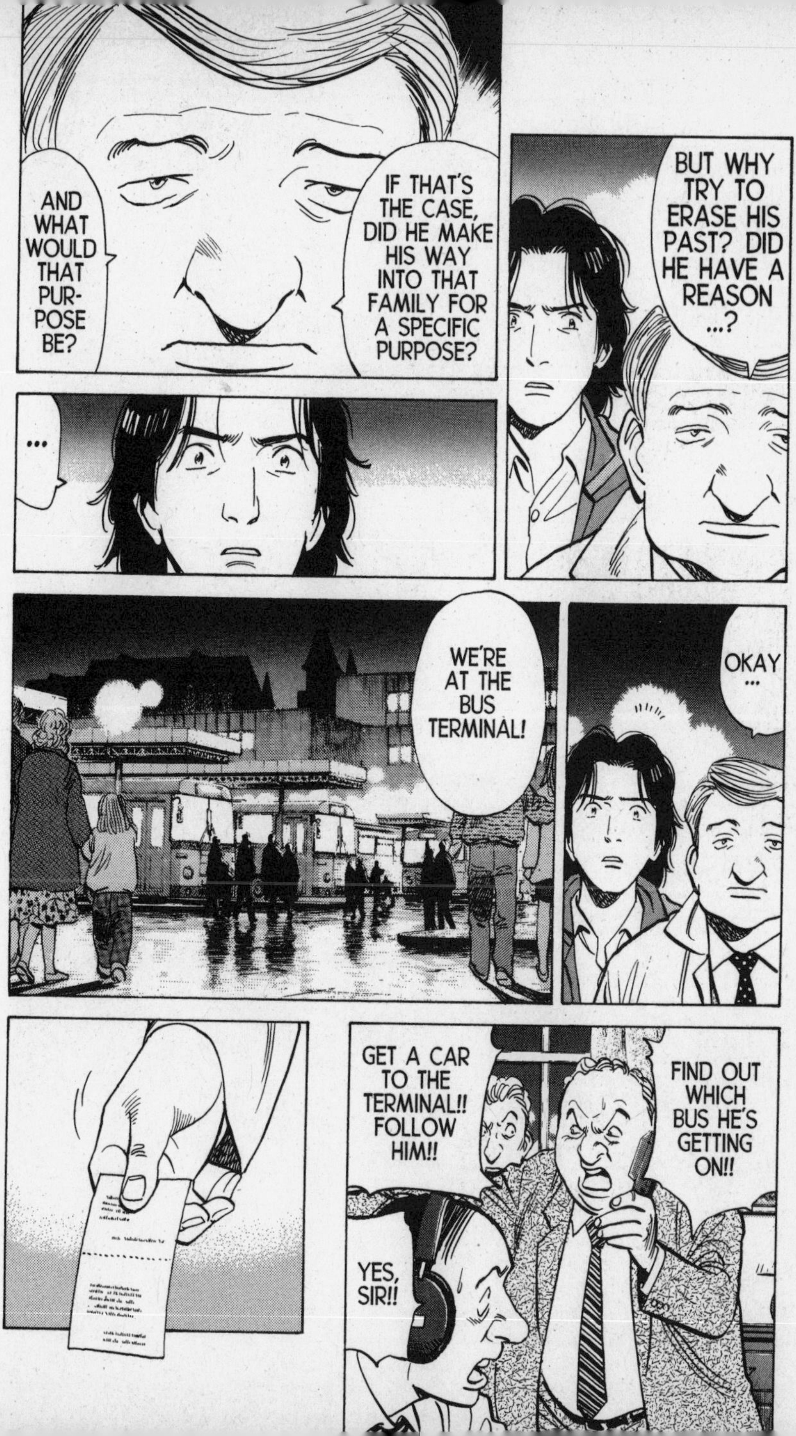
BUT WHY TRY TO ERASE HIS PAST? DID HE HAVE A REASON ...?
IF THAT'S THE CASE, DID HE MAKE HIS WAY INTO THAT FAMILY FOR A SPECIFIC PURPOSE?
AND WHAT WOULD THAT PUR-POSE BE?
...
OKAY ...
WE'RE AT THE BUS TERMINAL!
FIND OUT WHICH BUS HE'S GETTING ON!!
GET A CAR TO THE TERMINAL!! FOLLOW HIM!!
YES, SIR!!

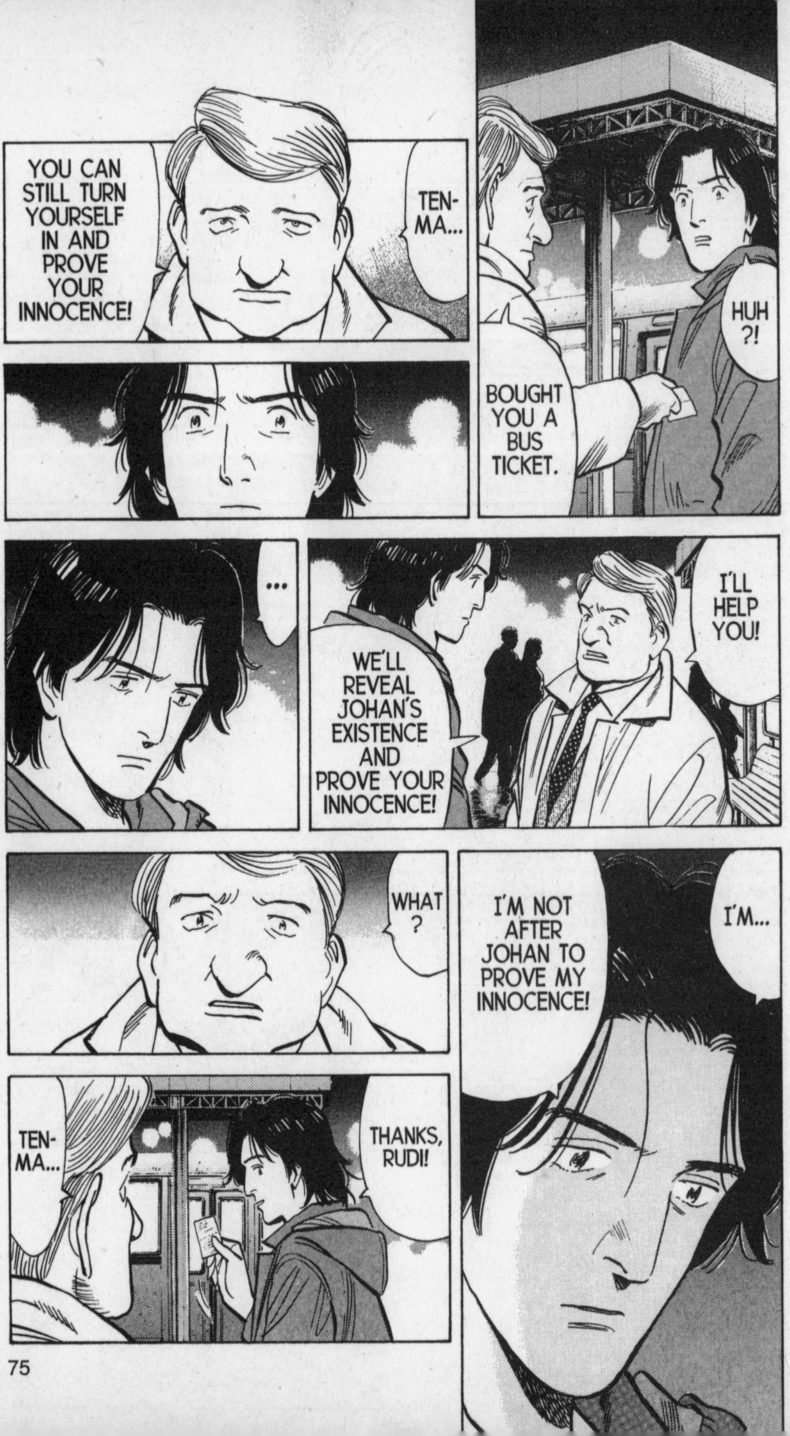
HUH ?!
BOUGHT YOU A BUS TICKET.
TEN-MA...
YOU CAN STILL TURN YOURSELF IN AND PROVE YOUR INNOCENCE!
I'LL HELP YOU!
WE'LL REVEAL JOHAN'S EXISTENCE AND PROVE YOUR INNOCENCE!
...
I'M...
I'M NOT AFTER JOHAN TO PROVE MY INNOCENCE!
WHAT ?
THANKS, RUDI!
TEN-MA...

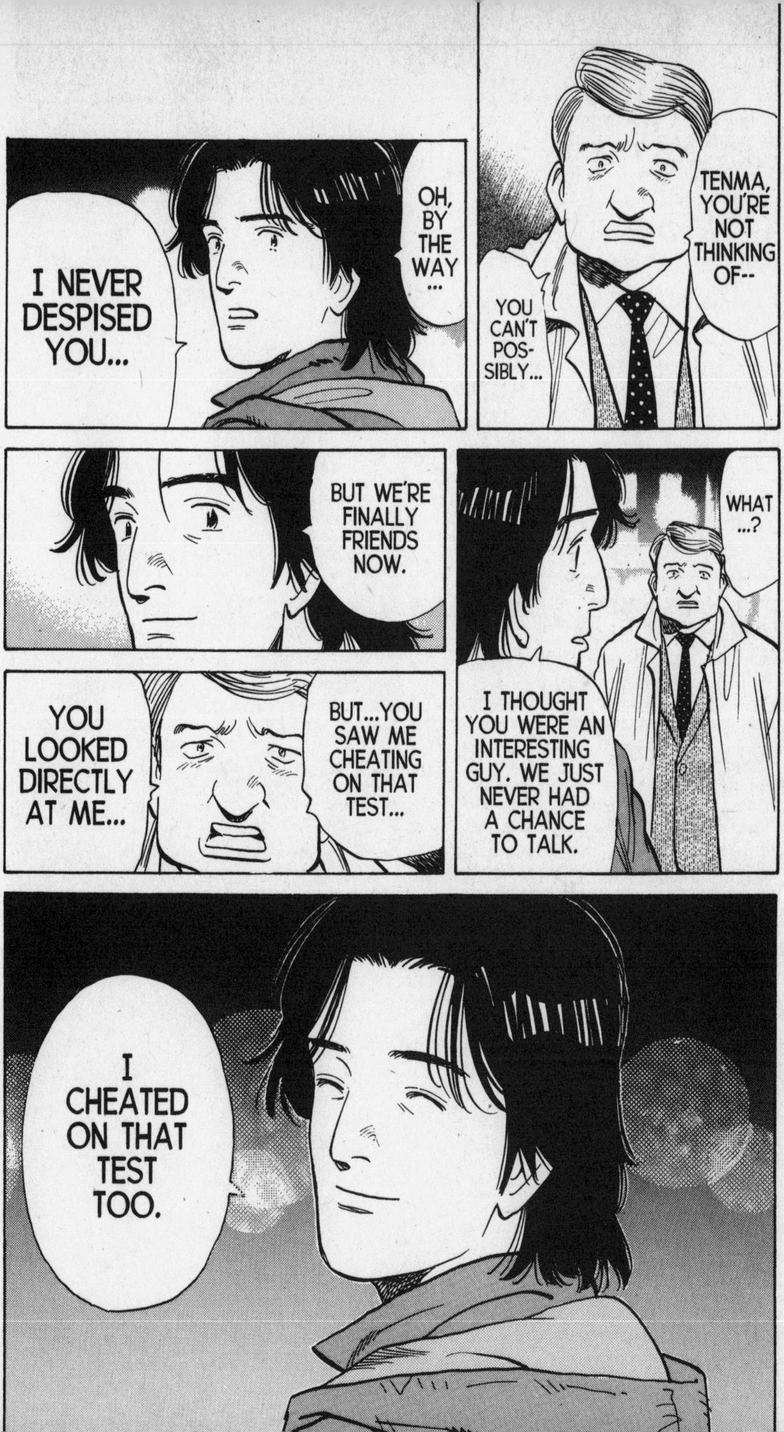
TENMA, YOU'RE NOT THINKING OF--
YOU CAN'T POS- SIBLY...
OH, BY THE WAY ...
I NEVER DESPISED YOU...
WHAT ...?
I THOUGHT YOU WERE AN INTERESTING GUY. WE JUST NEVER HAD A CHANCE TO TALK.
BUT WE'RE FINALLY FRIENDS NOW.
BUT...YOU SAW ME CHEATING ON THAT TEST...
YOU LOOKED DIRECTLY AT ME...
I CHEATED ON THAT TEST TOO.

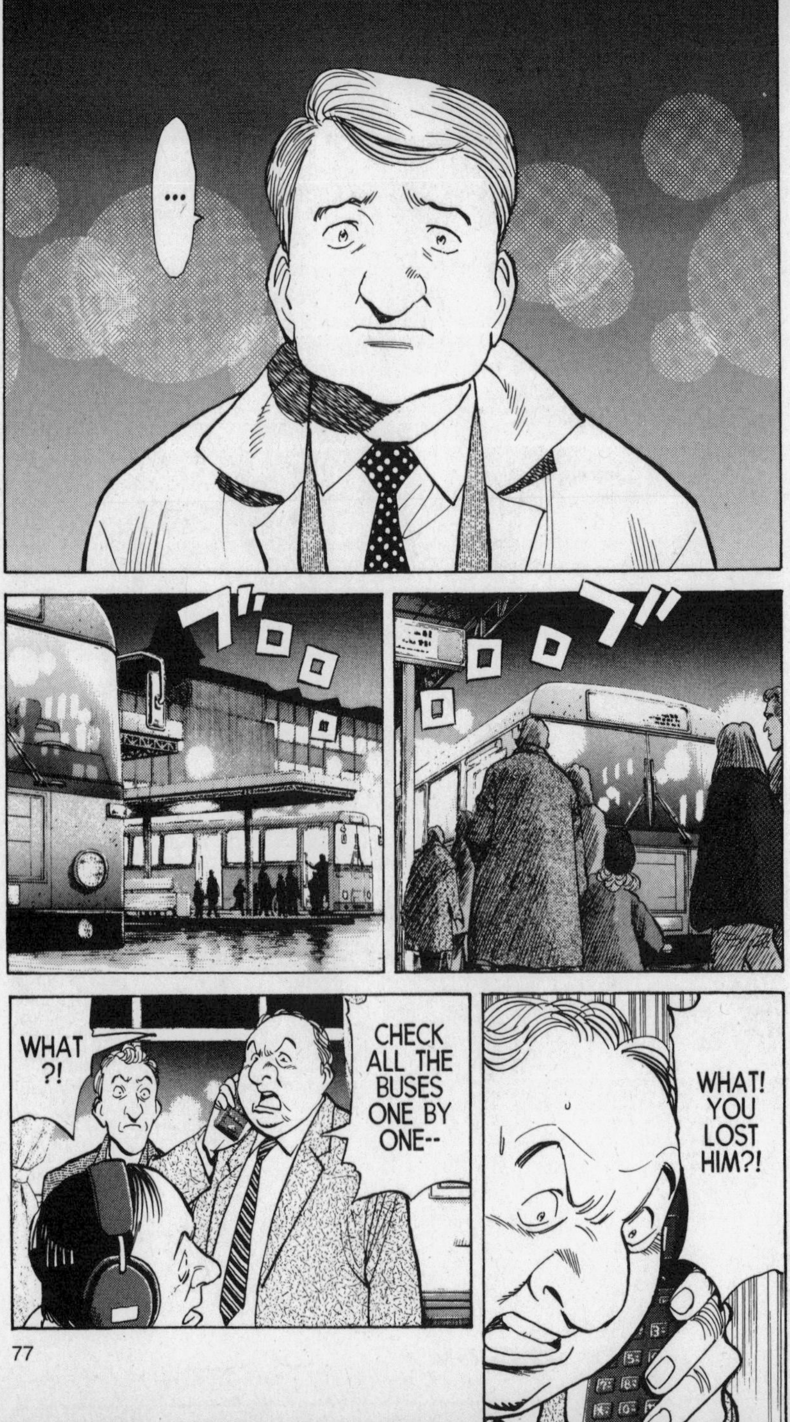
...
ブロロロ
ブロロロ
WHAT! YOU LOST HIM?!
CHECK ALL THE BUSES ONE BY ONE--
WHAT ?!

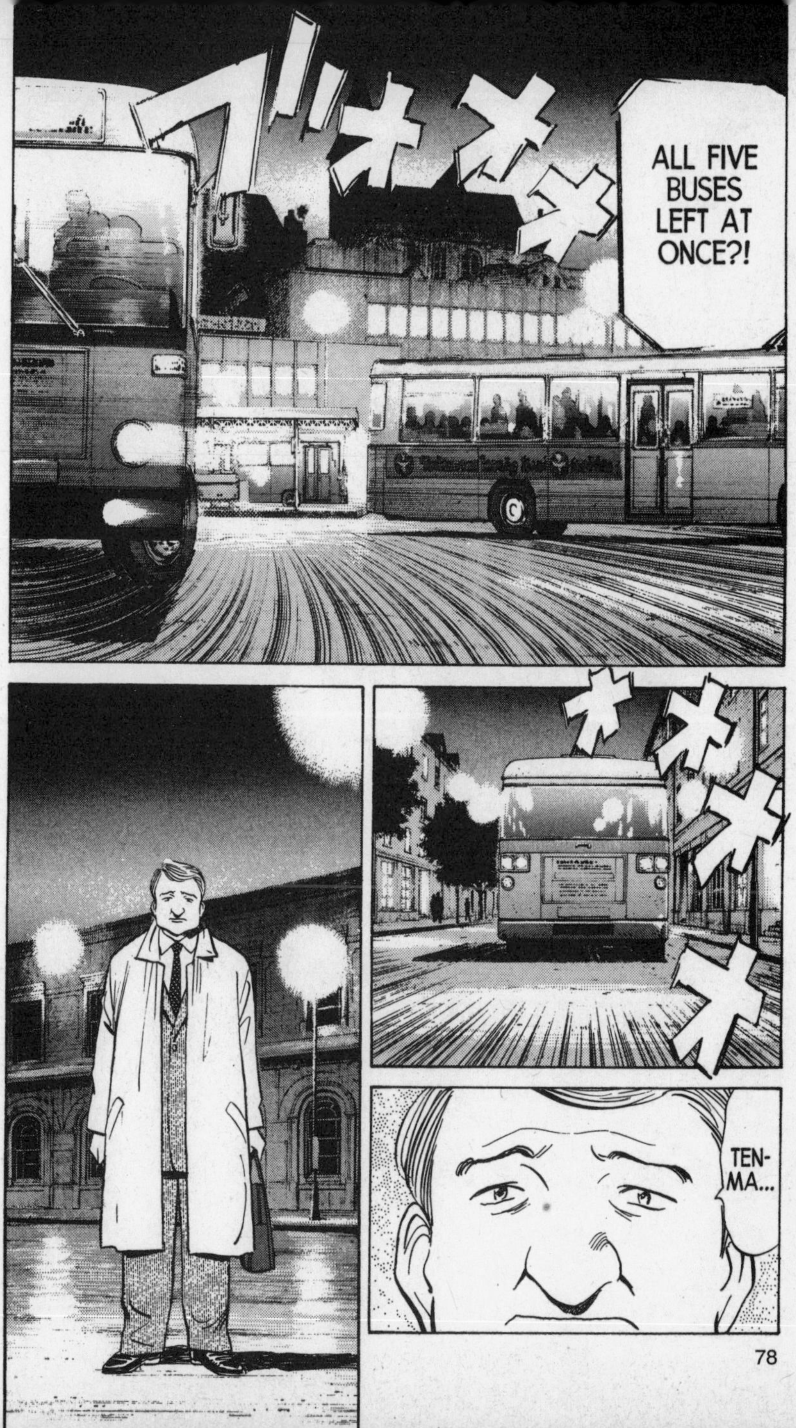
ALL FIVE BUSES LEFT AT ONCE?!
TEN-MA...

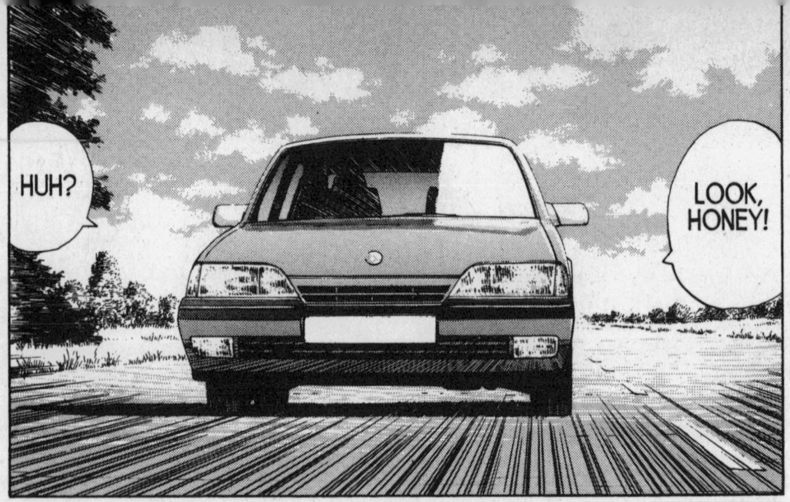
LOOK, HONEY!
HUH?

Chapter 4

Journey to Freiham

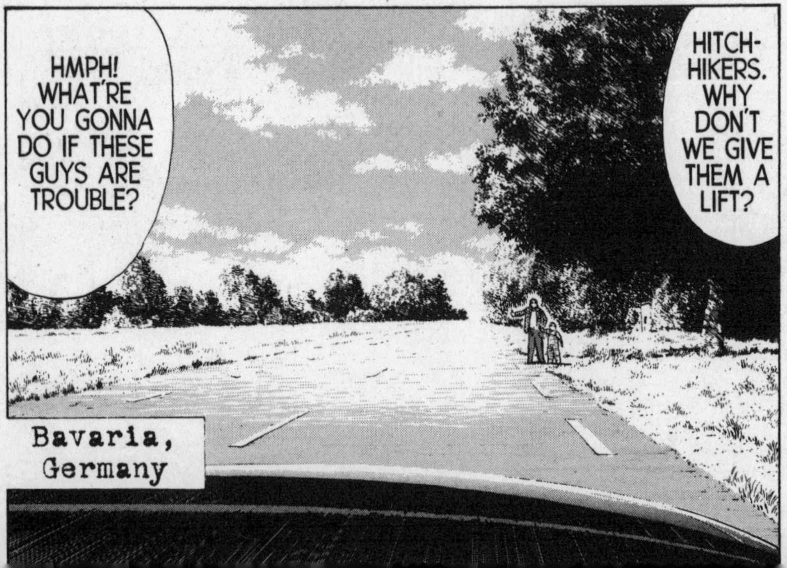
HITCH-HIKERS. WHY DON'T WE GIVE THEM A LIFT?
HMPH! WHAT'RE YOU GONNA DO IF THESE GUYS ARE TROUBLE?
Bavaria, Germany

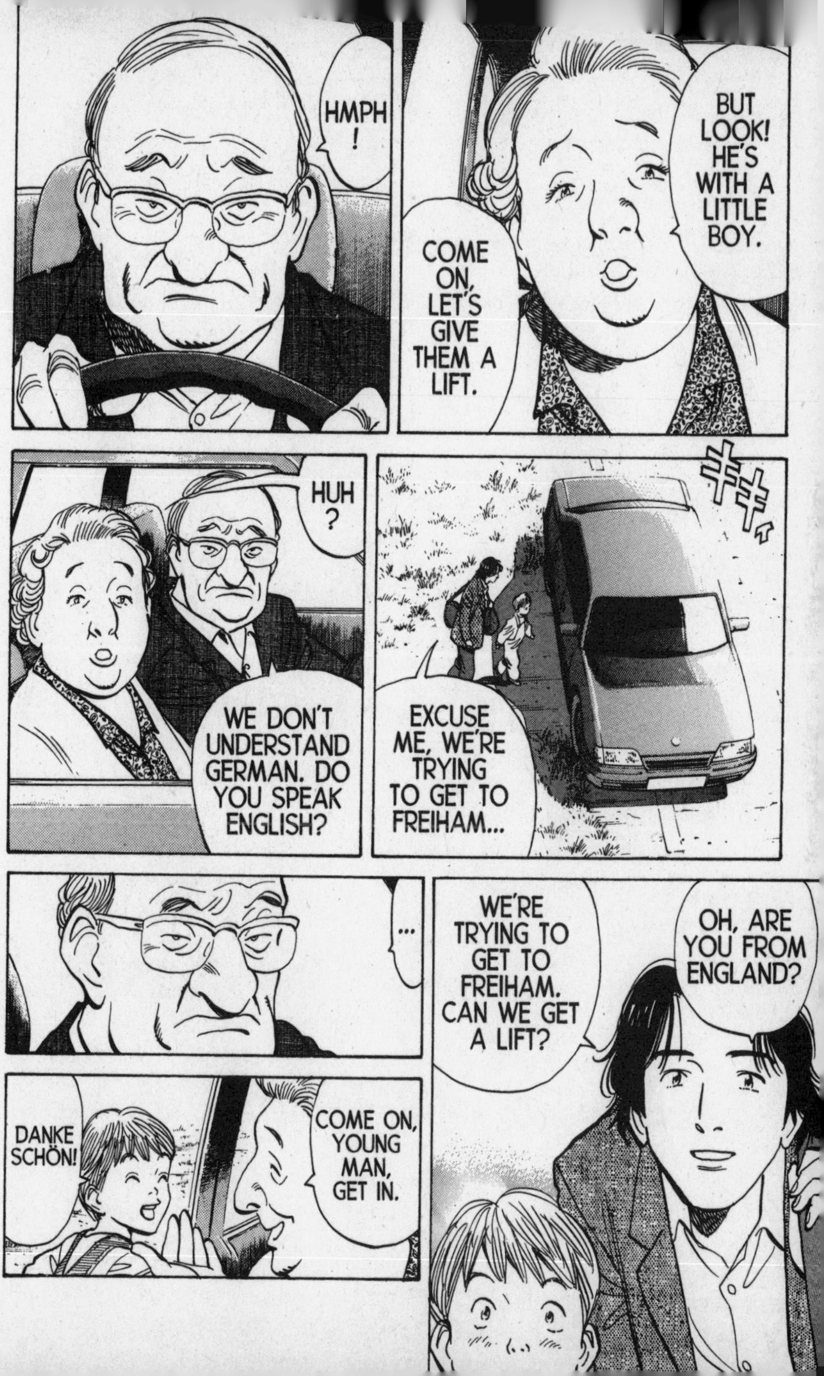
BUT LOOK! HE'S WITH A LITTLE BOY.
COME ON, LET'S GIVE THEM A LIFT.
HMPH!
EXCUSE ME, WE'RE TRYING TO GET TO FREIHAM...
HUH?
WE DON'T UNDERSTAND GERMAN. DO YOU SPEAK ENGLISH?
OH, ARE YOU FROM ENGLAND?
WE'RE TRYING TO GET TO FREIHAM. CAN WE GET A LIFT?
...
COME ON, YOUNG MAN, GET IN.
DANKE SCHÖN!

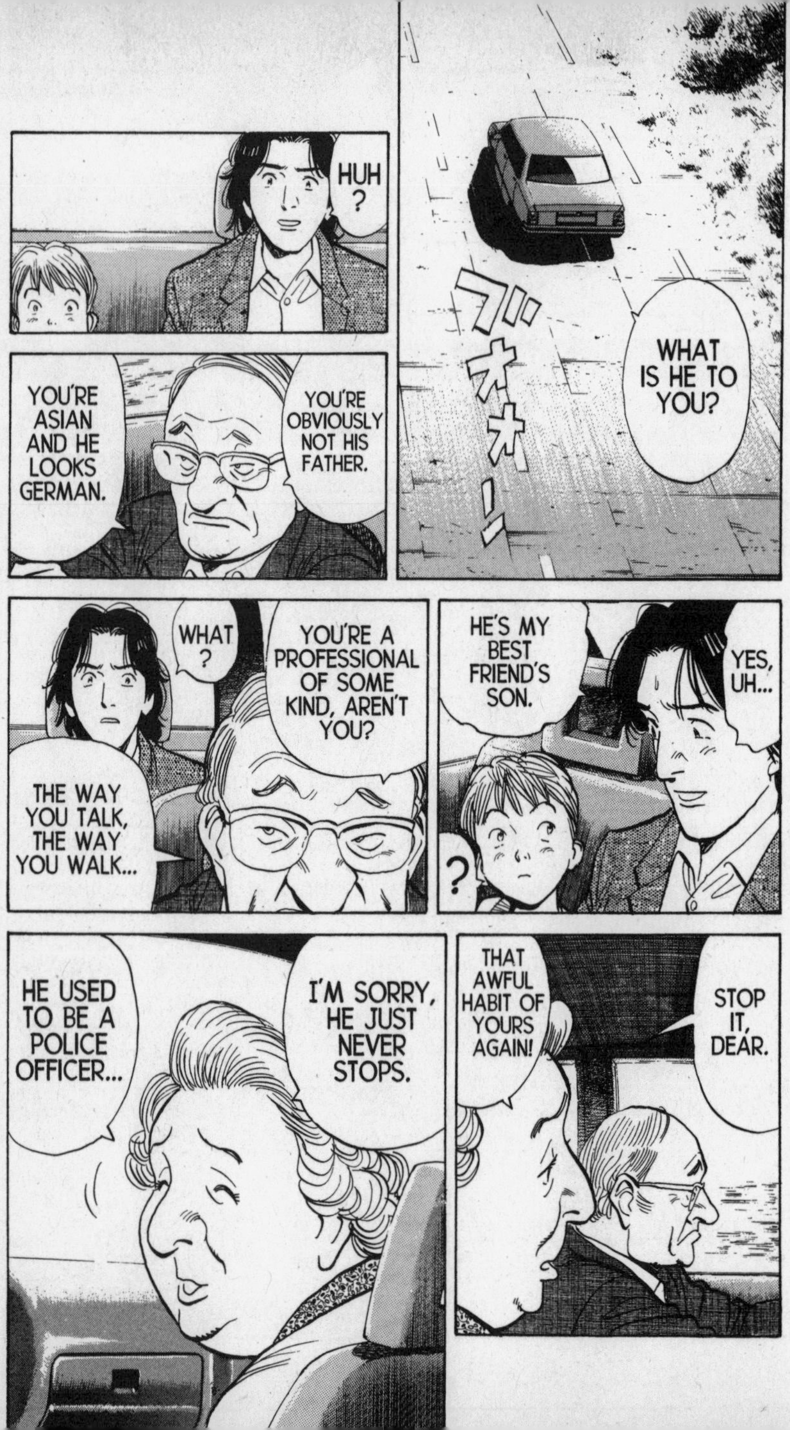
ブオォ!!
WHAT IS HE TO YOU?
HUH ?
YOU'RE OBVIOUSLY NOT HIS FATHER.
YOU'RE ASIAN AND HE LOOKS GERMAN.
YES, UH...
HE'S MY BEST FRIEND'S SON.
?
YOU'RE A PROFESSIONAL OF SOME KIND, AREN'T YOU?
WHAT ?
THE WAY YOU TALK, THE WAY YOU WALK...
STOP IT, DEAR.
THAT AWFUL HABIT OF YOURS AGAIN!
I'M SORRY, HE JUST NEVER STOPS.
HE USED TO BE A POLICE OFFICER...

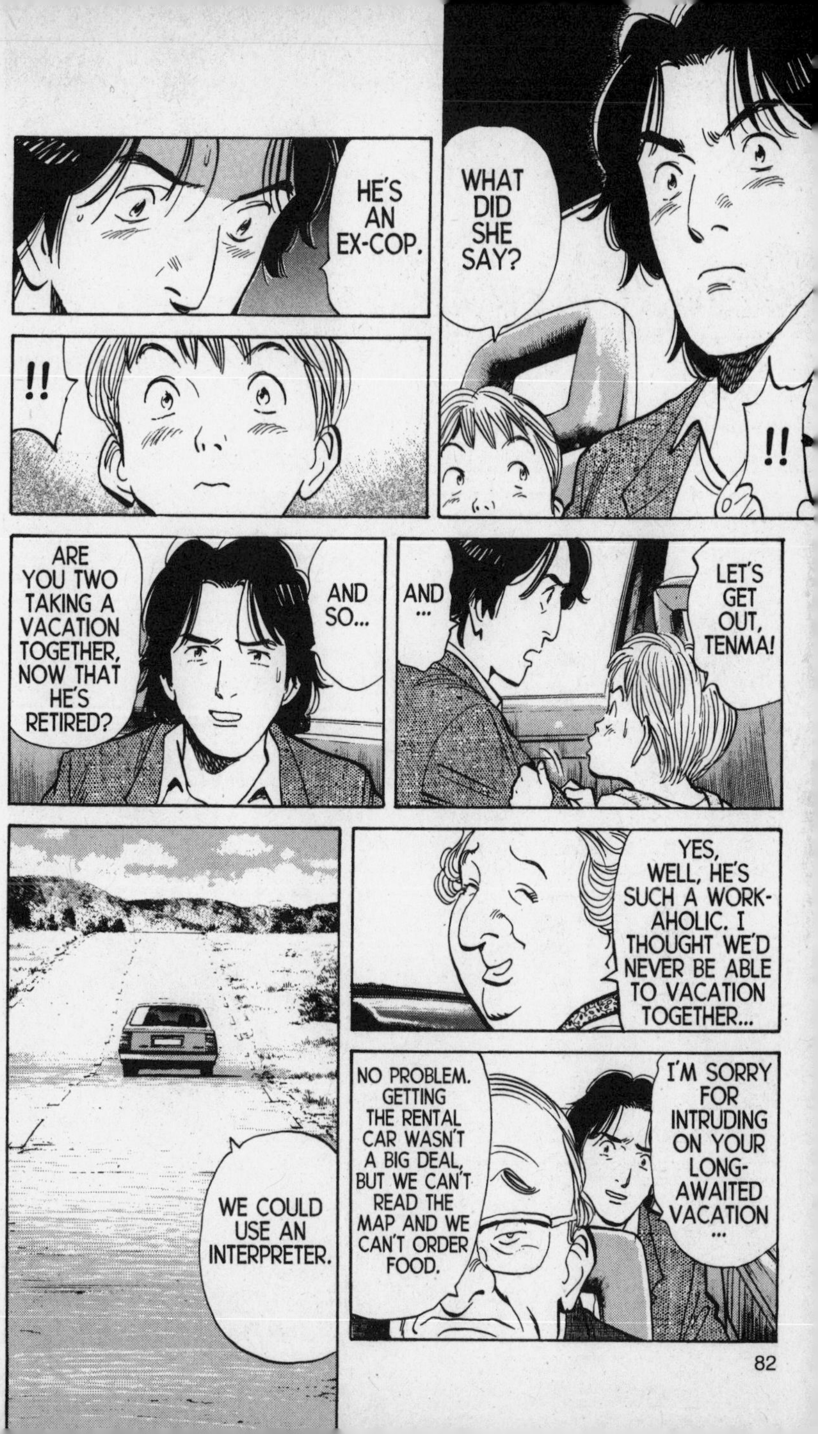
WHAT DID SHE SAY?
!!
HE'S AN EX-COP.
!!
LET'S GET OUT, TENMA!
AND ...
AND SO...
ARE YOU TWO TAKING A VACATION TOGETHER, NOW THAT HE'S RETIRED?
YES, WELL, HE'S SUCH A WORK-AHOLIC. I THOUGHT WE'D NEVER BE ABLE TO VACATION TOGETHER...
I'M SORRY FOR INTRUDING ON YOUR LONG-AWAITED VACATION ...
NO PROBLEM. GETTING THE RENTAL CAR WASN'T A BIG DEAL, BUT WE CAN'T READ THE MAP AND WE CAN'T ORDER FOOD.
WE COULD USE AN INTERPRETER.

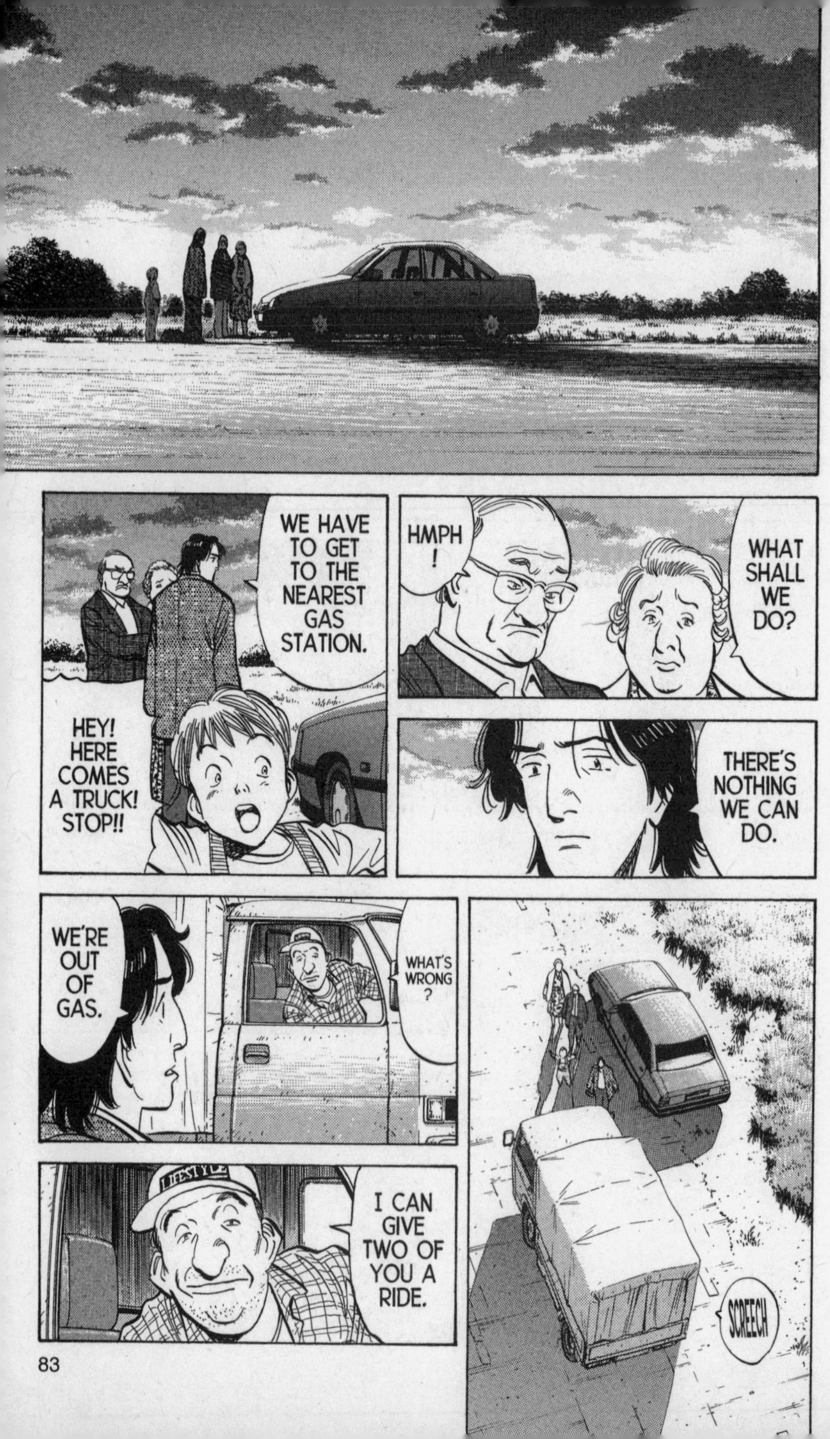
WHAT SHALL WE DO?
HMPH!
THERE'S NOTHING WE CAN DO.
WE HAVE TO GET TO THE NEAREST GAS STATION.
HEY! HERE COMES A TRUCK! STOP!!
SCREECH
WHAT'S WRONG?
WE'RE OUT OF GAS.
I CAN GIVE TWO OF YOU A RIDE.

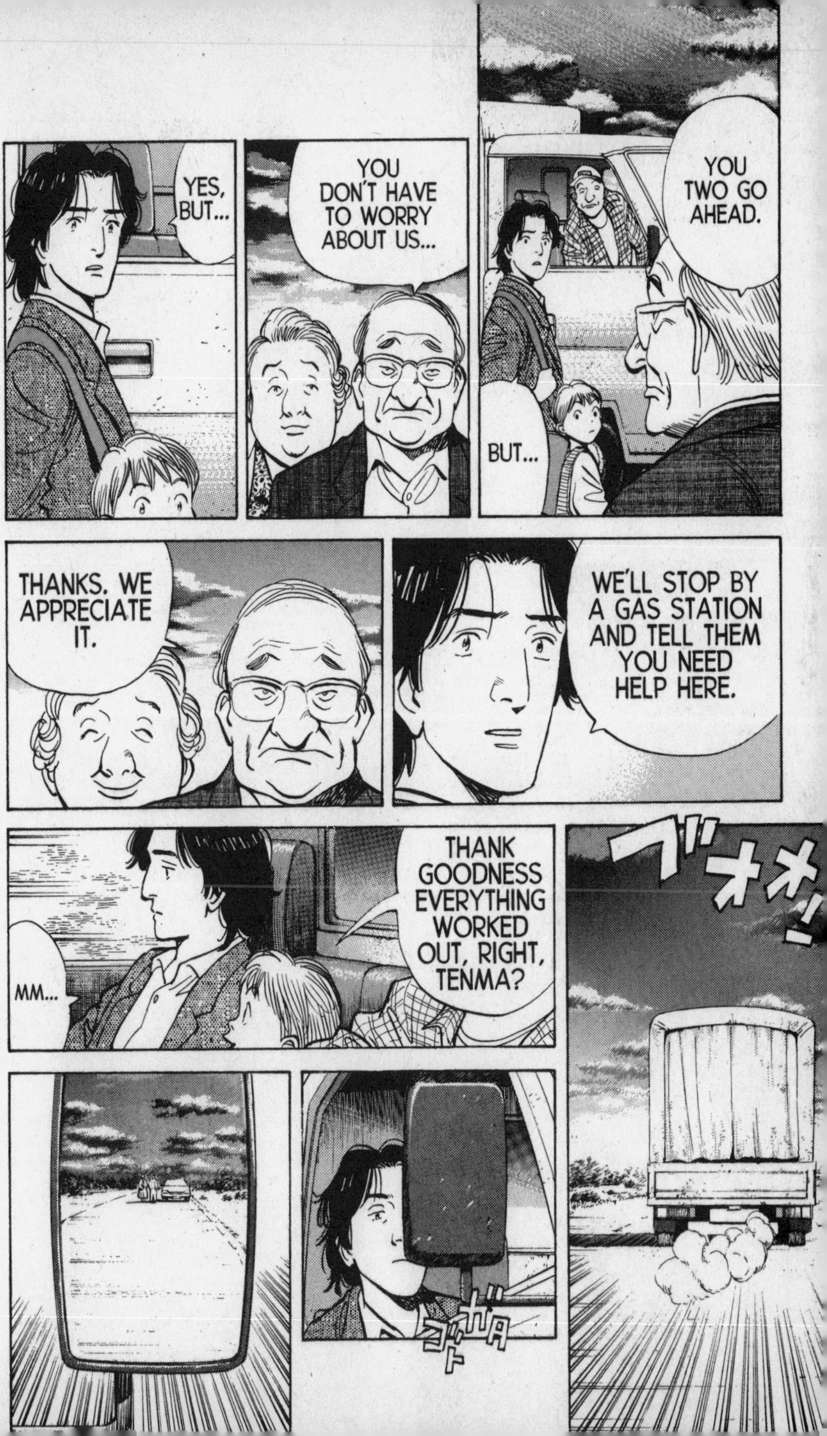
YOU TWO GO AHEAD.
BUT...
YOU DON'T HAVE TO WORRY ABOUT US...
YES, BUT...
WE'LL STOP BY A GAS STATION AND TELL THEM YOU NEED HELP HERE.
THANKS. WE APPRECIATE IT.
THANK GOODNESS EVERYTHING WORKED OUT, RIGHT, TENMA?
MM...

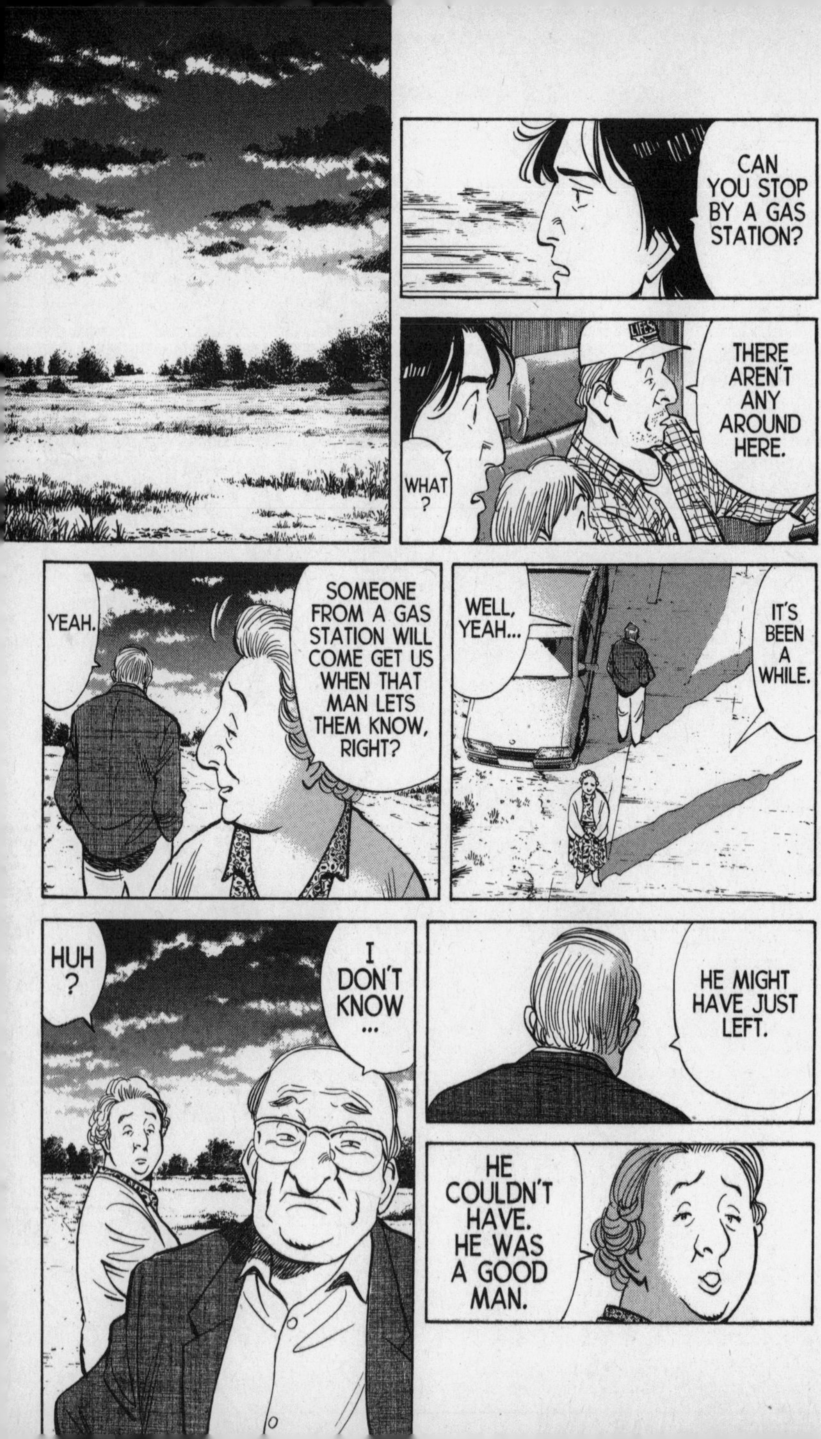
CAN YOU STOP BY A GAS STATION?
THERE AREN'T ANY AROUND HERE.
WHAT?
IT'S BEEN A WHILE.
WELL, YEAH...
SOMEONE FROM A GAS STATION WILL COME GET US WHEN THAT MAN LETS THEM KNOW, RIGHT?
YEAH.
HE MIGHT HAVE JUST LEFT.
HE COULDN'T HAVE. HE WAS A GOOD MAN.
I DON'T KNOW...
HUH?

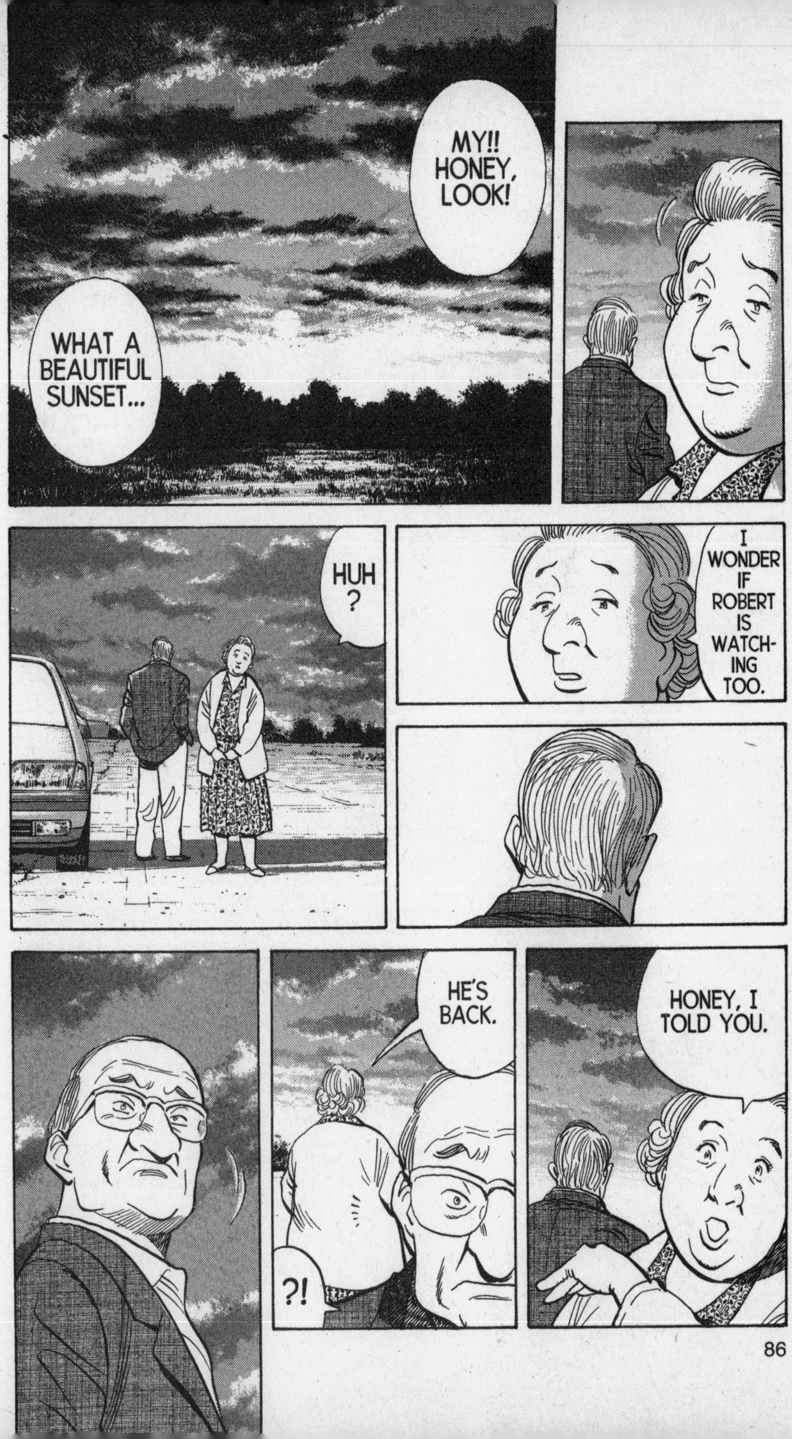
MY!! HONEY, LOOK!
WHAT A BEAUTIFUL SUNSET...
I WONDER IF ROBERT IS WATCHING TOO.
HUH?
HONEY, I TOLD YOU.
HE'S BACK.
?!

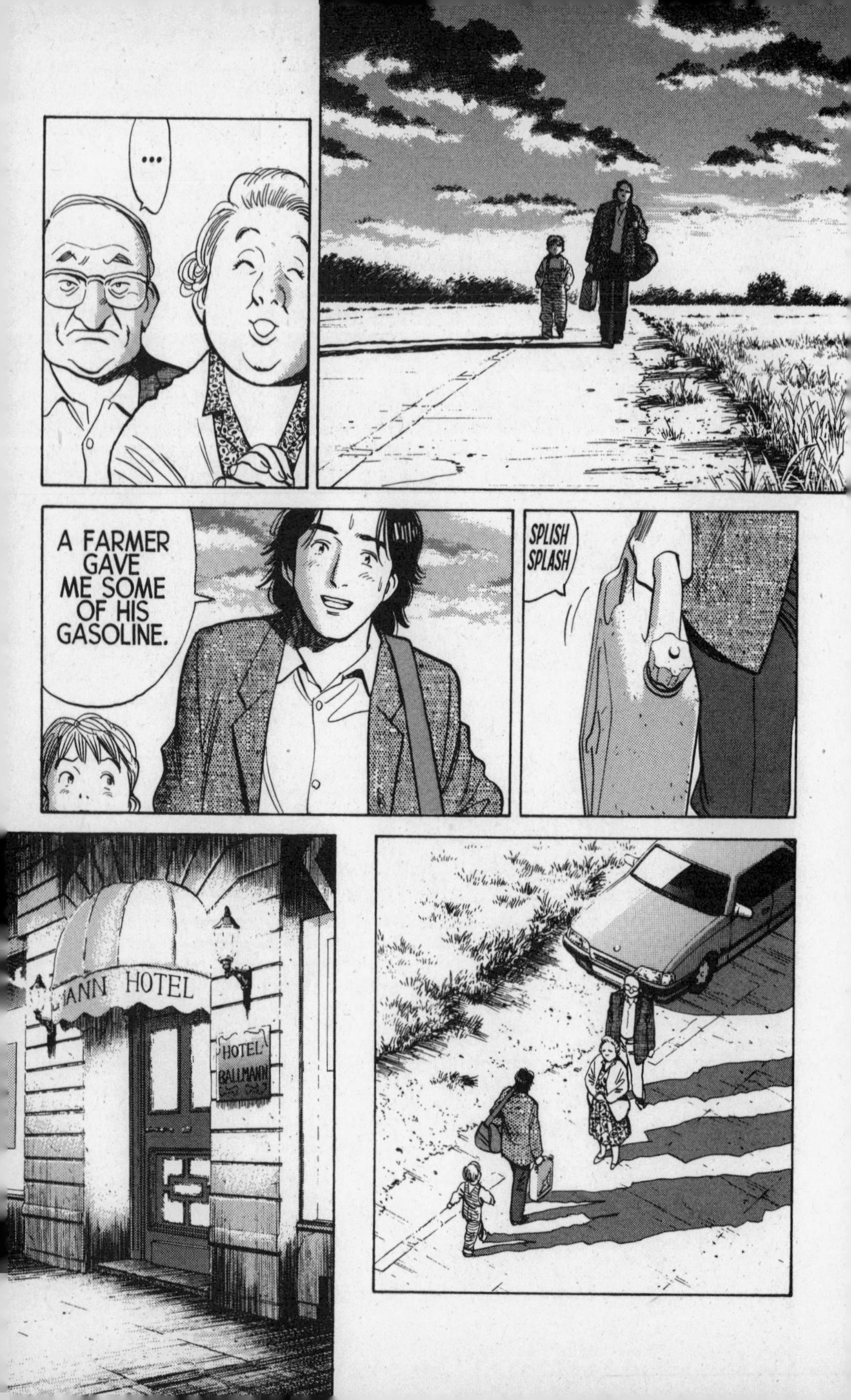
...
SPLISH SPLASH
A FARMER GAVE ME SOME OF HIS GASOLINE.
MANN HOTEL
HOTEL BALLMANN

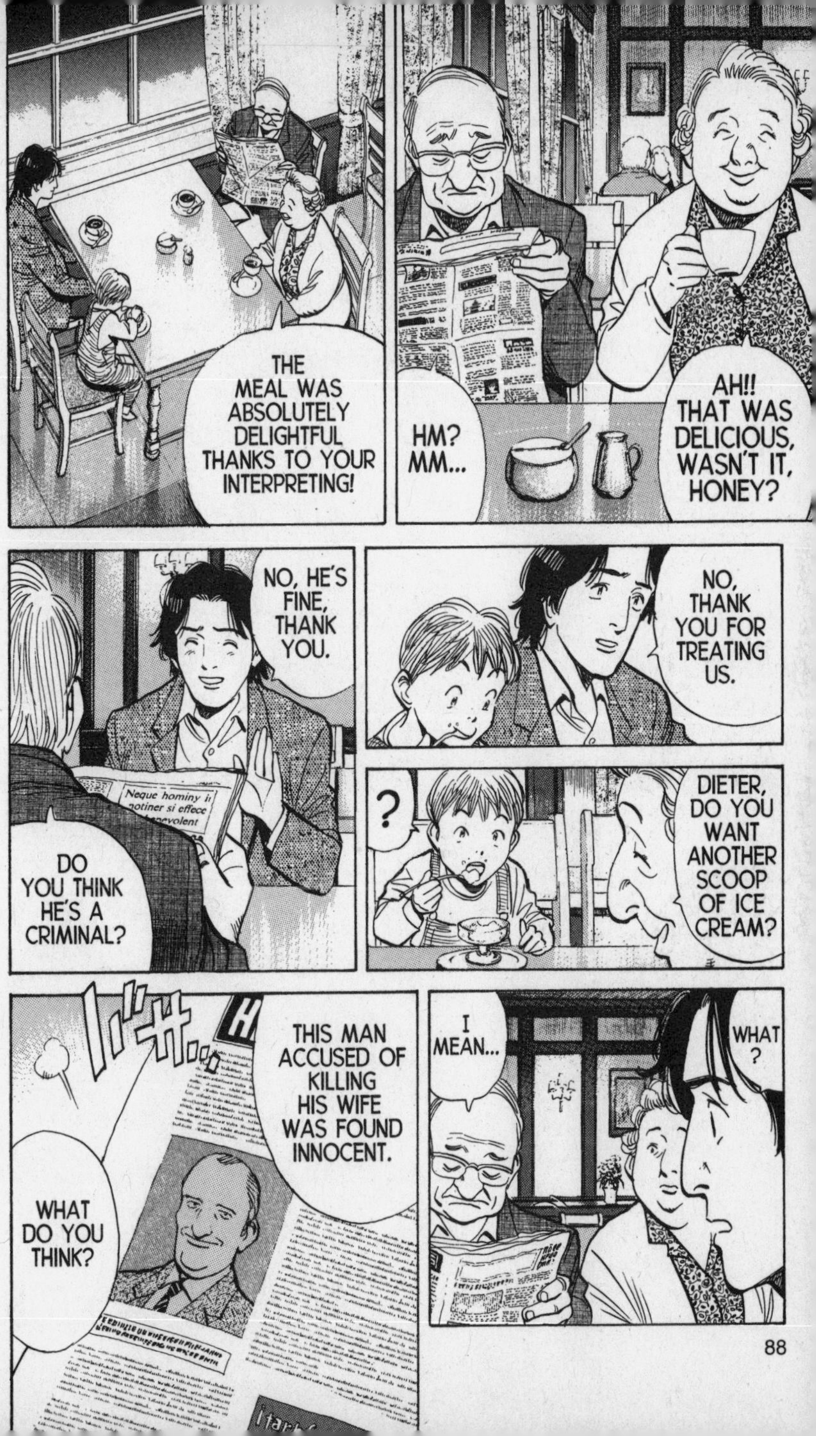
AH!! THAT WAS DELICIOUS, WASN'T IT, HONEY?
HM? MM...
THE MEAL WAS ABSOLUTELY DELIGHTFUL THANKS TO YOUR INTERPRETING!
NO, THANK YOU FOR TREATING US.
DIETER, DO YOU WANT ANOTHER SCOOP OF ICE CREAM?
?
NO, HE'S FINE, THANK YOU.
DO YOU THINK HE'S A CRIMINAL?
WHAT ?
I MEAN...
THIS MAN ACCUSED OF KILLING HIS WIFE WAS FOUND INNOCENT.
WHAT DO YOU THINK?

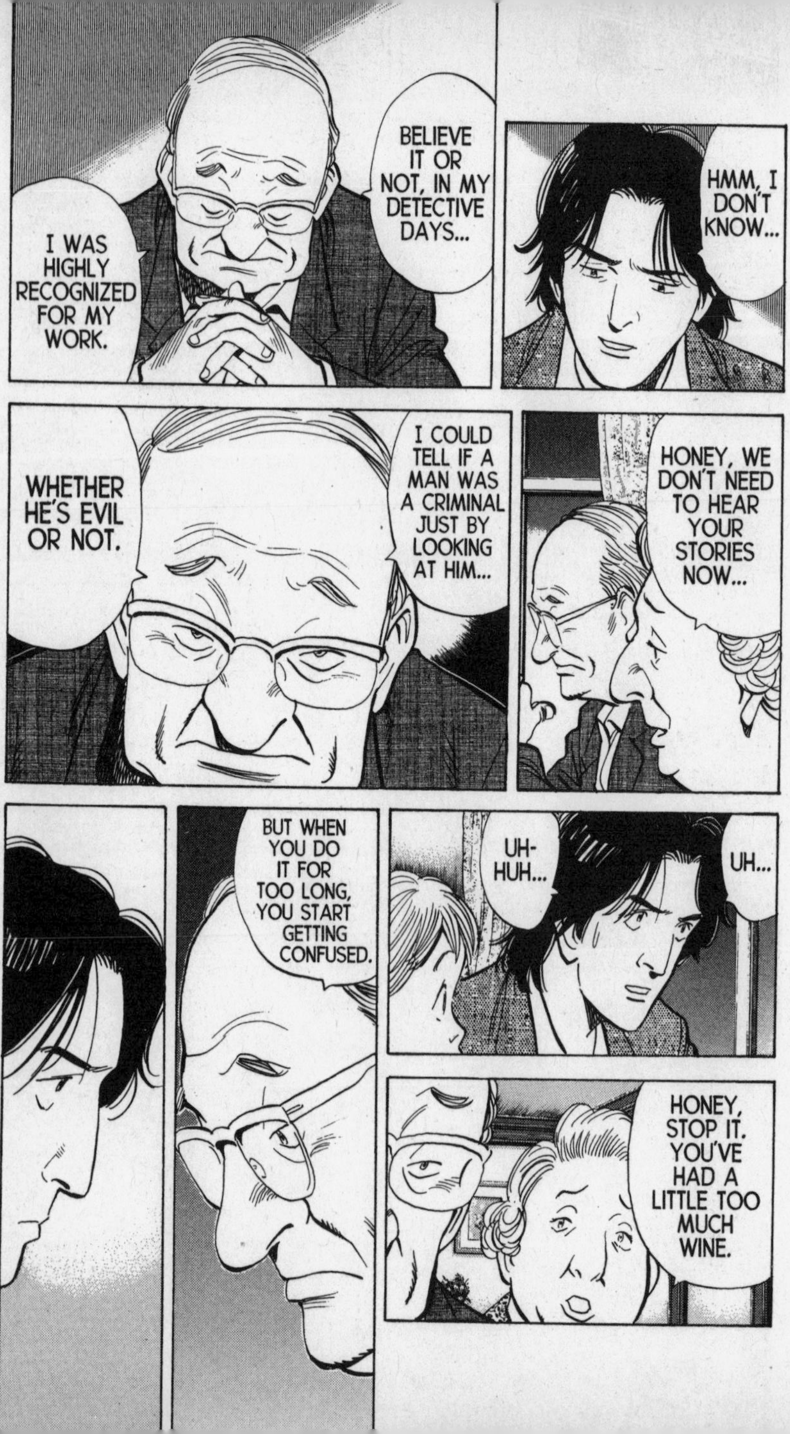
HMM, I DON'T KNOW...
BELIEVE IT OR NOT, IN MY DETECTIVE DAYS...
I WAS HIGHLY RECOGNIZED FOR MY WORK.
HONEY, WE DON'T NEED TO HEAR YOUR STORIES NOW...
I COULD TELL IF A MAN WAS A CRIMINAL JUST BY LOOKING AT HIM...
WHETHER HE'S EVIL OR NOT.
UH...
UH-HUH...
HONEY, STOP IT. YOU'VE HAD A LITTLE TOO MUCH WINE.
BUT WHEN YOU DO IT FOR TOO LONG, YOU START GETTING CONFUSED.

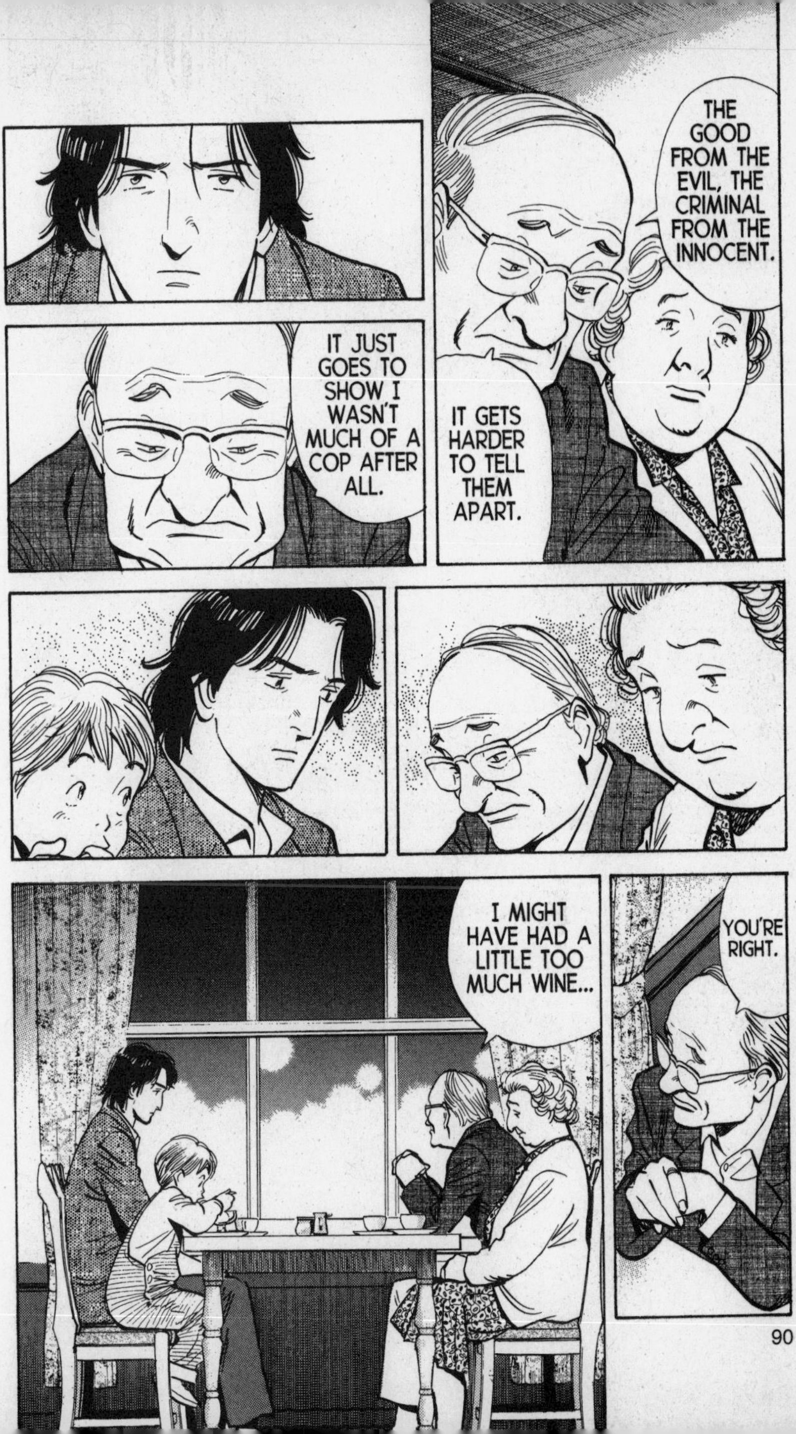
THE GOOD FROM THE EVIL, THE CRIMINAL FROM THE INNOCENT.
IT GETS HARDER TO TELL THEM APART.
IT JUST GOES TO SHOW I WASN'T MUCH OF A COP AFTER ALL.
YOU'RE RIGHT.
I MIGHT HAVE HAD A LITTLE TOO MUCH WINE...

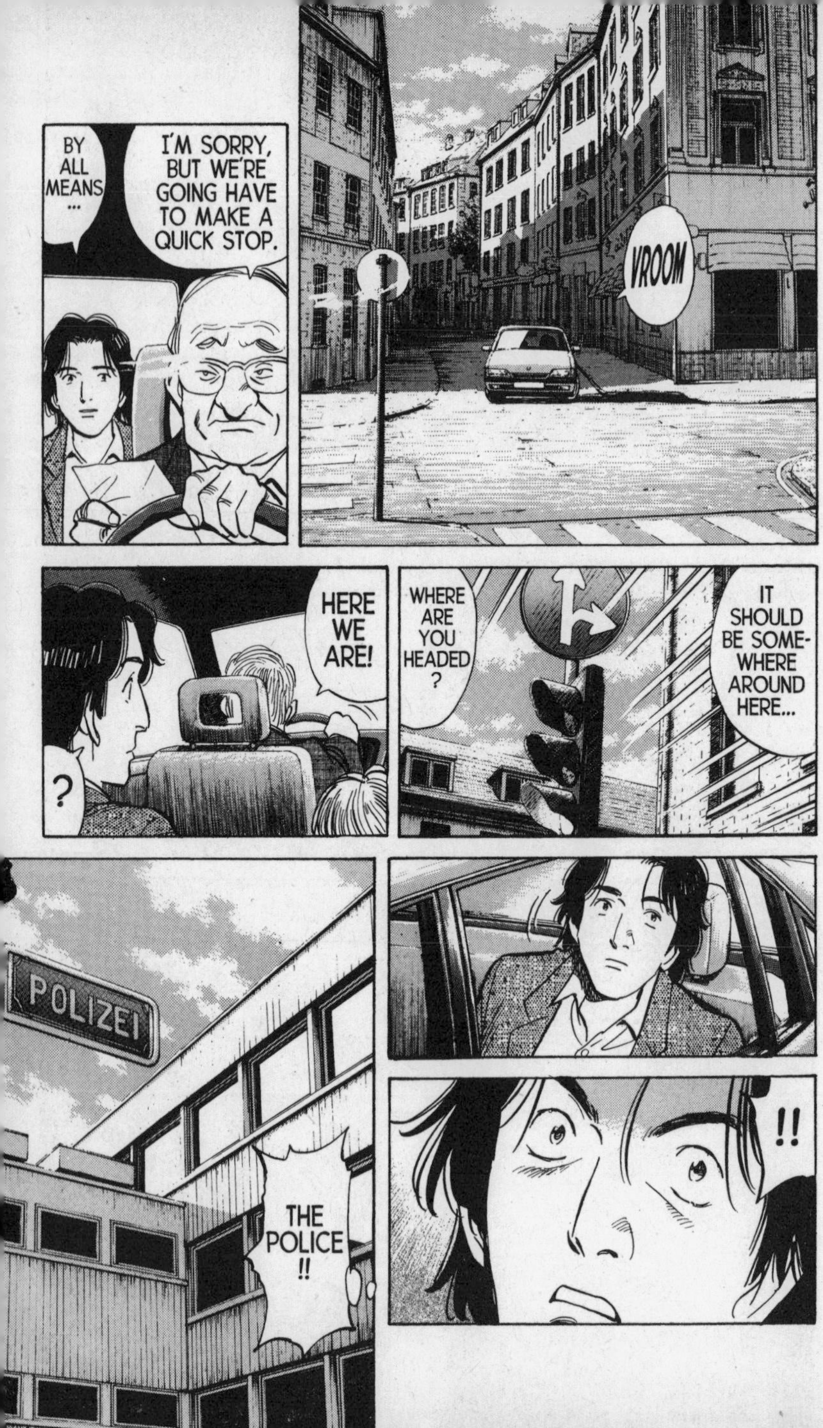
VROOM
I'M SORRY, BUT WE'RE GOING HAVE TO MAKE A QUICK STOP.
BY ALL MEANS ...
IT SHOULD BE SOME-WHERE AROUND HERE...
WHERE ARE YOU HEADED ?
HERE WE ARE!
?
!!
POLIZEI
THE POLICE !!

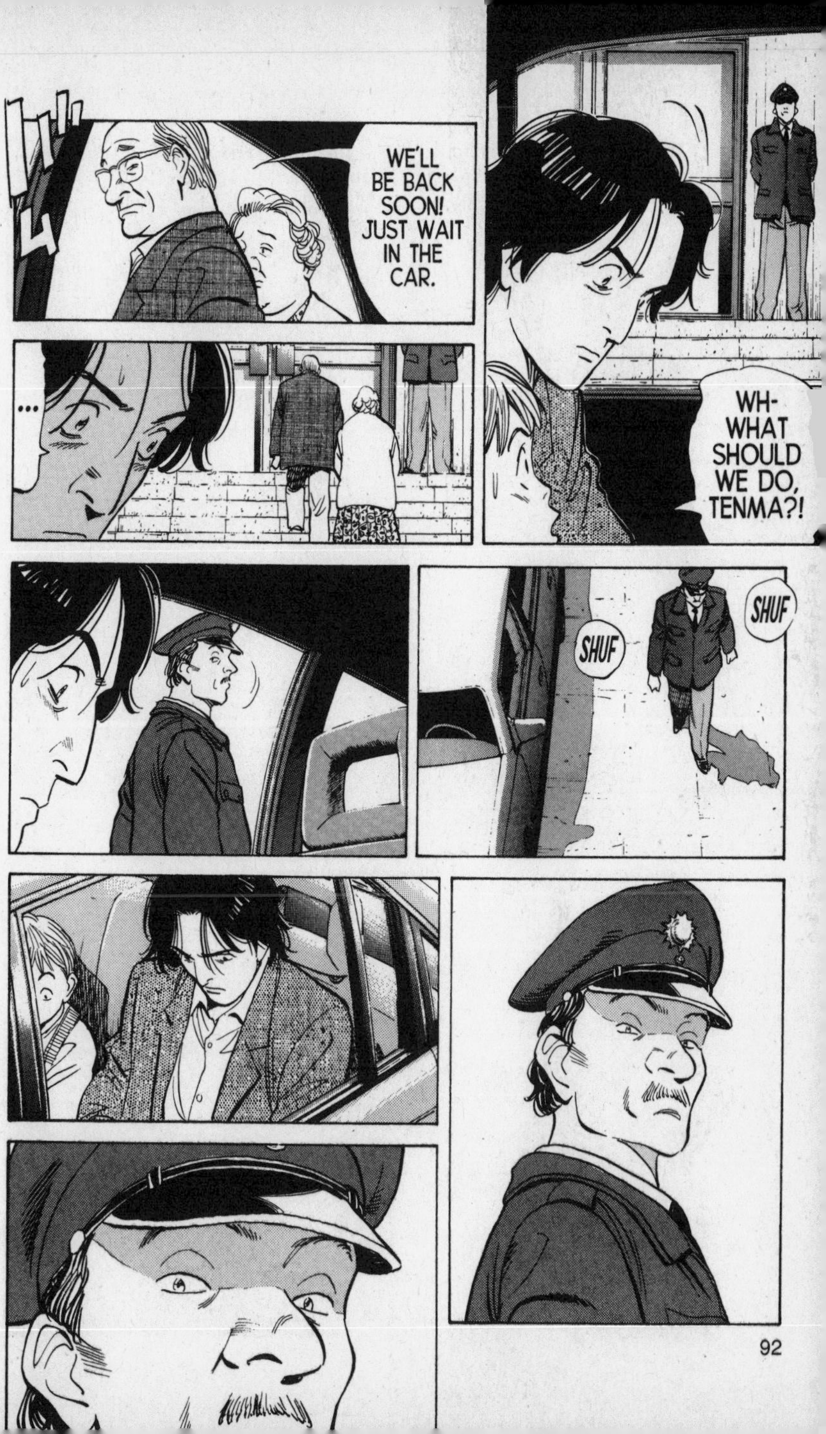
WH- WHAT SHOULD WE DO, TENMA?!
WE'LL BE BACK SOON! JUST WAIT IN THE CAR.
...
SHUF
SHUF

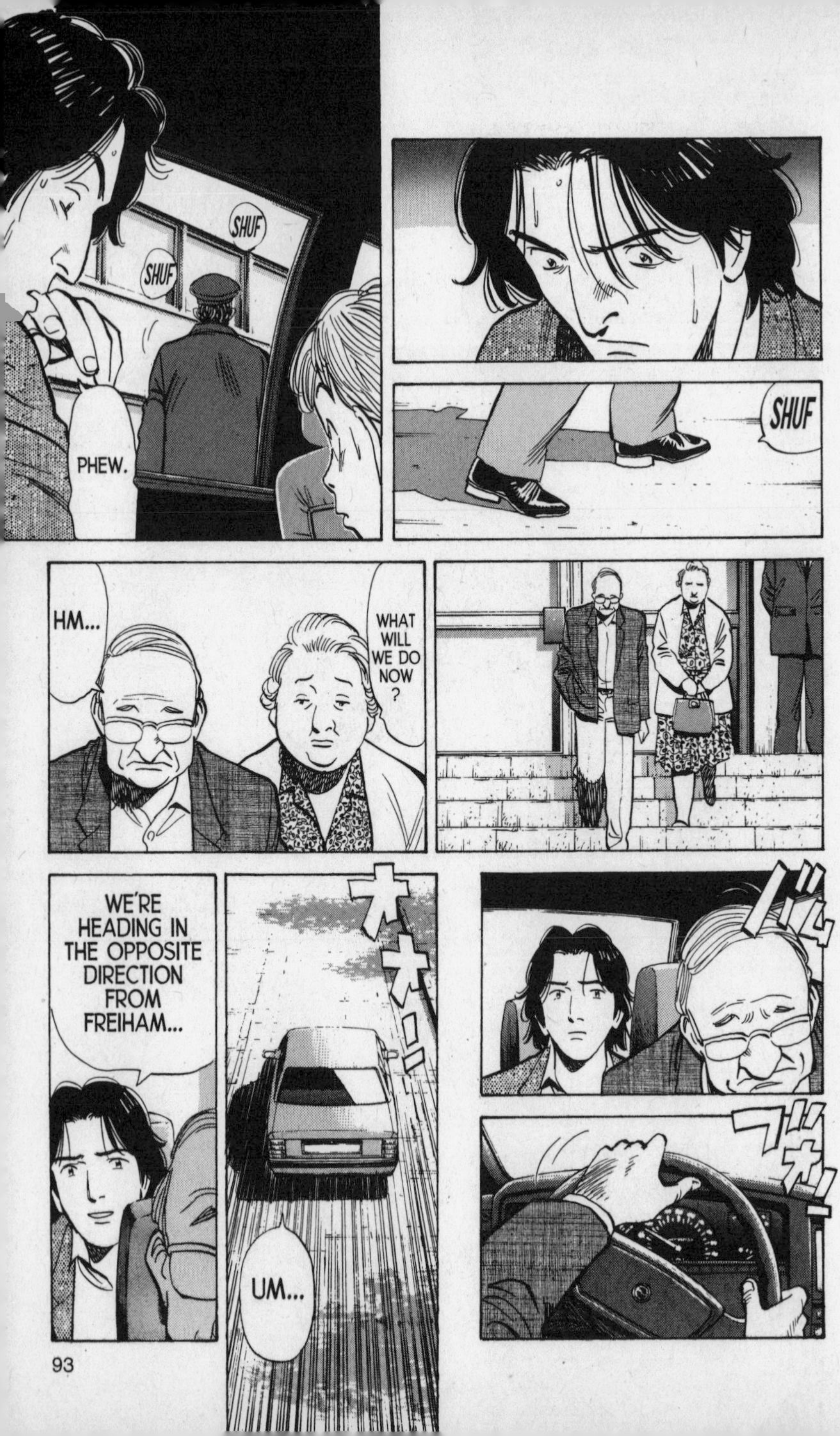
SHUF
SHUF
SHUF
PHEW.
WHAT WILL WE DO NOW?
HM...
UM...
WE'RE HEADING IN THE OPPOSITE DIRECTION FROM FREIHAM...

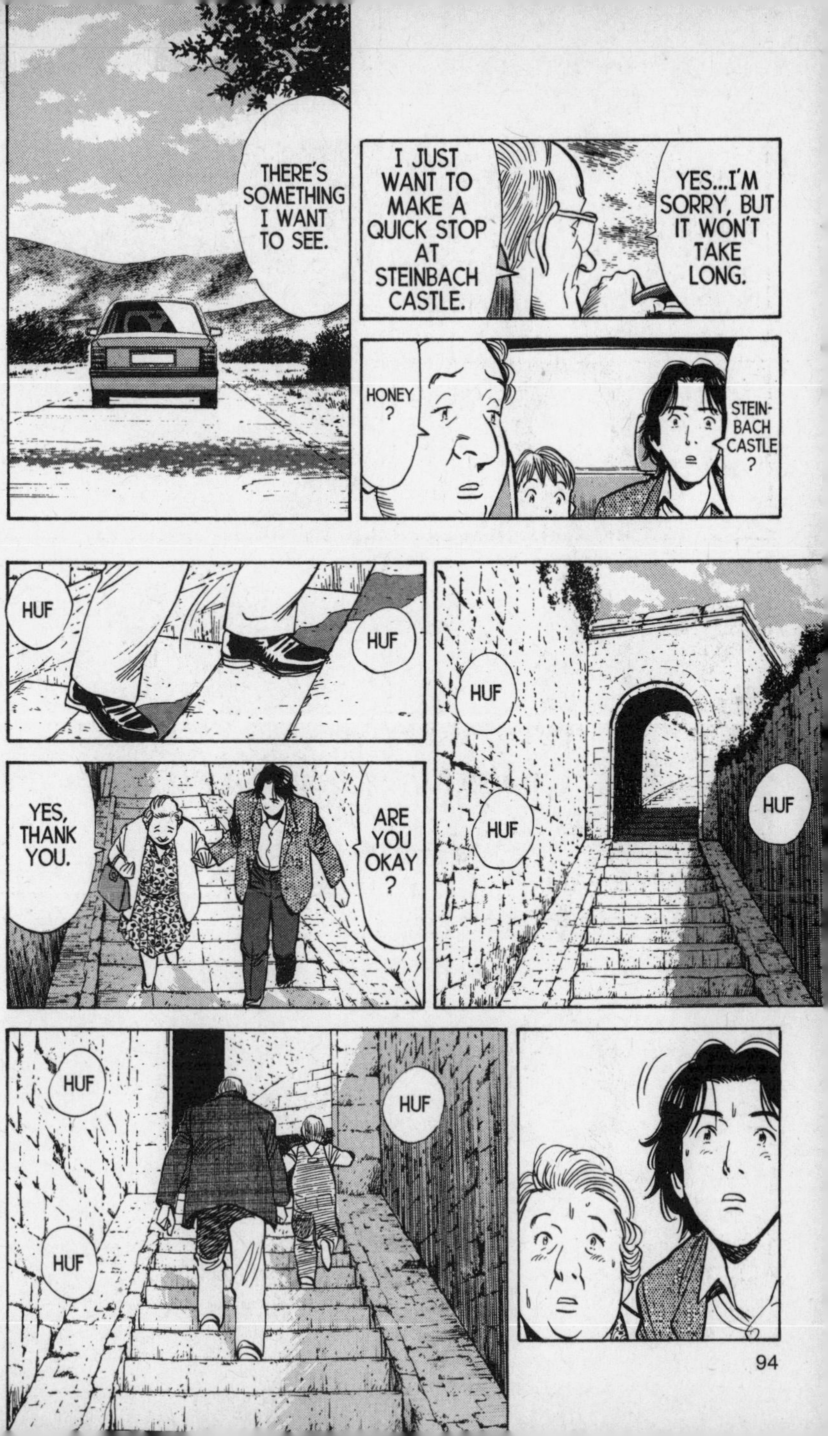
YES...I'M SORRY, BUT IT WON'T TAKE LONG.
I JUST WANT TO MAKE A QUICK STOP AT STEINBACH CASTLE.
STEIN-BACH CASTLE?
HONEY?
THERE'S SOMETHING I WANT TO SEE.
HUF
HUF
HUF
HUF
HUF
ARE YOU OKAY?
YES, THANK YOU.
HUF
HUF
HUF

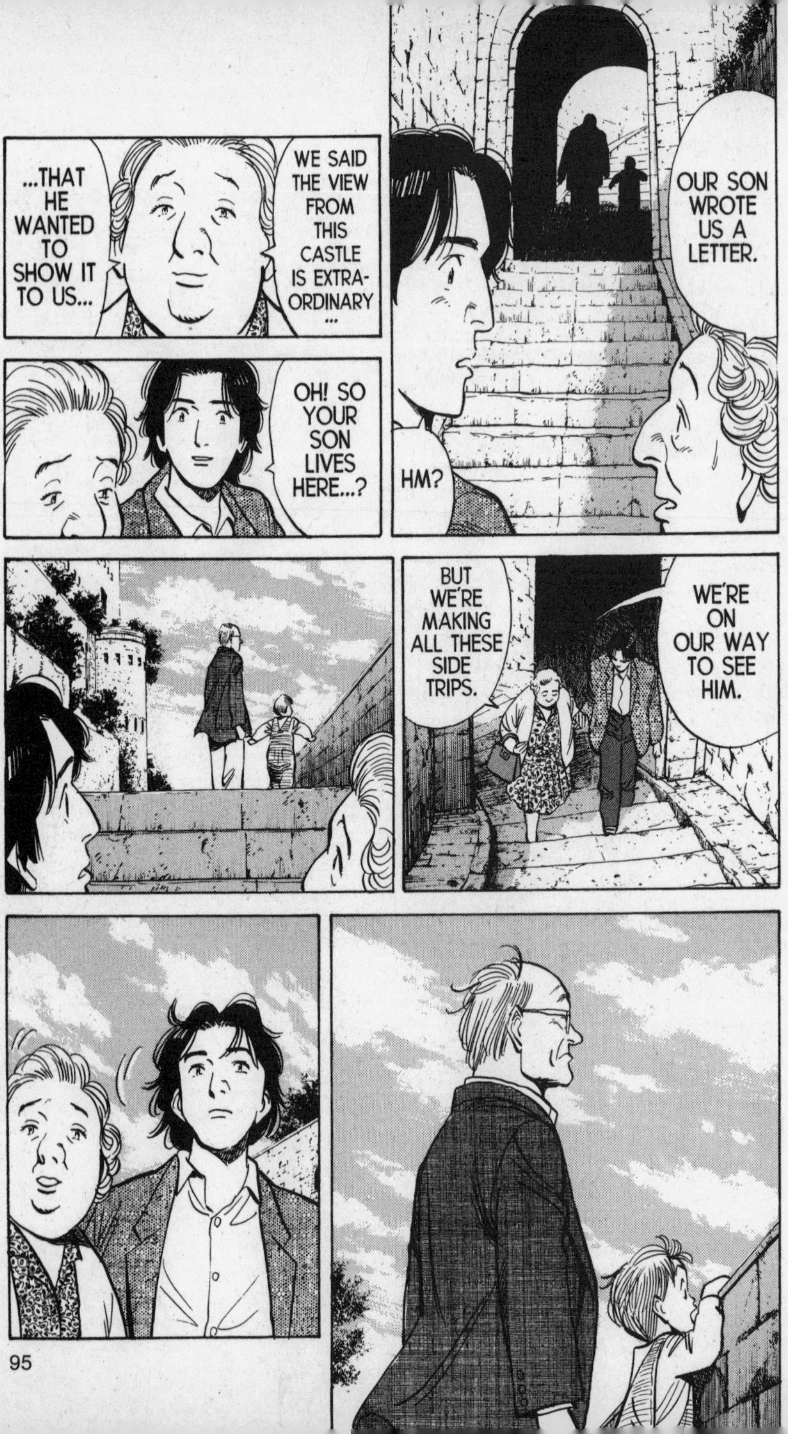
OUR SON WROTE US A LETTER.
HM?
WE SAID THE VIEW FROM THIS CASTLE IS EXTRAORDINARY...
...THAT HE WANTED TO SHOW IT TO US...
OH! SO YOUR SON LIVES HERE...?
WE'RE ON OUR WAY TO SEE HIM.
BUT WE'RE MAKING ALL THESE SIDE TRIPS.

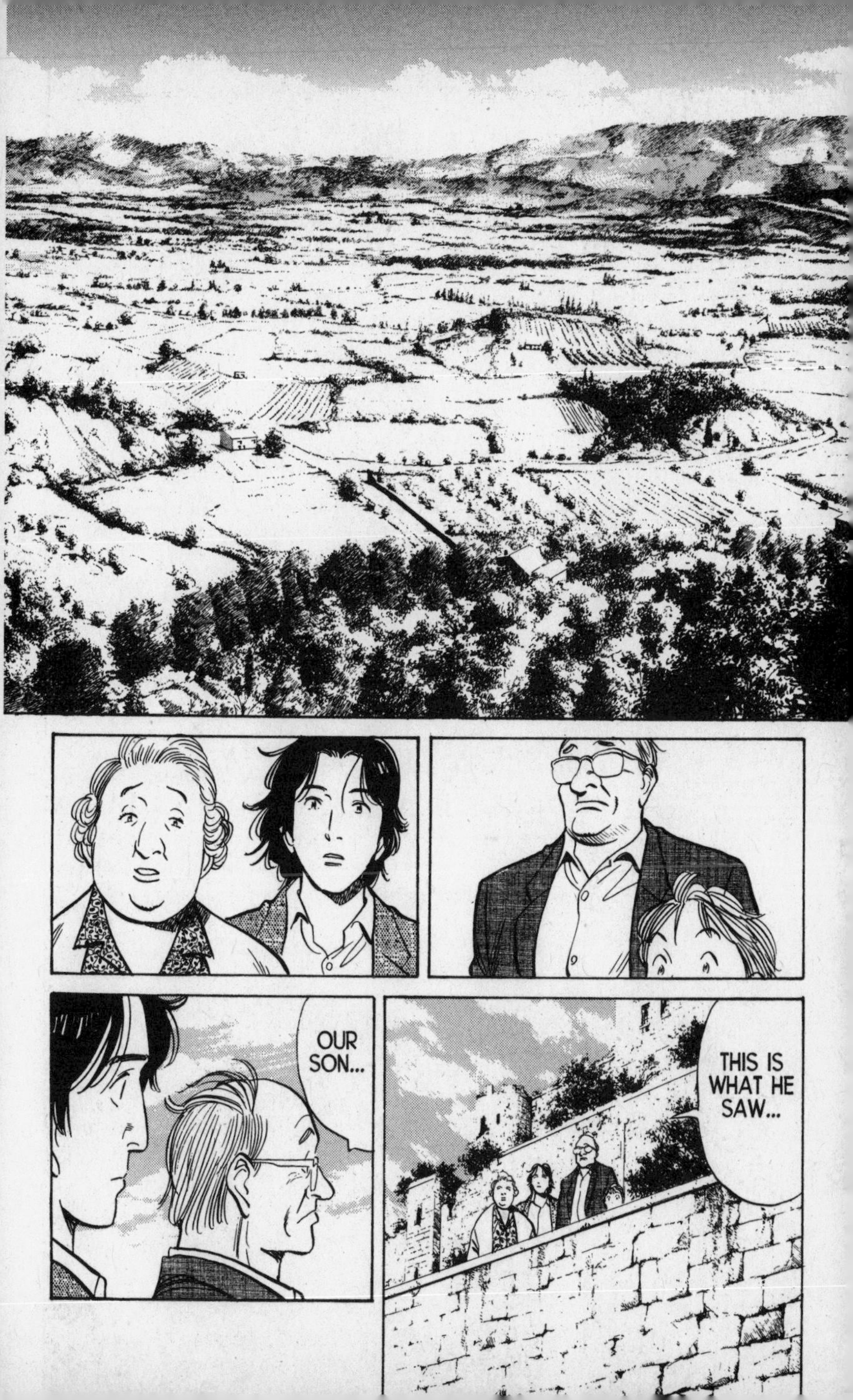
THIS IS WHAT HE SAW...
OUR SON...

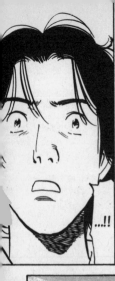

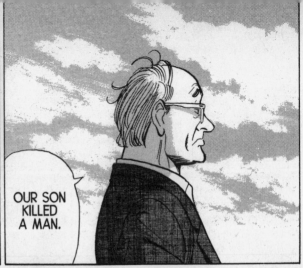

...!!

OUR SON KILLED A MAN.

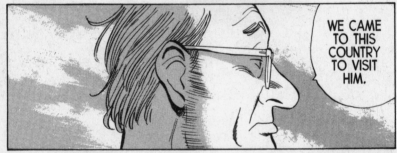

WE CAME TO THIS COUNTRY TO VISIT HIM.

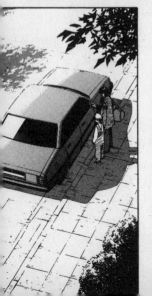

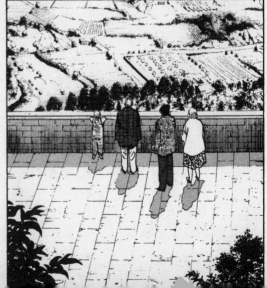

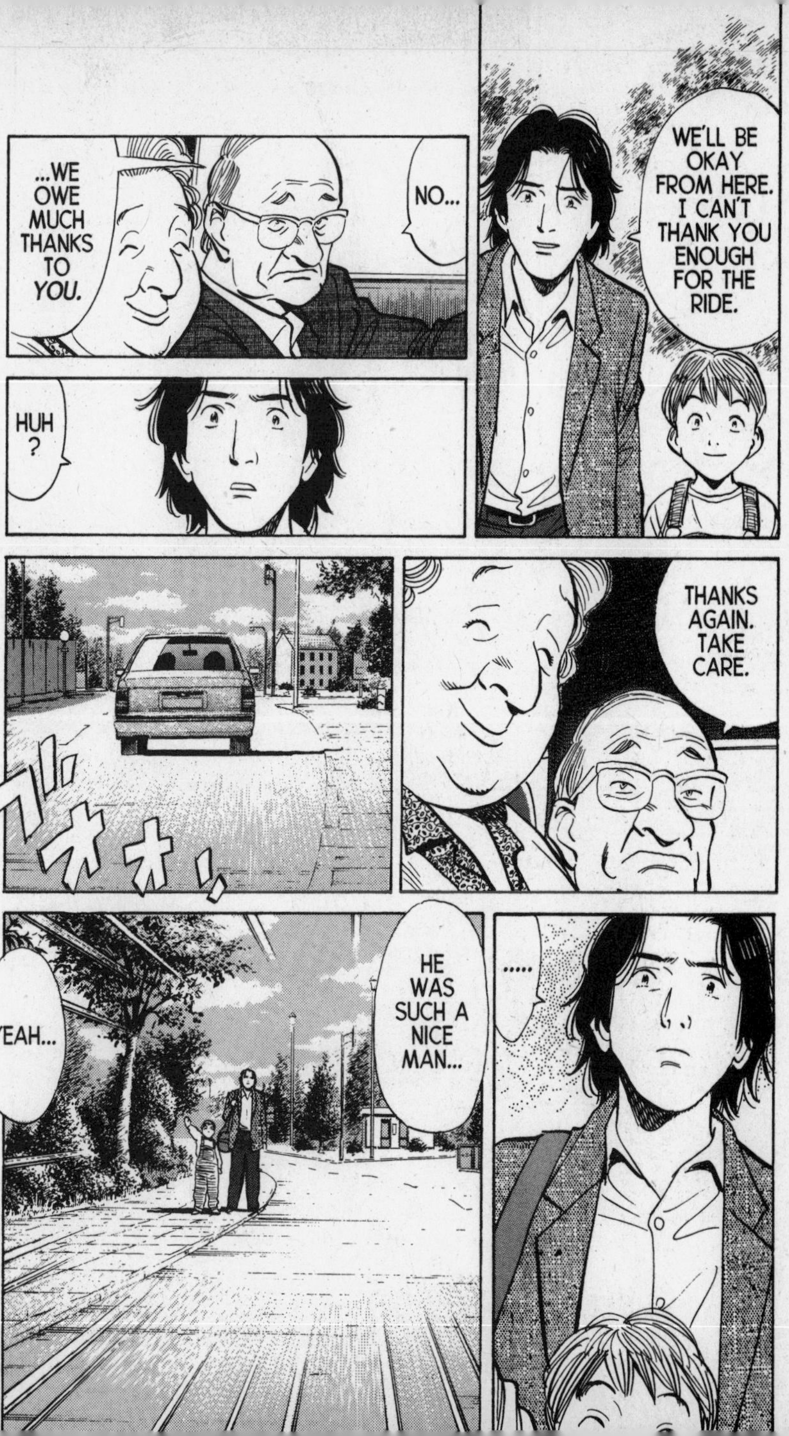
WE'LL BE OKAY FROM HERE. I CAN'T THANK YOU ENOUGH FOR THE RIDE.
NO...
...WE OWE MUCH THANKS TO *YOU.*
HUH?
THANKS AGAIN. TAKE CARE.
.....
HE WAS SUCH A NICE MAN...
YEAH...

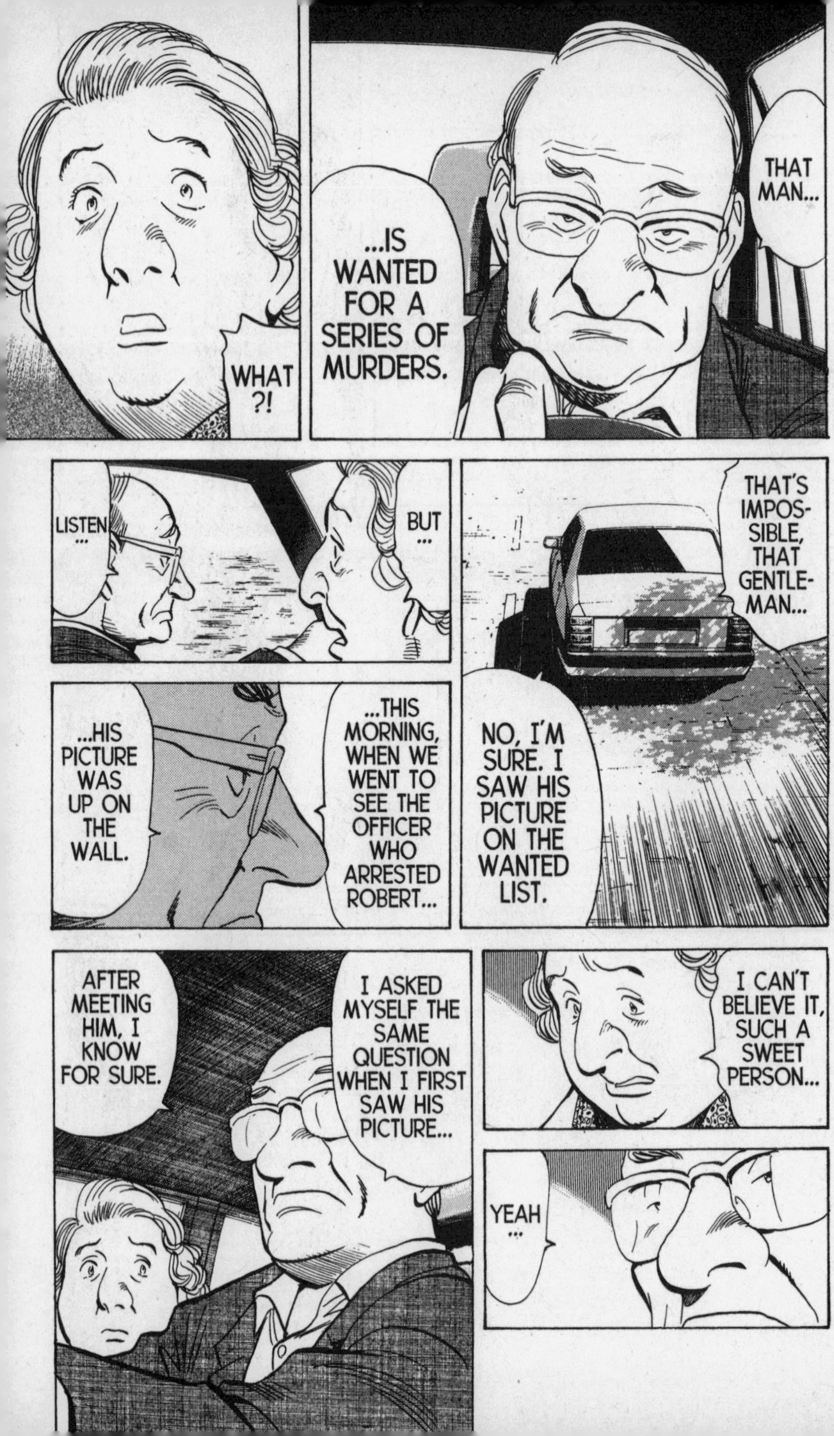
THAT MAN...
...IS WANTED FOR A SERIES OF MURDERS.
WHAT?!
THAT'S IMPOSSIBLE, THAT GENTLEMAN...
NO, I'M SURE. I SAW HIS PICTURE ON THE WANTED LIST.
BUT...
LISTEN...
...THIS MORNING, WHEN WE WENT TO SEE THE OFFICER WHO ARRESTED ROBERT...
...HIS PICTURE WAS UP ON THE WALL.
I CAN'T BELIEVE IT, SUCH A SWEET PERSON...
YEAH...
I ASKED MYSELF THE SAME QUESTION WHEN I FIRST SAW HIS PICTURE...
AFTER MEETING HIM, I KNOW FOR SURE.

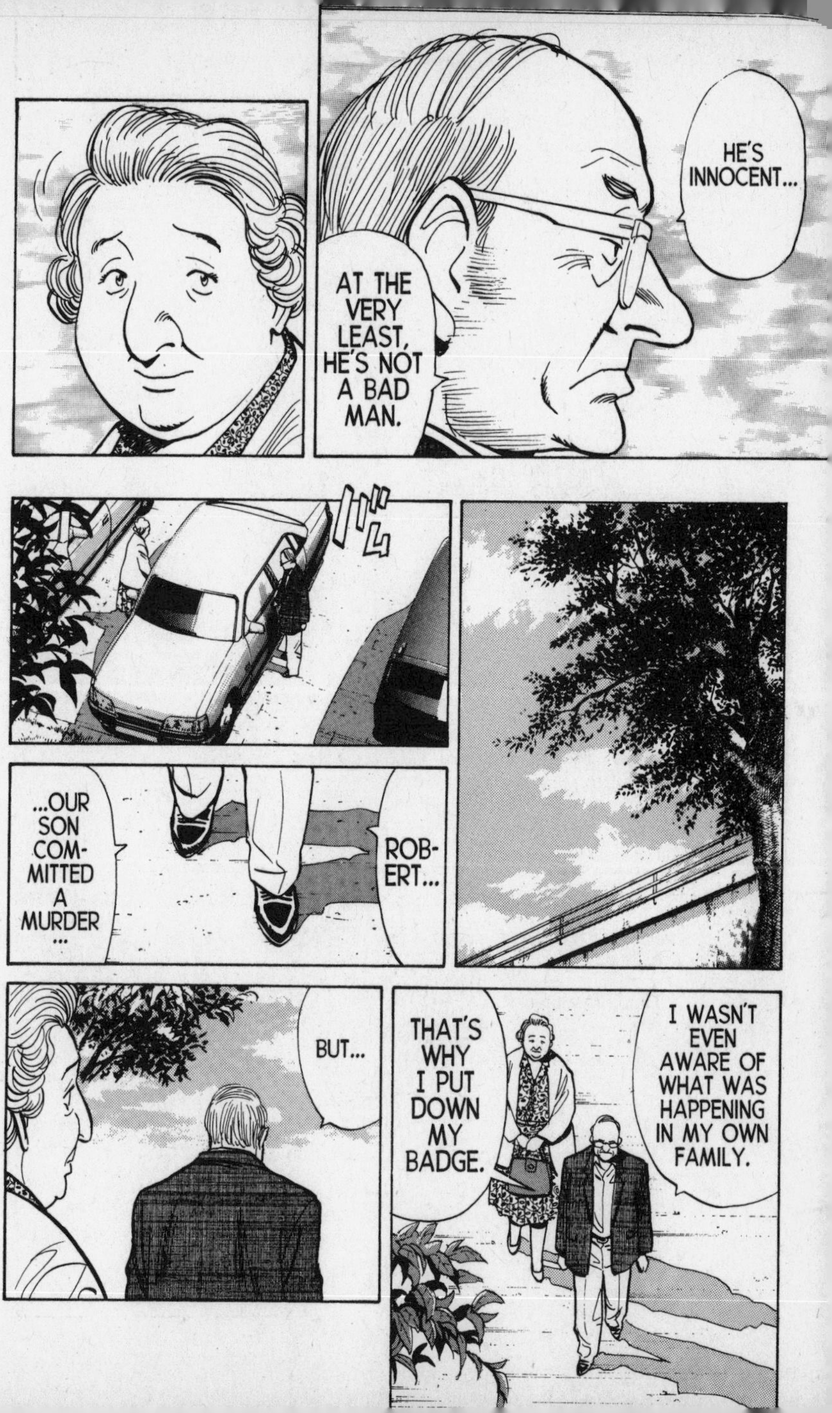
HE'S INNOCENT...
AT THE VERY LEAST, HE'S NOT A BAD MAN.
ROB-ERT...
...OUR SON COM-MITTED A MURDER...
I WASN'T EVEN AWARE OF WHAT WAS HAPPENING IN MY OWN FAMILY.
THAT'S WHY I PUT DOWN MY BADGE.
BUT...

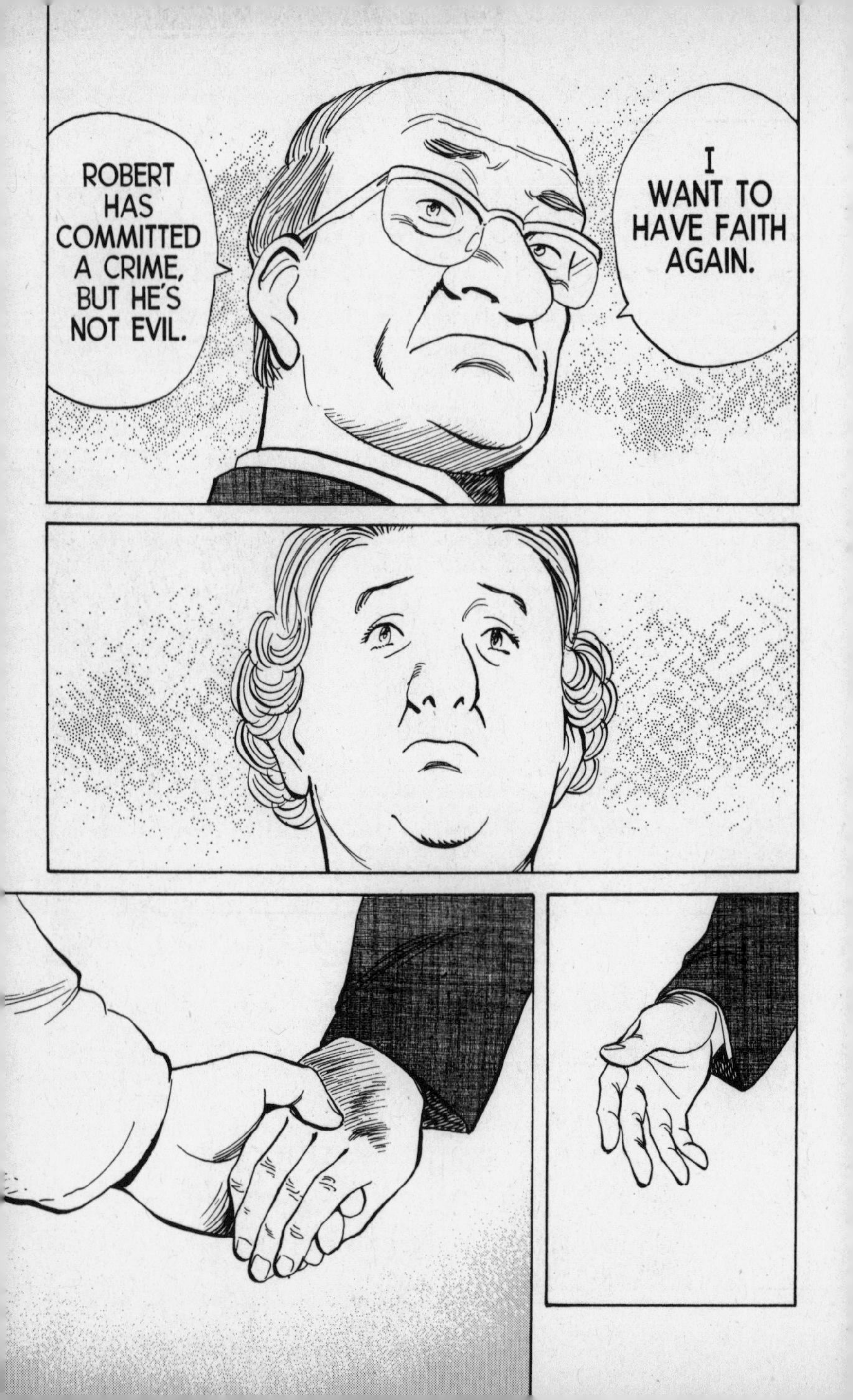
I WANT TO HAVE FAITH AGAIN.
ROBERT HAS COMMITTED A CRIME, BUT HE'S NOT EVIL.

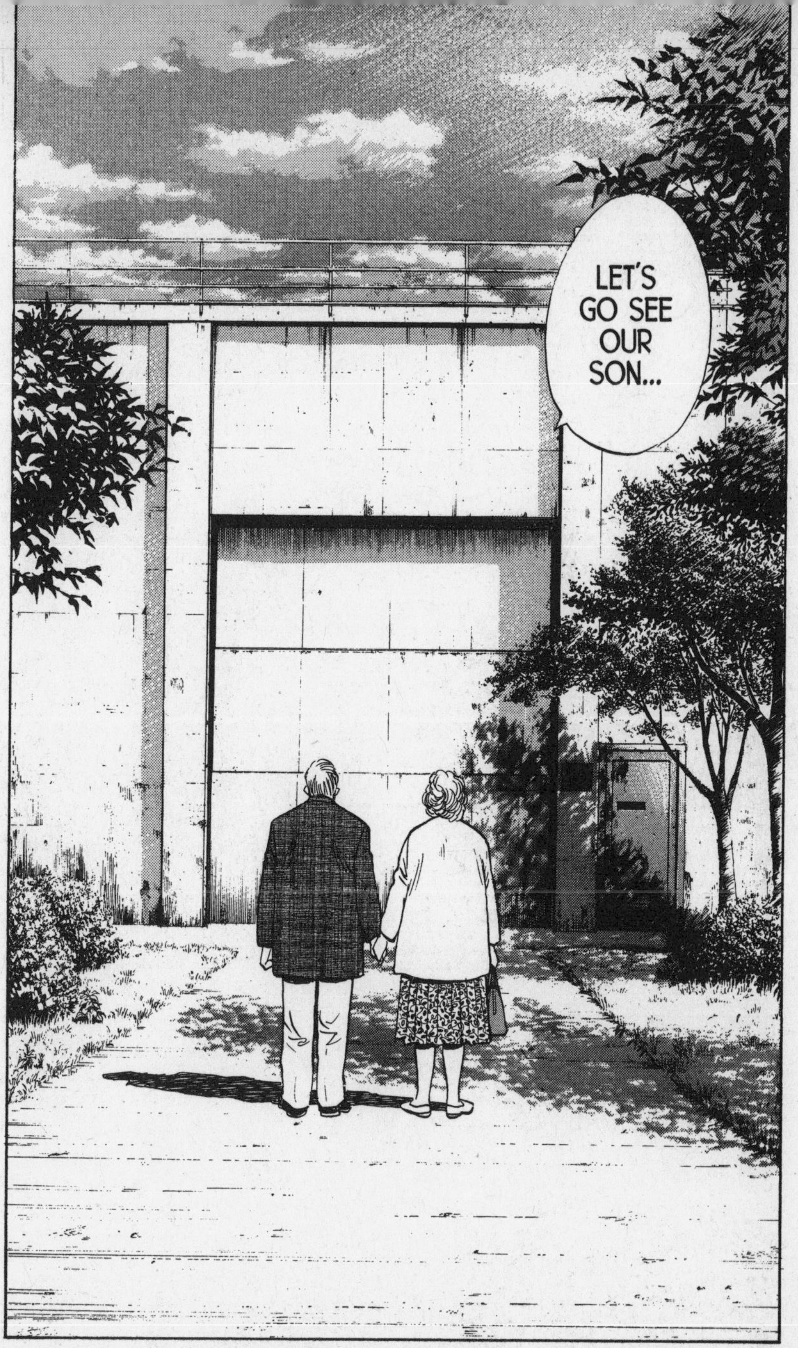
LET'S GO SEE OUR SON...

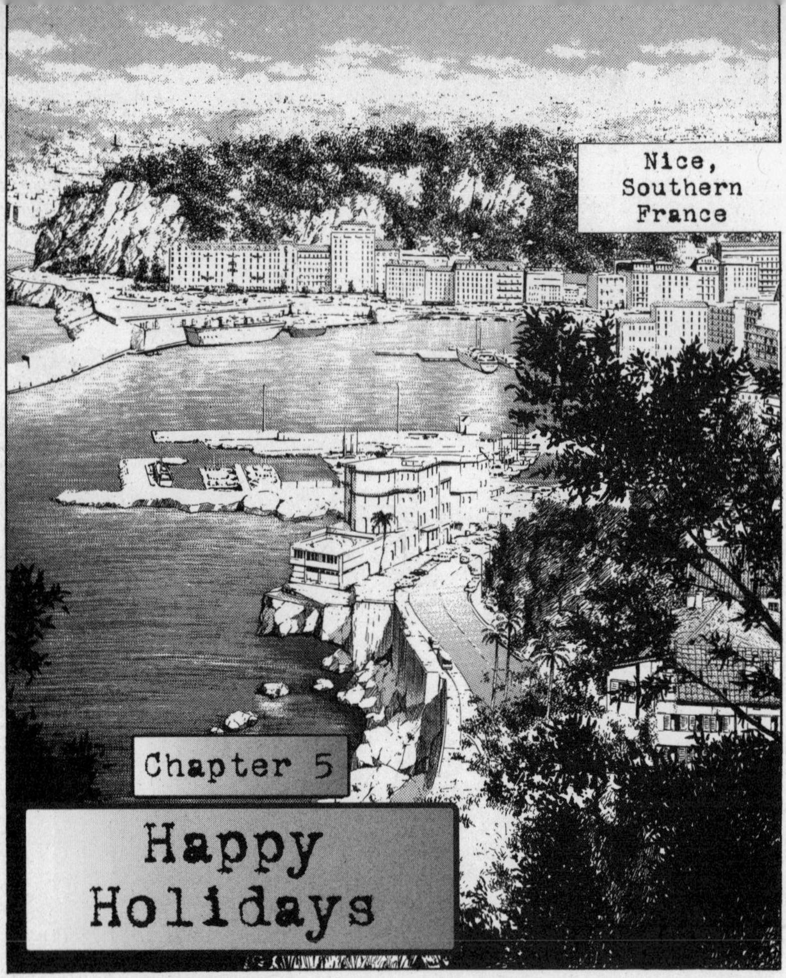
Nice,
Southern
France
Chapter 5
Happy
Holidays
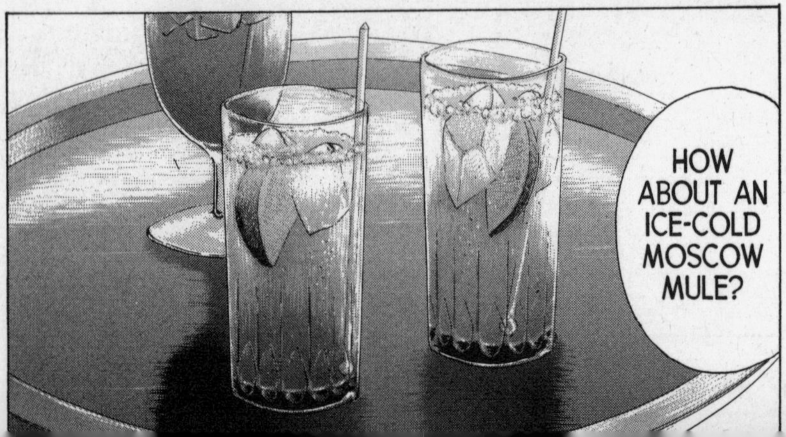
HOW ABOUT AN ICE-COLD MOSCOW MULE?

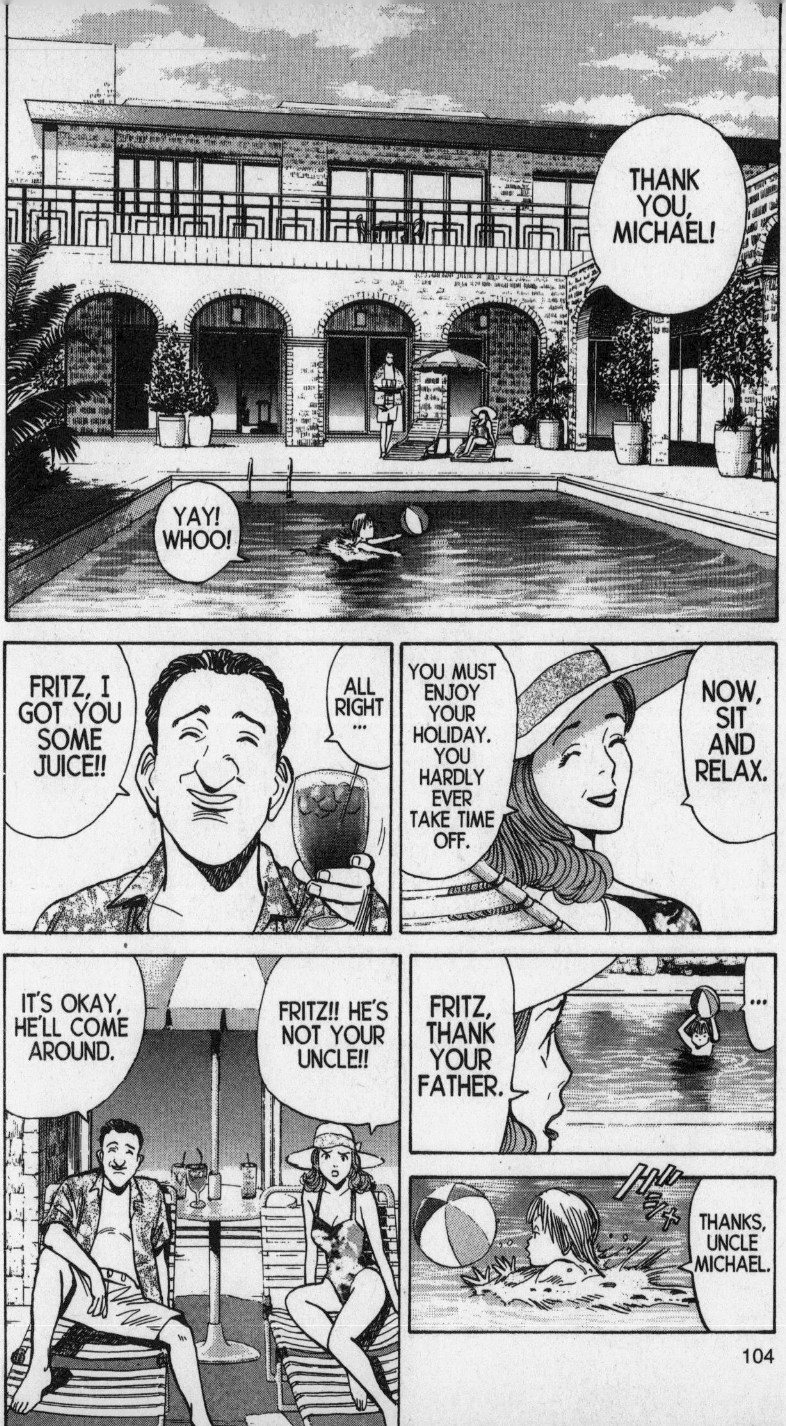
THANK YOU, MICHAEL!
YAY! WHOO!
NOW, SIT AND RELAX.
YOU MUST ENJOY YOUR HOLIDAY. YOU HARDLY EVER TAKE TIME OFF.
ALL RIGHT...
FRITZ, I GOT YOU SOME JUICE!!
...
FRITZ, THANK YOUR FATHER.
THANKS, UNCLE MICHAEL.
FRITZ!! HE'S NOT YOUR UNCLE!!
IT'S OKAY, HE'LL COME AROUND.

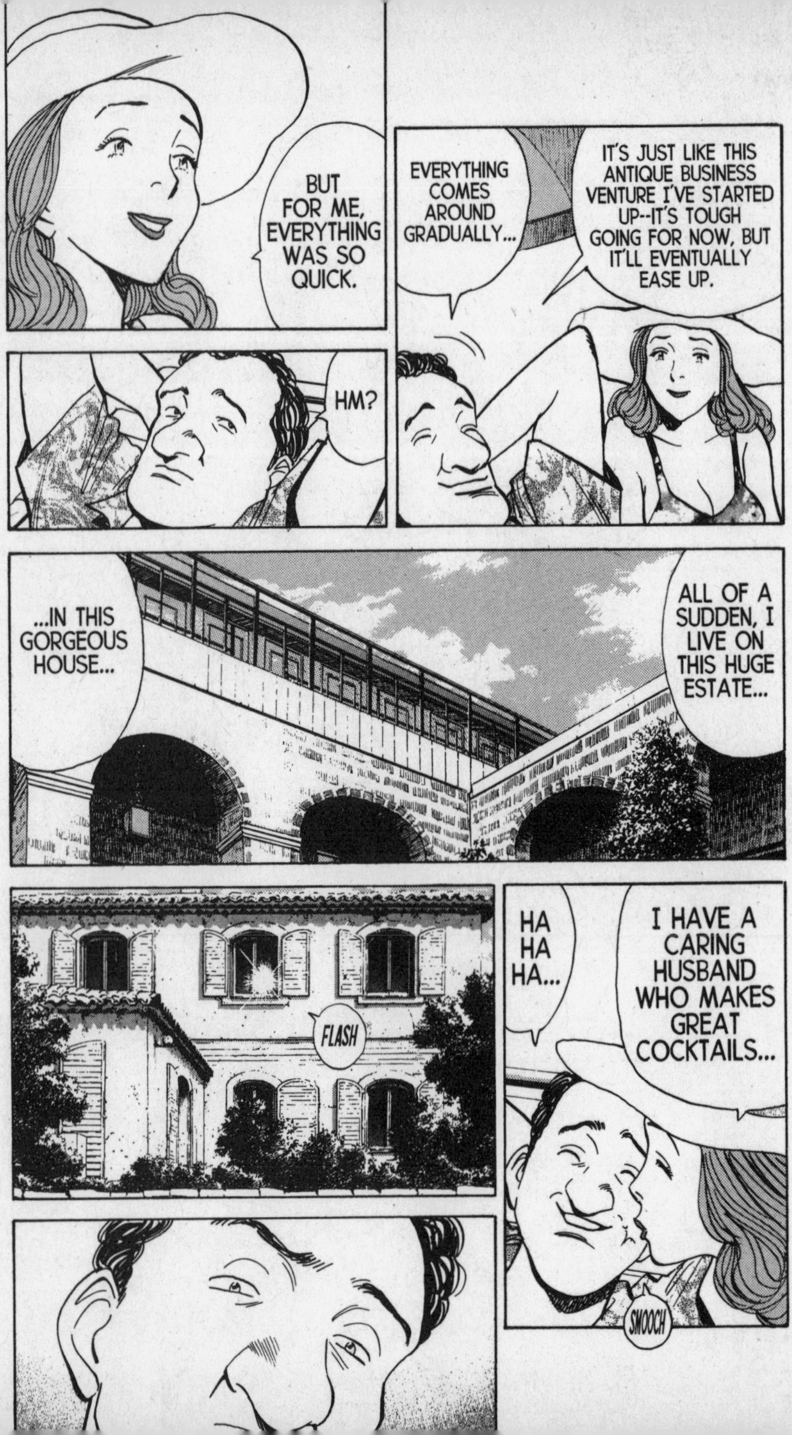
IT'S JUST LIKE THIS ANTIQUE BUSINESS VENTURE I'VE STARTED UP--IT'S TOUGH GOING FOR NOW, BUT IT'LL EVENTUALLY EASE UP.
EVERYTHING COMES AROUND GRADUALLY...
BUT FOR ME, EVERYTHING WAS SO QUICK.
HM?
ALL OF A SUDDEN, I LIVE ON THIS HUGE ESTATE...
...IN THIS GORGEOUS HOUSE...
I HAVE A CARING HUSBAND WHO MAKES GREAT COCKTAILS...
HA HA HA...
SMOOCH
FLASH

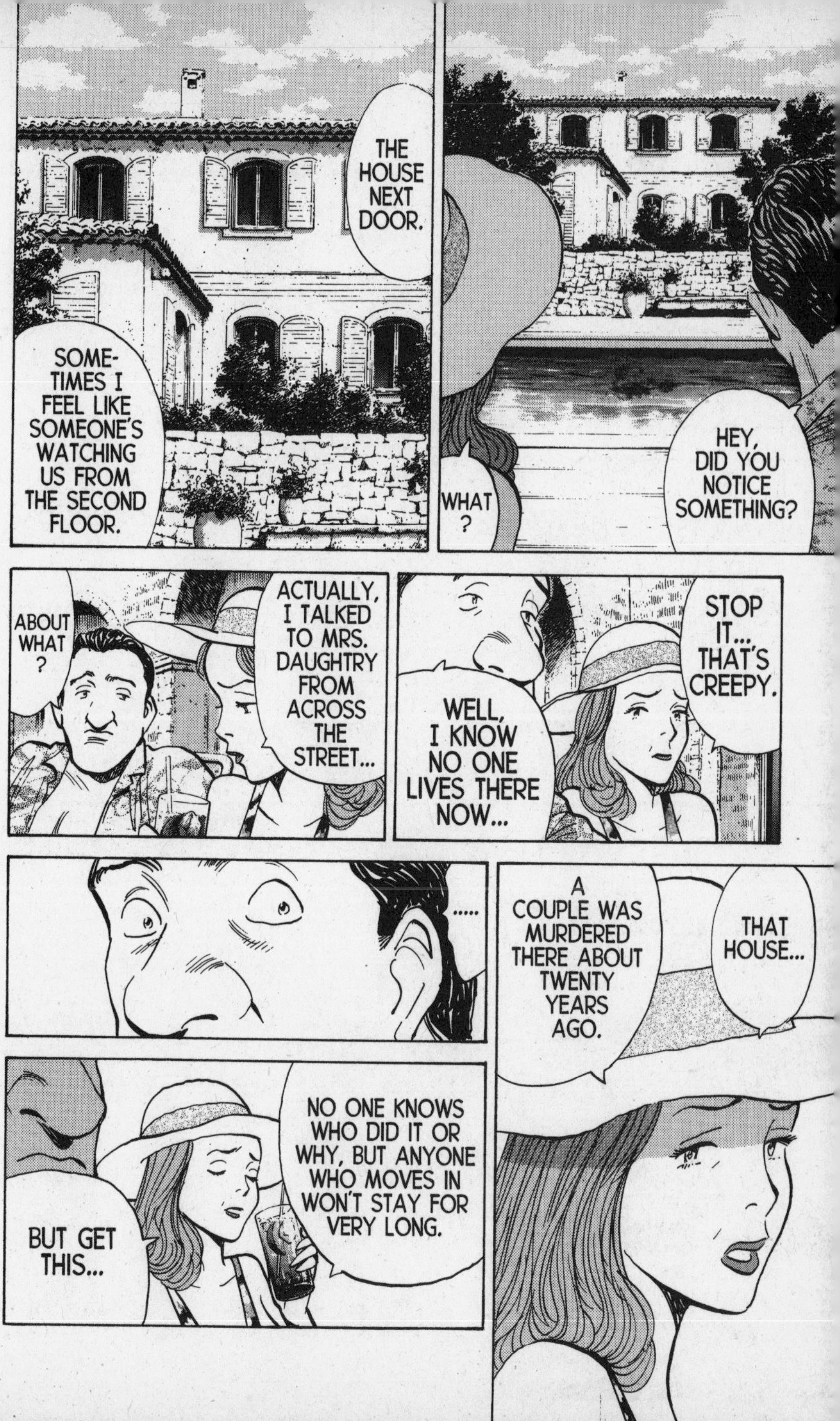
HEY, DID YOU NOTICE SOMETHING?
WHAT?
THE HOUSE NEXT DOOR.
SOMETIMES I FEEL LIKE SOMEONE'S WATCHING US FROM THE SECOND FLOOR.
STOP IT... THAT'S CREEPY.
WELL, I KNOW NO ONE LIVES THERE NOW...
ACTUALLY, I TALKED TO MRS. DAUGHTRY FROM ACROSS THE STREET...
ABOUT WHAT?
THAT HOUSE...
A COUPLE WAS MURDERED THERE ABOUT TWENTY YEARS AGO.
.....
NO ONE KNOWS WHO DID IT OR WHY, BUT ANYONE WHO MOVES IN WON'T STAY FOR VERY LONG.
BUT GET THIS...

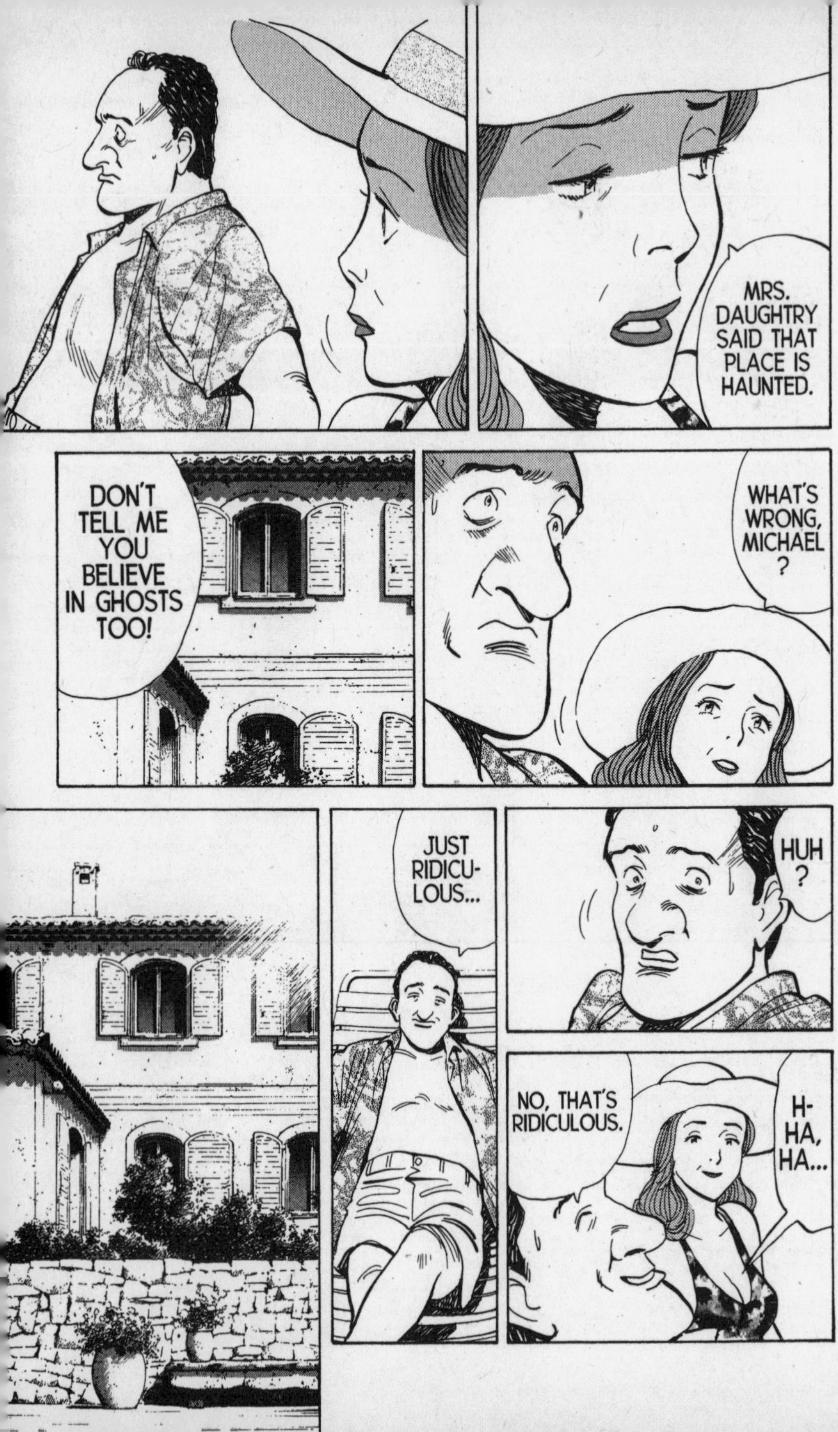
MRS. DAUGHTRY SAID THAT PLACE IS HAUNTED.
WHAT'S WRONG, MICHAEL?
DON'T TELL ME YOU BELIEVE IN GHOSTS TOO!
HUH?
H-HA, HA...
NO, THAT'S RIDICULOUS.
JUST RIDICULOUS...

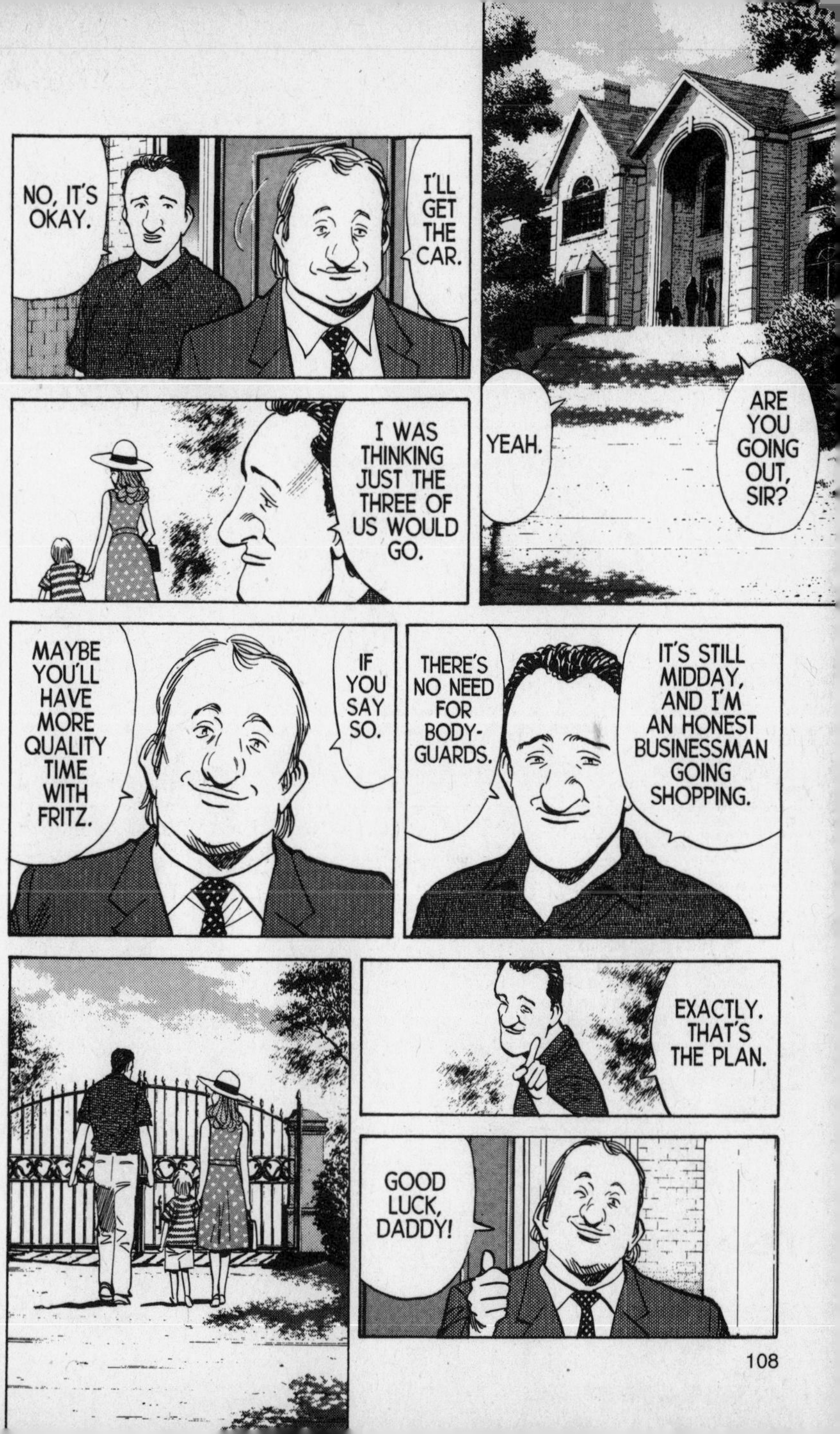
ARE YOU GOING OUT, SIR?
YEAH.
I'LL GET THE CAR.
NO, IT'S OKAY.
I WAS THINKING JUST THE THREE OF US WOULD GO.
IT'S STILL MIDDAY, AND I'M AN HONEST BUSINESSMAN GOING SHOPPING.
THERE'S NO NEED FOR BODY-GUARDS.
IF YOU SAY SO.
MAYBE YOU'LL HAVE MORE QUALITY TIME WITH FRITZ.
EXACTLY. THAT'S THE PLAN.
GOOD LUCK, DADDY!

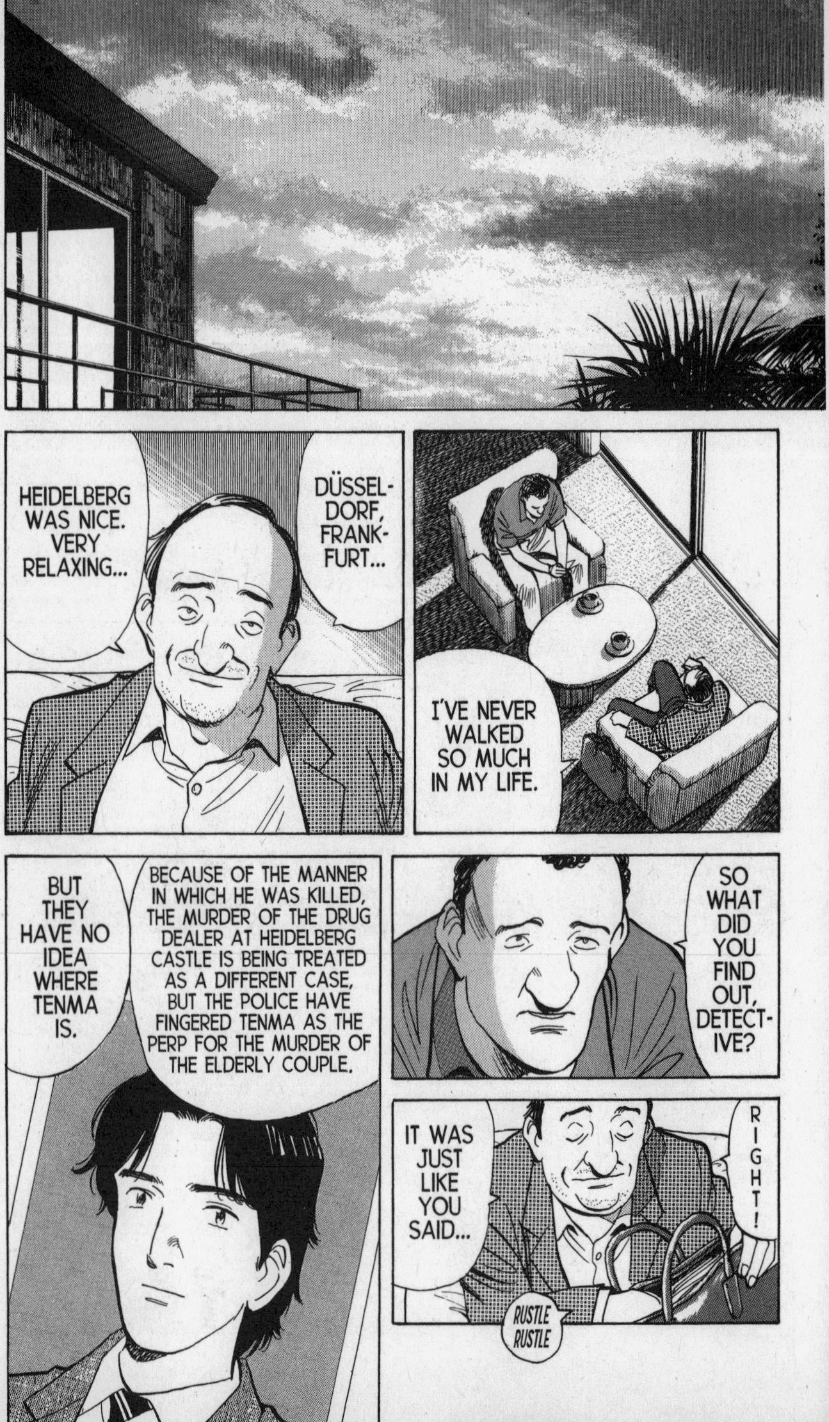
I'VE NEVER WALKED SO MUCH IN MY LIFE.
DÜSSEL-DORF, FRANK-FURT...
HEIDELBERG WAS NICE. VERY RELAXING...
SO WHAT DID YOU FIND OUT, DETECT-IVE?
RIGHT!
IT WAS JUST LIKE YOU SAID...
RUSTLE RUSTLE
BECAUSE OF THE MANNER IN WHICH HE WAS KILLED, THE MURDER OF THE DRUG DEALER AT HEIDELBERG CASTLE IS BEING TREATED AS A DIFFERENT CASE, BUT THE POLICE HAVE FINGERED TENMA AS THE PERP FOR THE MURDER OF THE ELDERLY COUPLE.
BUT THEY HAVE NO IDEA WHERE TENMA IS.

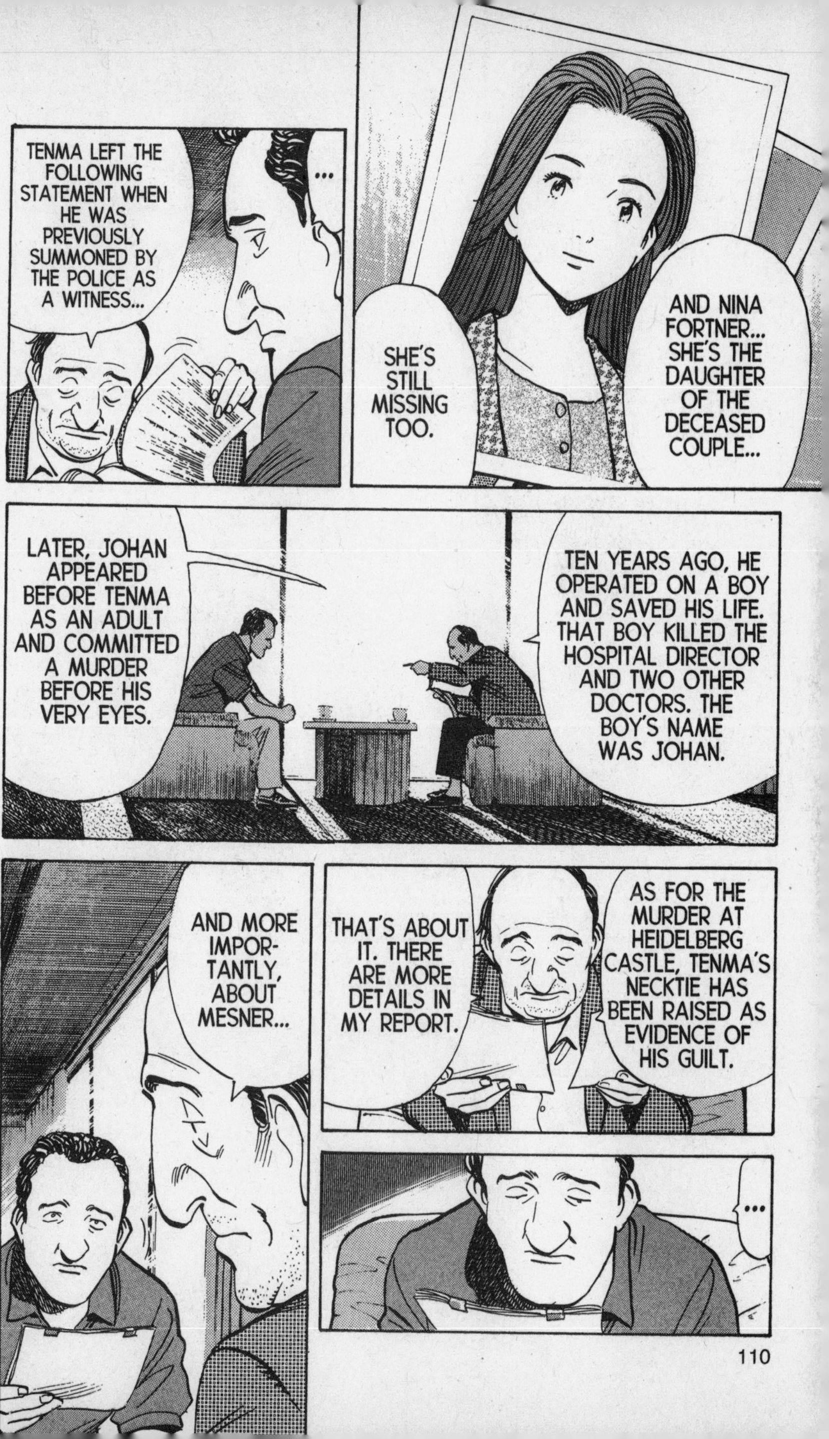
AND NINA FORTNER... SHE'S THE DAUGHTER OF THE DECEASED COUPLE...
SHE'S STILL MISSING TOO.
TENMA LEFT THE FOLLOWING STATEMENT WHEN HE WAS PREVIOUSLY SUMMONED BY THE POLICE AS A WITNESS...
...
TEN YEARS AGO, HE OPERATED ON A BOY AND SAVED HIS LIFE. THAT BOY KILLED THE HOSPITAL DIRECTOR AND TWO OTHER DOCTORS. THE BOY'S NAME WAS JOHAN.
LATER, JOHAN APPEARED BEFORE TENMA AS AN ADULT AND COMMITTED A MURDER BEFORE HIS VERY EYES.
AS FOR THE MURDER AT HEIDELBERG CASTLE, TENMA'S NECKTIE HAS BEEN RAISED AS EVIDENCE OF HIS GUILT.
THAT'S ABOUT IT. THERE ARE MORE DETAILS IN MY REPORT.
...
AND MORE IMPOR-TANTLY, ABOUT MESNER...

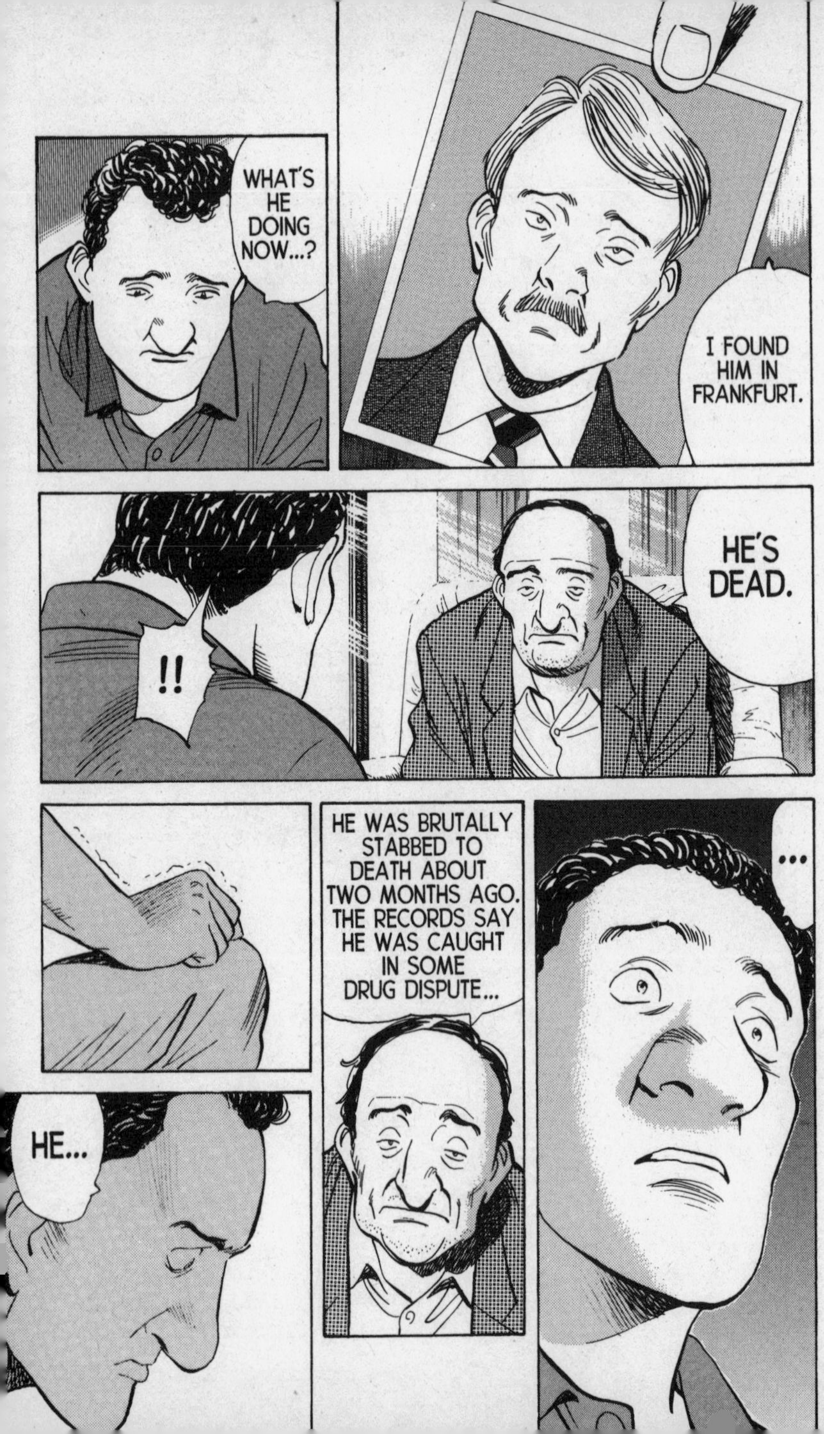
I FOUND HIM IN FRANKFURT.
WHAT'S HE DOING NOW...?
HE'S DEAD.
!!
...
HE WAS BRUTALLY STABBED TO DEATH ABOUT TWO MONTHS AGO. THE RECORDS SAY HE WAS CAUGHT IN SOME DRUG DISPUTE...
HE...

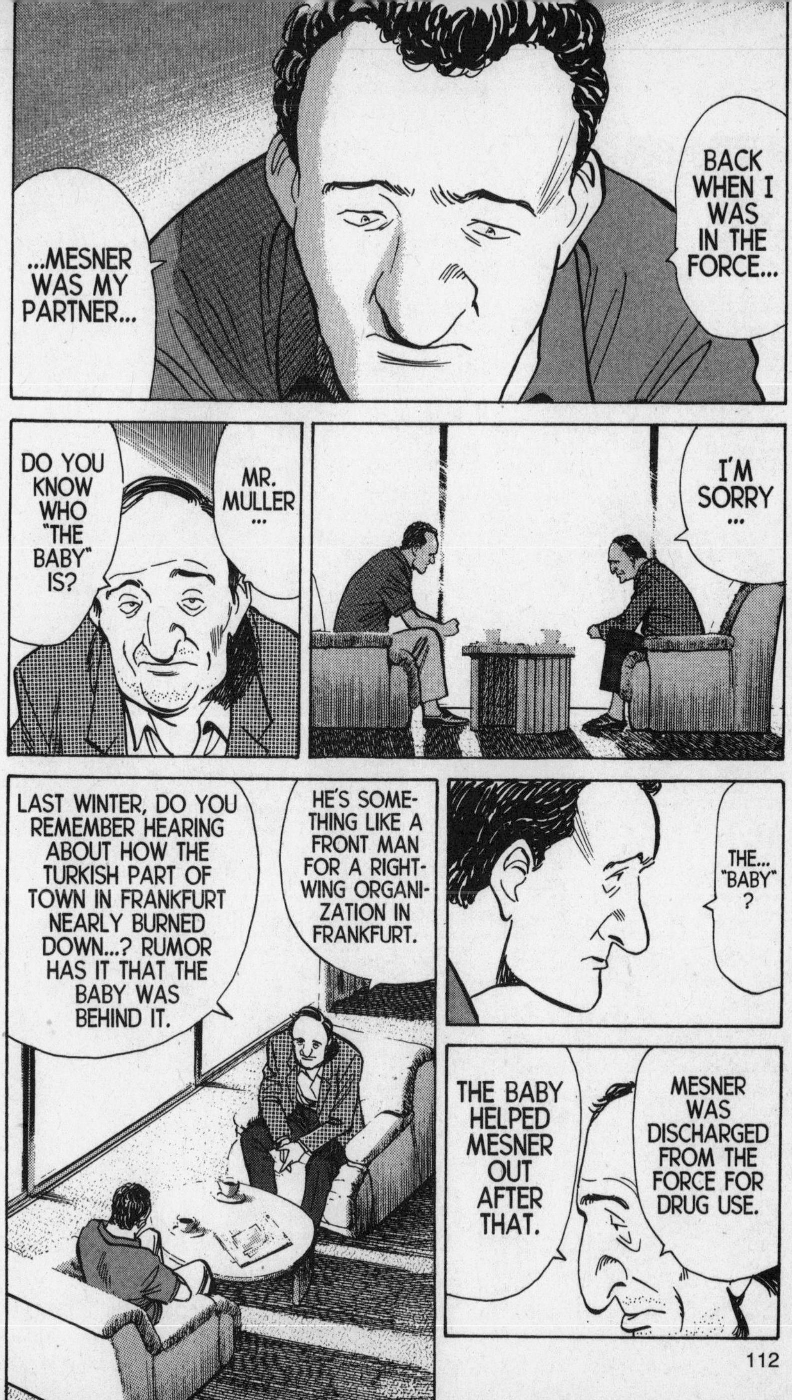
BACK WHEN I WAS IN THE FORCE...
...MESNER WAS MY PARTNER...
I'M SORRY...
MR. MULLER...
DO YOU KNOW WHO "THE BABY" IS?
THE... "BABY"?
MESNER WAS DISCHARGED FROM THE FORCE FOR DRUG USE.
THE BABY HELPED MESNER OUT AFTER THAT.
HE'S SOMETHING LIKE A FRONT MAN FOR A RIGHT-WING ORGANIZATION IN FRANKFURT.
LAST WINTER, DO YOU REMEMBER HEARING ABOUT HOW THE TURKISH PART OF TOWN IN FRANKFURT NEARLY BURNED DOWN...? RUMOR HAS IT THAT THE BABY WAS BEHIND IT.

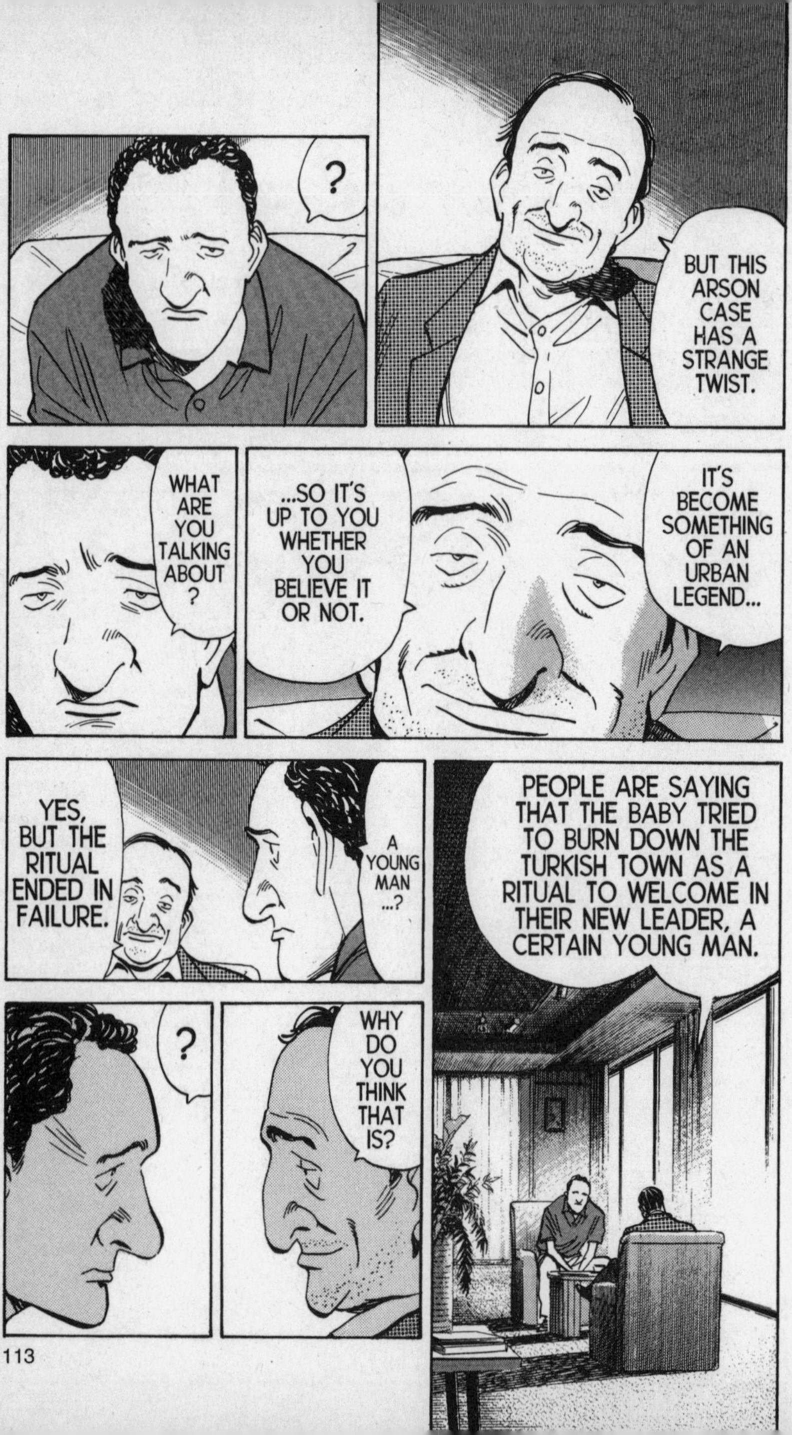
BUT THIS ARSON CASE HAS A STRANGE TWIST.
?
IT'S BECOME SOMETHING OF AN URBAN LEGEND...
...SO IT'S UP TO YOU WHETHER YOU BELIEVE IT OR NOT.
WHAT ARE YOU TALKING ABOUT?
PEOPLE ARE SAYING THAT THE BABY TRIED TO BURN DOWN THE TURKISH TOWN AS A RITUAL TO WELCOME IN THEIR NEW LEADER, A CERTAIN YOUNG MAN.
A YOUNG MAN...?
YES, BUT THE RITUAL ENDED IN FAILURE.
WHY DO YOU THINK THAT IS?
?

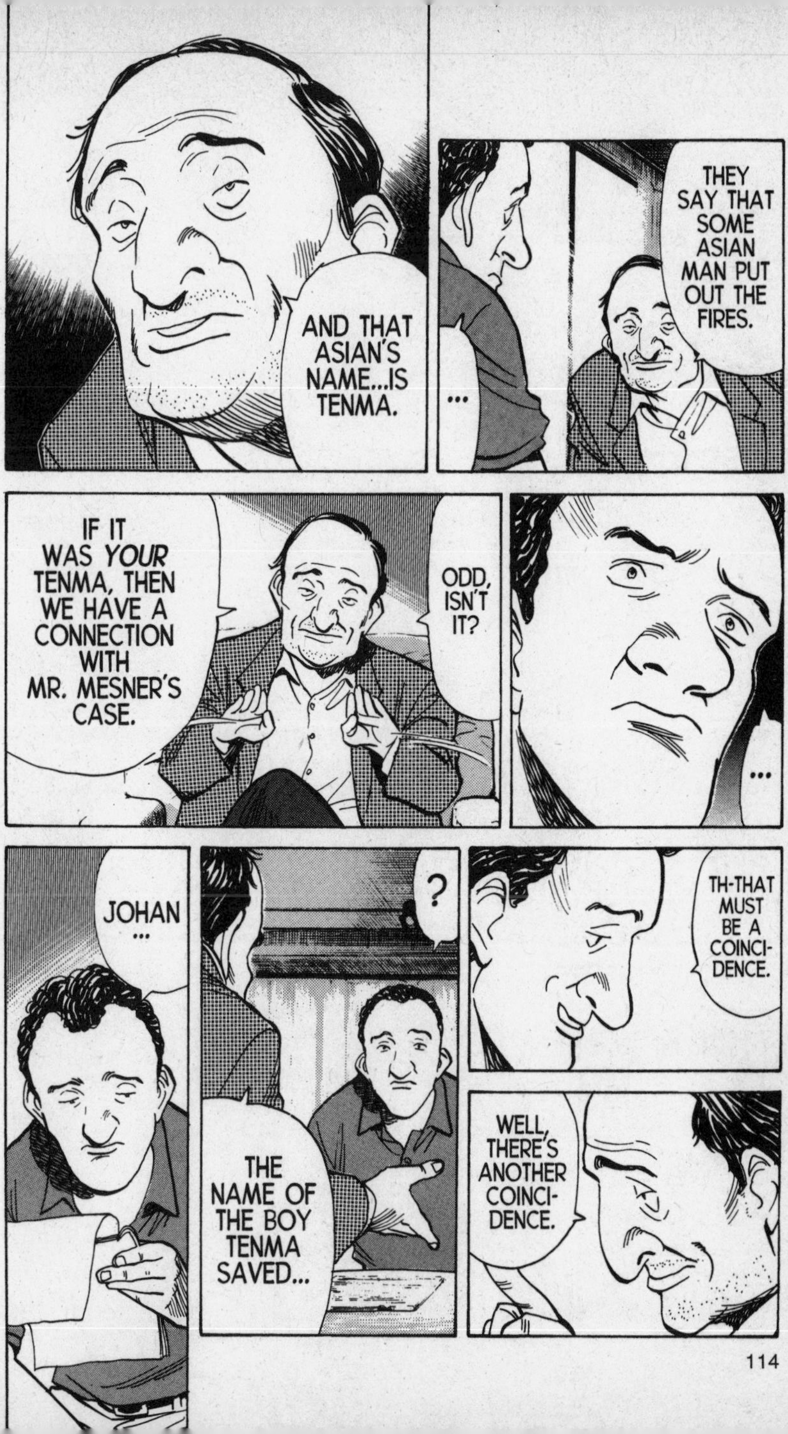

THEY SAY THAT SOME ASIAN MAN PUT OUT THE FIRES.
...
AND THAT ASIAN'S NAME...IS TENMA.
...
ODD, ISN'T IT?
IF IT WAS *YOUR* TENMA, THEN WE HAVE A CONNECTION WITH MR. MESNER'S CASE.
TH-THAT MUST BE A COINCI-DENCE.
WELL, THERE'S ANOTHER COINCI-DENCE.
?
THE NAME OF THE BOY TENMA SAVED...
JOHAN...

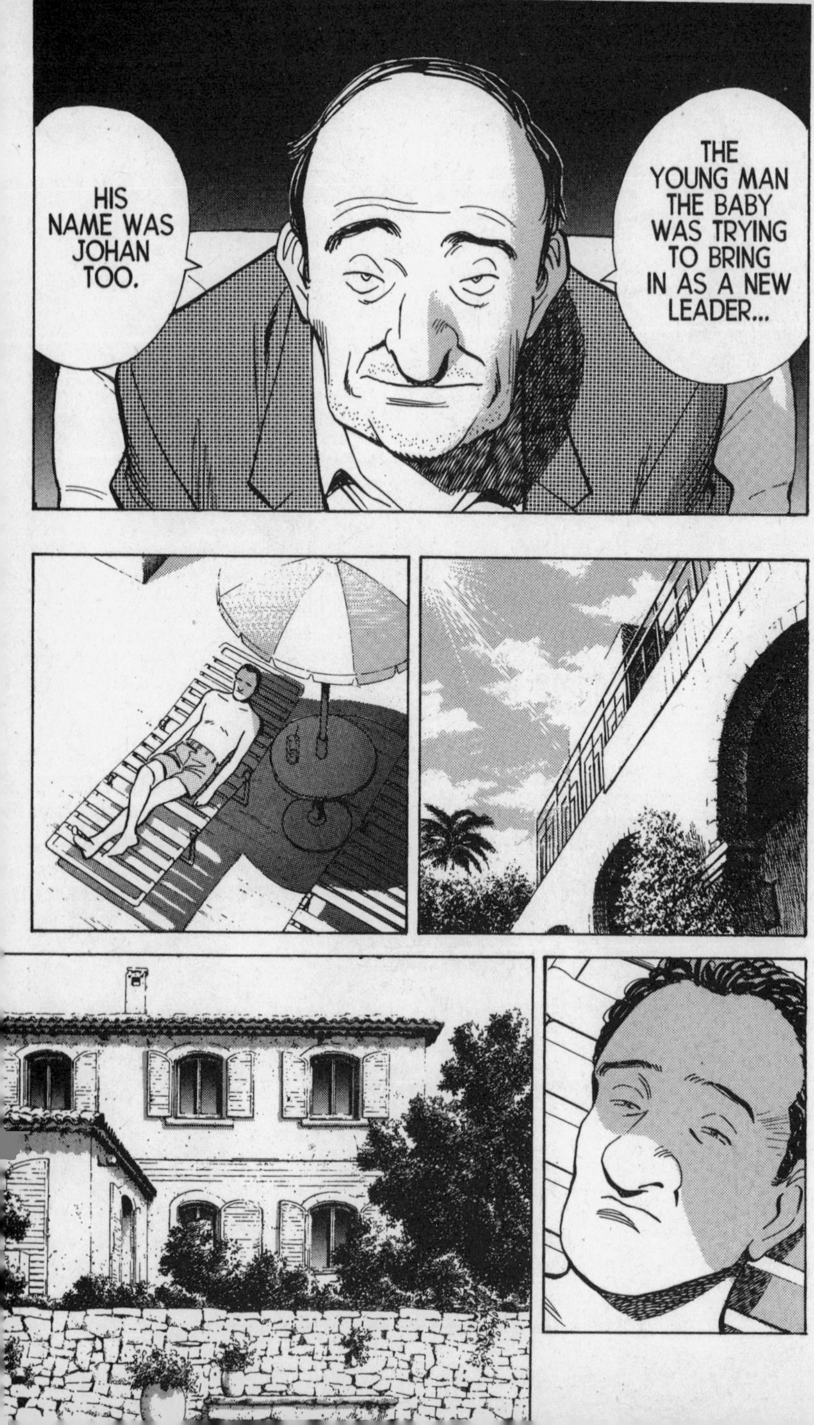
THE YOUNG MAN THE BABY WAS TRYING TO BRING IN AS A NEW LEADER...
HIS NAME WAS JOHAN TOO.

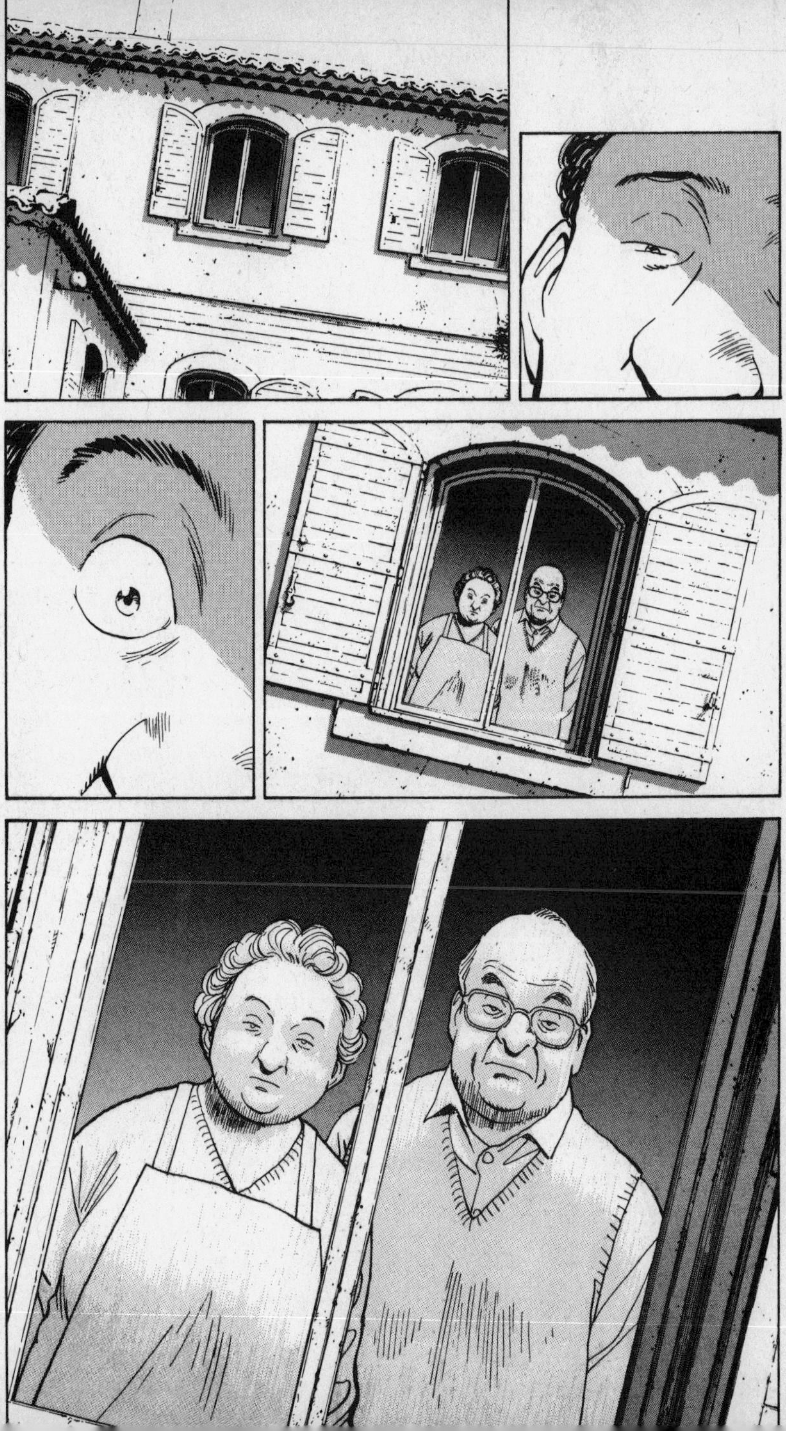

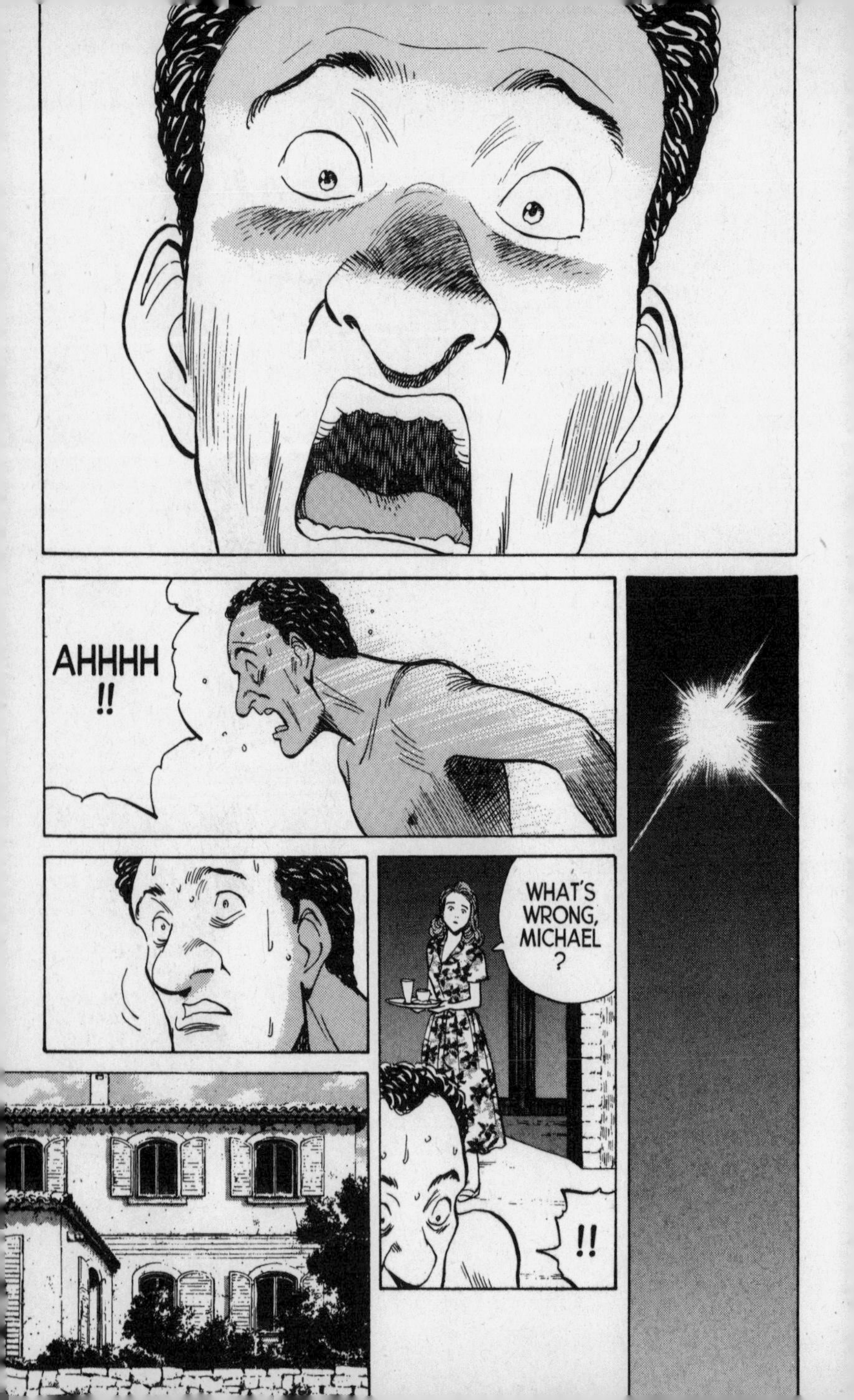
AHHHH !!
WHAT'S WRONG, MICHAEL ?
!!

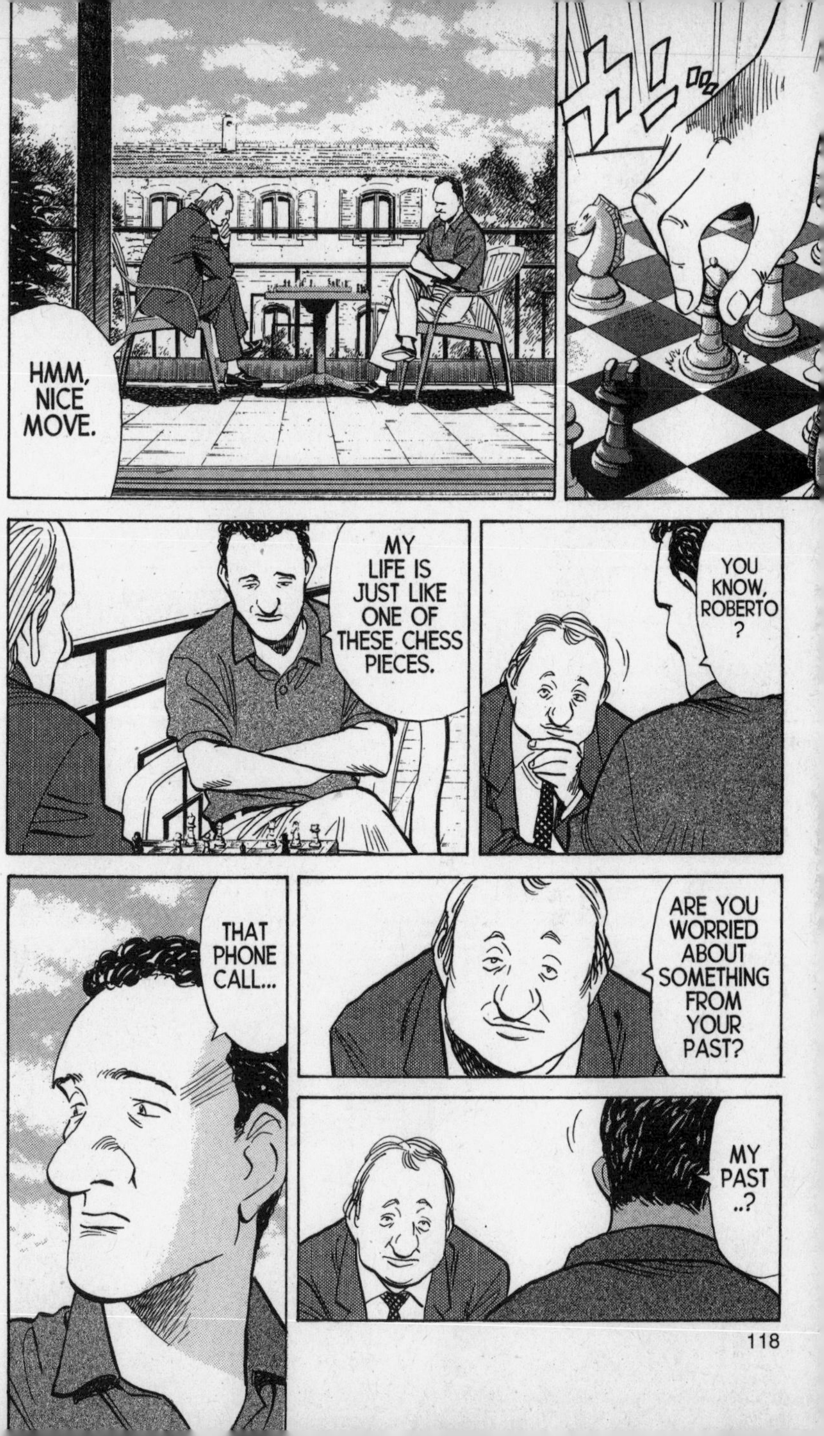
HMM, NICE MOVE.
YOU KNOW, ROBERTO?
MY LIFE IS JUST LIKE ONE OF THESE CHESS PIECES.
ARE YOU WORRIED ABOUT SOMETHING FROM YOUR PAST?
MY PAST ..?
THAT PHONE CALL...

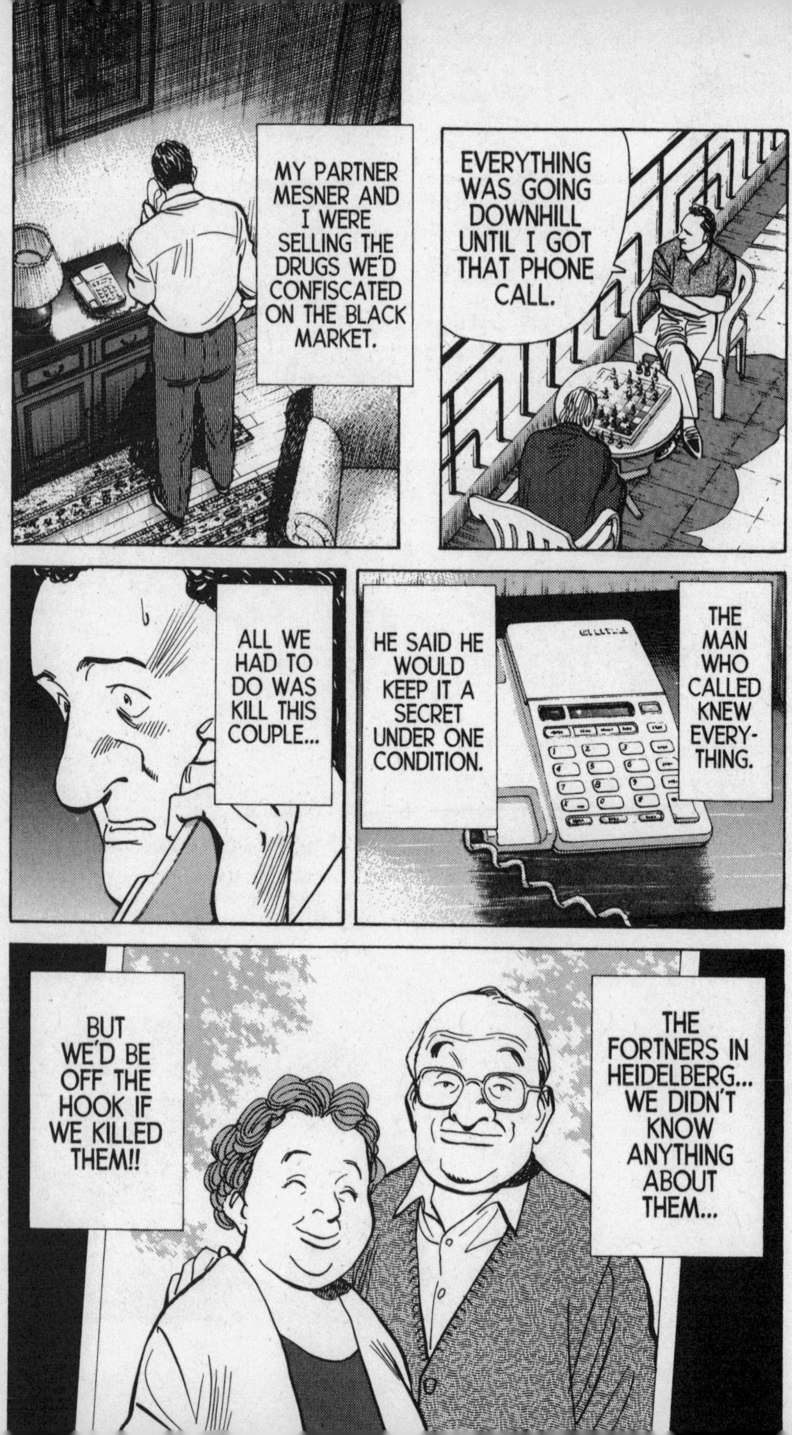
EVERYTHING WAS GOING DOWNHILL UNTIL I GOT THAT PHONE CALL.
MY PARTNER MESNER AND I WERE SELLING THE DRUGS WE'D CONFISCATED ON THE BLACK MARKET.
THE MAN WHO CALLED KNEW EVERY-THING.
HE SAID HE WOULD KEEP IT A SECRET UNDER ONE CONDITION.
ALL WE HAD TO DO WAS KILL THIS COUPLE...
THE FORTNERS IN HEIDELBERG... WE DIDN'T KNOW ANYTHING ABOUT THEM...
BUT WE'D BE OFF THE HOOK IF WE KILLED THEM!!

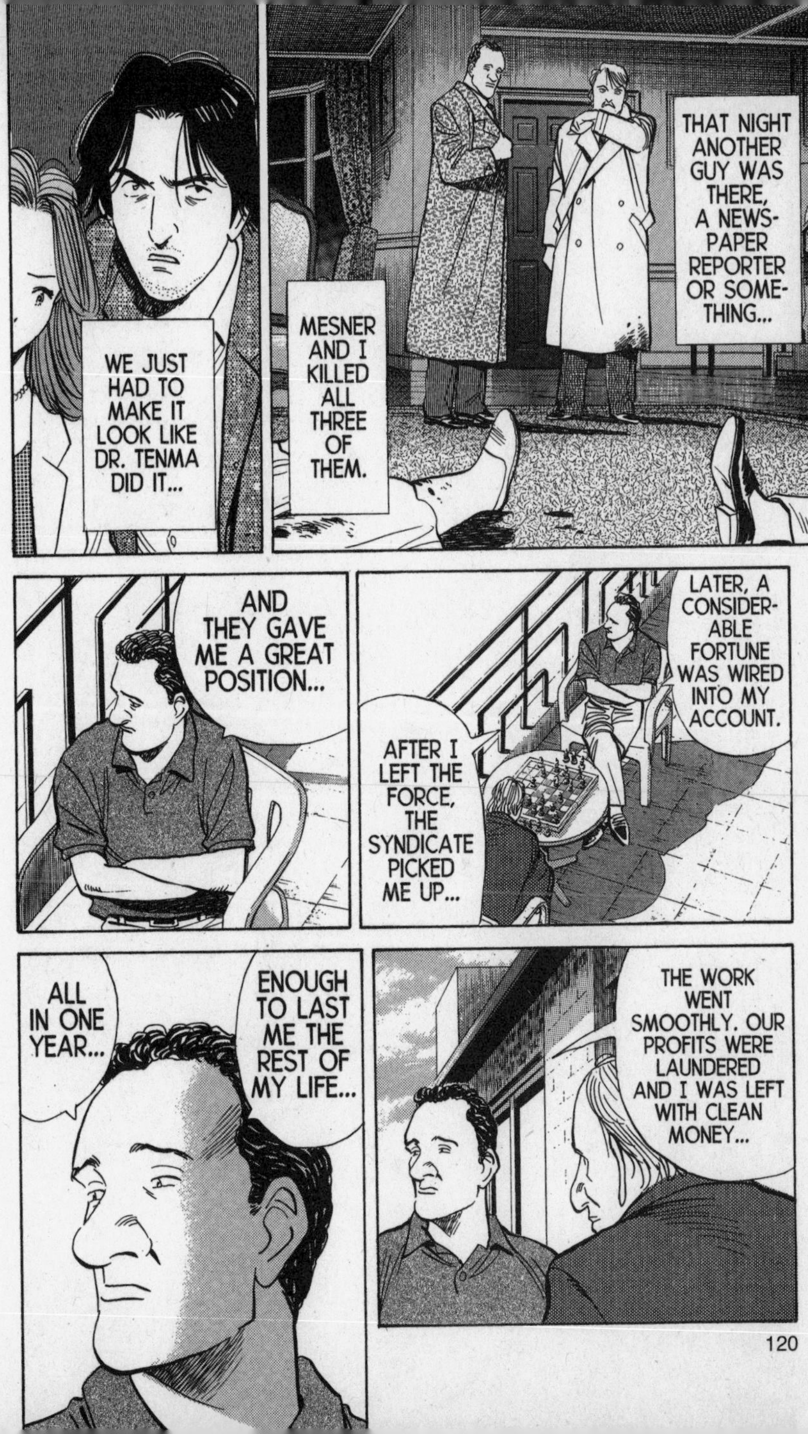
THAT NIGHT ANOTHER GUY WAS THERE, A NEWSPAPER REPORTER OR SOMETHING...
MESNER AND I KILLED ALL THREE OF THEM.
WE JUST HAD TO MAKE IT LOOK LIKE DR. TENMA DID IT...
LATER, A CONSIDERABLE FORTUNE WAS WIRED INTO MY ACCOUNT.
AFTER I LEFT THE FORCE, THE SYNDICATE PICKED ME UP...
AND THEY GAVE ME A GREAT POSITION...
THE WORK WENT SMOOTHLY. OUR PROFITS WERE LAUNDERED AND I WAS LEFT WITH CLEAN MONEY...
ENOUGH TO LAST ME THE REST OF MY LIFE...
ALL IN ONE YEAR...

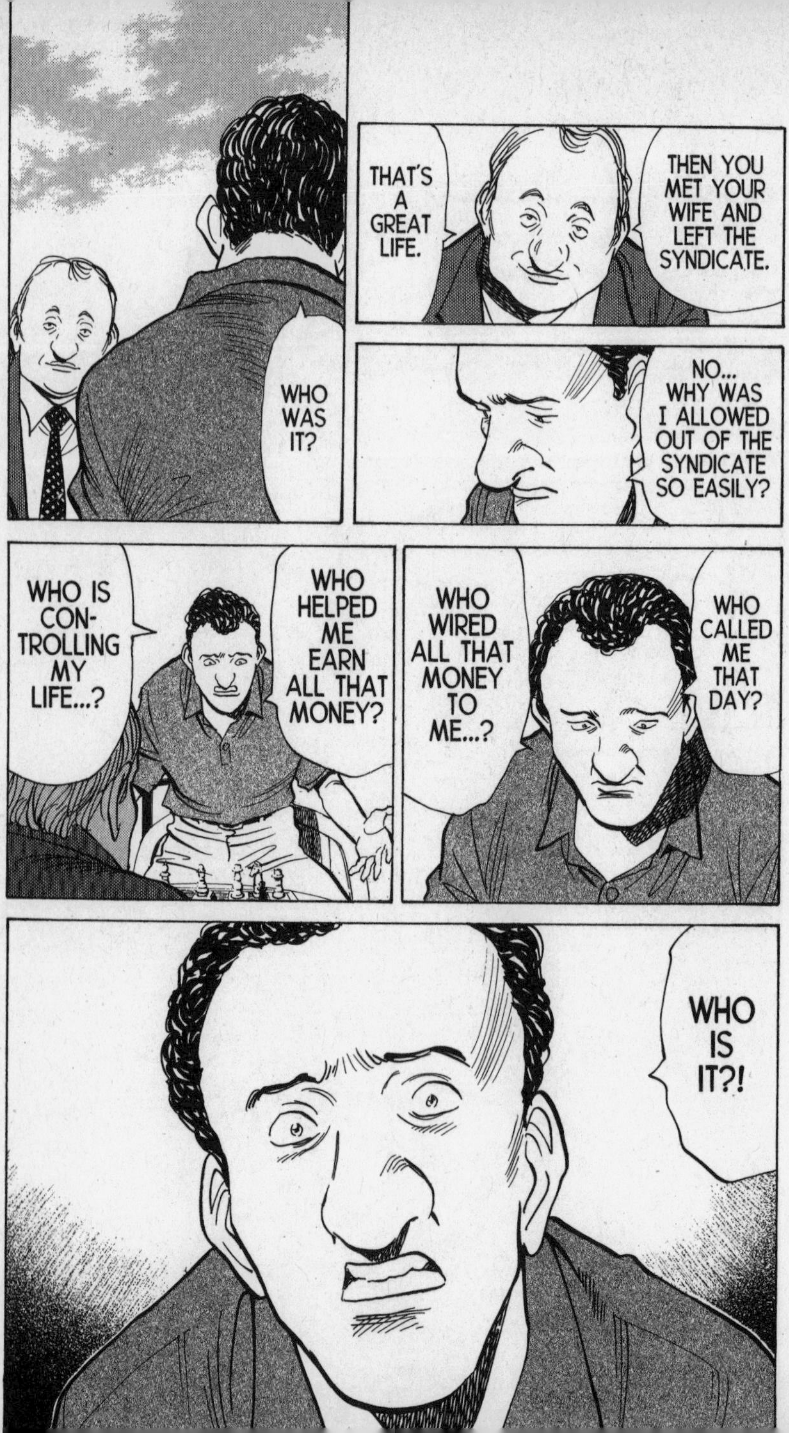
THEN YOU MET YOUR WIFE AND LEFT THE SYNDICATE.
THAT'S A GREAT LIFE.
NO... WHY WAS I ALLOWED OUT OF THE SYNDICATE SO EASILY?
WHO WAS IT?
WHO CALLED ME THAT DAY?
WHO WIRED ALL THAT MONEY TO ME...?
WHO HELPED ME EARN ALL THAT MONEY?
WHO IS CON-TROLLING MY LIFE...?
WHO IS IT?!

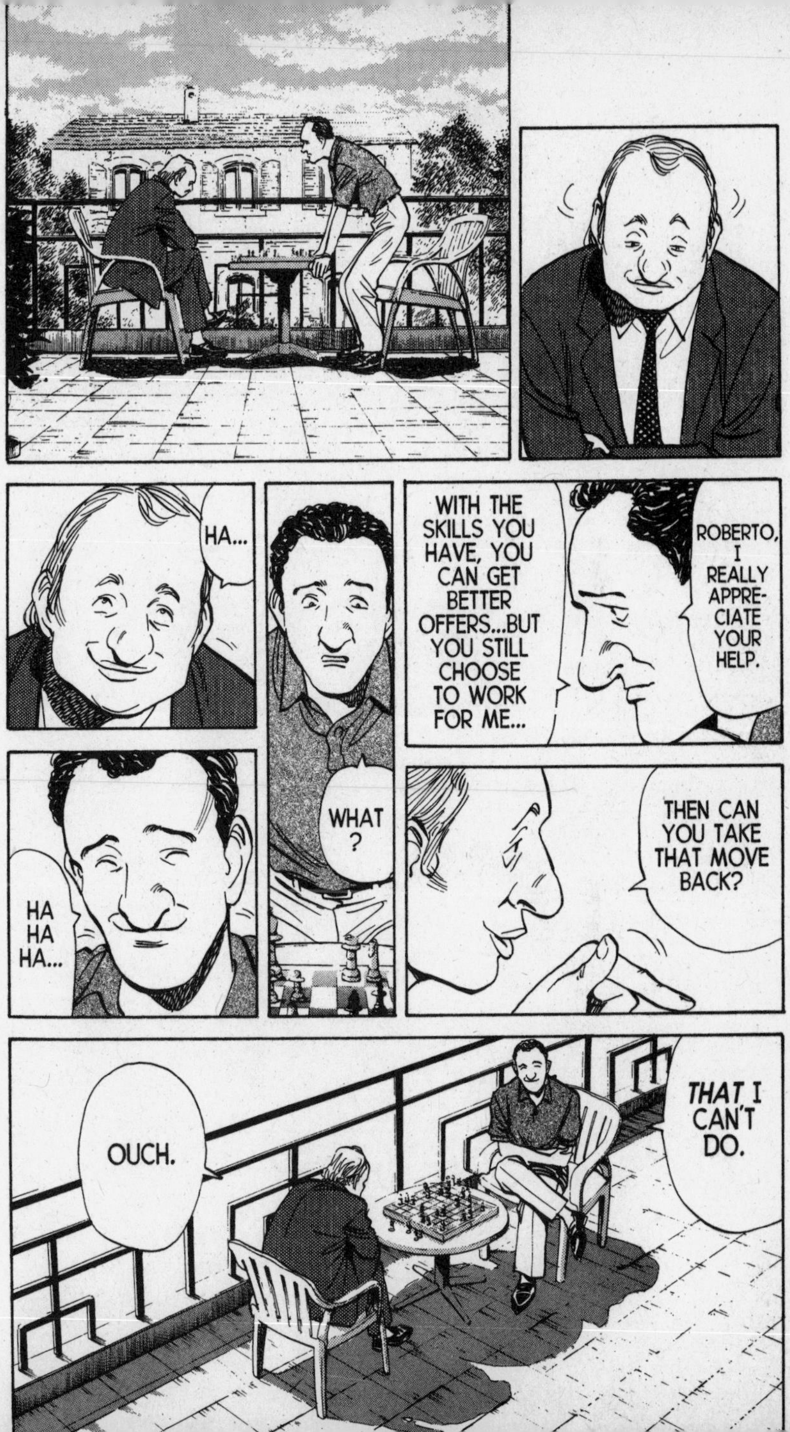
ROBERTO, I REALLY APPRECIATE YOUR HELP.
WITH THE SKILLS YOU HAVE, YOU CAN GET BETTER OFFERS...BUT YOU STILL CHOOSE TO WORK FOR ME...
THEN CAN YOU TAKE THAT MOVE BACK?
WHAT?
HA...
HA HA HA...
THAT I CAN'T DO.
OUCH.

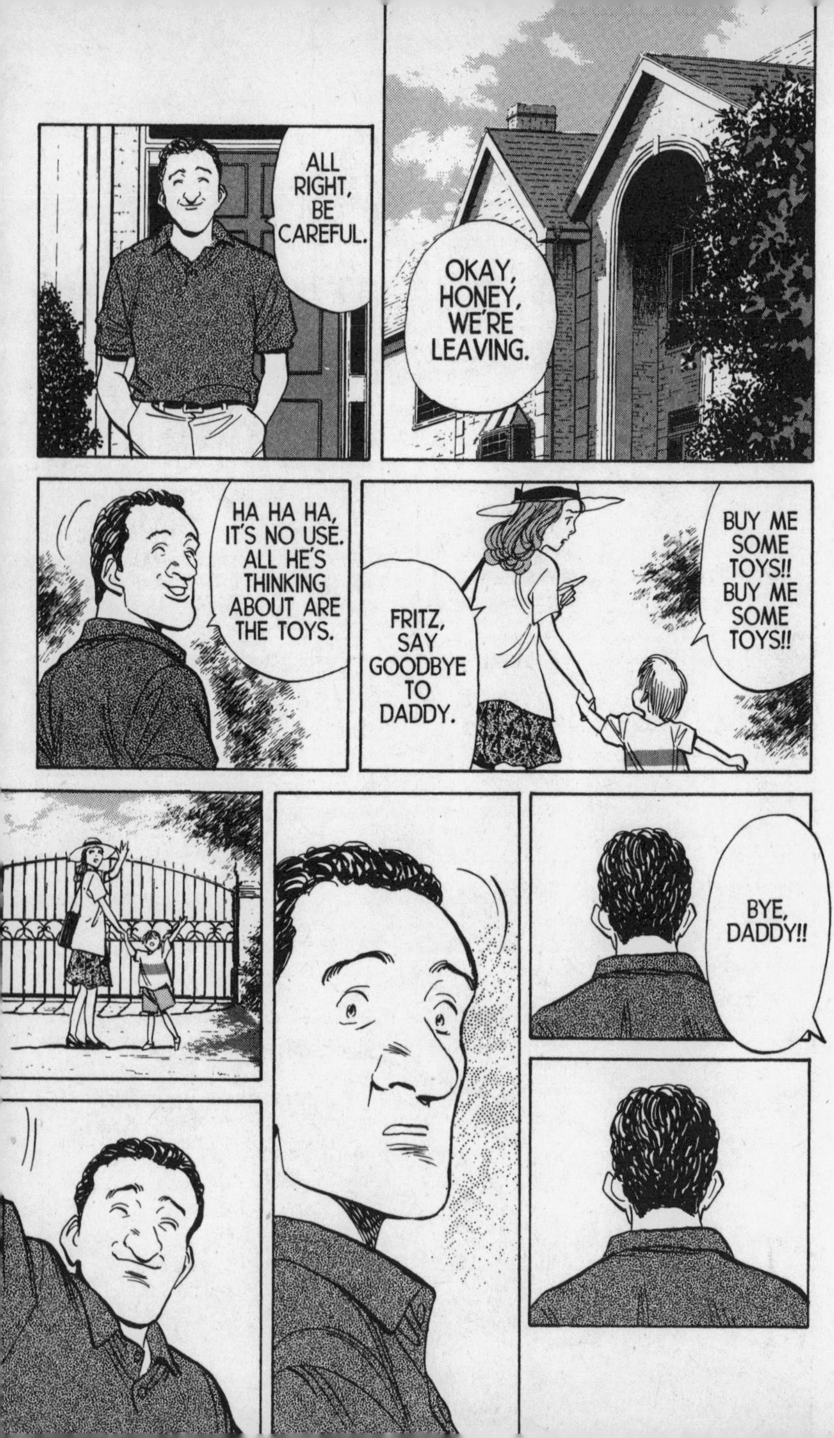
OKAY, HONEY, WE'RE LEAVING.
ALL RIGHT, BE CAREFUL.
BUY ME SOME TOYS!! BUY ME SOME TOYS!!
FRITZ, SAY GOODBYE TO DADDY.
HA HA HA, IT'S NO USE. ALL HE'S THINKING ABOUT ARE THE TOYS.
BYE, DADDY!!

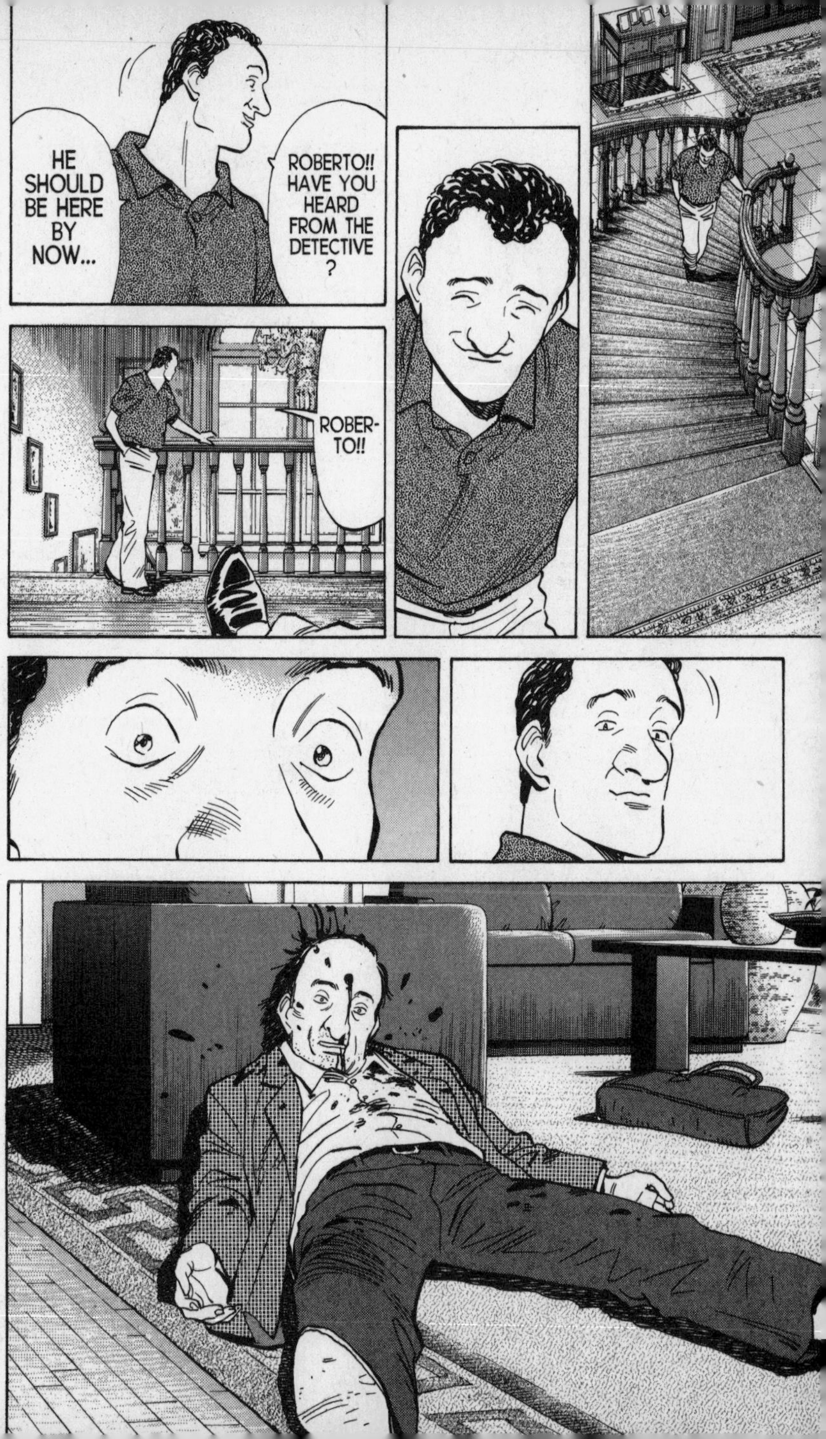
ROBERTO!! HAVE YOU HEARD FROM THE DETECTIVE?
HE SHOULD BE HERE BY NOW...
ROBER-TO!!

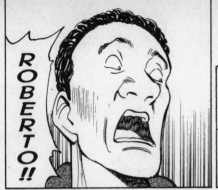

ROBERTO!!

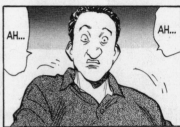

AH...

AH...

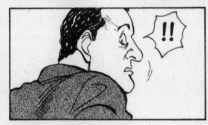

!!

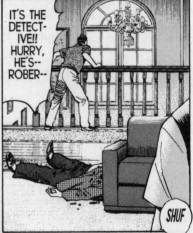

IT'S THE DETECT-IVE!! HURRY, HE'S-- ROBER--

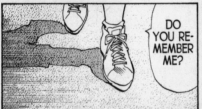

DO YOU RE-MEMBER ME?

SHUF

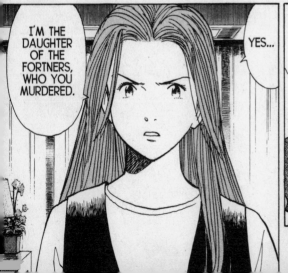

I'M THE DAUGHTER OF THE FORTNERS, WHO YOU MURDERED.

YES...

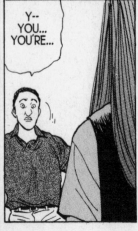

Y-- YOU... YOU'RE...

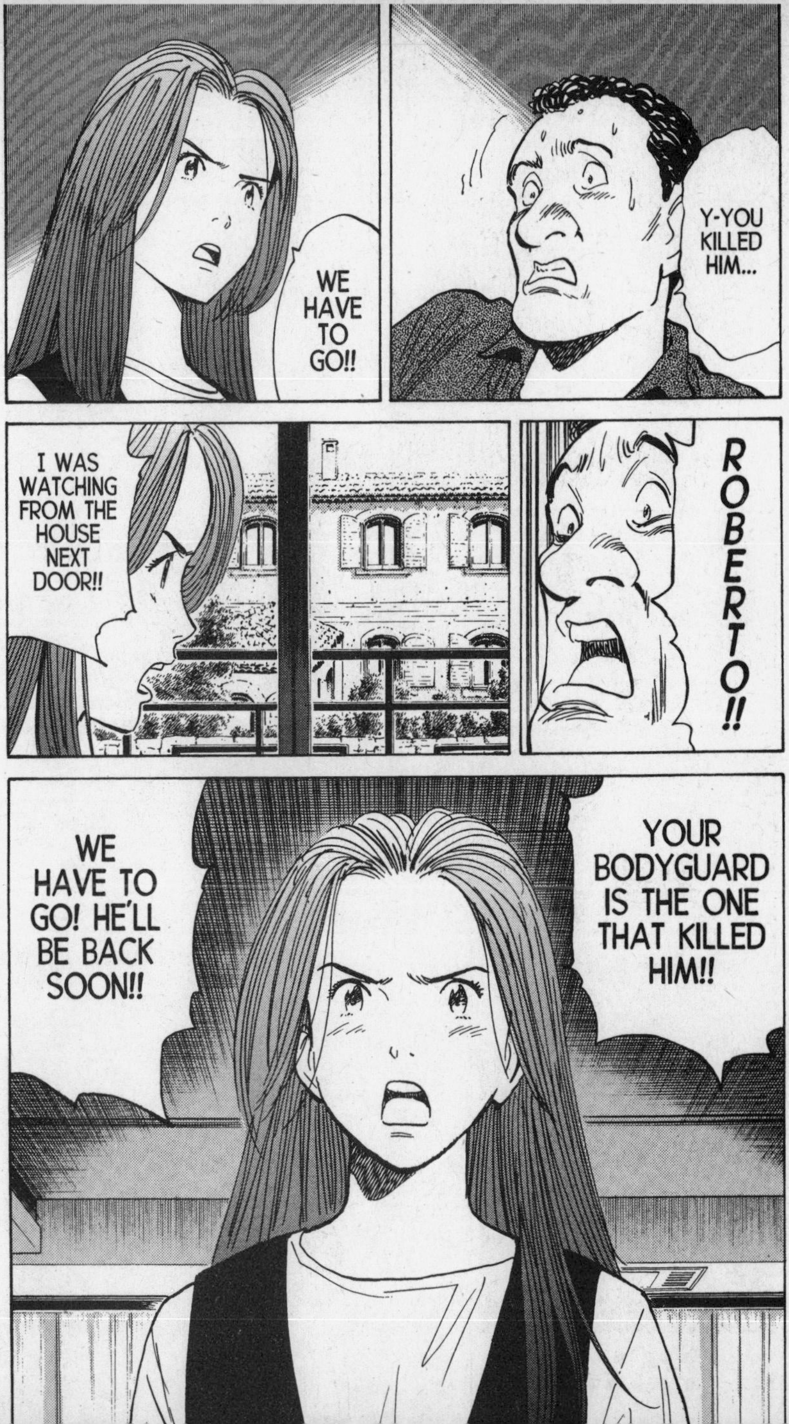
Y-YOU KILLED HIM...
WE HAVE TO GO!!
ROBERTO!!
I WAS WATCHING FROM THE HOUSE NEXT DOOR!!
YOUR BODYGUARD IS THE ONE THAT KILLED HIM!!
WE HAVE TO GO! HE'LL BE BACK SOON!!

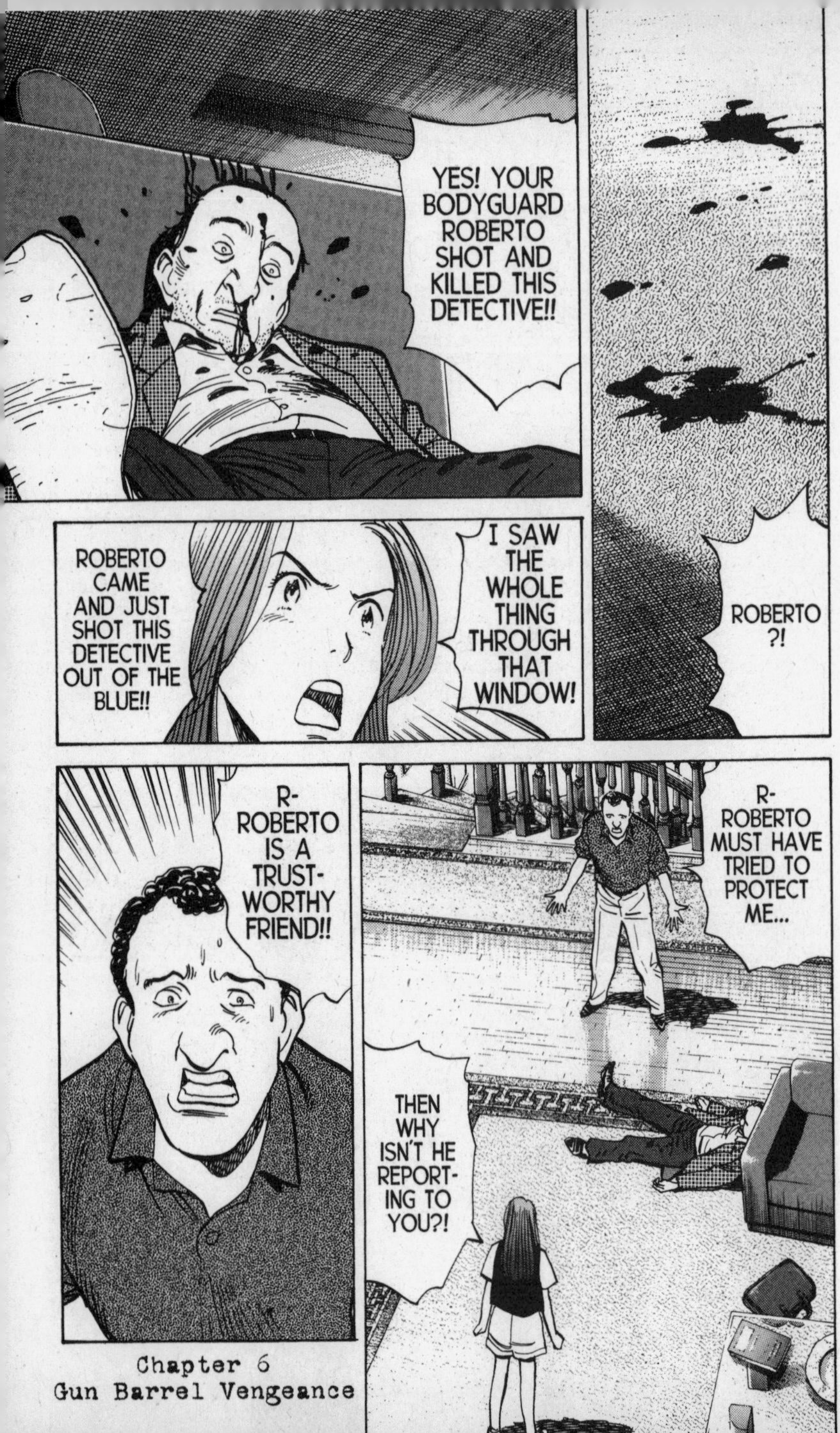
ROBERTO ?!
YES! YOUR BODYGUARD ROBERTO SHOT AND KILLED THIS DETECTIVE!!
I SAW THE WHOLE THING THROUGH THAT WINDOW!
ROBERTO CAME AND JUST SHOT THIS DETECTIVE OUT OF THE BLUE!!
R-ROBERTO MUST HAVE TRIED TO PROTECT ME...
THEN WHY ISN'T HE REPORTING TO YOU?!
R-ROBERTO IS A TRUSTWORTHY FRIEND!!

Chapter 6
Gun Barrel Vengeance

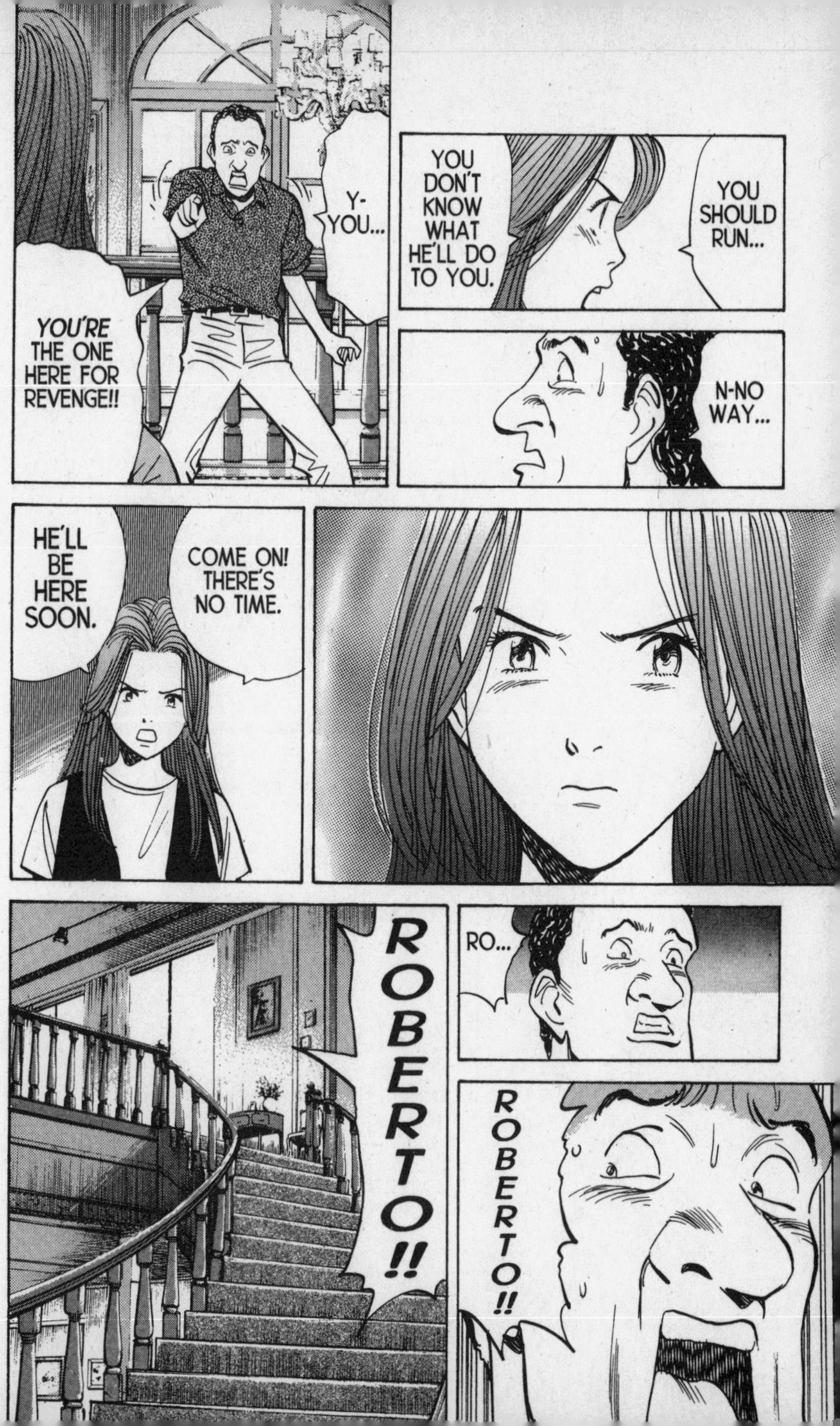

YOU SHOULD RUN...
YOU DON'T KNOW WHAT HE'LL DO TO YOU.
N-NO WAY...
Y-YOU...
YOU'RE THE ONE HERE FOR REVENGE!!
COME ON! THERE'S NO TIME.
HE'LL BE HERE SOON.
RO...
ROBERTO!!
ROBERTO!!

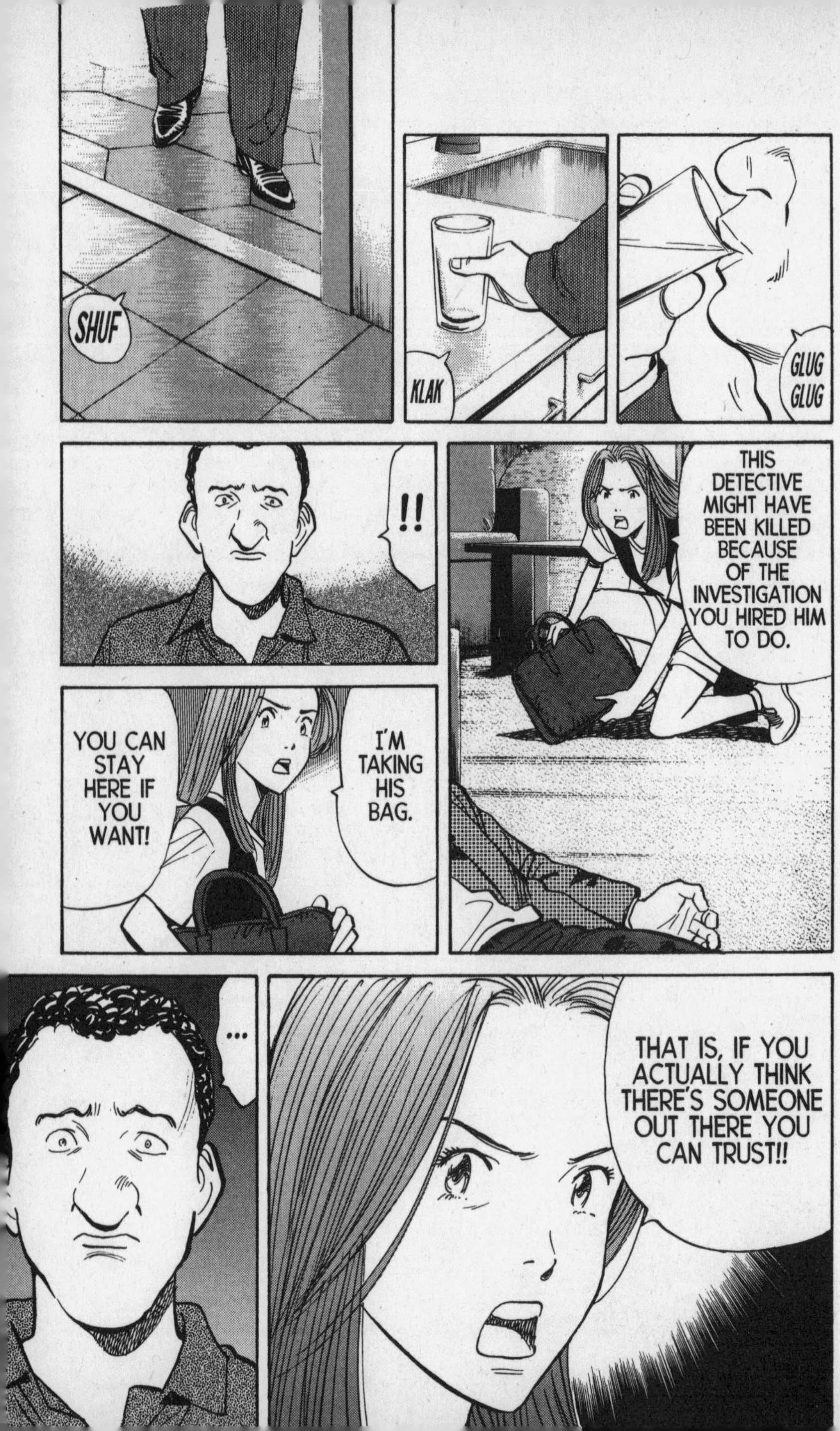
GLUG GLUG
KLAK
SHUF
THIS DETECTIVE MIGHT HAVE BEEN KILLED BECAUSE OF THE INVESTIGATION YOU HIRED HIM TO DO.
!!
I'M TAKING HIS BAG.
YOU CAN STAY HERE IF YOU WANT!
THAT IS, IF YOU ACTUALLY THINK THERE'S SOMEONE OUT THERE YOU CAN TRUST!!
...

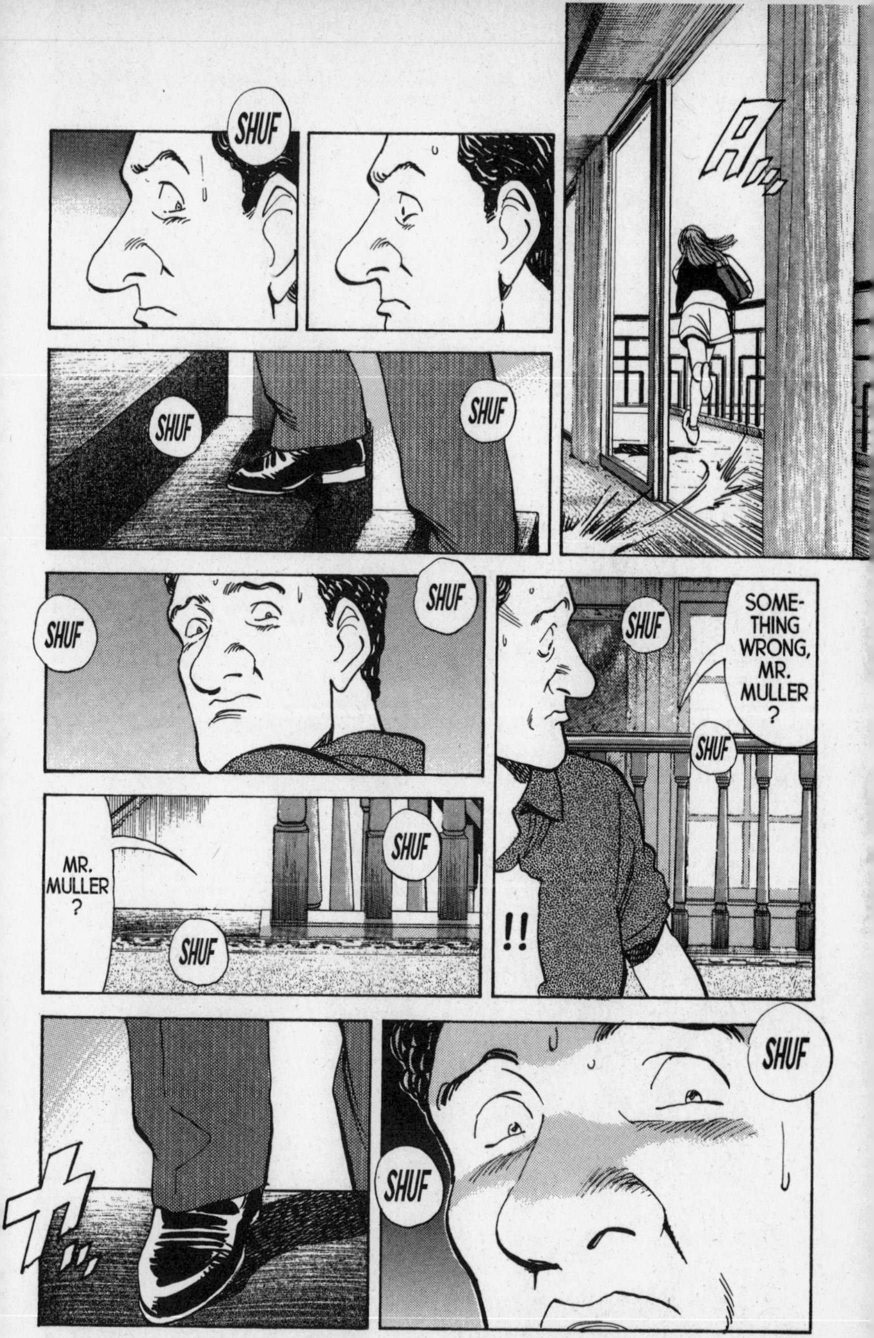
SHUF
SHUF
SHUF
SOME-THING WRONG, MR. MULLER?
SHUF
SHUF
!!
SHUF
SHUF
SHUF
MR. MULLER?
SHUF
SHUF
SHUF

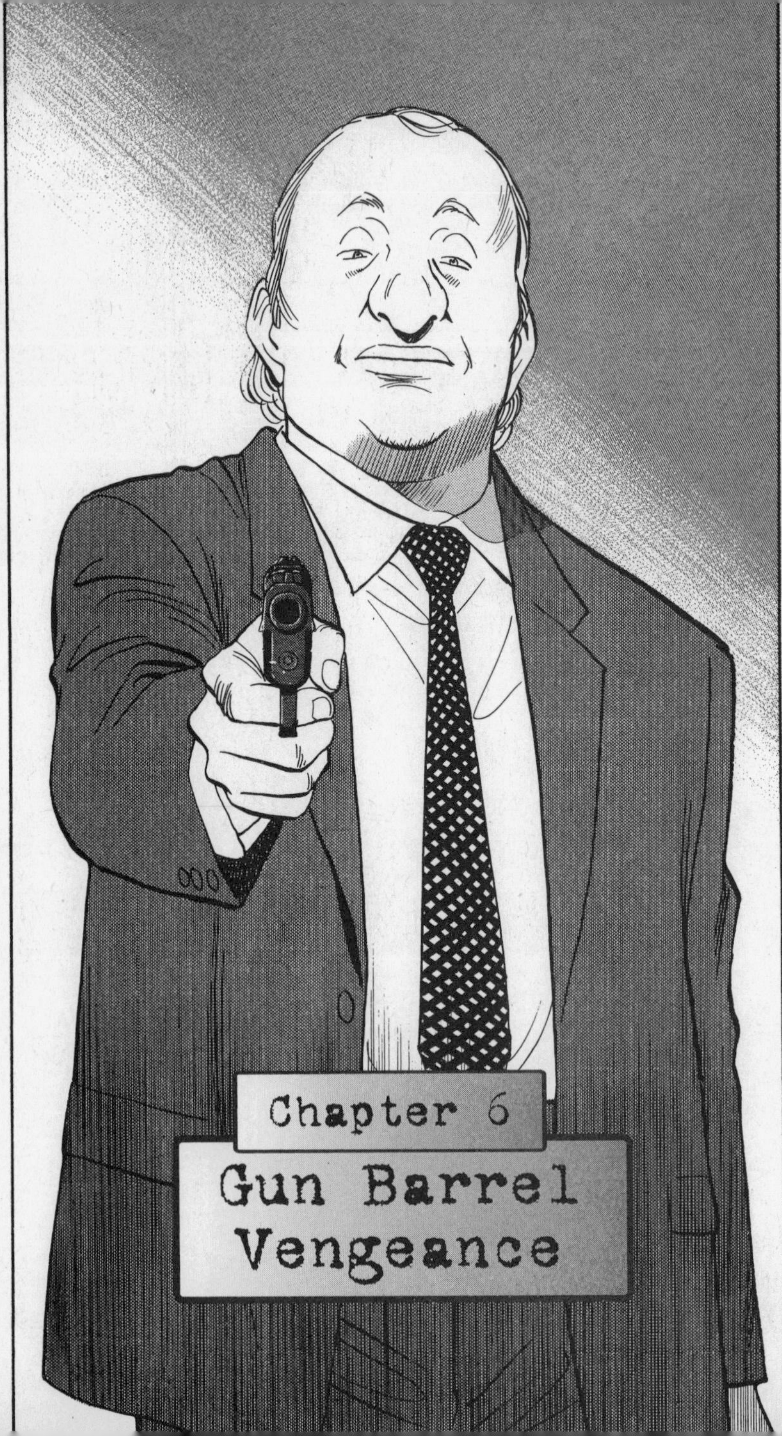
Chapter 6
Gun Barrel Vengeance

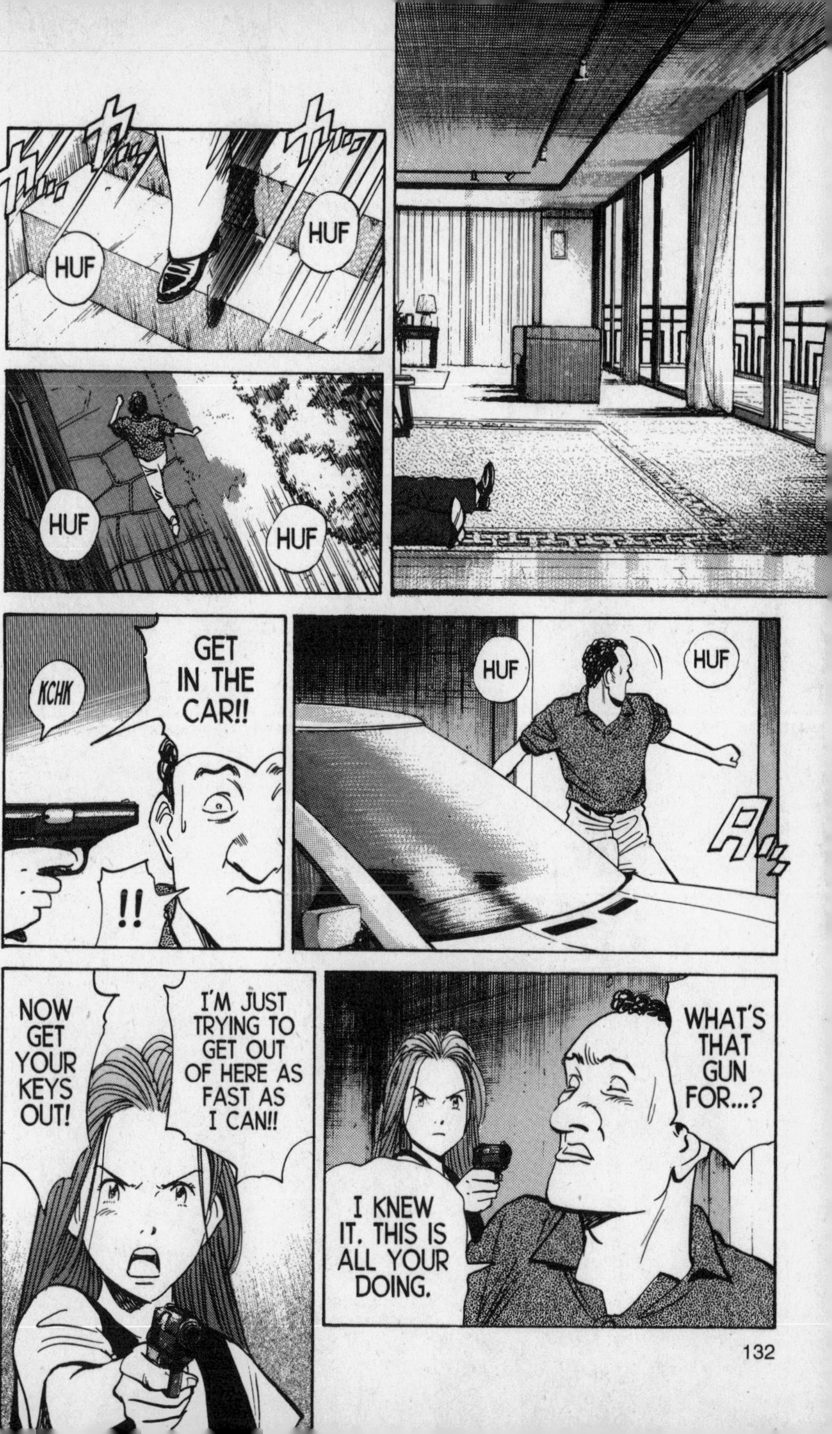
HUF
HUF
HUF
HUF
HUF
HUF
GET IN THE CAR!!
KCHK
!!
WHAT'S THAT GUN FOR...?
I KNEW IT. THIS IS ALL YOUR DOING.
I'M JUST TRYING TO GET OUT OF HERE AS FAST AS I CAN!!
NOW GET YOUR KEYS OUT!

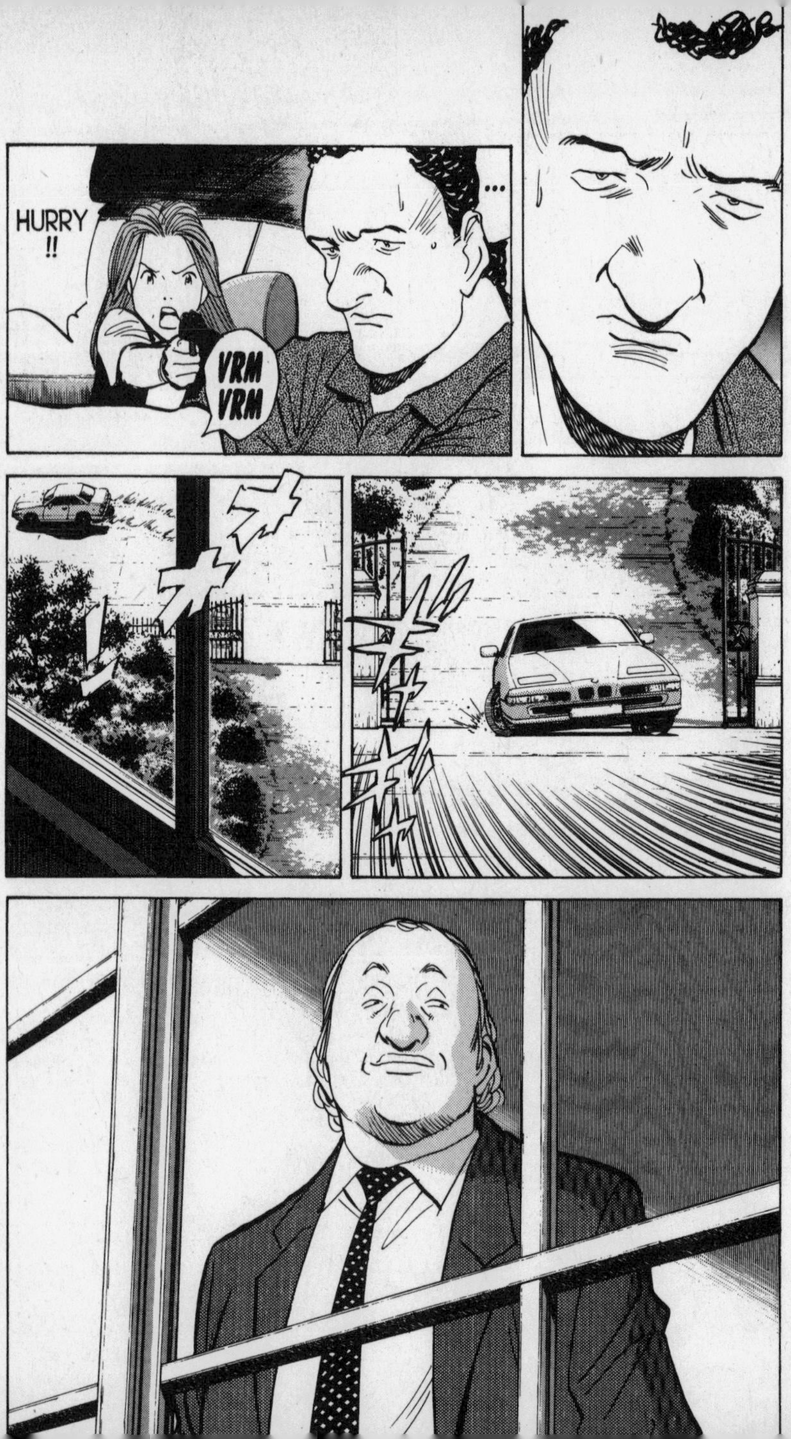
...
HURRY !!
VRM VRM

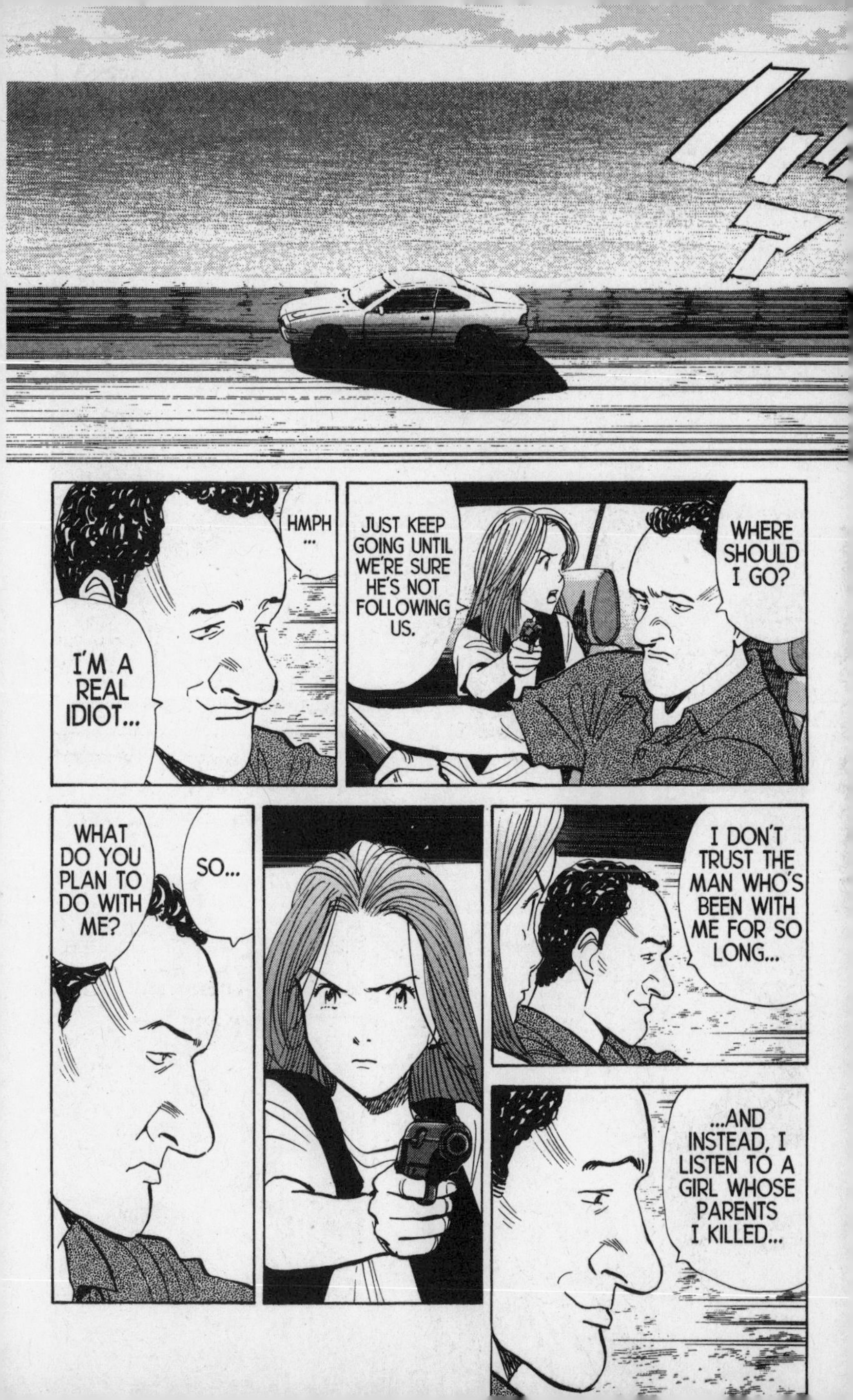
WHERE SHOULD I GO?
JUST KEEP GOING UNTIL WE'RE SURE HE'S NOT FOLLOWING US.
HMPH ...
I'M A REAL IDIOT...
I DON'T TRUST THE MAN WHO'S BEEN WITH ME FOR SO LONG...
...AND INSTEAD, I LISTEN TO A GIRL WHOSE PARENTS I KILLED...
SO...
WHAT DO YOU PLAN TO DO WITH ME?

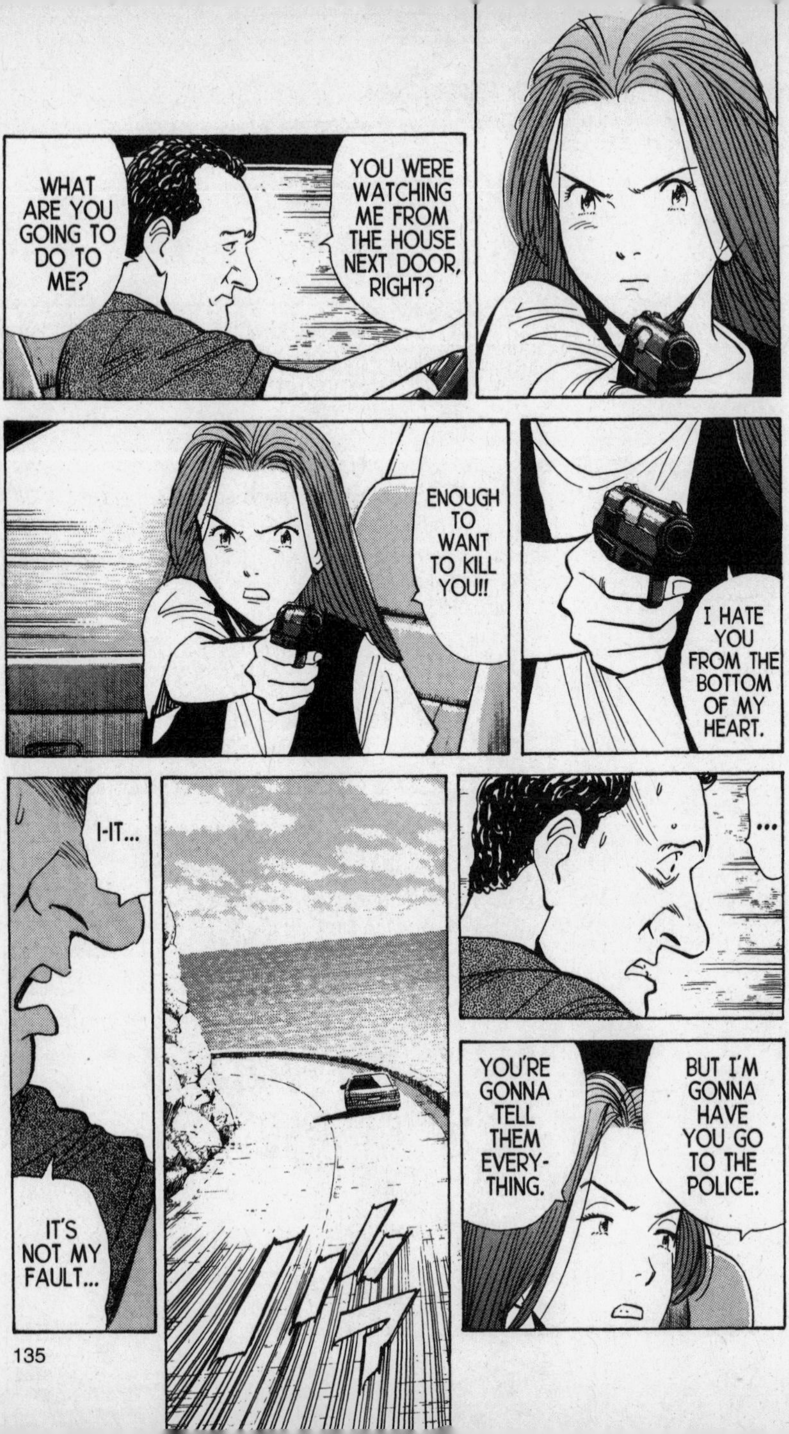
YOU WERE WATCHING ME FROM THE HOUSE NEXT DOOR, RIGHT?
WHAT ARE YOU GOING TO DO TO ME?
I HATE YOU FROM THE BOTTOM OF MY HEART.
ENOUGH TO WANT TO KILL YOU!!
...
BUT I'M GONNA HAVE YOU GO TO THE POLICE.
YOU'RE GONNA TELL THEM EVERY-THING.
I-IT...
IT'S NOT MY FAULT...

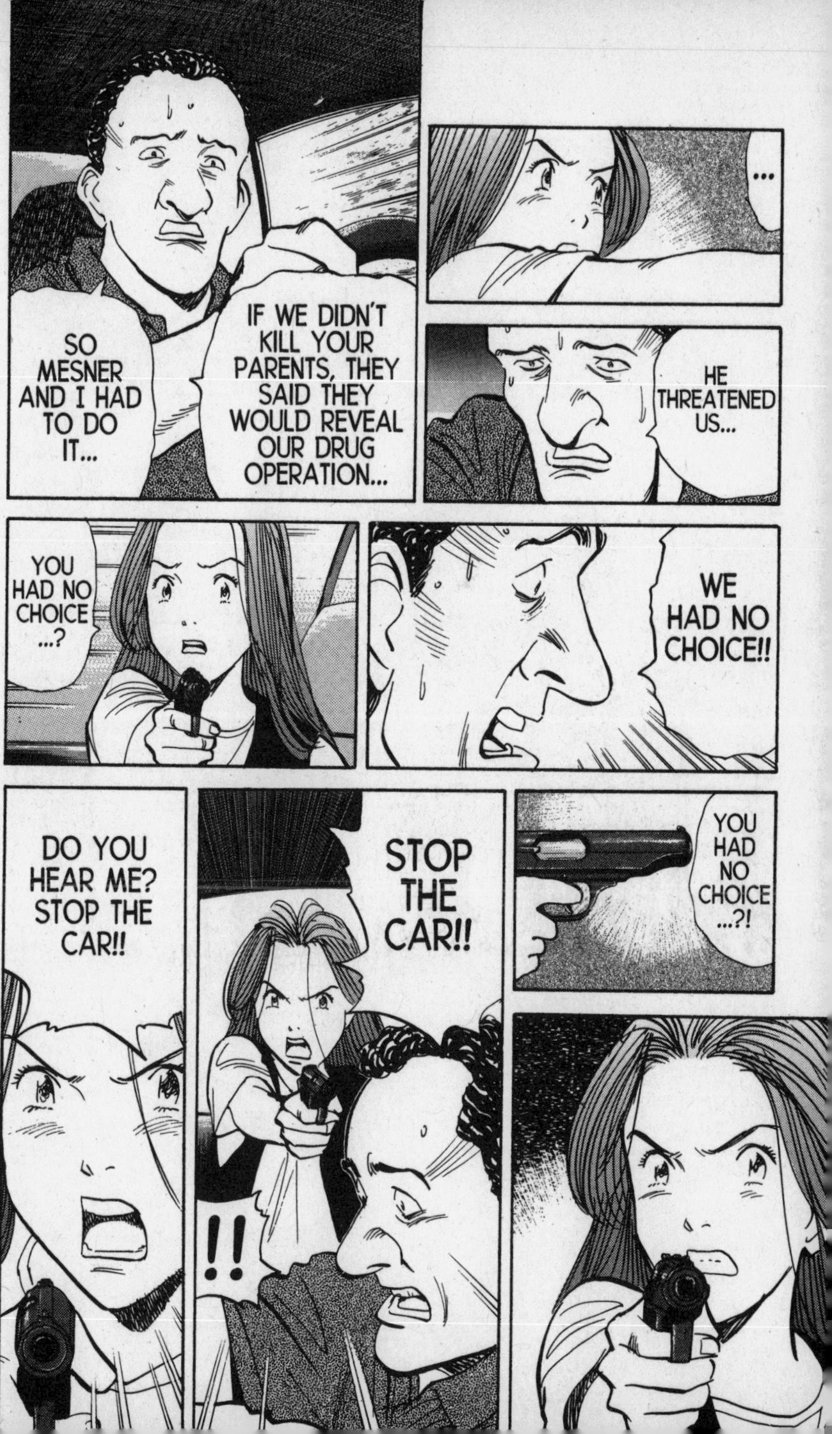
...
HE THREATENED US...
IF WE DIDN'T KILL YOUR PARENTS, THEY SAID THEY WOULD REVEAL OUR DRUG OPERATION...
SO MESNER AND I HAD TO DO IT...
WE HAD NO CHOICE!!
YOU HAD NO CHOICE ...?
YOU HAD NO CHOICE ...?!
STOP THE CAR!!
!!
DO YOU HEAR ME? STOP THE CAR!!

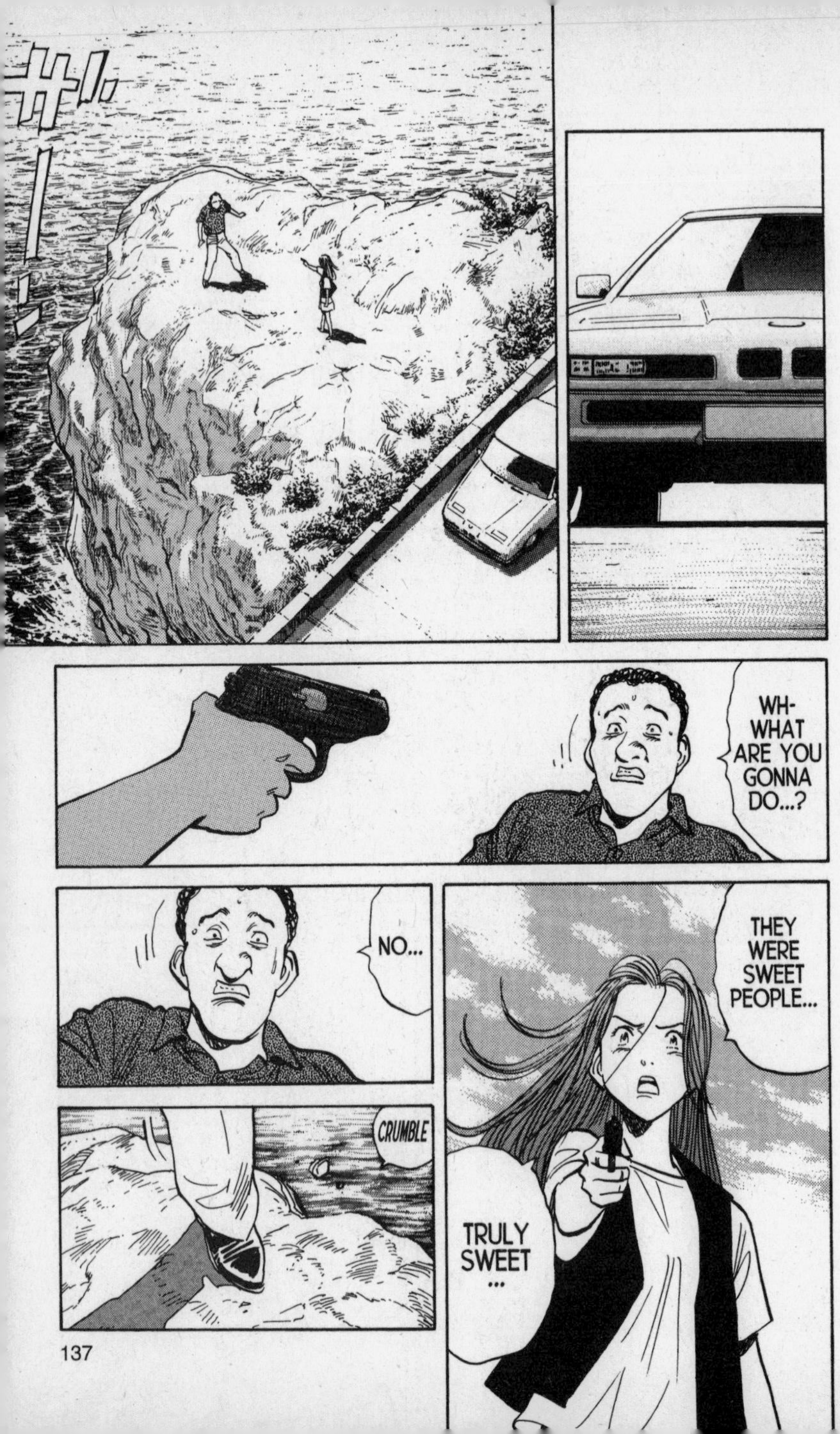
WH- WHAT ARE YOU GONNA DO...?
THEY WERE SWEET PEOPLE...
TRULY SWEET ...
NO...
CRUMBLE

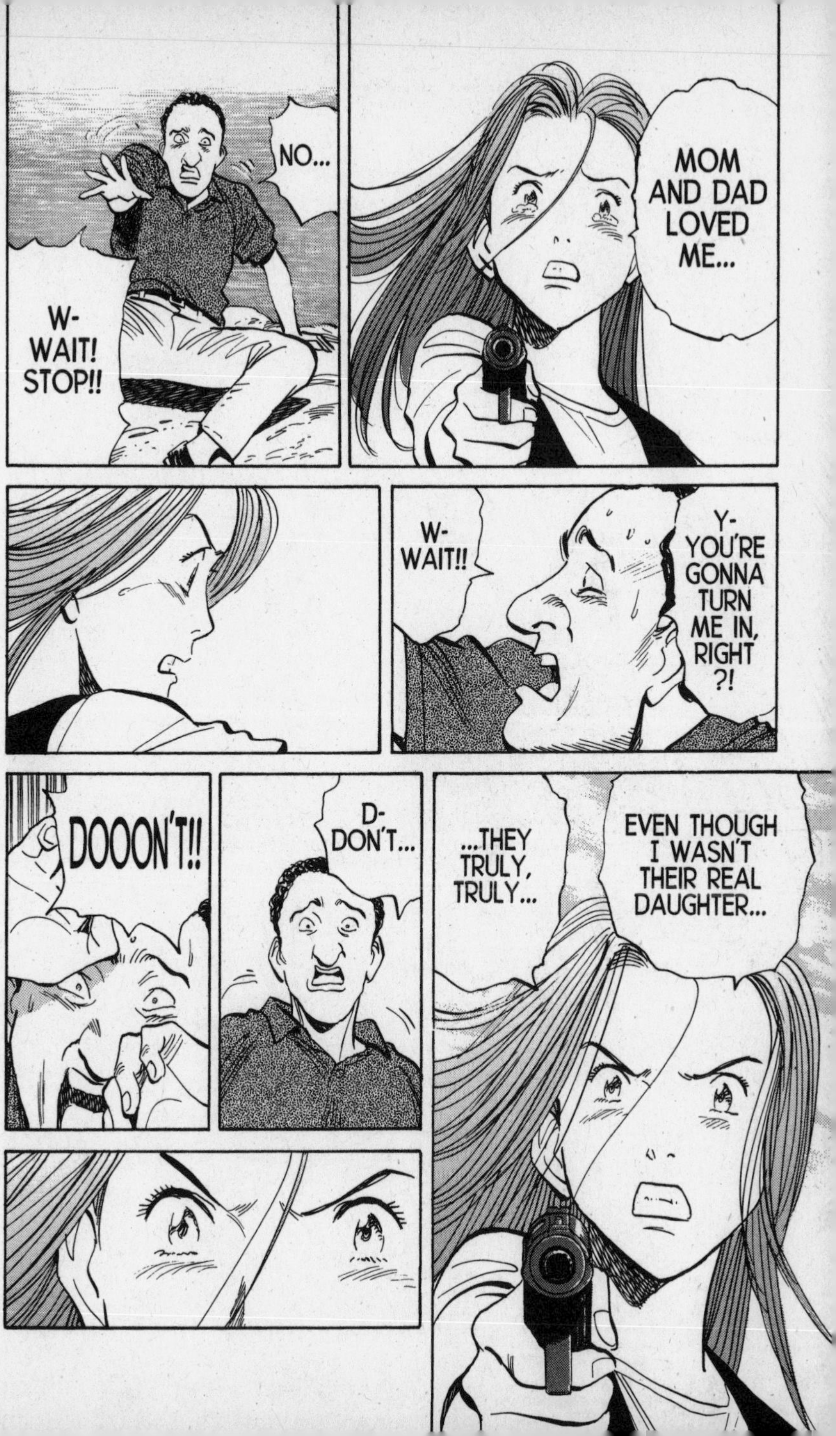
MOM AND DAD LOVED ME...
NO...
W- WAIT! STOP!!
Y- YOU'RE GONNA TURN ME IN, RIGHT ?!
W- WAIT!!
EVEN THOUGH I WASN'T THEIR REAL DAUGHTER...
...THEY TRULY, TRULY...
D- DON'T...
DOOON'T!!

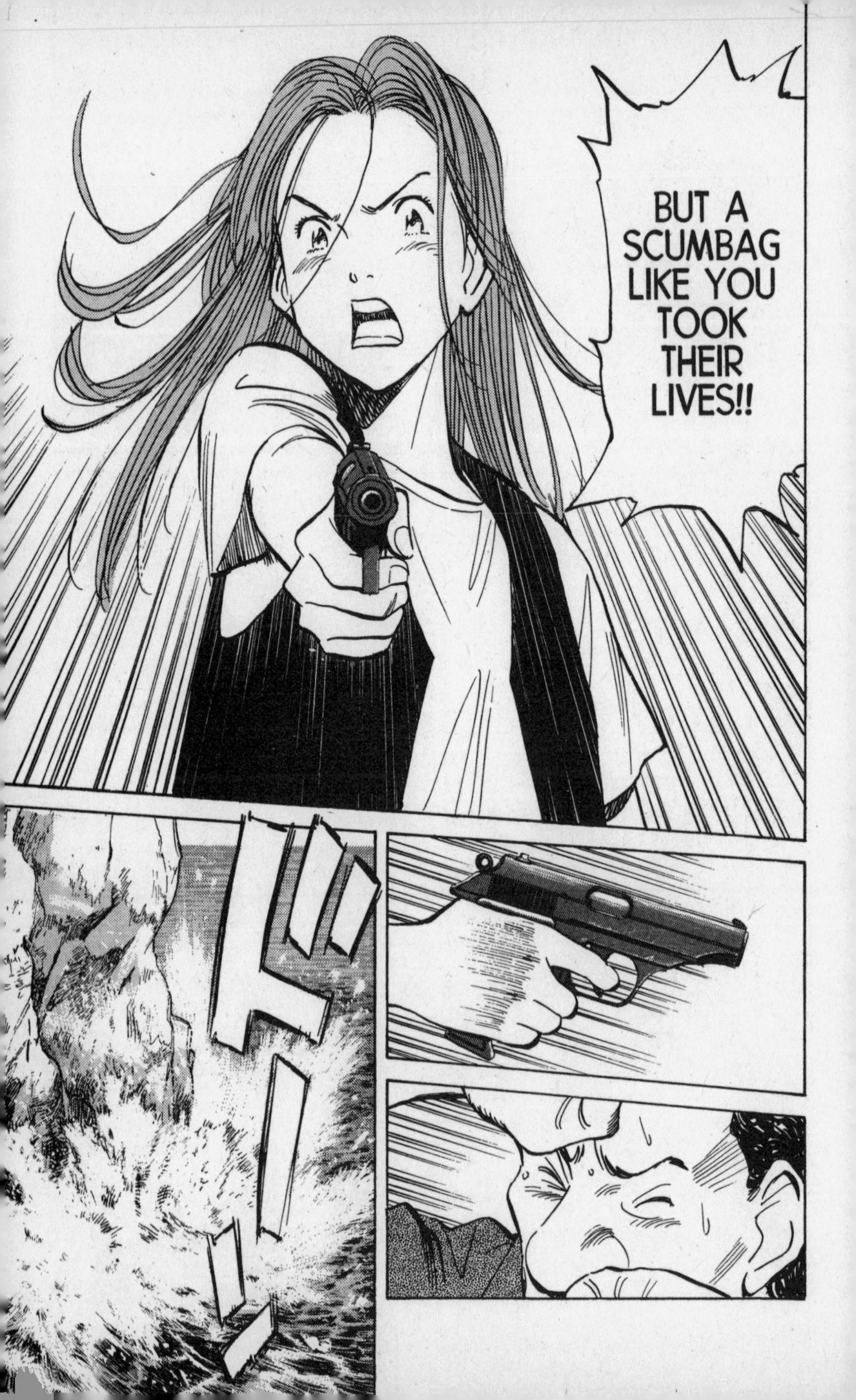
BUT A SCUMBAG LIKE YOU TOOK THEIR LIVES!!

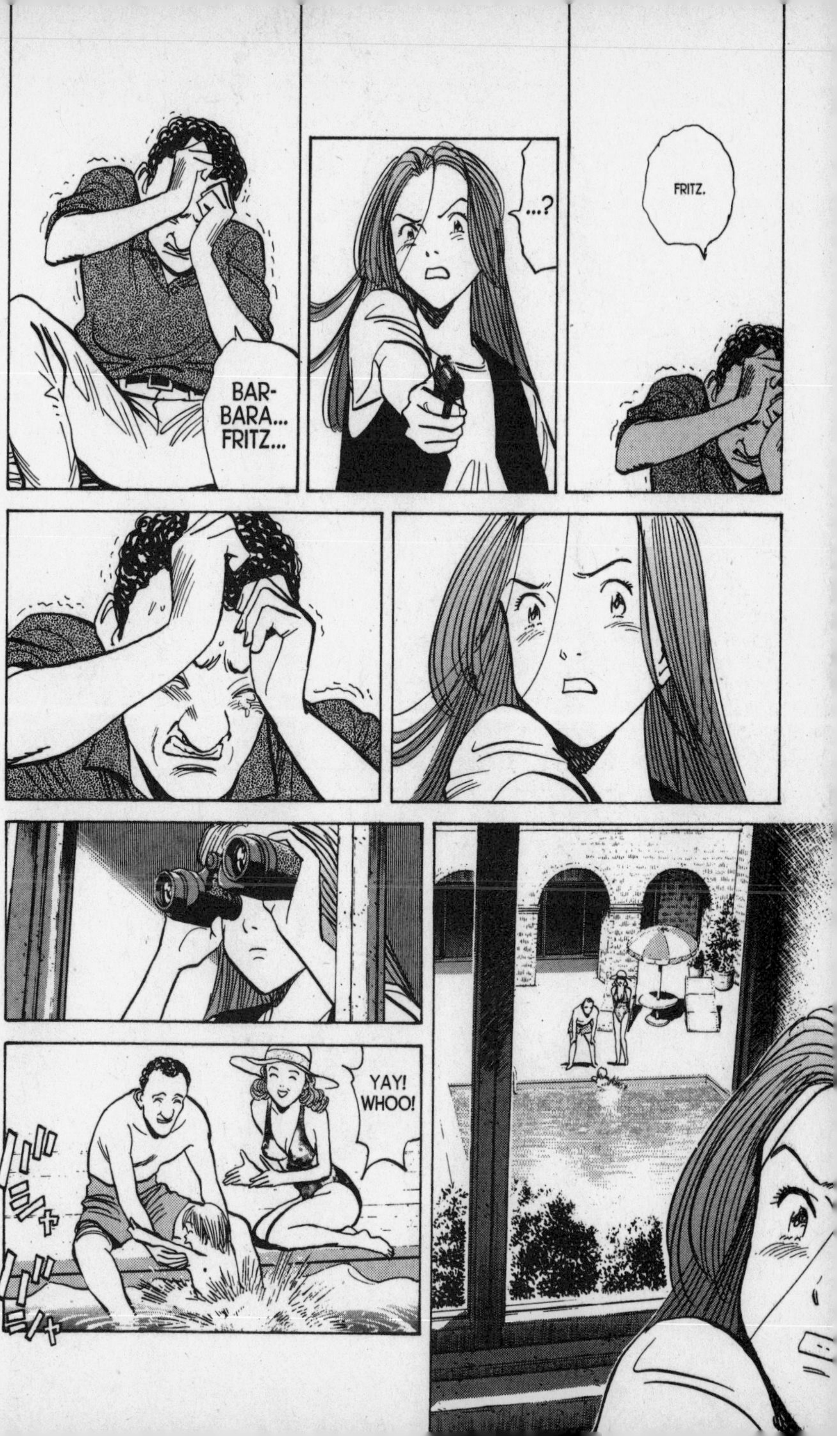
FRITZ.
...?
BAR-BARA... FRITZ...
YAY! WHOO!

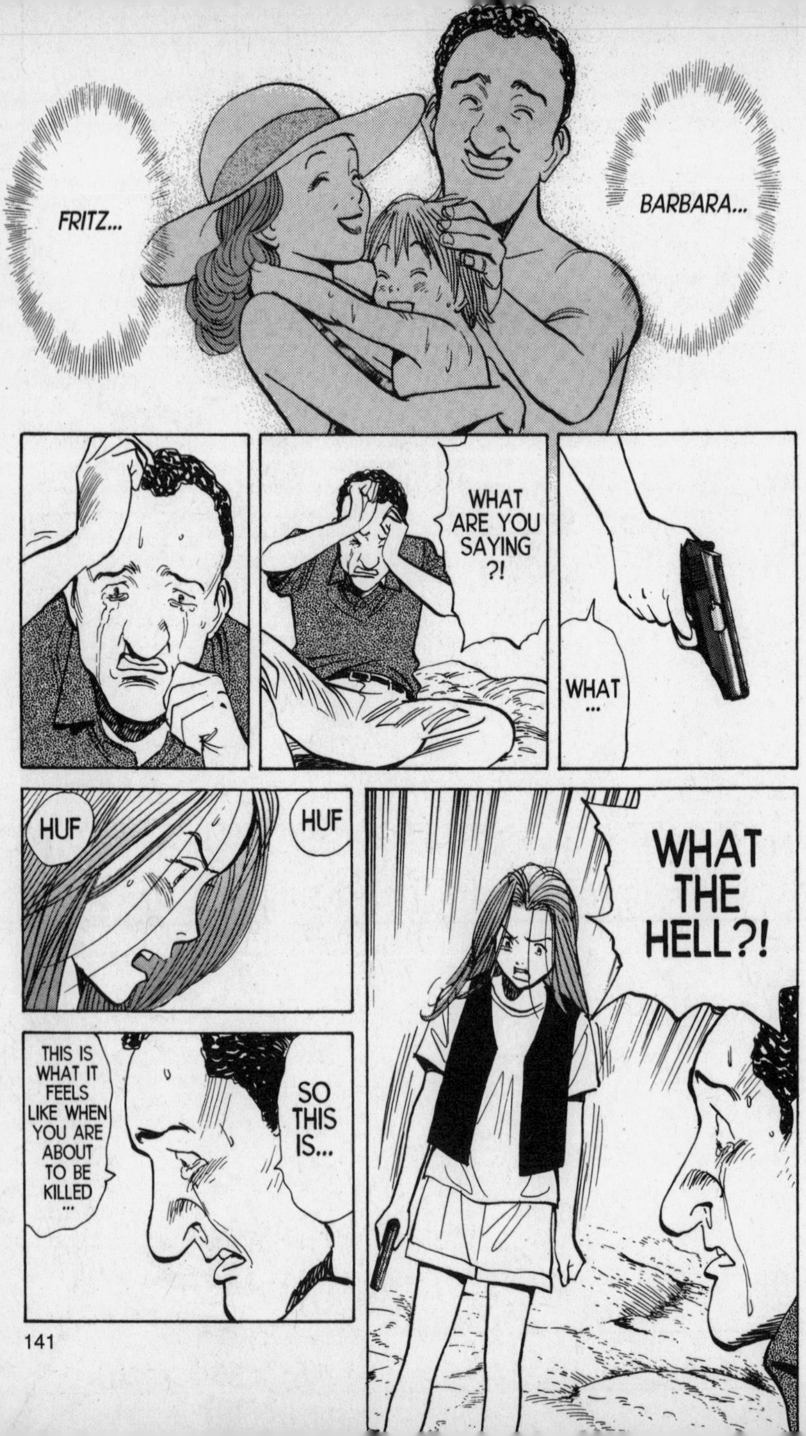
BARBARA...
FRITZ...
WHAT ...
WHAT ARE YOU SAYING ?!
WHAT THE HELL?!
HUF
HUF
SO THIS IS...
THIS IS WHAT IT FEELS LIKE WHEN YOU ARE ABOUT TO BE KILLED ...

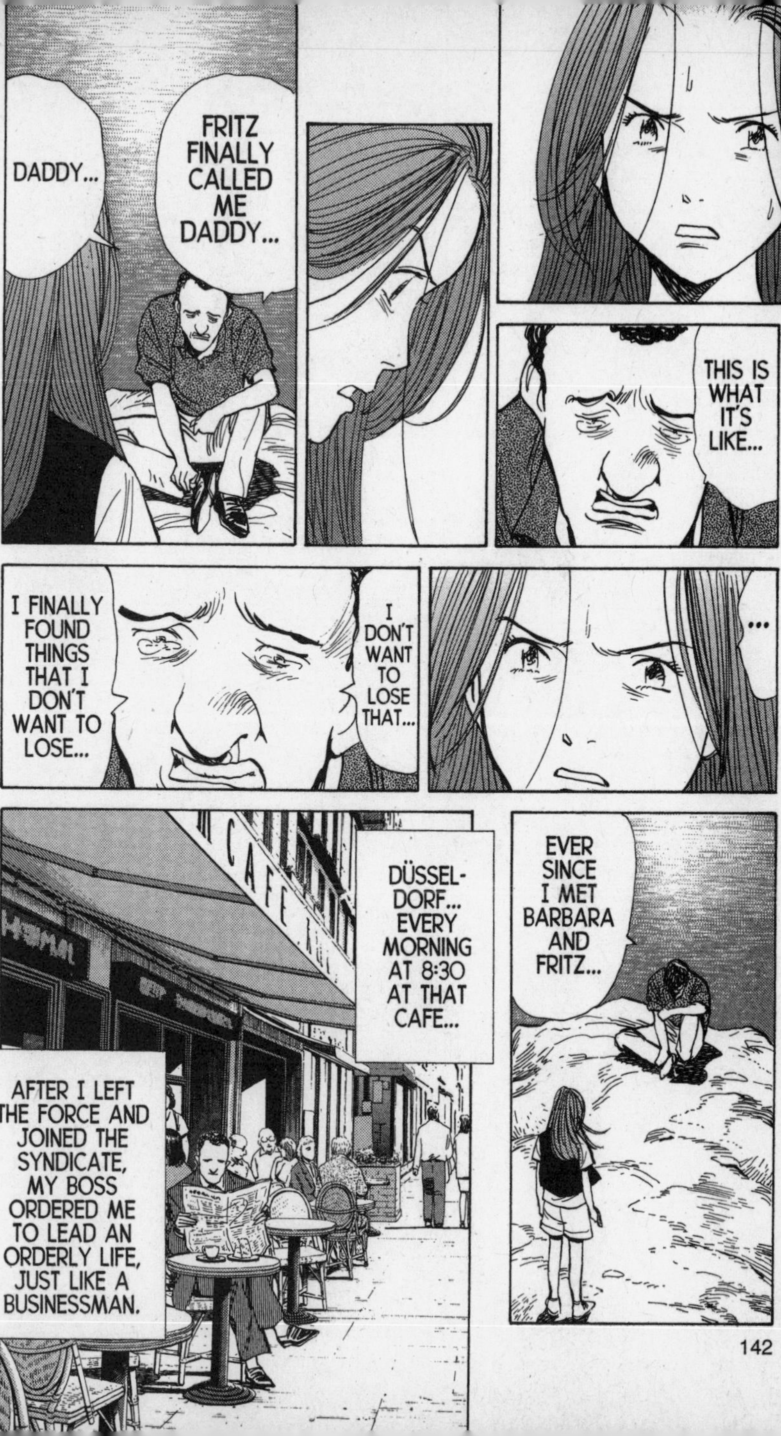
THIS IS WHAT IT'S LIKE...
FRITZ FINALLY CALLED ME DADDY...
DADDY...
...
I DON'T WANT TO LOSE THAT...
I FINALLY FOUND THINGS THAT I DON'T WANT TO LOSE...
EVER SINCE I MET BARBARA AND FRITZ...
CAFE
DÜSSEL-DORF... EVERY MORNING AT 8:30 AT THAT CAFE...
AFTER I LEFT THE FORCE AND JOINED THE SYNDICATE, MY BOSS ORDERED ME TO LEAD AN ORDERLY LIFE, JUST LIKE A BUSINESSMAN.

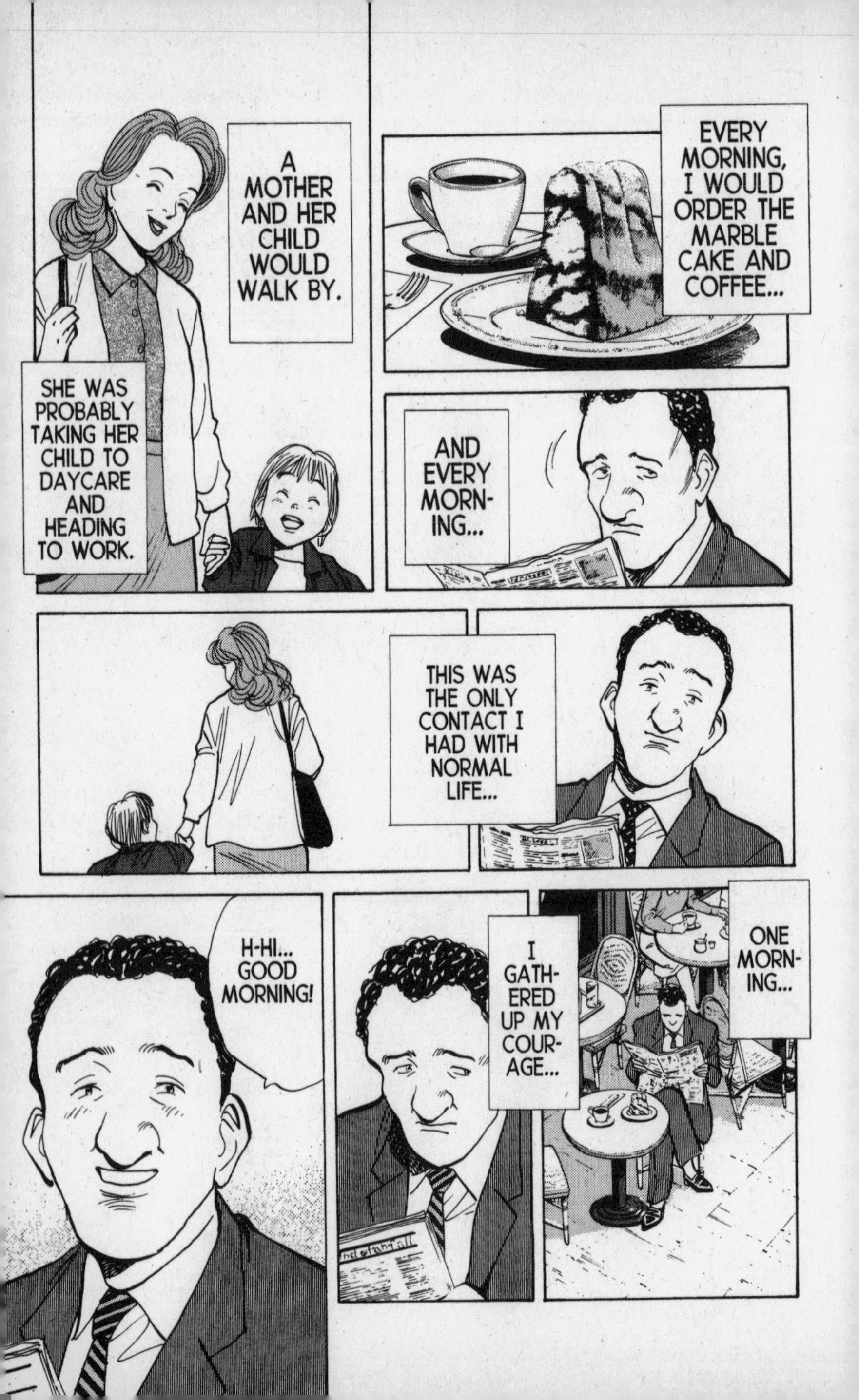
EVERY MORNING, I WOULD ORDER THE MARBLE CAKE AND COFFEE...
AND EVERY MORN-ING...
A MOTHER AND HER CHILD WOULD WALK BY.
SHE WAS PROBABLY TAKING HER CHILD TO DAYCARE AND HEADING TO WORK.
THIS WAS THE ONLY CONTACT I HAD WITH NORMAL LIFE...
ONE MORN-ING...
I GATH-ERED UP MY COUR-AGE...
H-HI... GOOD MORNING!

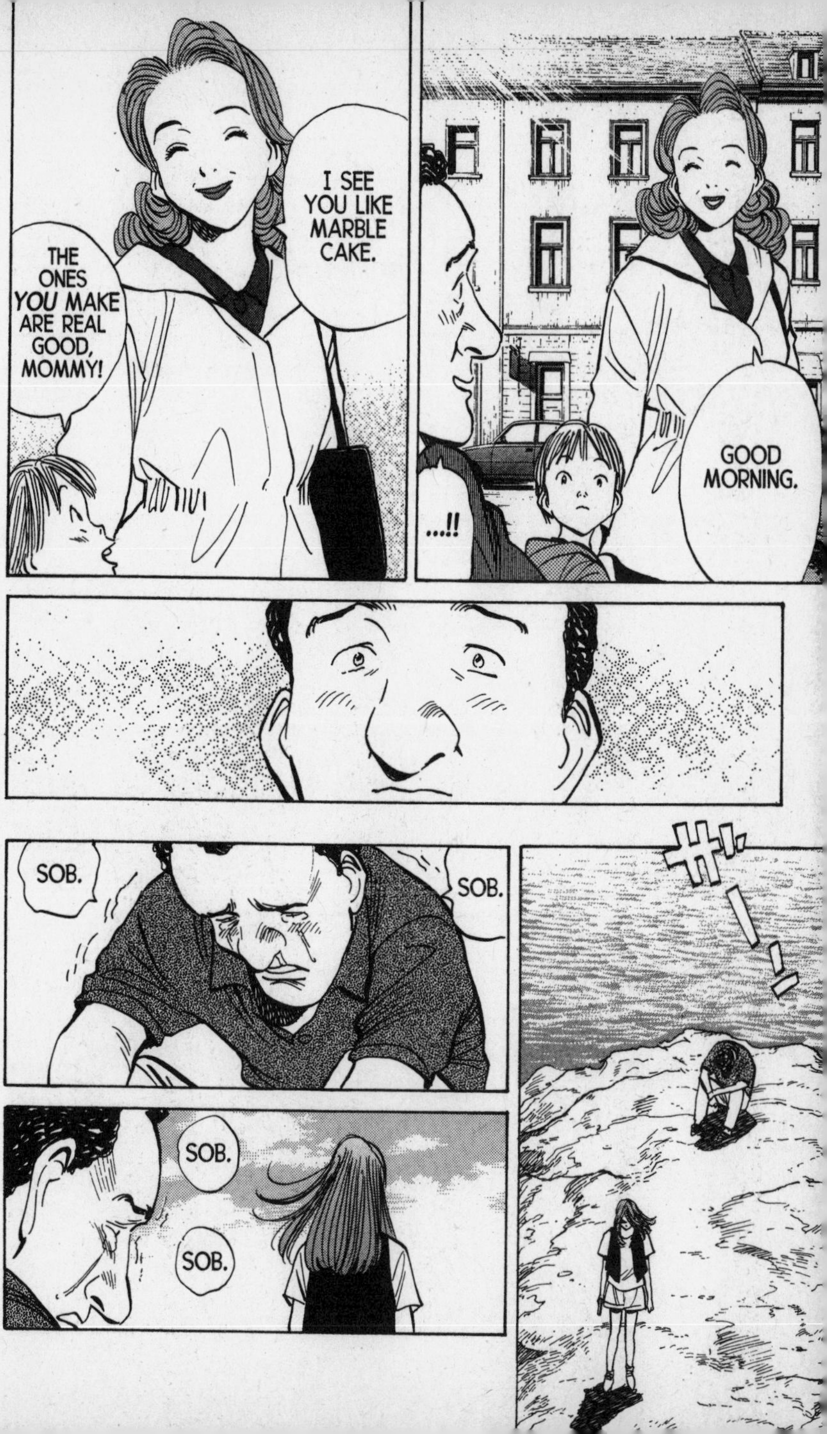
GOOD MORNING.
...!!
I SEE YOU LIKE MARBLE CAKE.
THE ONES *YOU* MAKE ARE REAL GOOD, MOMMY!
SOB.
SOB.
SOB.
SOB.

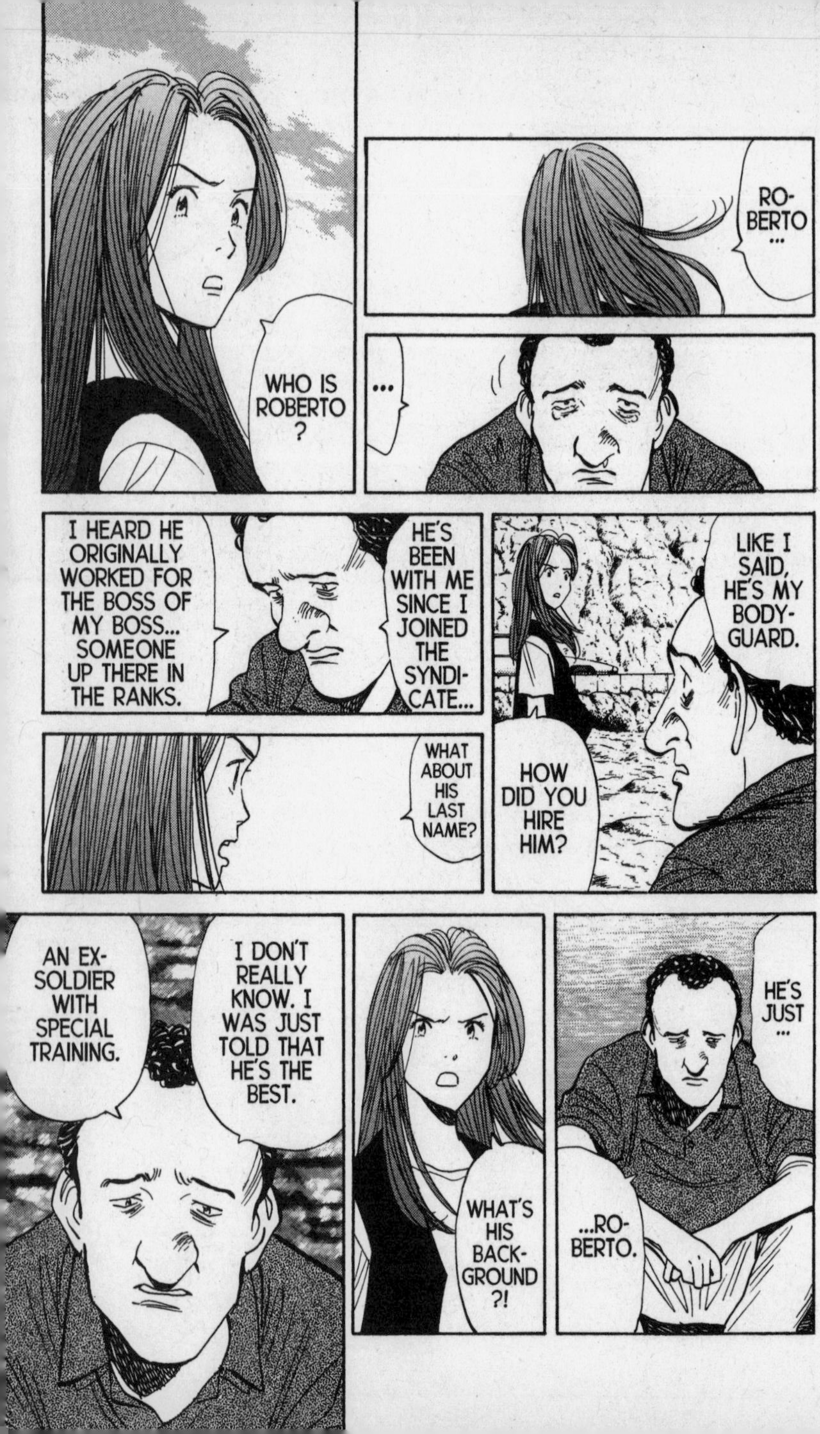
RO-BERTO...
...
WHO IS ROBERTO?
LIKE I SAID, HE'S MY BODY-GUARD.
HOW DID YOU HIRE HIM?
HE'S BEEN WITH ME SINCE I JOINED THE SYNDI-CATE...
I HEARD HE ORIGINALLY WORKED FOR THE BOSS OF MY BOSS... SOMEONE UP THERE IN THE RANKS.
WHAT ABOUT HIS LAST NAME?
HE'S JUST...
...RO-BERTO.
WHAT'S HIS BACK-GROUND?!
I DON'T REALLY KNOW. I WAS JUST TOLD THAT HE'S THE BEST.
AN EX-SOLDIER WITH SPECIAL TRAINING.

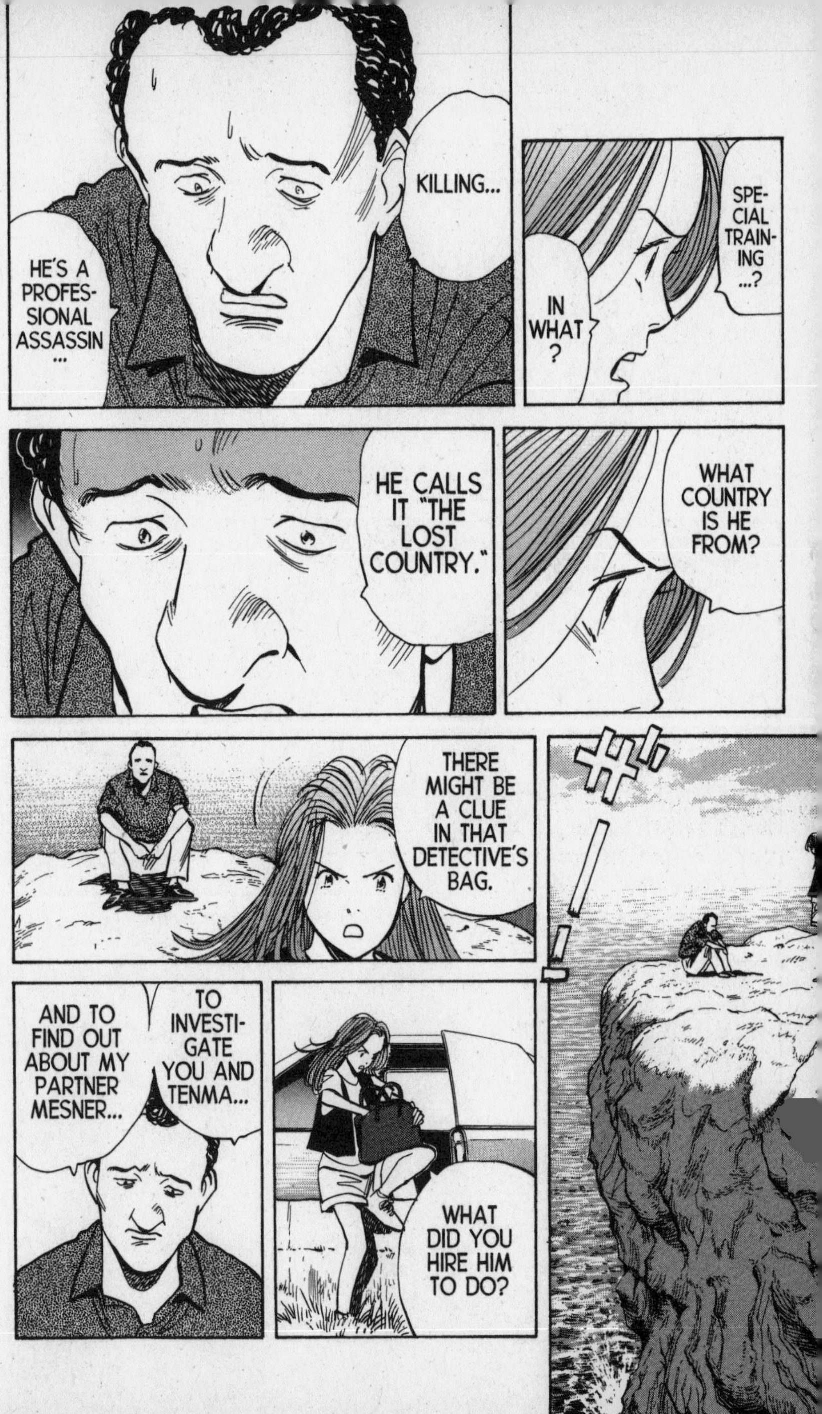
SPECIAL TRAINING...?
IN WHAT?
KILLING...
HE'S A PROFESSIONAL ASSASSIN...
WHAT COUNTRY IS HE FROM?
HE CALLS IT "THE LOST COUNTRY."
THERE MIGHT BE A CLUE IN THAT DETECTIVE'S BAG.
WHAT DID YOU HIRE HIM TO DO?
TO INVESTIGATE YOU AND TENMA...
AND TO FIND OUT ABOUT MY PARTNER MESNER...

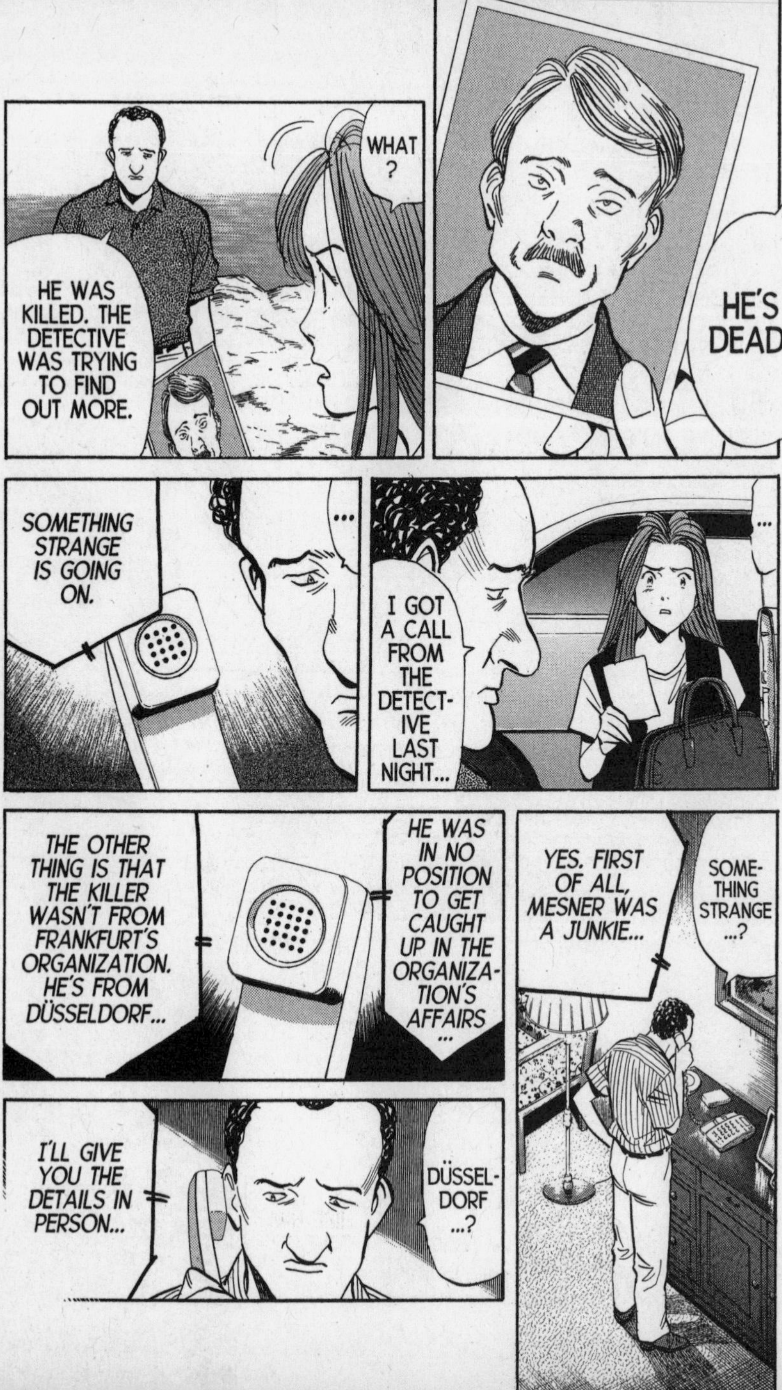
HE'S DEAD.
WHAT ?
HE WAS KILLED. THE DETECTIVE WAS TRYING TO FIND OUT MORE.
...
I GOT A CALL FROM THE DETECT-IVE LAST NIGHT...
...
SOMETHING STRANGE IS GOING ON.
SOME-THING STRANGE ...?
YES. FIRST OF ALL, MESNER WAS A JUNKIE...
HE WAS IN NO POSITION TO GET CAUGHT UP IN THE ORGANIZA-TION'S AFFAIRS ...
THE OTHER THING IS THAT THE KILLER WASN'T FROM FRANKFURT'S ORGANIZATION. HE'S FROM DÜSSELDORF...
DÜSSEL-DORF ...?
I'LL GIVE YOU THE DETAILS IN PERSON...

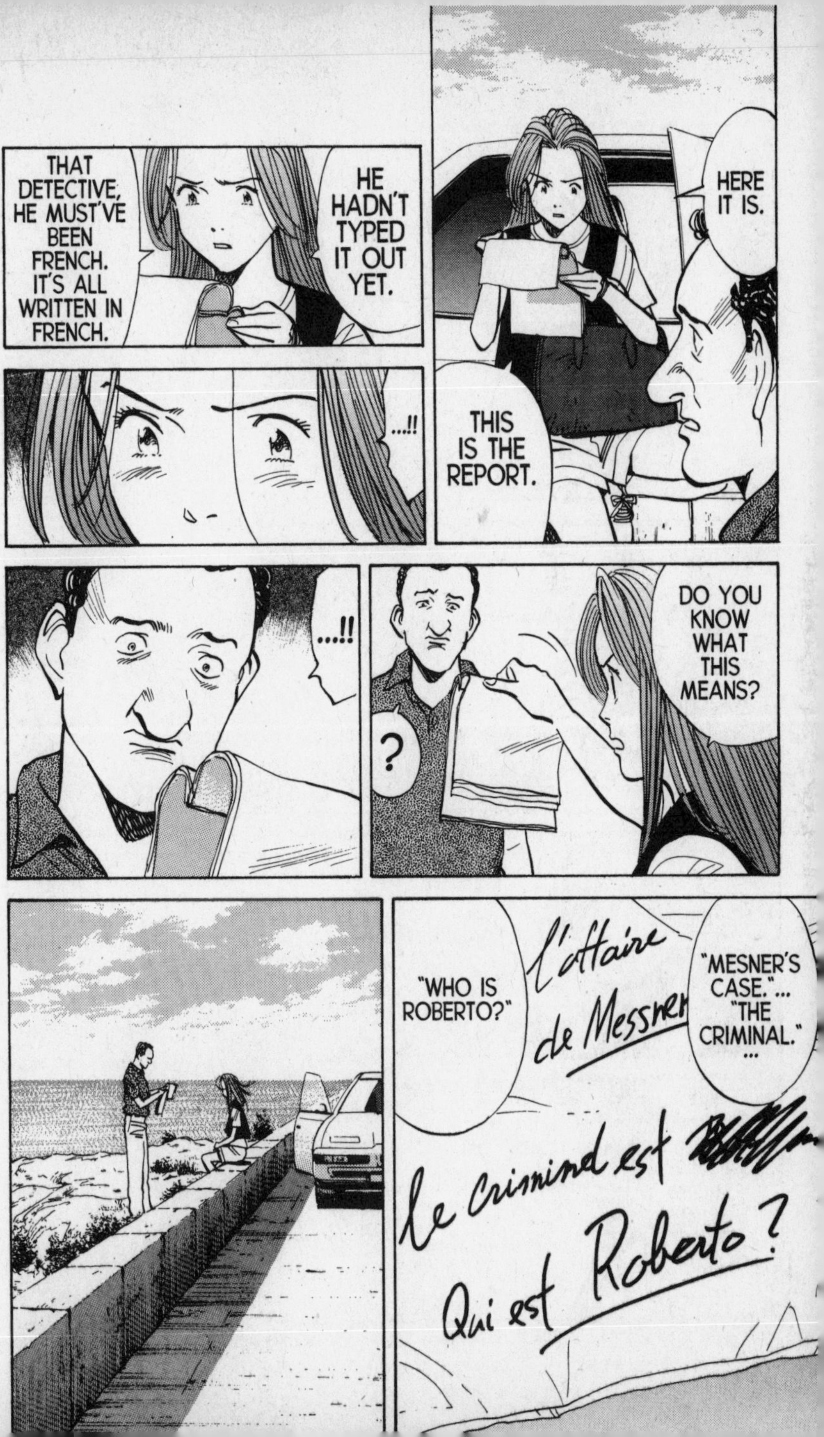

HERE IT IS.
THIS IS THE REPORT.
HE HADN'T TYPED IT OUT YET.
THAT DETECTIVE, HE MUST'VE BEEN FRENCH. IT'S ALL WRITTEN IN FRENCH.
...!!
DO YOU KNOW WHAT THIS MEANS?
?
...!!
"MESNER'S CASE."... "THE CRIMINAL."...
"WHO IS ROBERTO?"
l'affaire de Messner
le criminel est
Qui est Roberto?

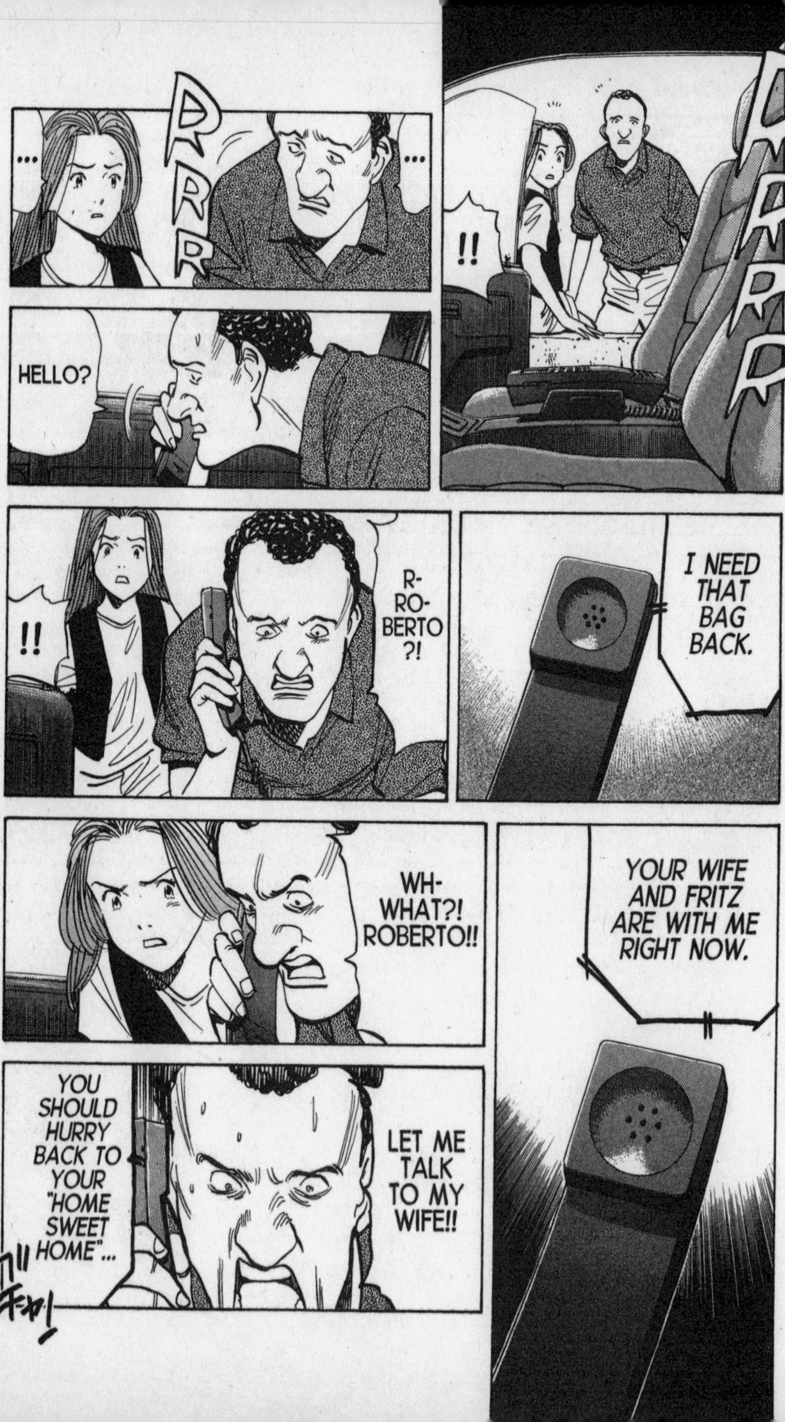
DRRRR
!!
...
RRR
...
HELLO?
I NEED THAT BAG BACK.
!!
R-RO-BERTO?!
YOUR WIFE AND FRITZ ARE WITH ME RIGHT NOW.
WH-WHAT?! ROBERTO!!
YOU SHOULD HURRY BACK TO YOUR "HOME SWEET HOME"...
LET ME TALK TO MY WIFE!!
ガチャ!

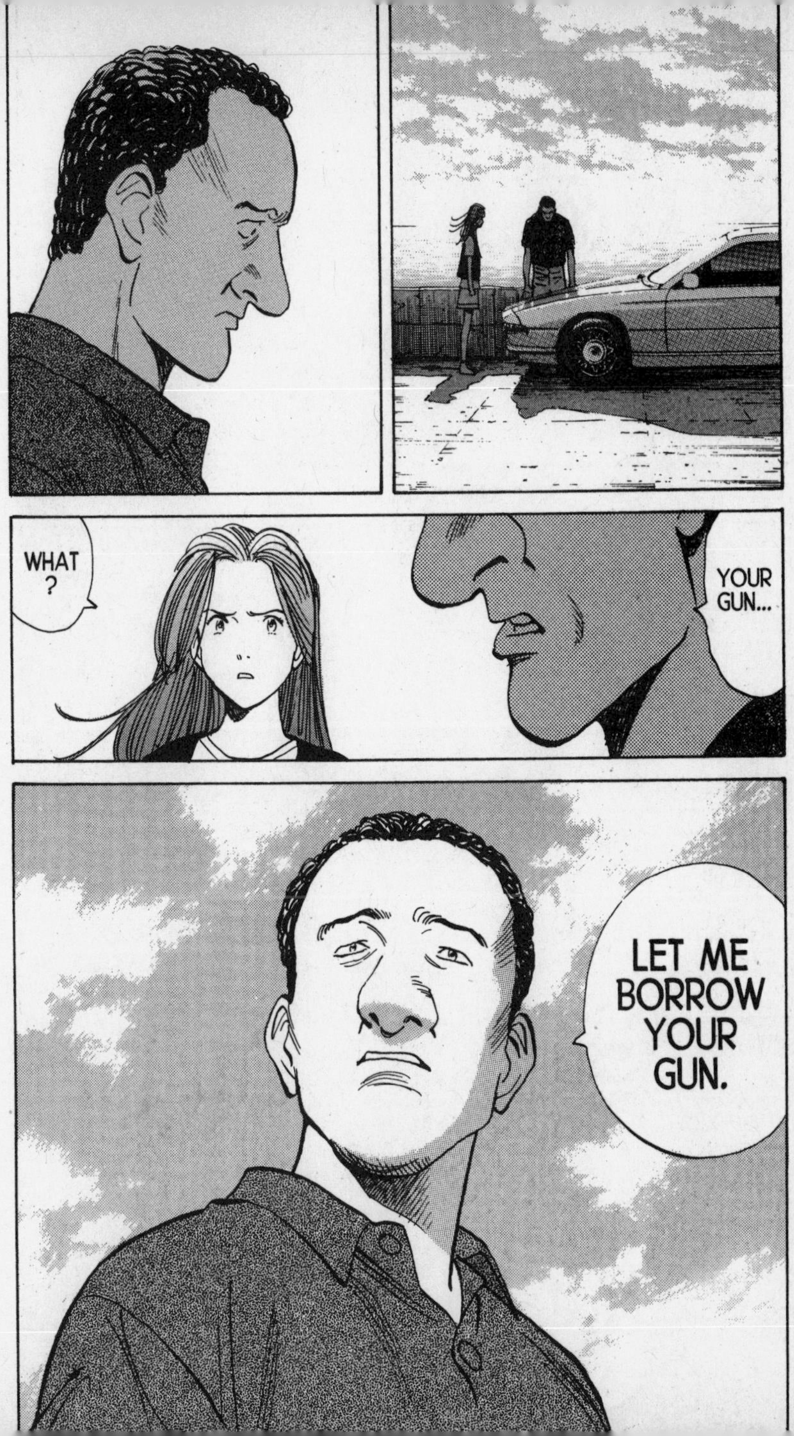
YOUR GUN...
WHAT ?
LET ME BORROW YOUR GUN.

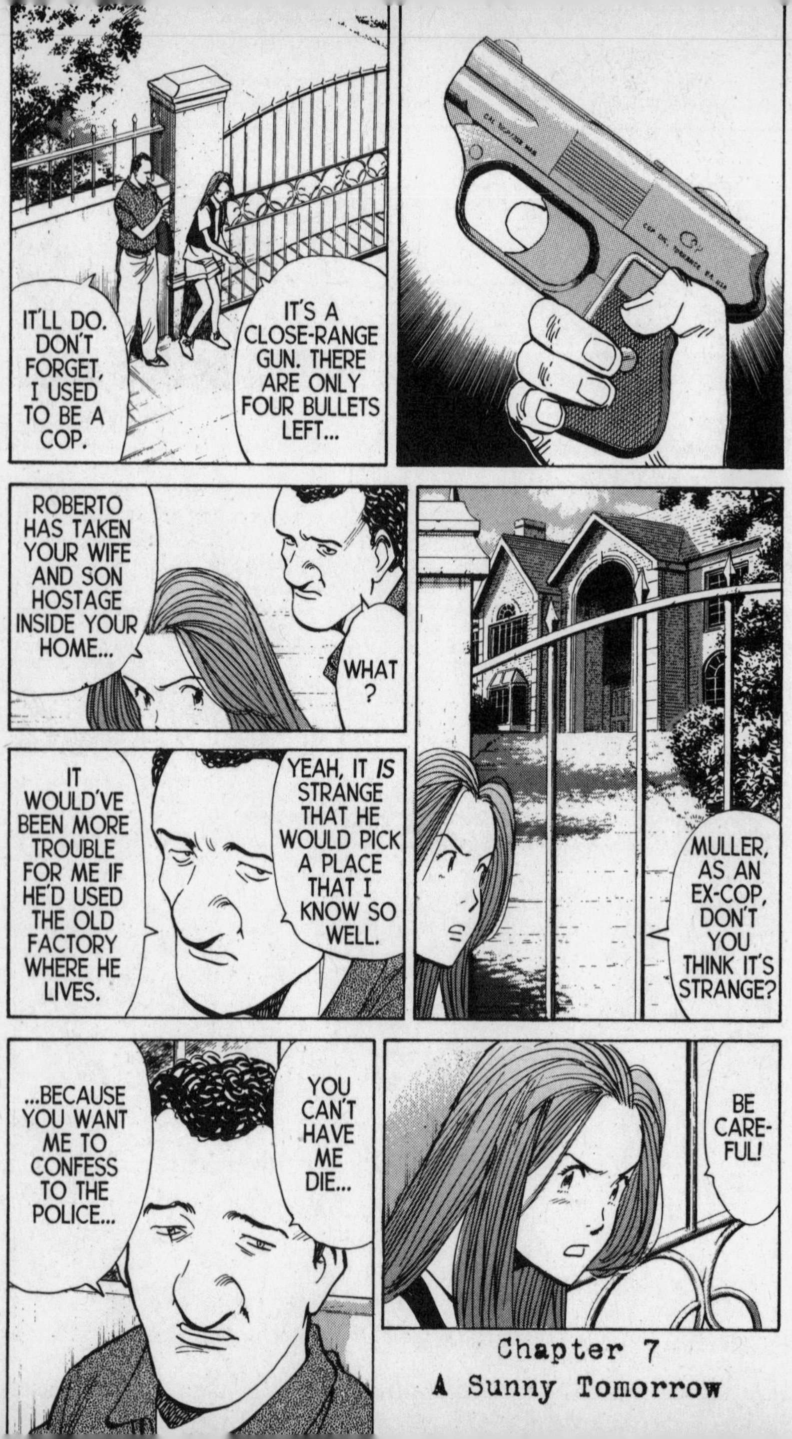
IT'S A CLOSE-RANGE GUN. THERE ARE ONLY FOUR BULLETS LEFT...
IT'LL DO. DON'T FORGET, I USED TO BE A COP.
MULLER, AS AN EX-COP, DON'T YOU THINK IT'S STRANGE?
ROBERTO HAS TAKEN YOUR WIFE AND SON HOSTAGE INSIDE YOUR HOME...
WHAT?
YEAH, IT *IS* STRANGE THAT HE WOULD PICK A PLACE THAT I KNOW SO WELL.
IT WOULD'VE BEEN MORE TROUBLE FOR ME IF HE'D USED THE OLD FACTORY WHERE HE LIVES.
BE CARE-FUL!
YOU CAN'T HAVE ME DIE...
...BECAUSE YOU WANT ME TO CONFESS TO THE POLICE...

Chapter 7
A Sunny Tomorrow

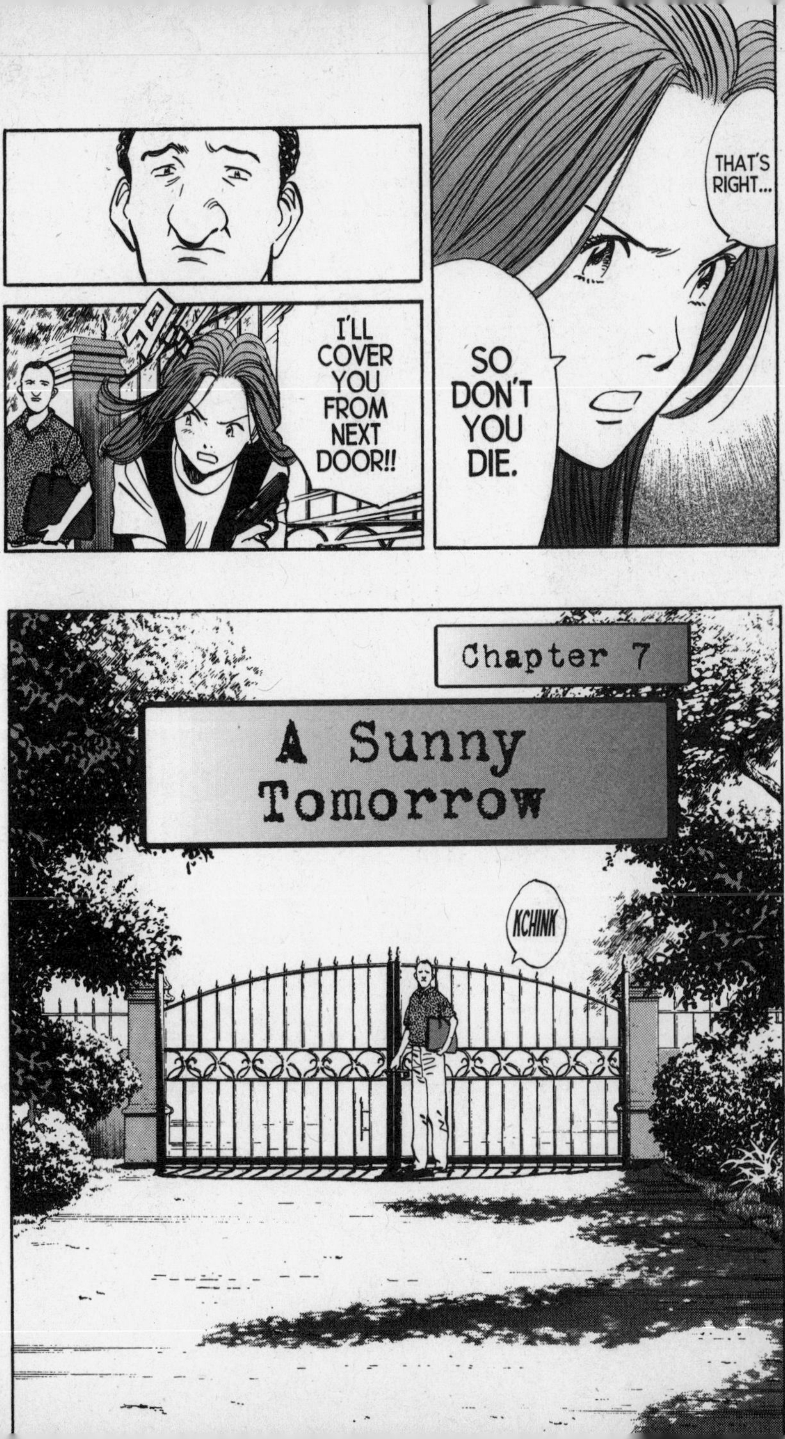
THAT'S RIGHT...
SO DON'T YOU DIE.
I'LL COVER YOU FROM NEXT DOOR!!
Chapter 7
A Sunny Tomorrow
KCHINK

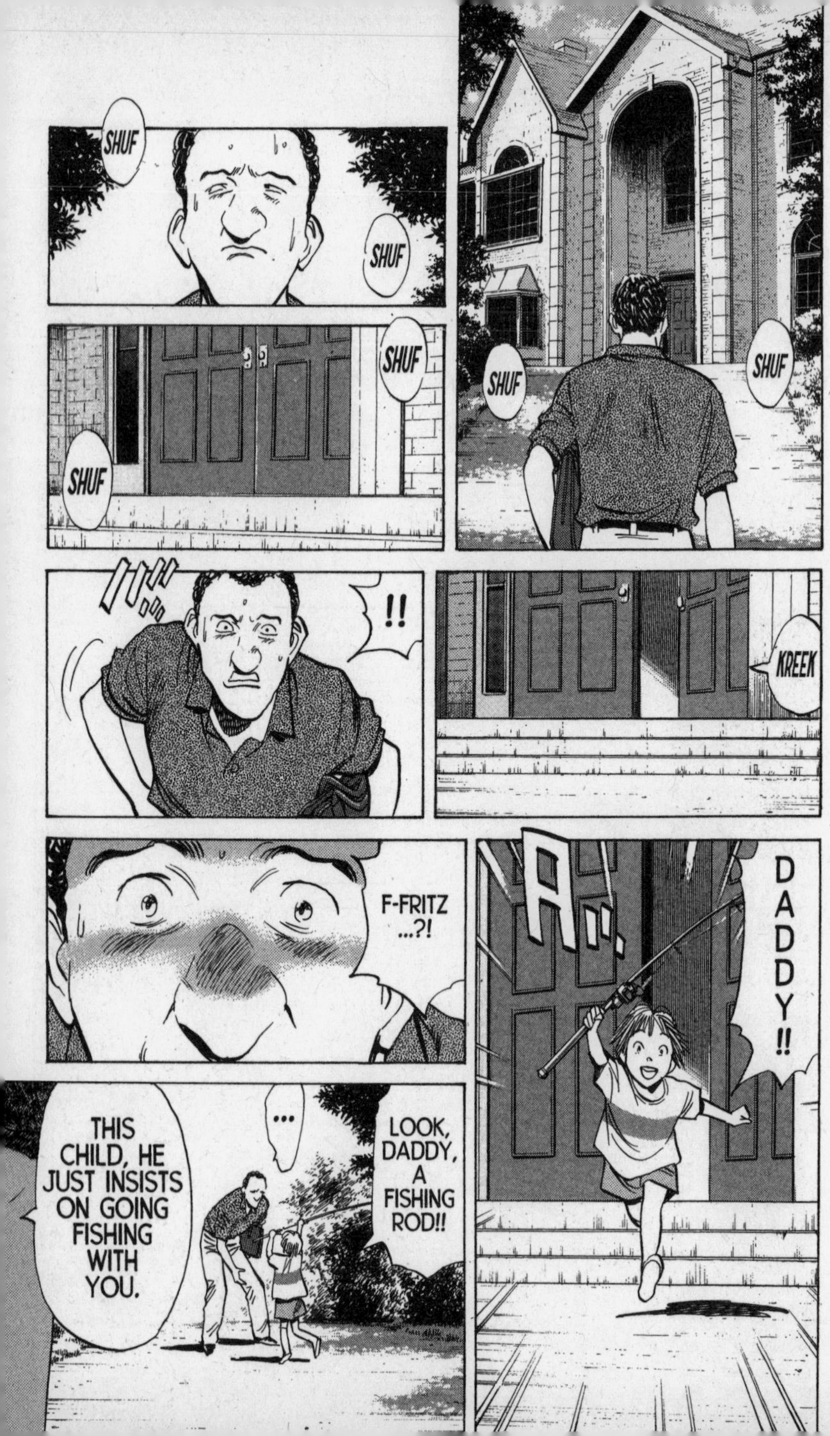
SHUF
SHUF
SHUF
SHUF
SHUF
SHUF
KREEK
!!
DADDY!!
A..
F-FRITZ ...?!
LOOK, DADDY, A FISHING ROD!!
...
THIS CHILD, HE JUST INSISTS ON GOING FISHING WITH YOU.

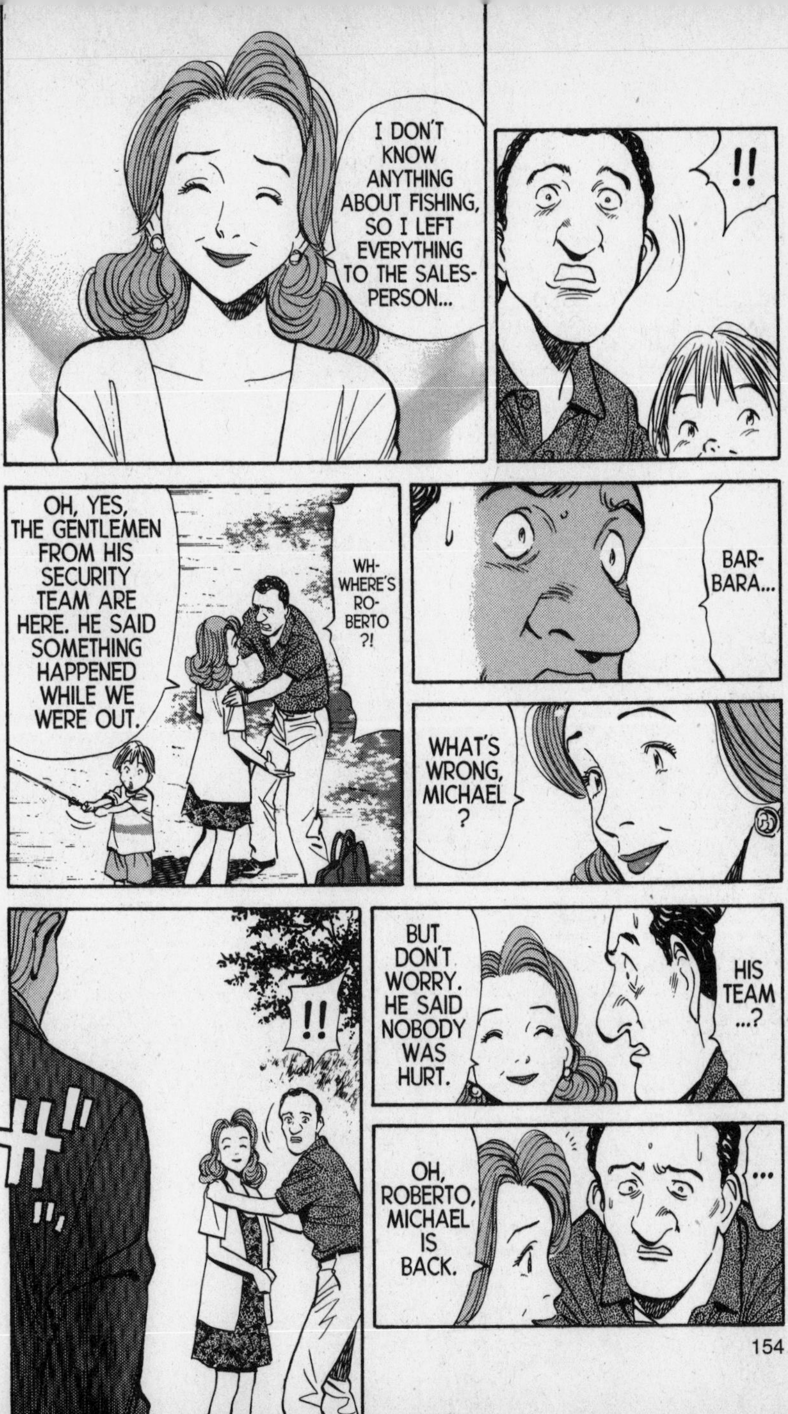
!!
I DON'T KNOW ANYTHING ABOUT FISHING, SO I LEFT EVERYTHING TO THE SALES-PERSON...
BAR-BARA...
WHAT'S WRONG, MICHAEL?
WH-WHERE'S ROBERTO?!
OH, YES, THE GENTLEMEN FROM HIS SECURITY TEAM ARE HERE. HE SAID SOMETHING HAPPENED WHILE WE WERE OUT.
HIS TEAM...?
BUT DON'T WORRY. HE SAID NOBODY WAS HURT.
...
OH, ROBERTO, MICHAEL IS BACK.
!!

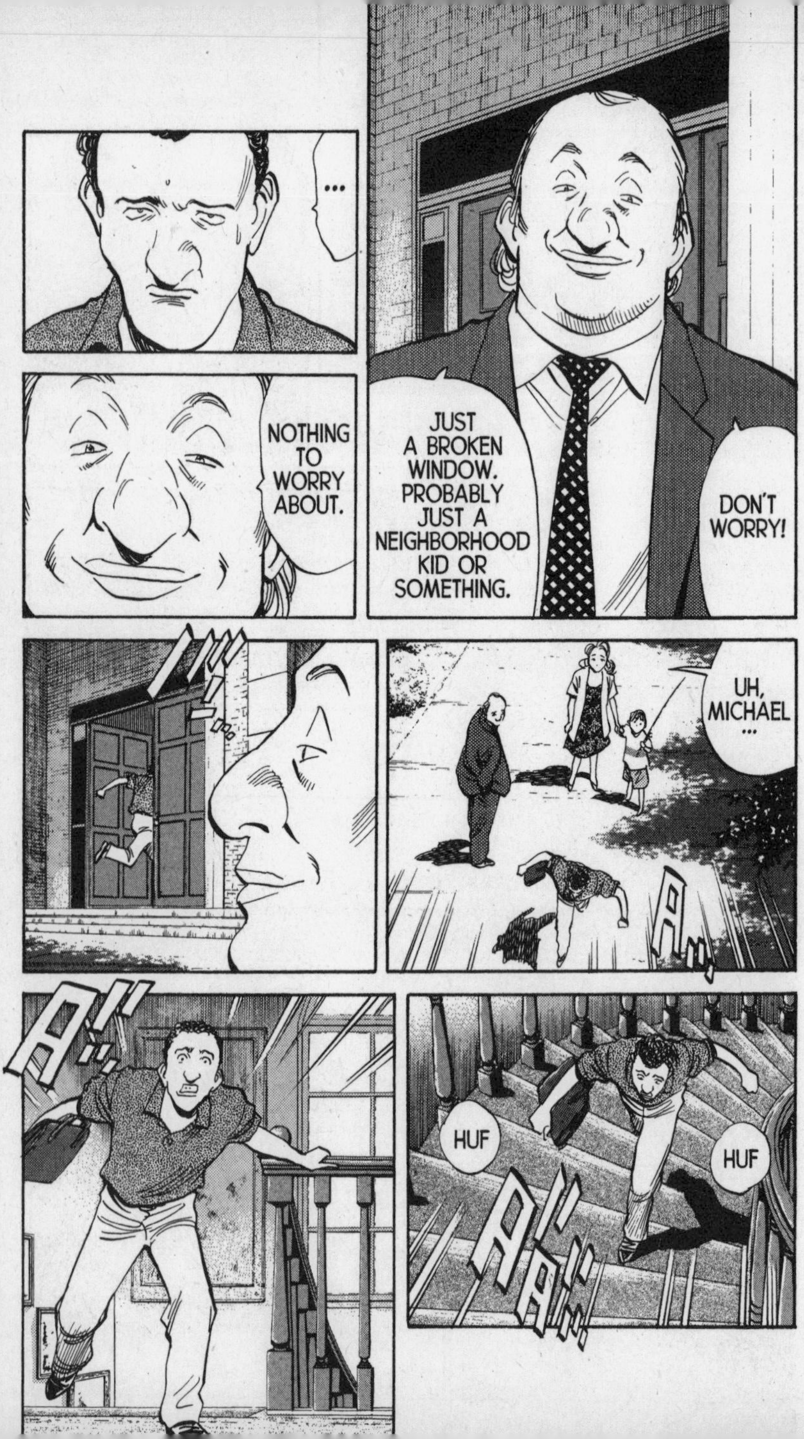
DON'T WORRY!
JUST A BROKEN WINDOW. PROBABLY JUST A NEIGHBORHOOD KID OR SOMETHING.
...
NOTHING TO WORRY ABOUT.
UH, MICHAEL ...
HUF
HUF
A!!
A!!
A!!

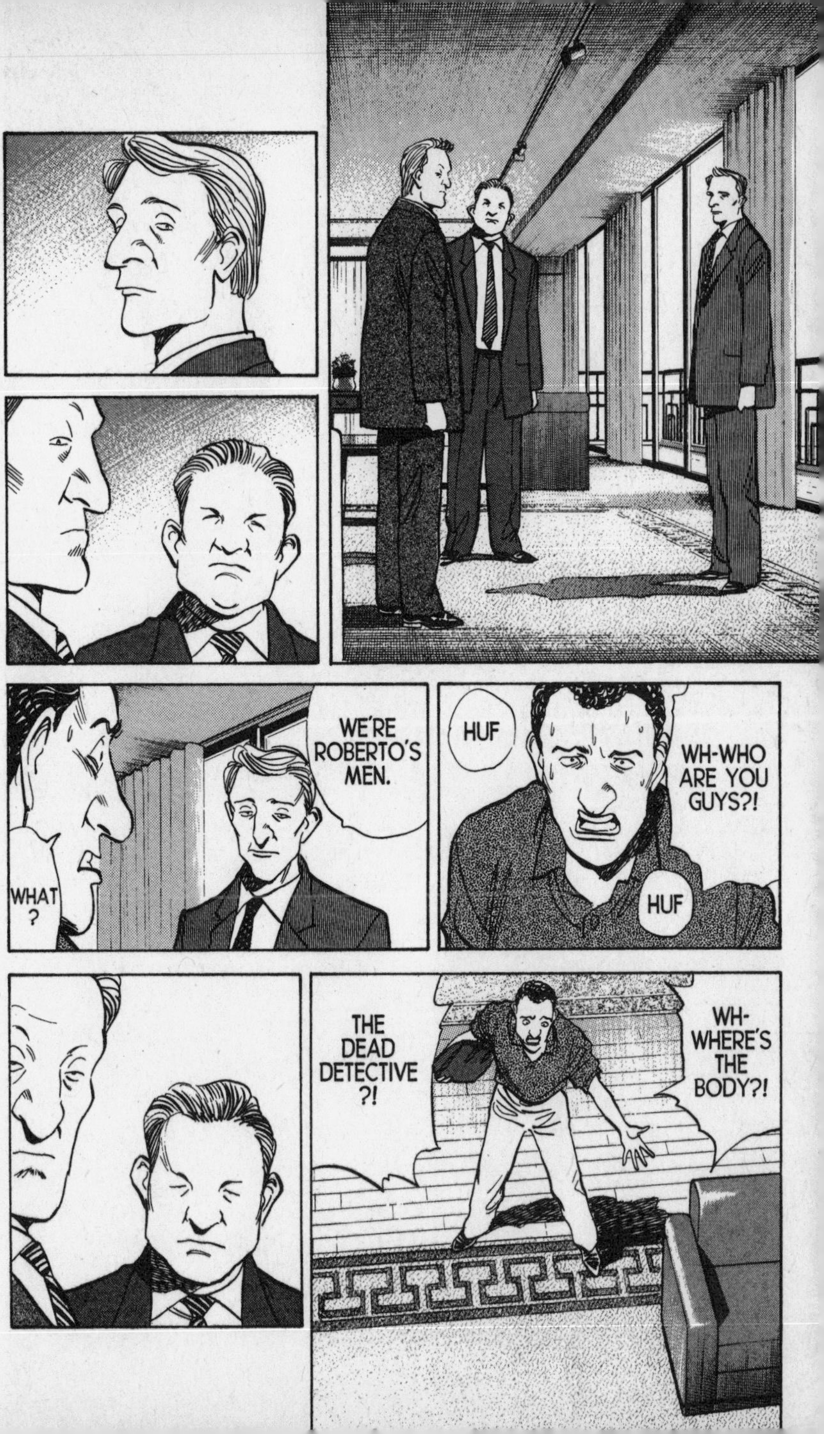
WH-WHO ARE YOU GUYS?!
HUF
HUF
WE'RE ROBERTO'S MEN.
WHAT?
WH-WHERE'S THE BODY?!
THE DEAD DETECTIVE?!

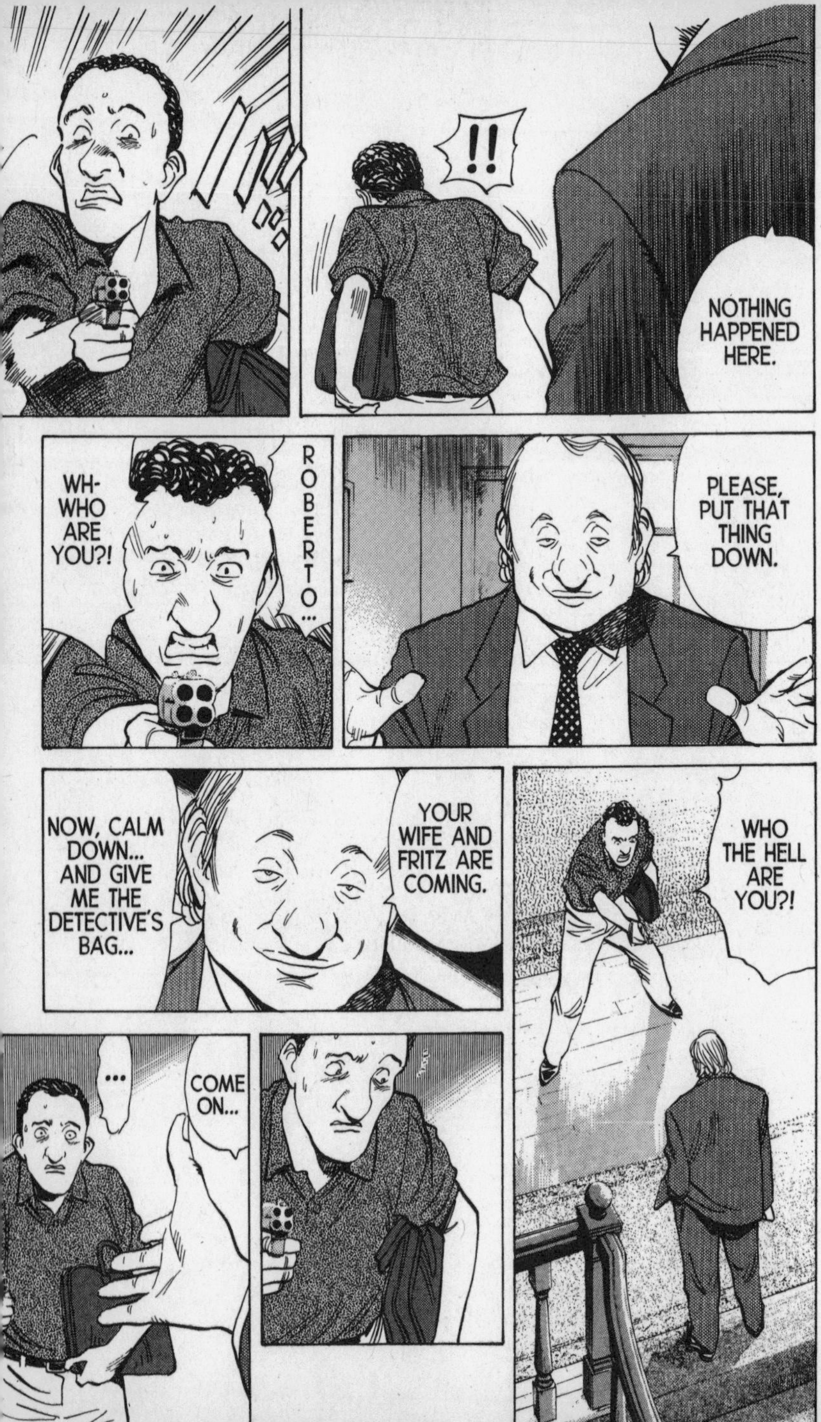
NOTHING HAPPENED HERE.
!!
PLEASE, PUT THAT THING DOWN.
ROBERTO...
WH- WHO ARE YOU?!
WHO THE HELL ARE YOU?!
YOUR WIFE AND FRITZ ARE COMING.
NOW, CALM DOWN... AND GIVE ME THE DETECTIVE'S BAG...
COME ON...
...

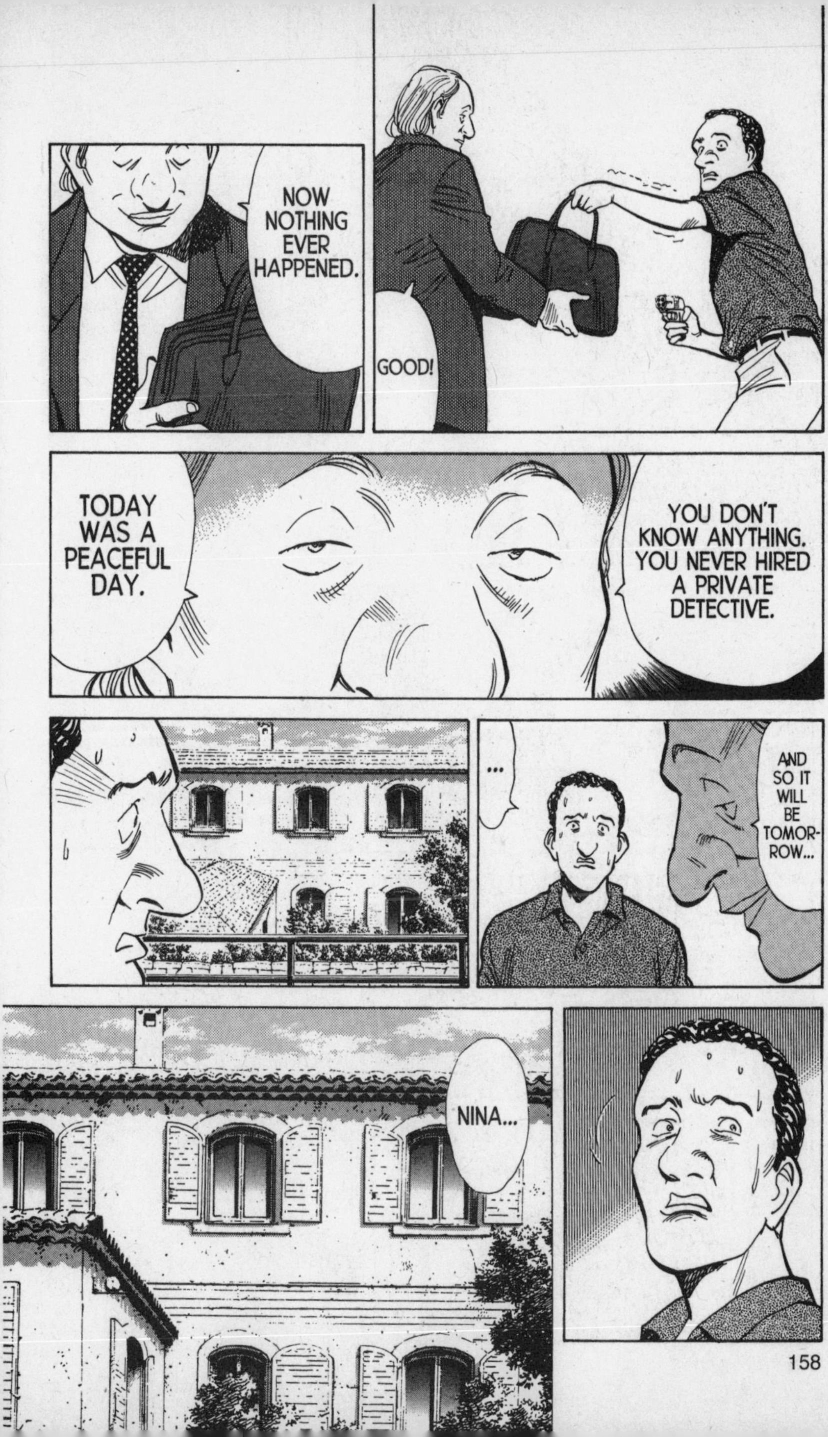
GOOD!
NOW NOTHING EVER HAPPENED.
YOU DON'T KNOW ANYTHING. YOU NEVER HIRED A PRIVATE DETECTIVE.
TODAY WAS A PEACEFUL DAY.
AND SO IT WILL BE TOMORROW...
...
NINA...

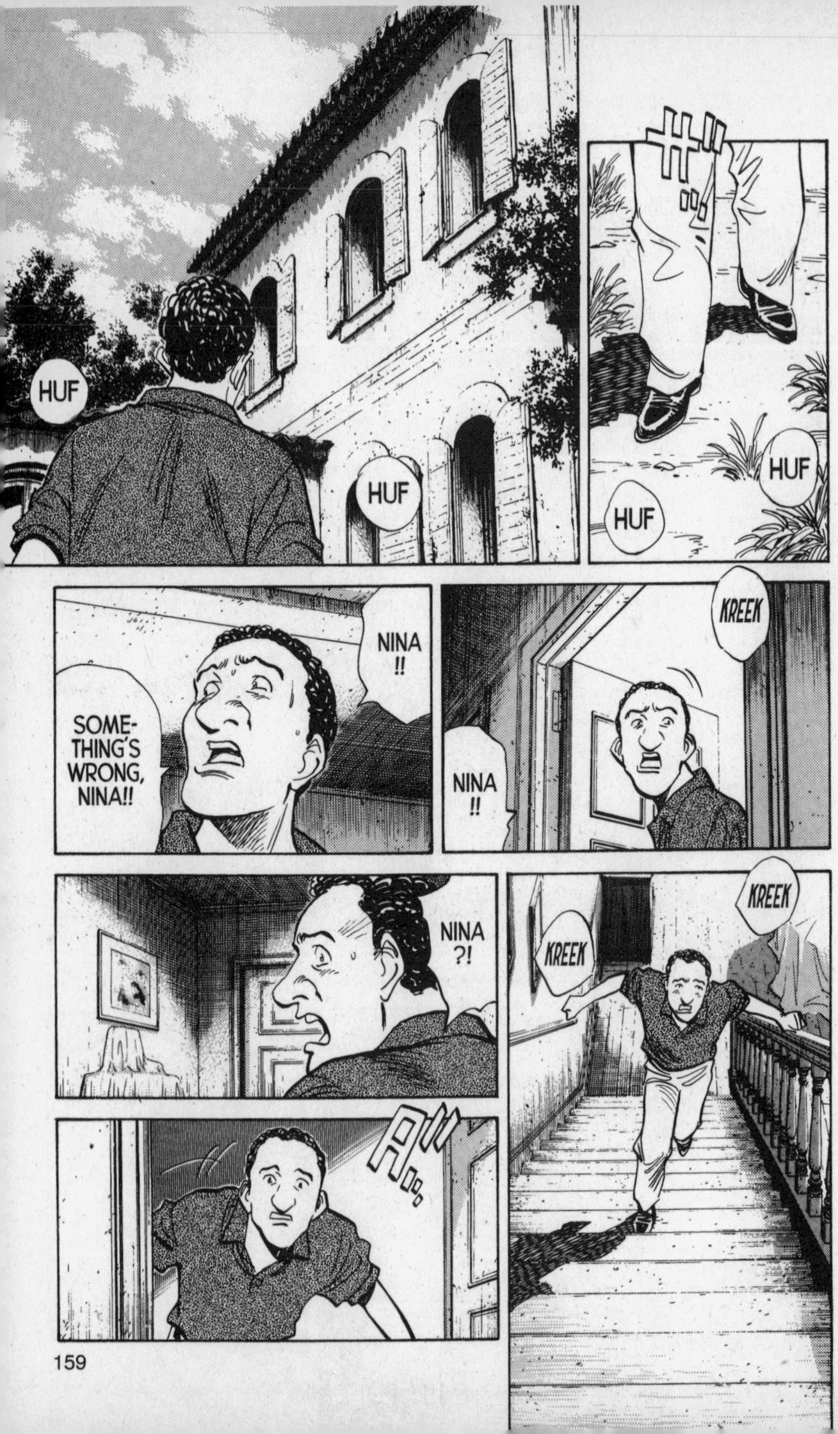
HUF
HUF
HUF
HUF
KREEK
NINA!!
NINA!!
SOME-THING'S WRONG, NINA!!
KREEK
KREEK
NINA?!

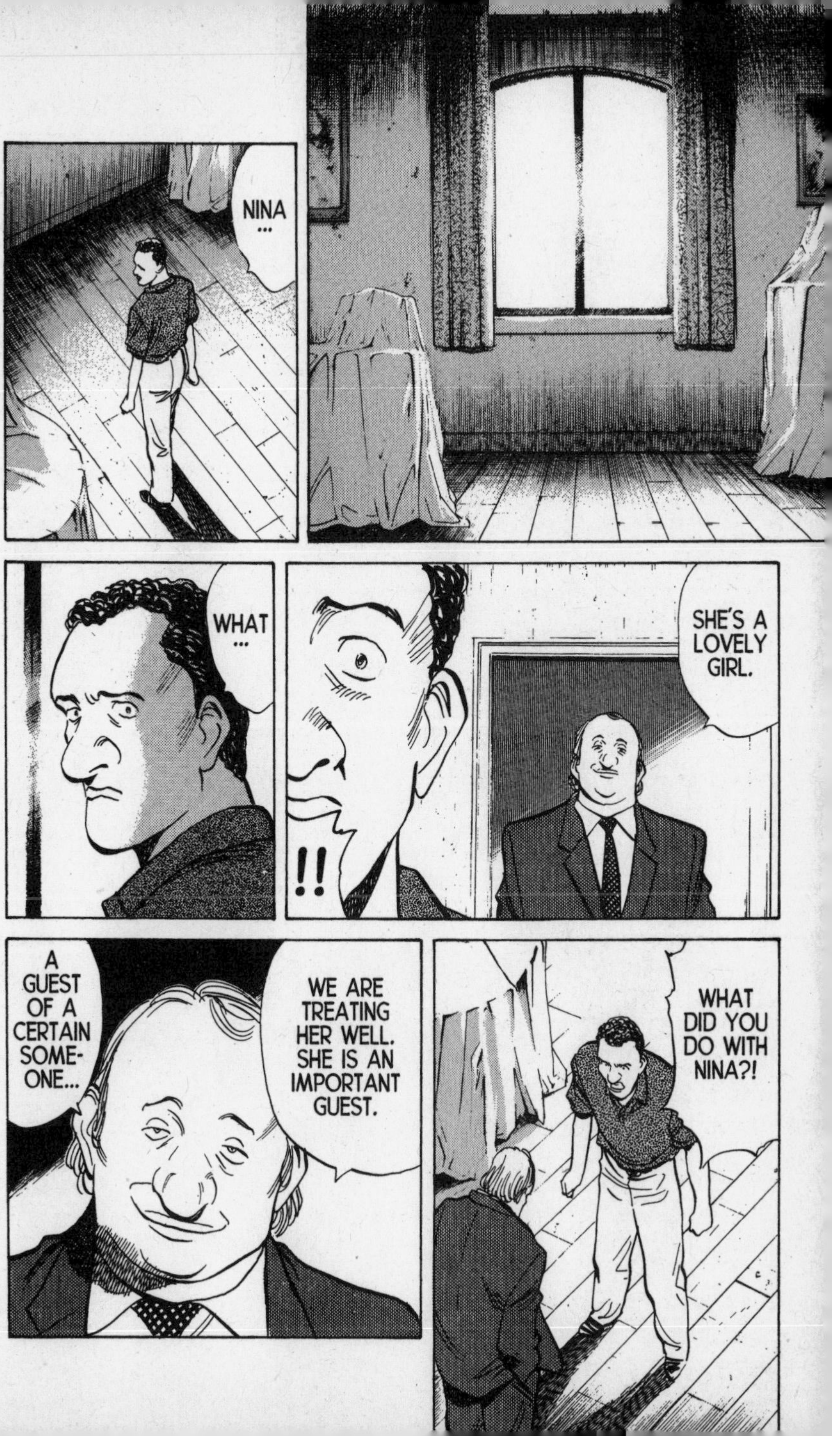
NINA...
SHE'S A LOVELY GIRL.
!!
WHAT...
WHAT DID YOU DO WITH NINA?!
WE ARE TREATING HER WELL. SHE IS AN IMPORTANT GUEST.
A GUEST OF A CERTAIN SOME-ONE...

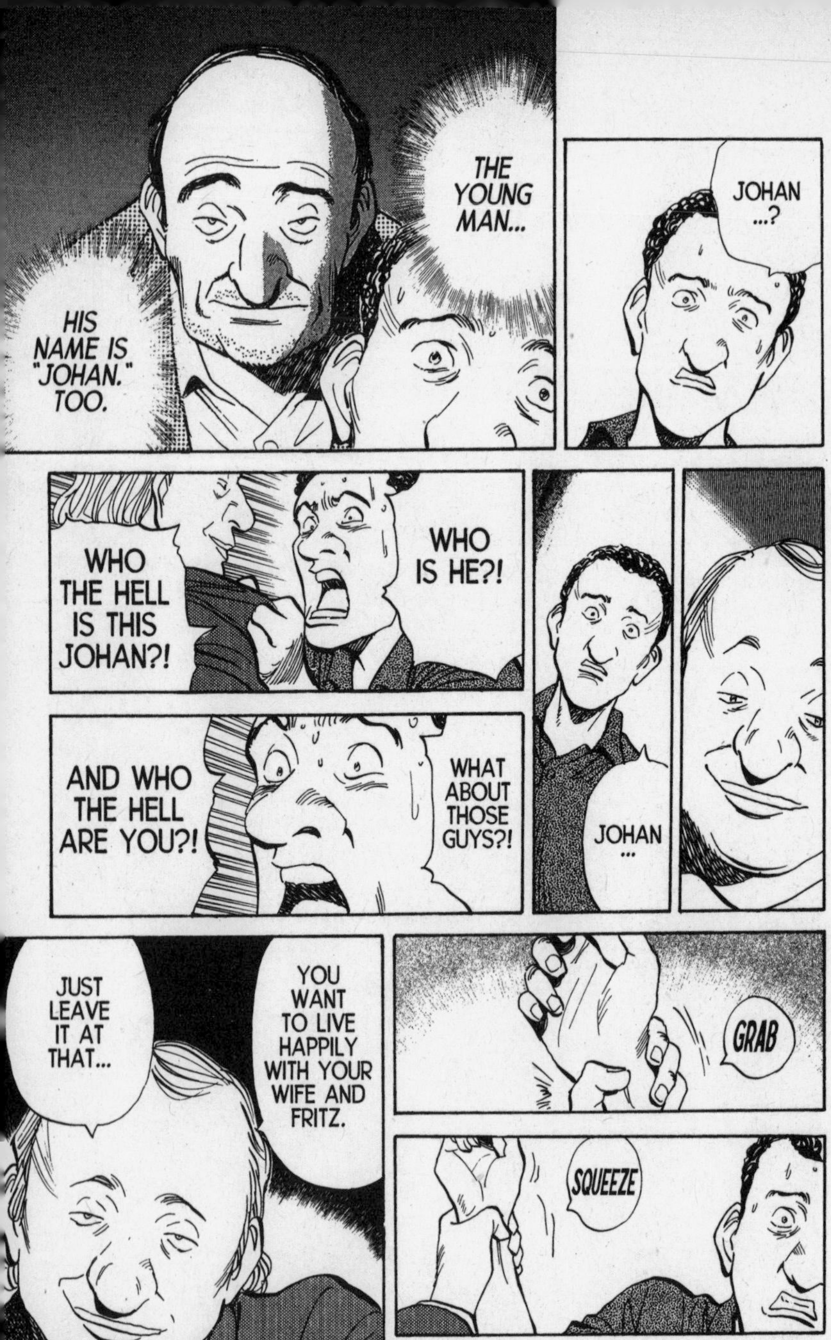
JOHAN ...?
THE YOUNG MAN...
HIS NAME IS "JOHAN," TOO.
JOHAN ...
WHO IS HE?!
WHO THE HELL IS THIS JOHAN?!
WHAT ABOUT THOSE GUYS?!
AND WHO THE HELL ARE YOU?!
GRAB
SQUEEZE
YOU WANT TO LIVE HAPPILY WITH YOUR WIFE AND FRITZ.
JUST LEAVE IT AT THAT...

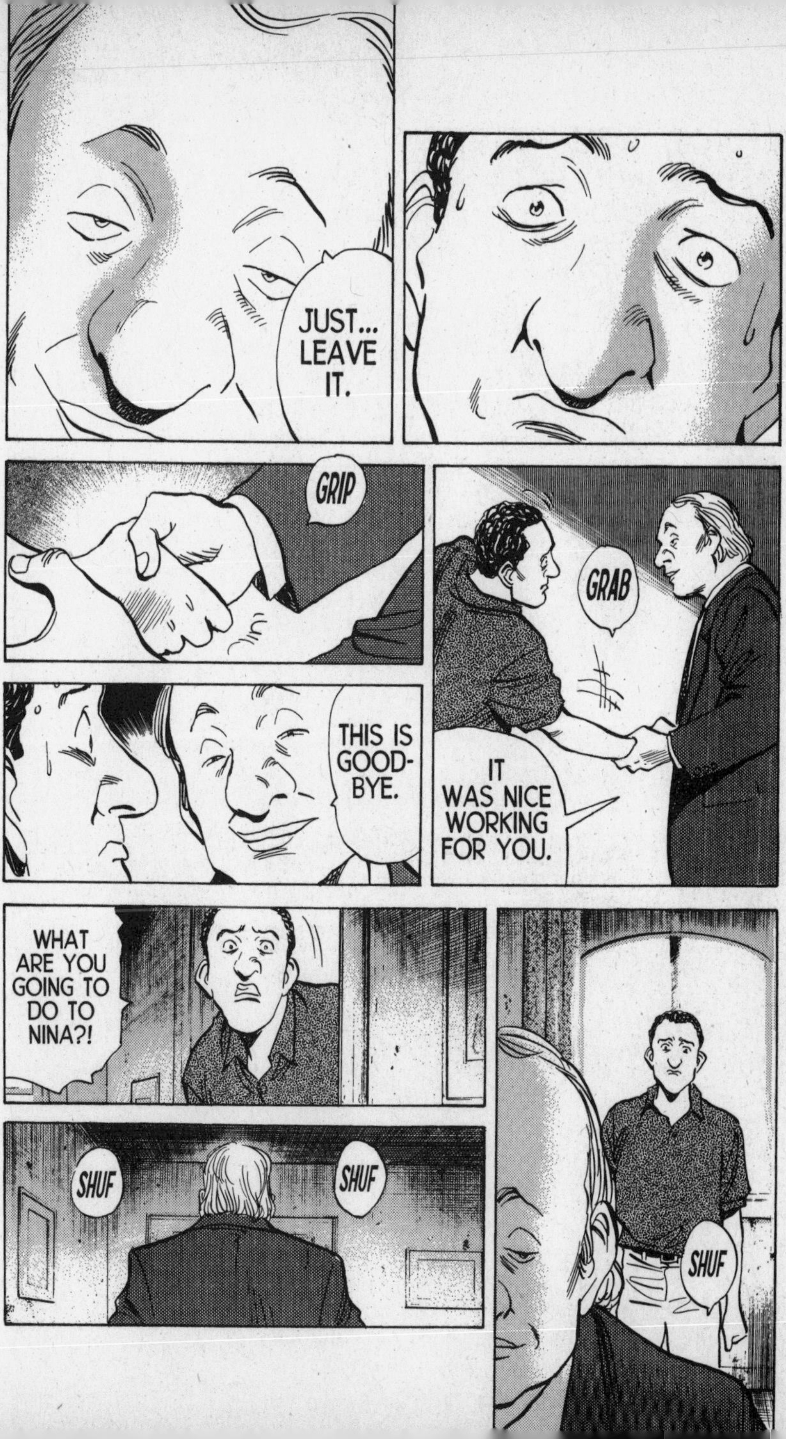
JUST... LEAVE IT.
GRAB
IT WAS NICE WORKING FOR YOU.
GRIP
THIS IS GOOD-BYE.
SHUF
WHAT ARE YOU GOING TO DO TO NINA?!
SHUF
SHUF

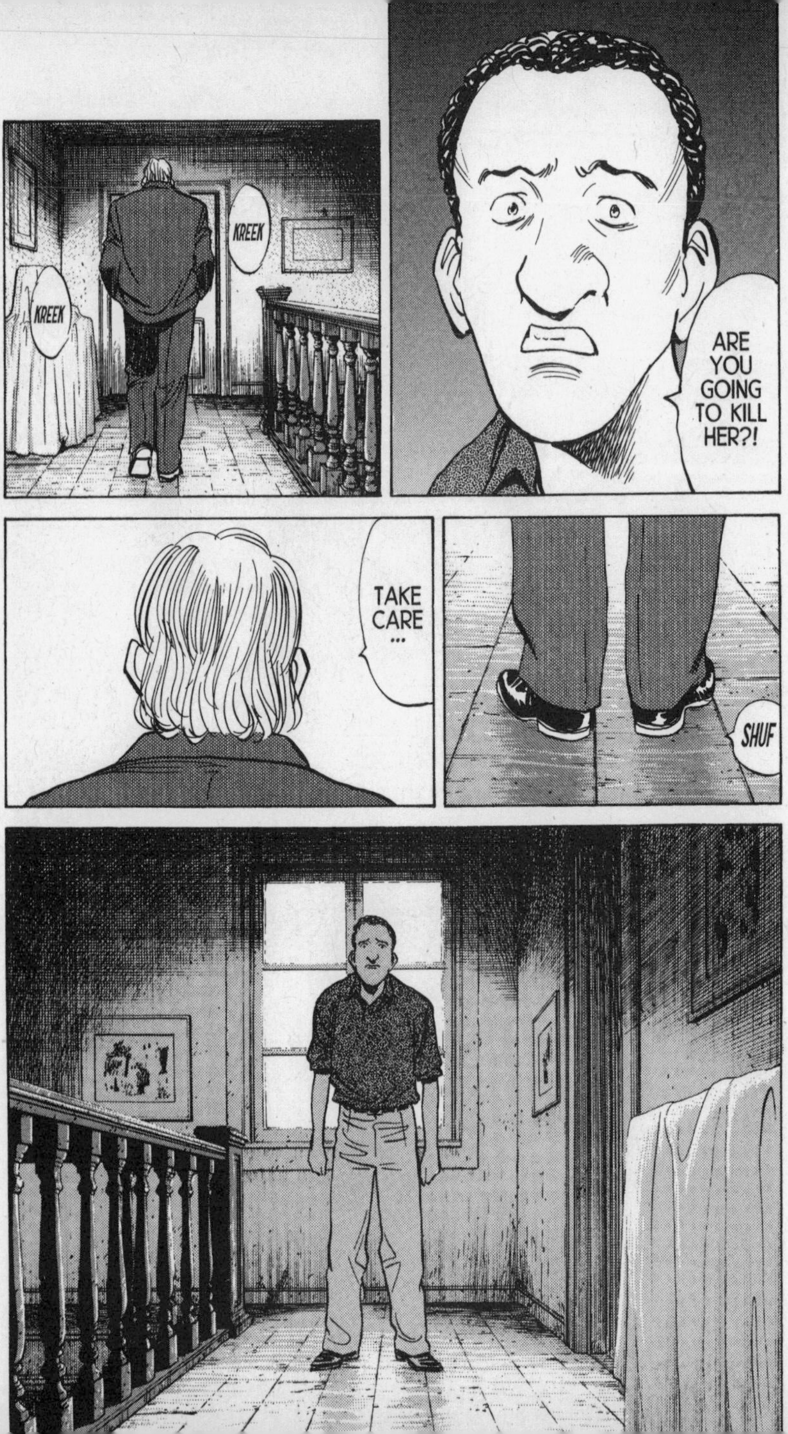
ARE YOU GOING TO KILL HER?!
KREEK
KREEK
SHUF
TAKE CARE ...

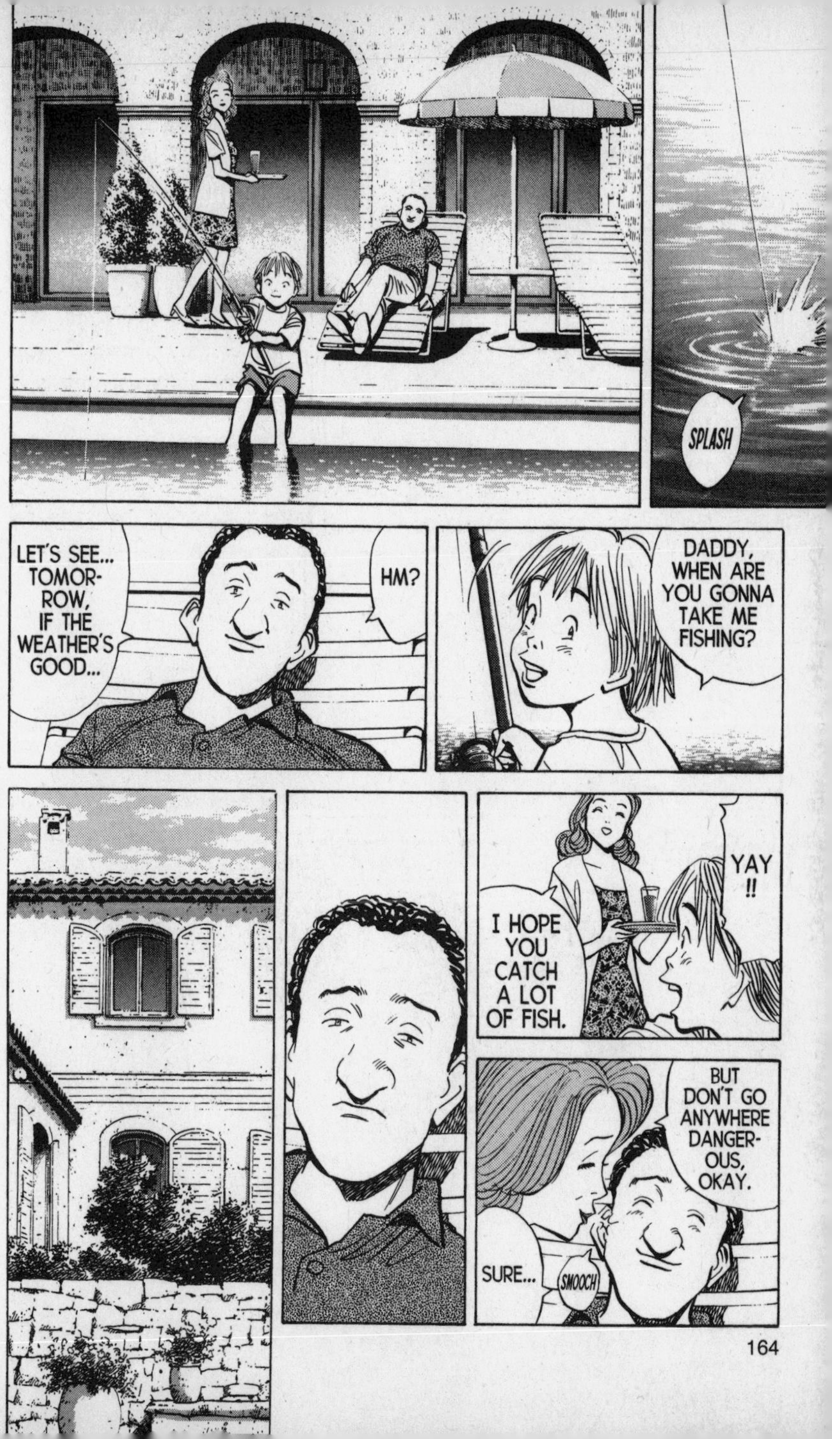
SPLASH
DADDY, WHEN ARE YOU GONNA TAKE ME FISHING?
HM?
LET'S SEE... TOMOR-ROW, IF THE WEATHER'S GOOD...
YAY !!
I HOPE YOU CATCH A LOT OF FISH.
BUT DON'T GO ANYWHERE DANGER-OUS, OKAY.
SMOOCH
SURE...

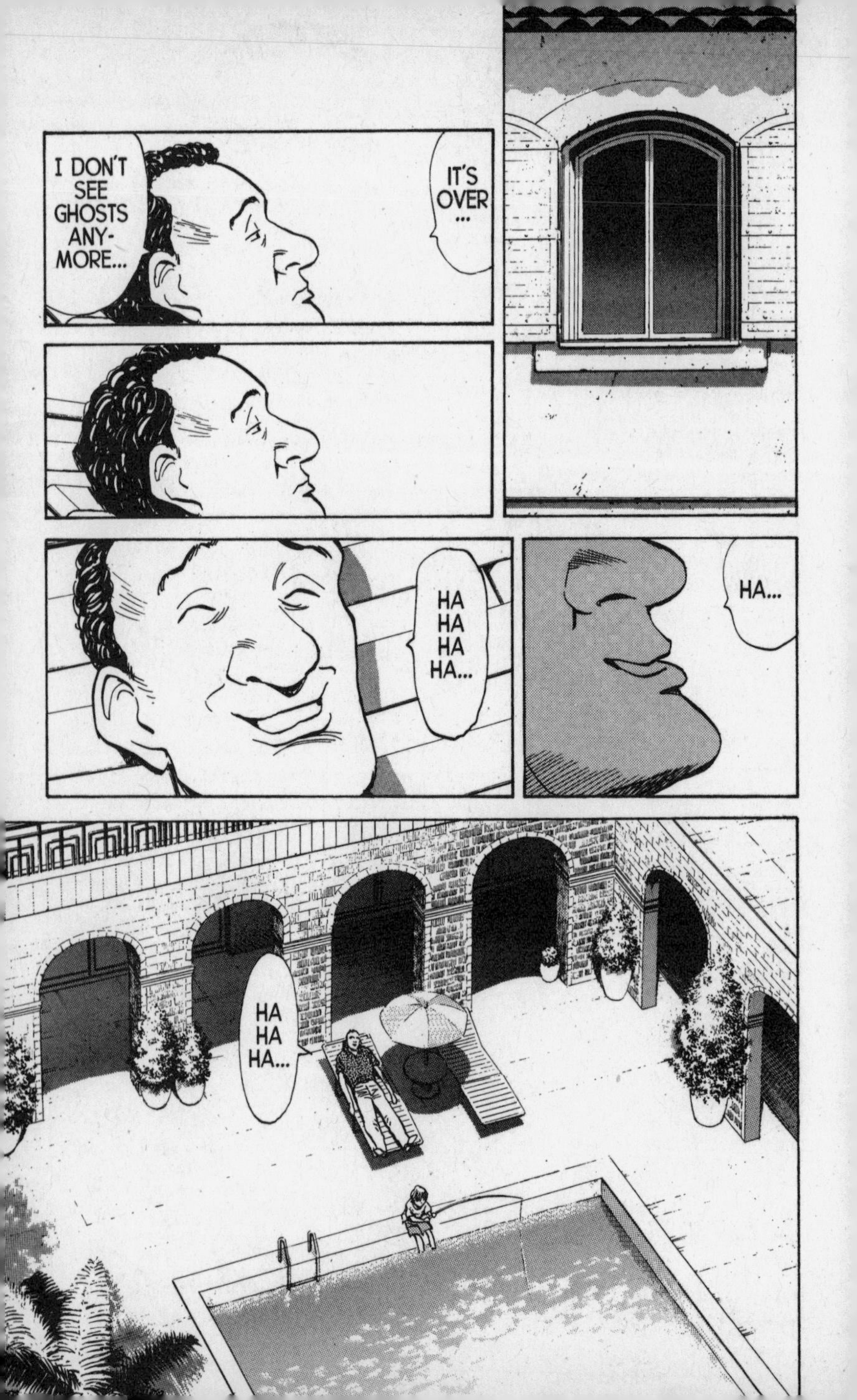
IT'S OVER...
I DON'T SEE GHOSTS ANY-MORE...
HA...
HA HA HA HA...
HA HA HA...

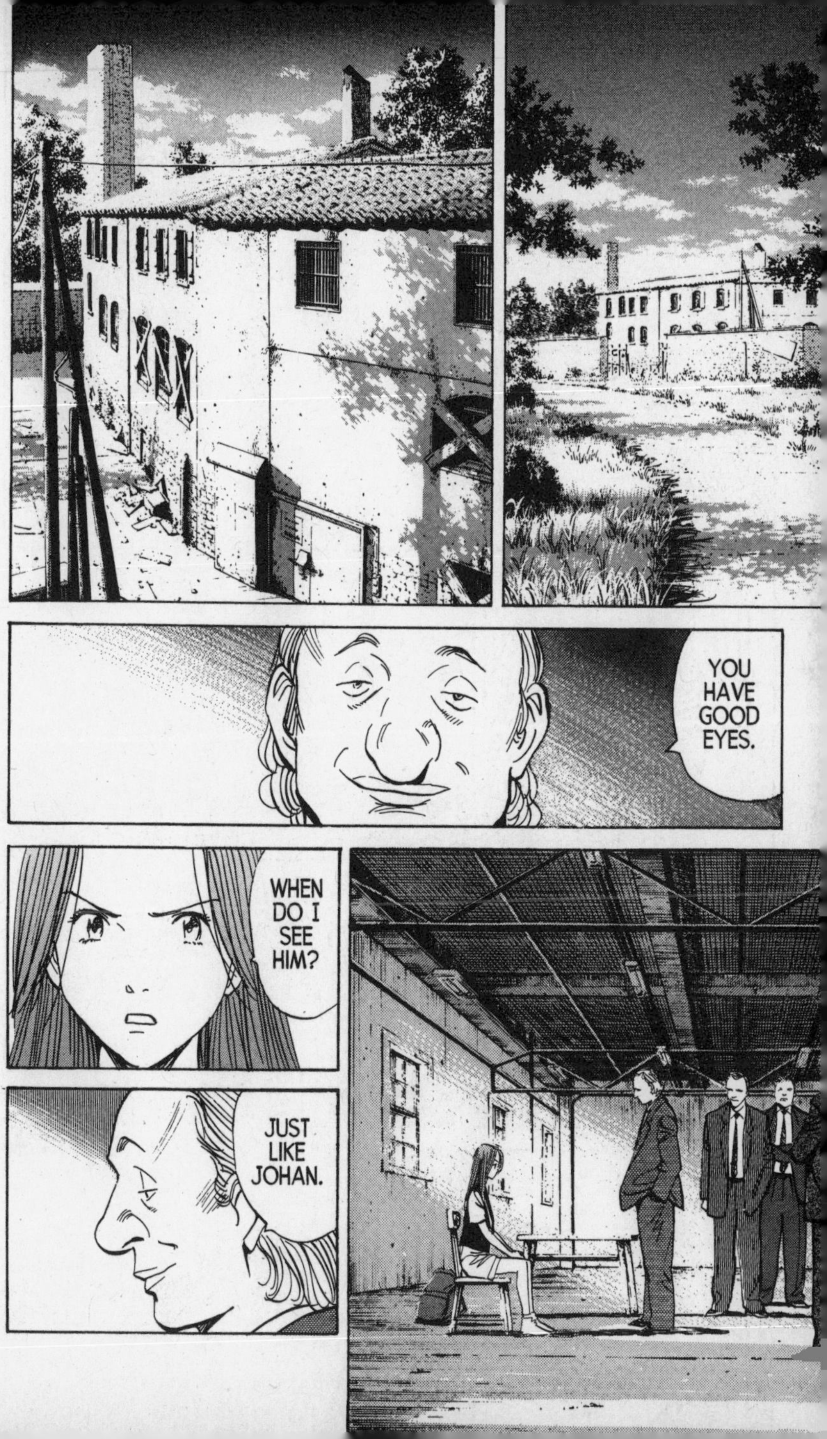
YOU HAVE GOOD EYES.
WHEN DO I SEE HIM?
JUST LIKE JOHAN.

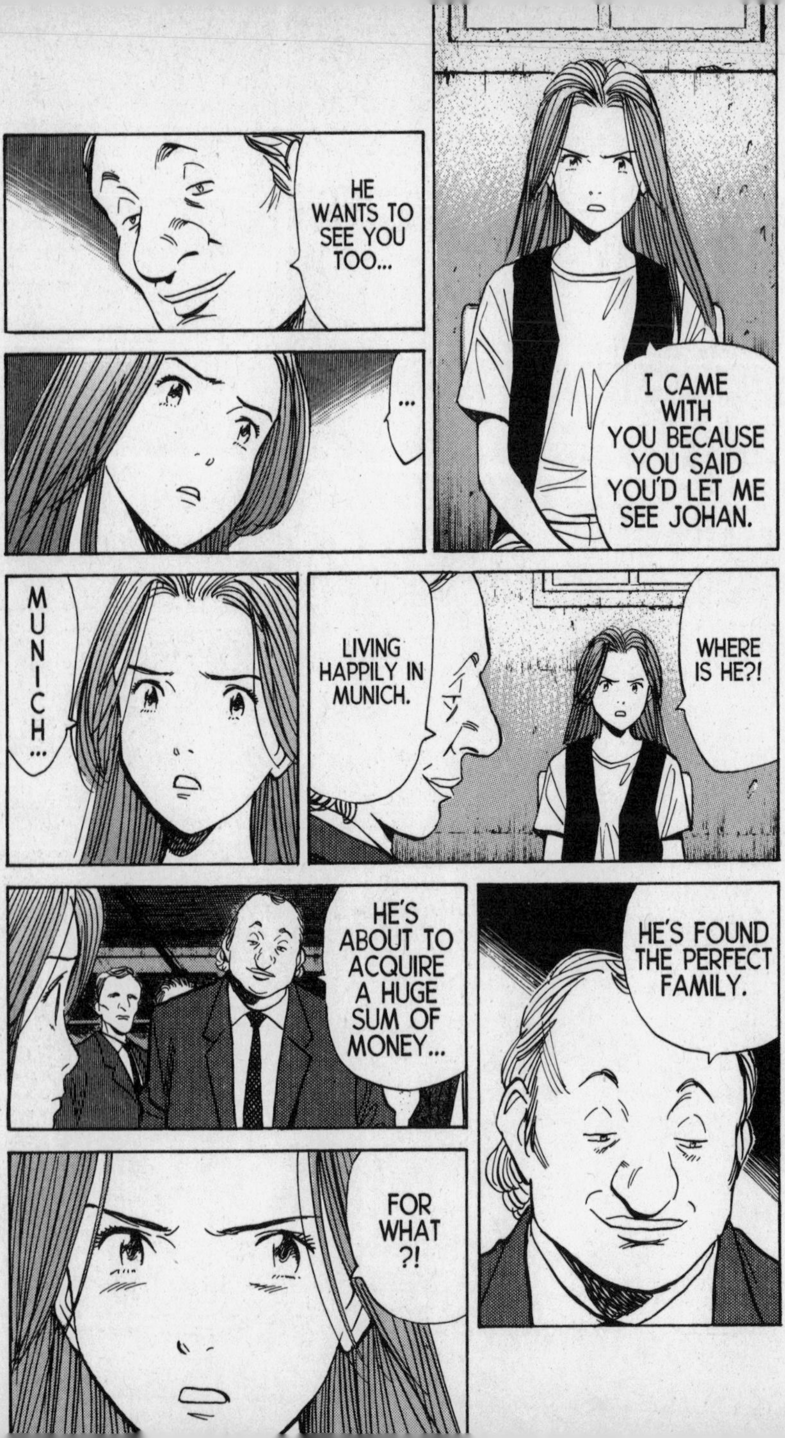
I CAME WITH YOU BECAUSE YOU SAID YOU'D LET ME SEE JOHAN.
HE WANTS TO SEE YOU TOO...
...
WHERE IS HE?!
LIVING HAPPILY IN MUNICH.
MUNICH...
HE'S FOUND THE PERFECT FAMILY.
HE'S ABOUT TO ACQUIRE A HUGE SUM OF MONEY...
FOR WHAT?!

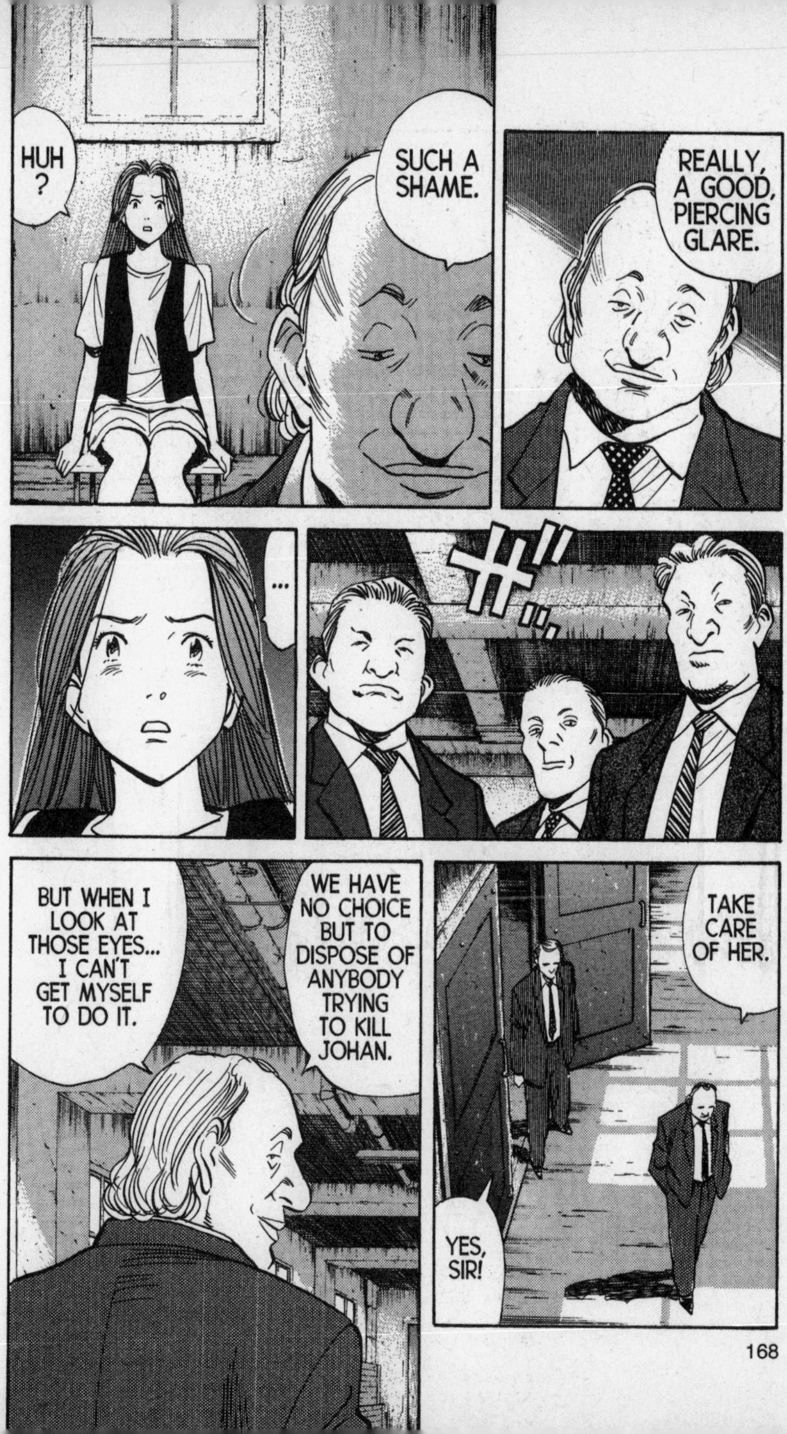
REALLY, A GOOD, PIERCING GLARE.
SUCH A SHAME.
HUH ?
...
TAKE CARE OF HER.
YES, SIR!
WE HAVE NO CHOICE BUT TO DISPOSE OF ANYBODY TRYING TO KILL JOHAN.
BUT WHEN I LOOK AT THOSE EYES... I CAN'T GET MYSELF TO DO IT.

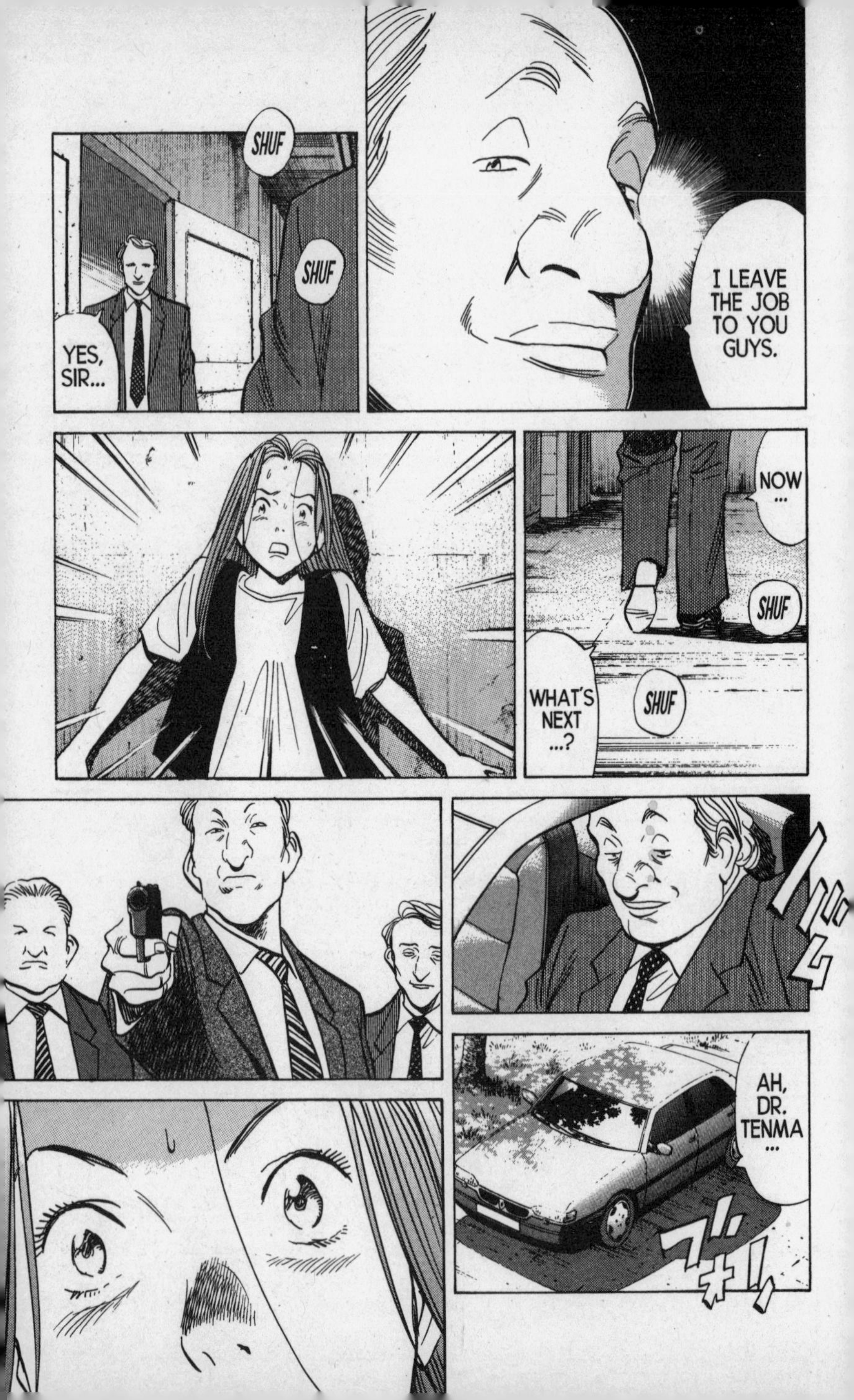
I LEAVE THE JOB TO YOU GUYS.
SHUF
SHUF
YES, SIR...
NOW...
SHUF
WHAT'S NEXT...?
SHUF
AH, DR. TENMA...

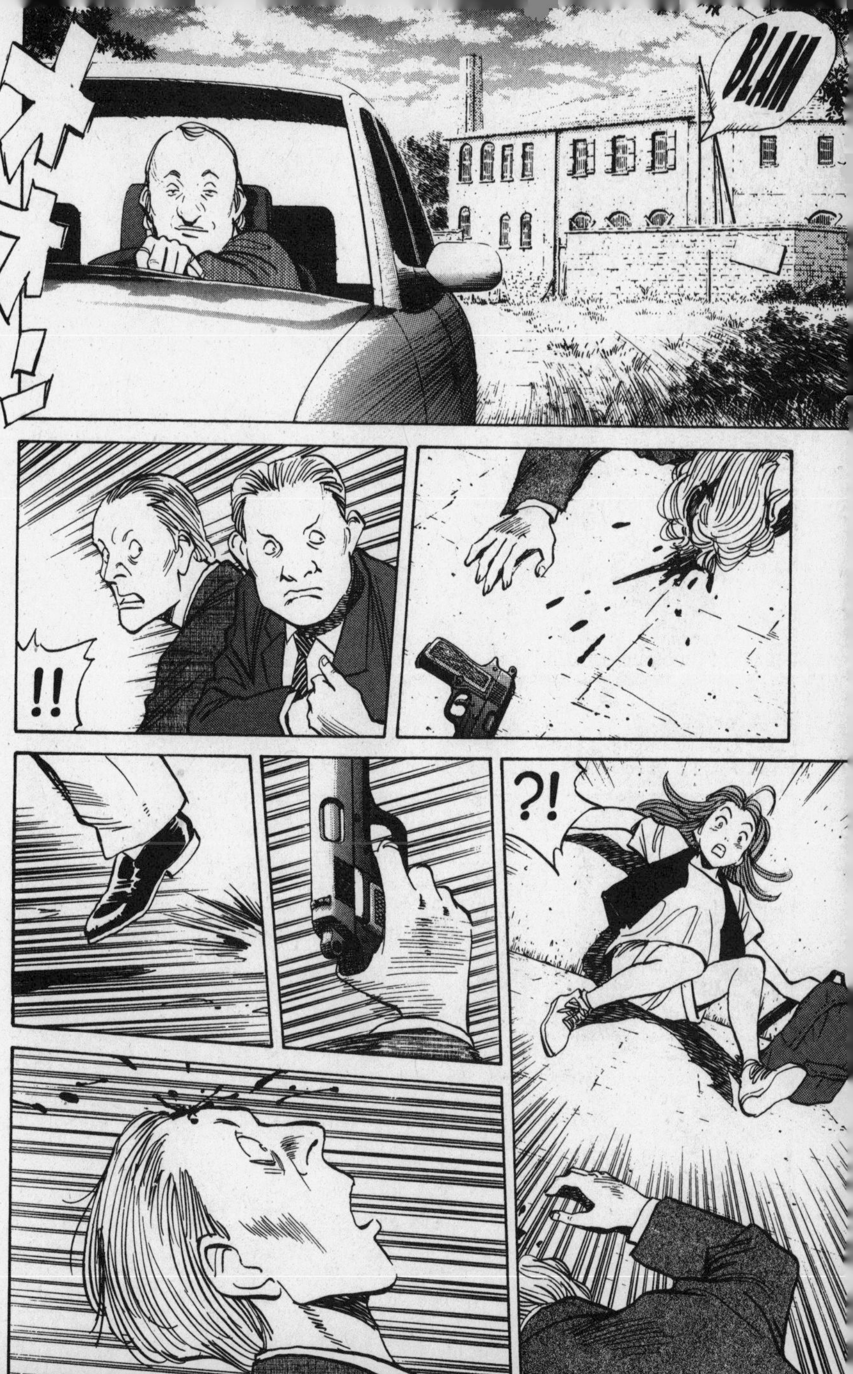
BLAM
ドオオーン
!!
?!

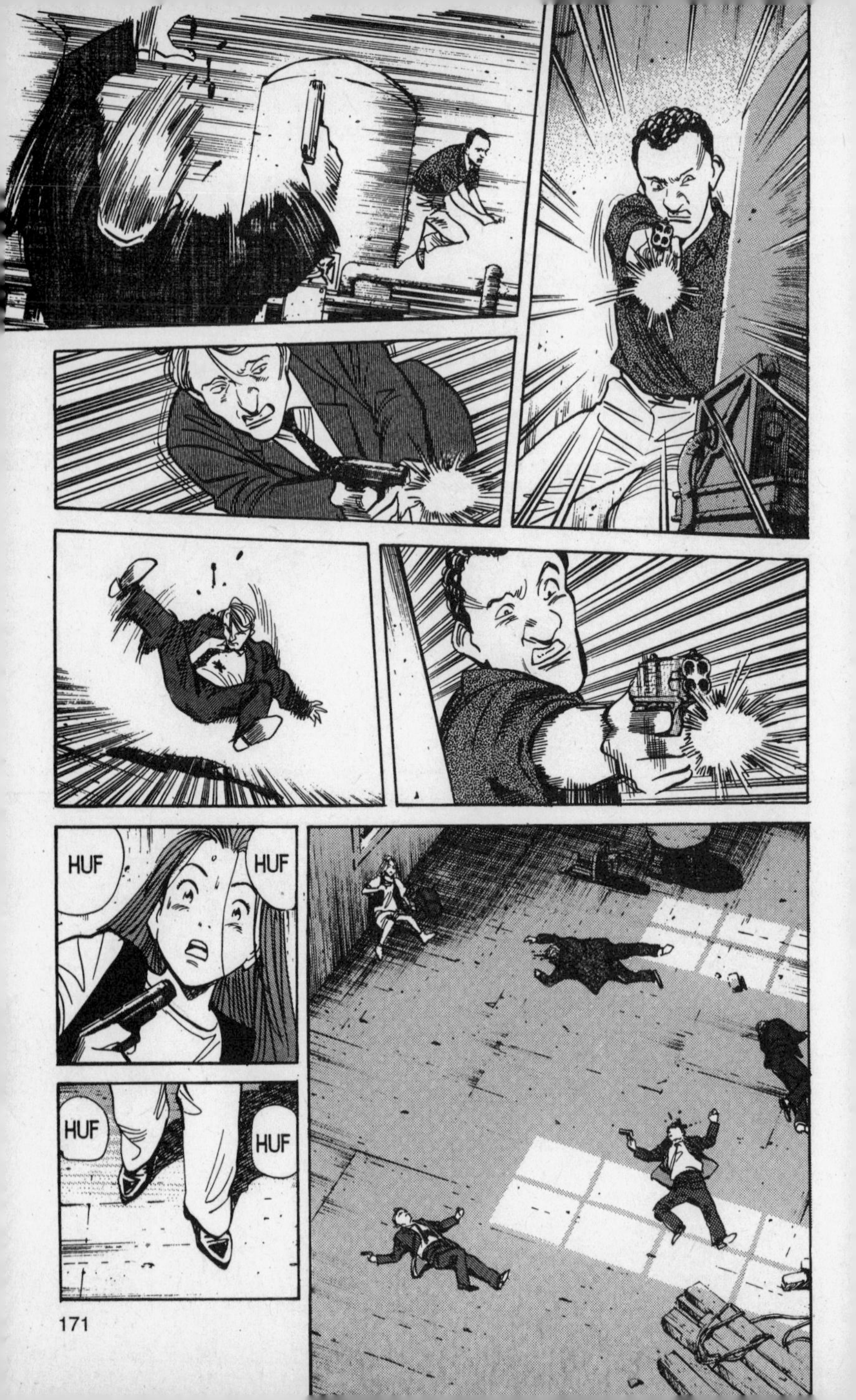
HUF
HUF
HUF
HUF

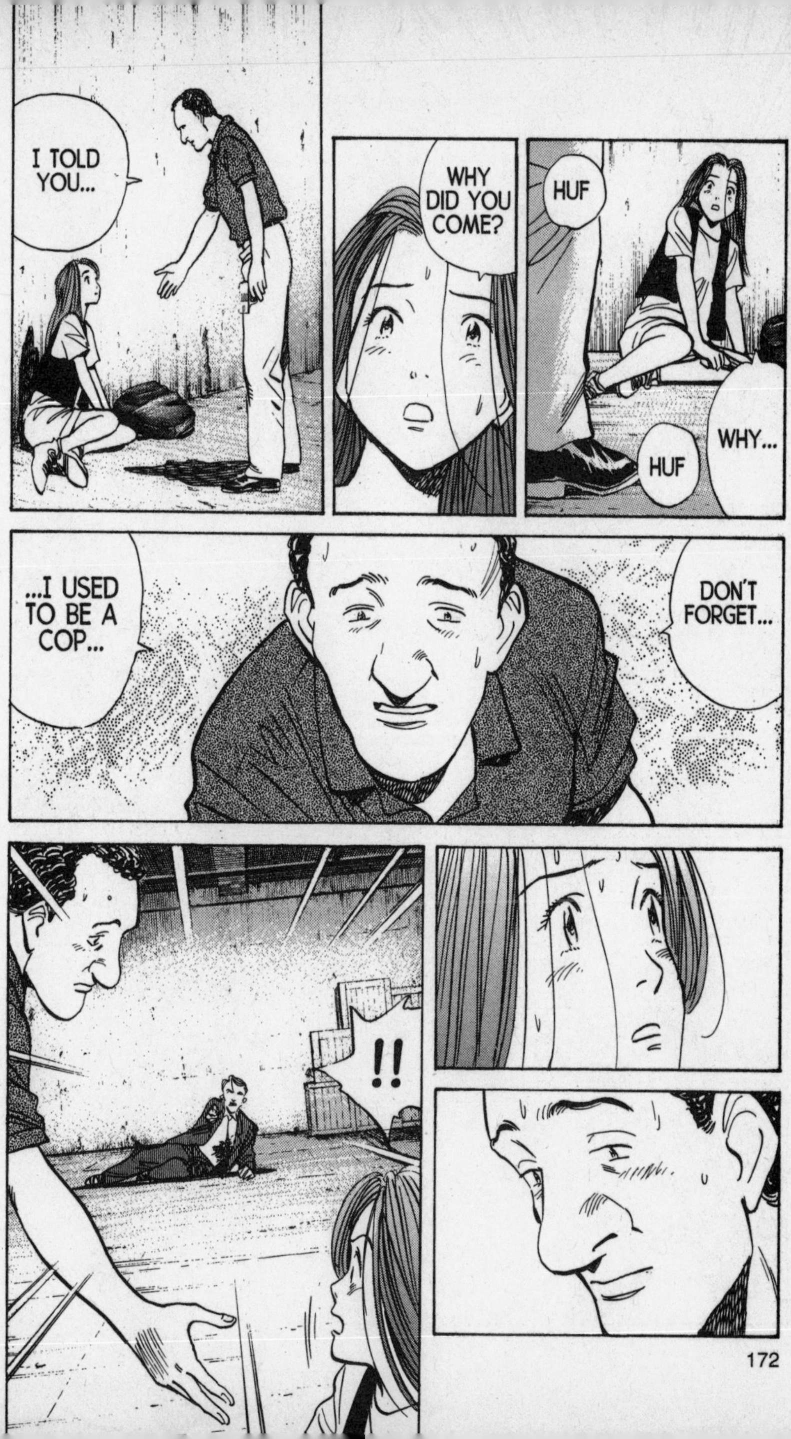
HUF
WHY...
HUF
WHY DID YOU COME?
I TOLD YOU...
DON'T FORGET...
...I USED TO BE A COP...
!!

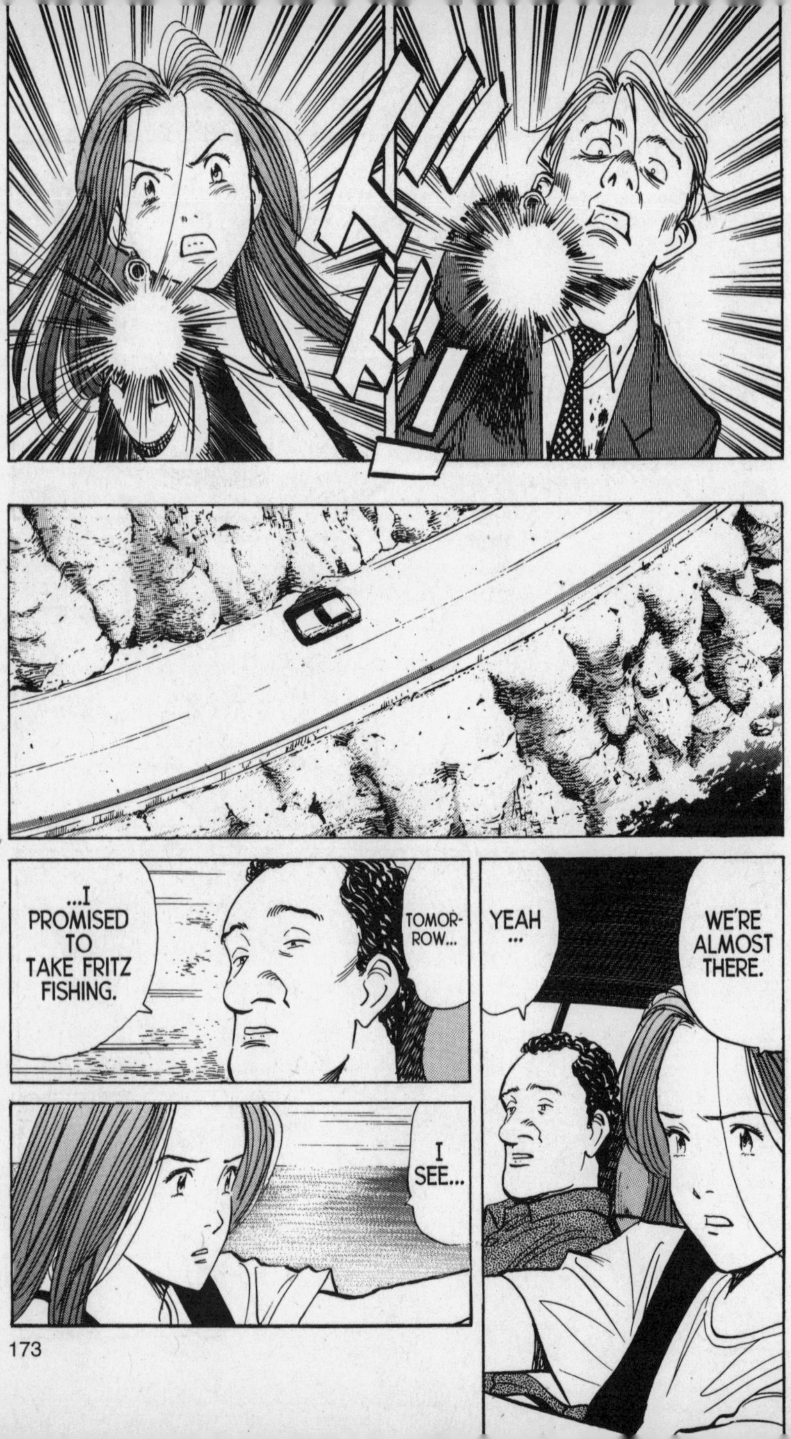
WE'RE ALMOST THERE.
YEAH ...
TOMORROW...
...I PROMISED TO TAKE FRITZ FISHING.
I SEE...

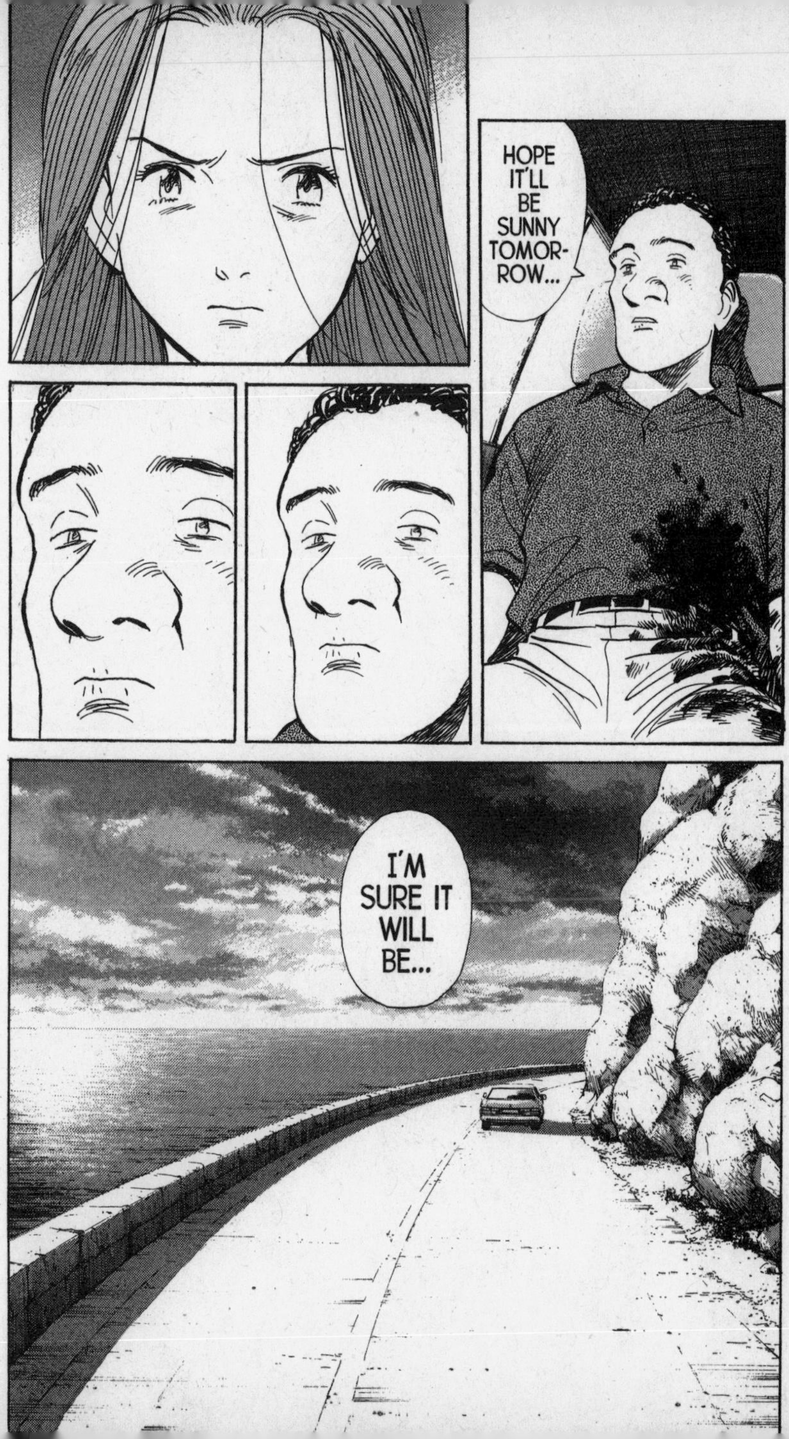
HOPE IT'LL BE SUNNY TOMORROW...
I'M SURE IT WILL BE...

Chapter 8 Lunge's Hope

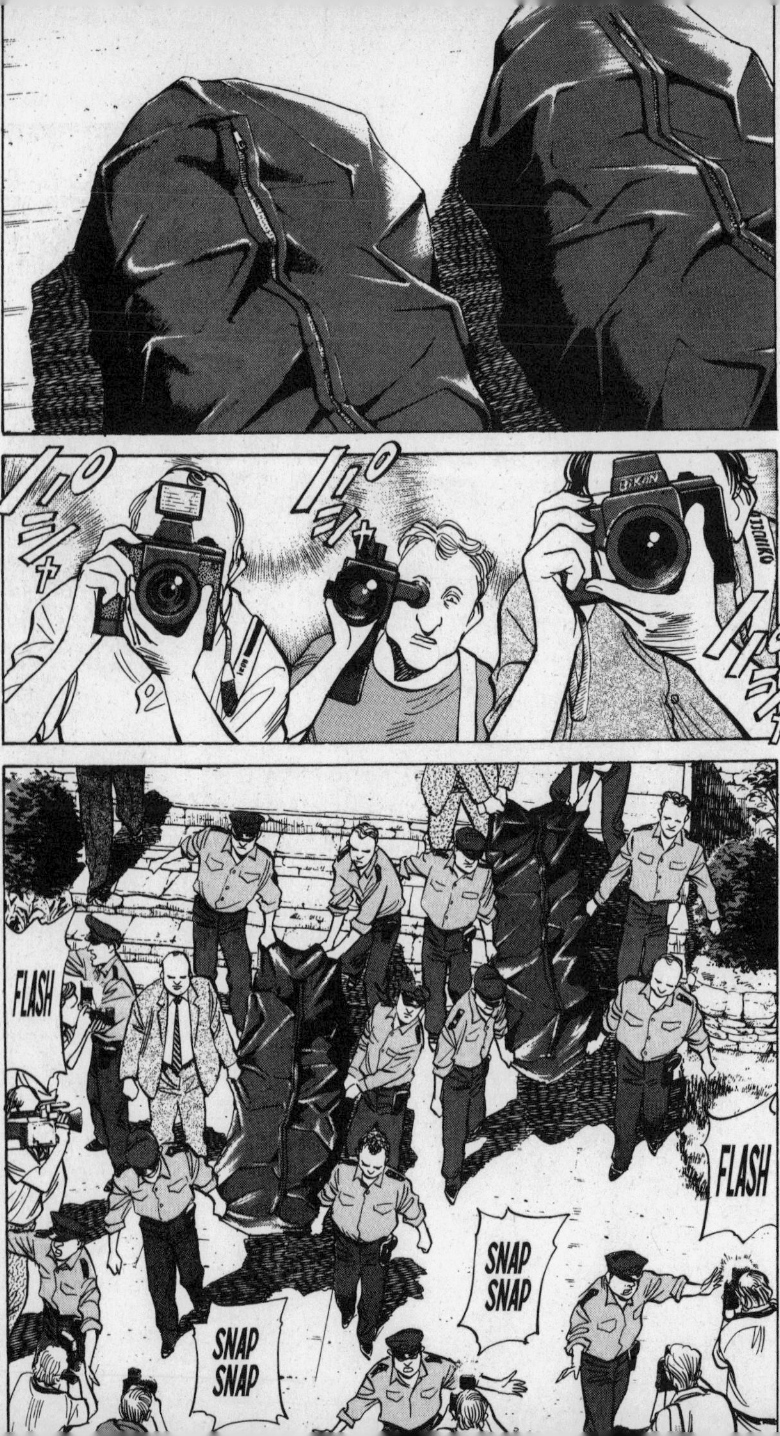
パシャ
パシャ
パシャ
FLASH
SNAP
SNAP
FLASH
SNAP
SNAP

Chapter 8

Lunge's Hope

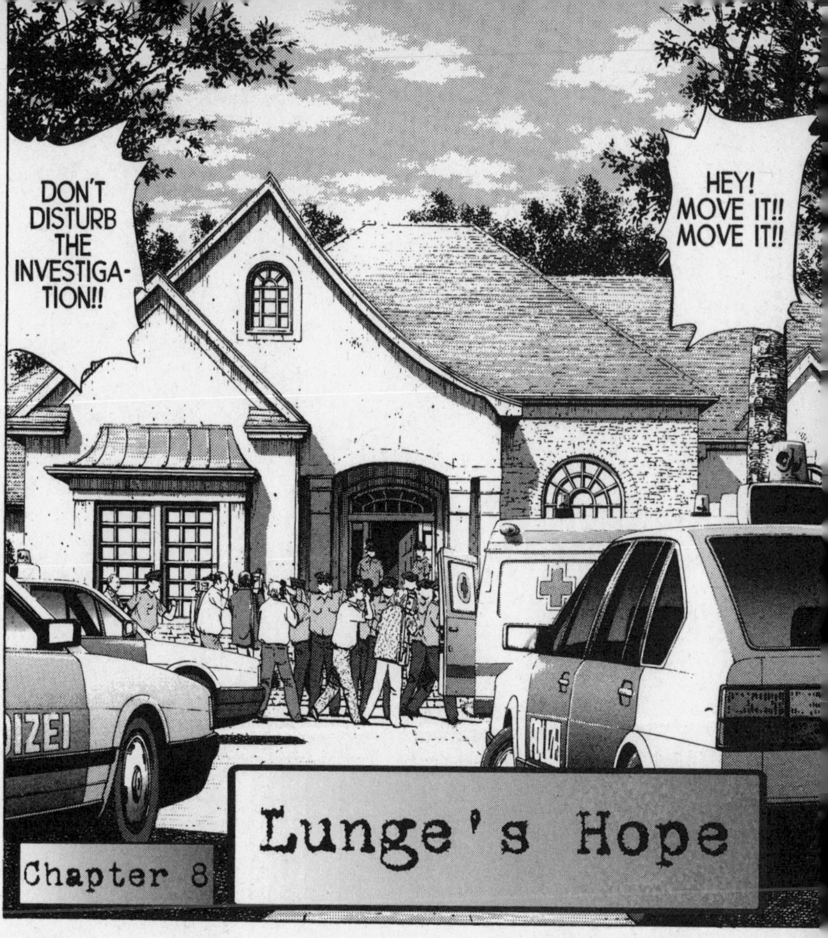
HEY! MOVE IT!! MOVE IT!!
DON'T DISTURB THE INVESTIGATION!!

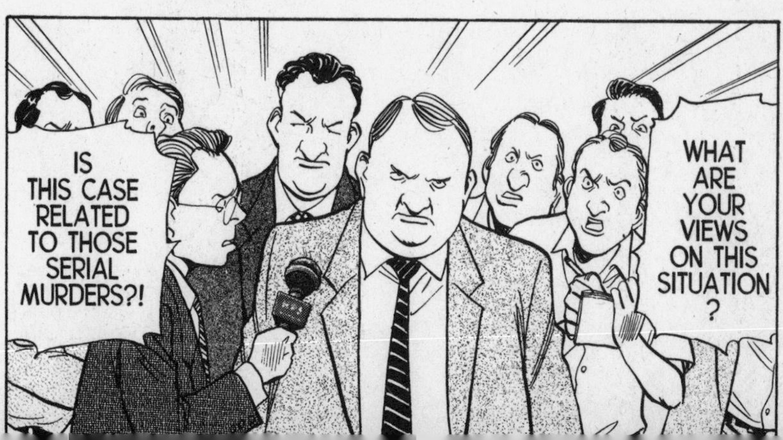
WHAT ARE YOUR VIEWS ON THIS SITUATION?
IS THIS CASE RELATED TO THOSE SERIAL MURDERS?!

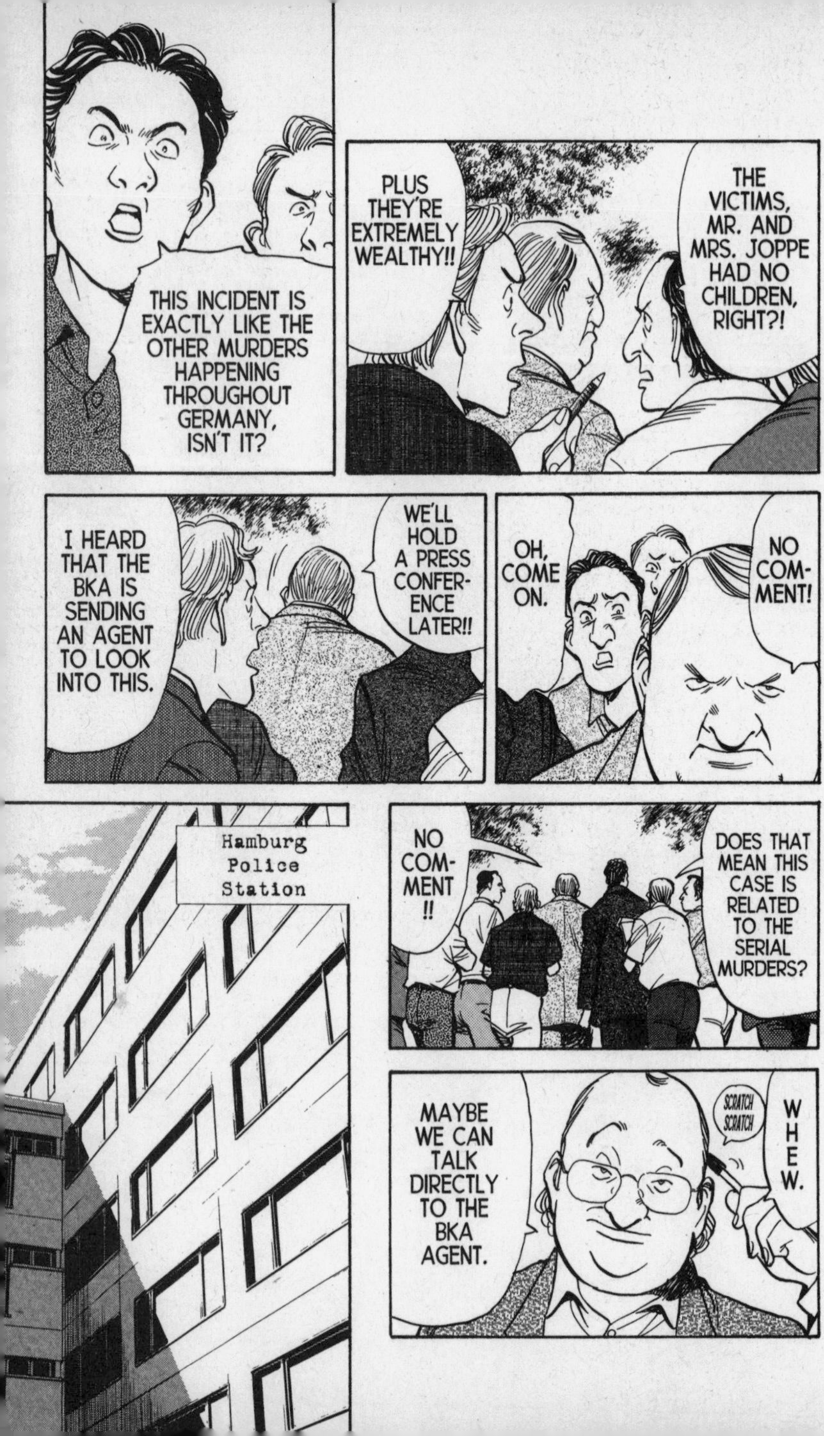
THE VICTIMS, MR. AND MRS. JOPPE HAD NO CHILDREN, RIGHT?!
PLUS THEY'RE EXTREMELY WEALTHY!!
THIS INCIDENT IS EXACTLY LIKE THE OTHER MURDERS HAPPENING THROUGHOUT GERMANY, ISN'T IT?
NO COMMENT!
OH, COME ON.
WE'LL HOLD A PRESS CONFERENCE LATER!!
I HEARD THAT THE BKA IS SENDING AN AGENT TO LOOK INTO THIS.
DOES THAT MEAN THIS CASE IS RELATED TO THE SERIAL MURDERS?
NO COMMENT!!
WHEW.
SCRATCH SCRATCH
MAYBE WE CAN TALK DIRECTLY TO THE BKA AGENT.
Hamburg Police Station

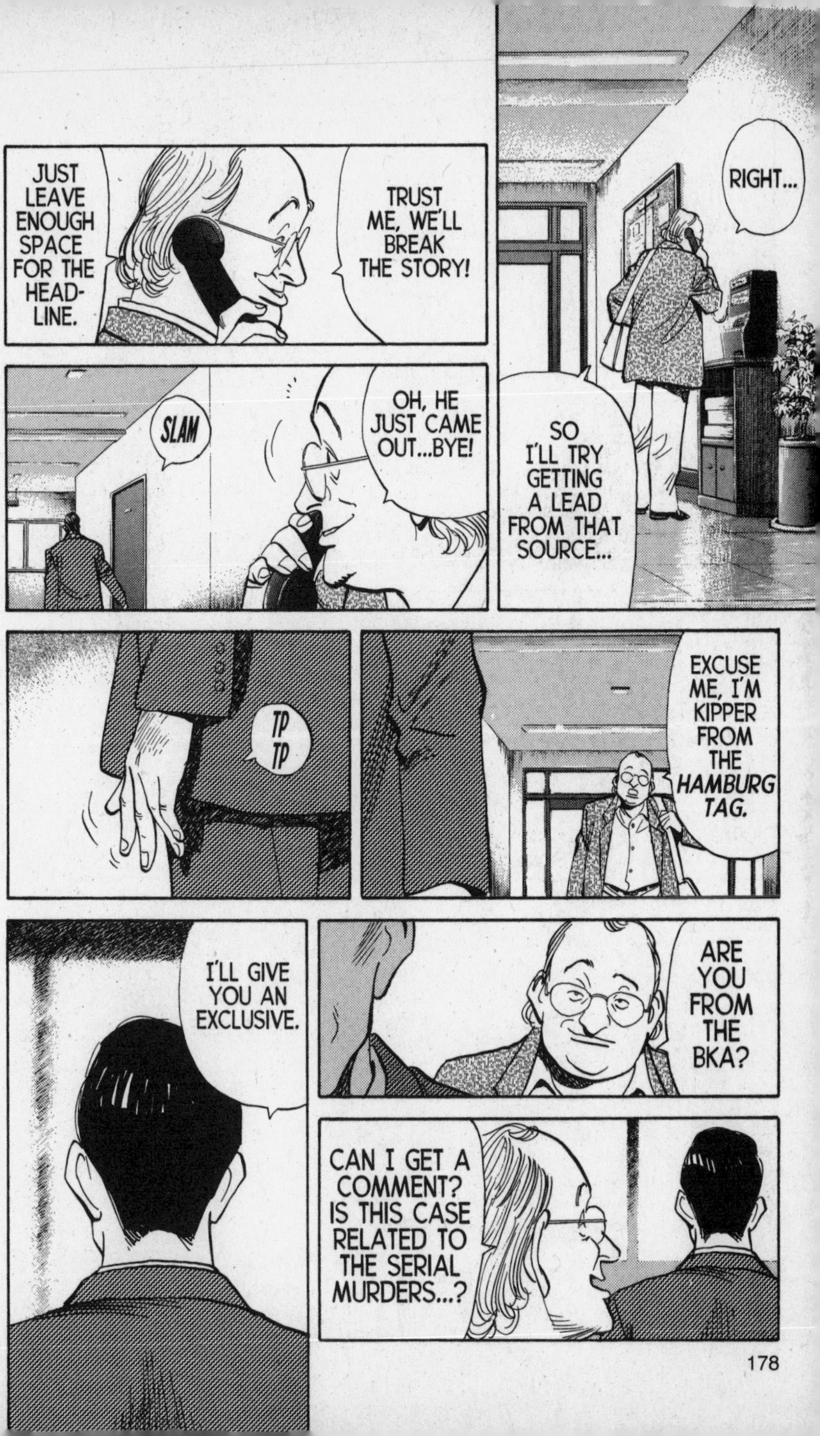
RIGHT...
SO I'LL TRY GETTING A LEAD FROM THAT SOURCE...
TRUST ME, WE'LL BREAK THE STORY!
JUST LEAVE ENOUGH SPACE FOR THE HEAD-LINE.
OH, HE JUST CAME OUT...BYE!
SLAM
EXCUSE ME, I'M KIPPER FROM THE *HAMBURG TAG.*
TP TP
ARE YOU FROM THE BKA?
CAN I GET A COMMENT? IS THIS CASE RELATED TO THE SERIAL MURDERS...?
I'LL GIVE YOU AN EXCLUSIVE.

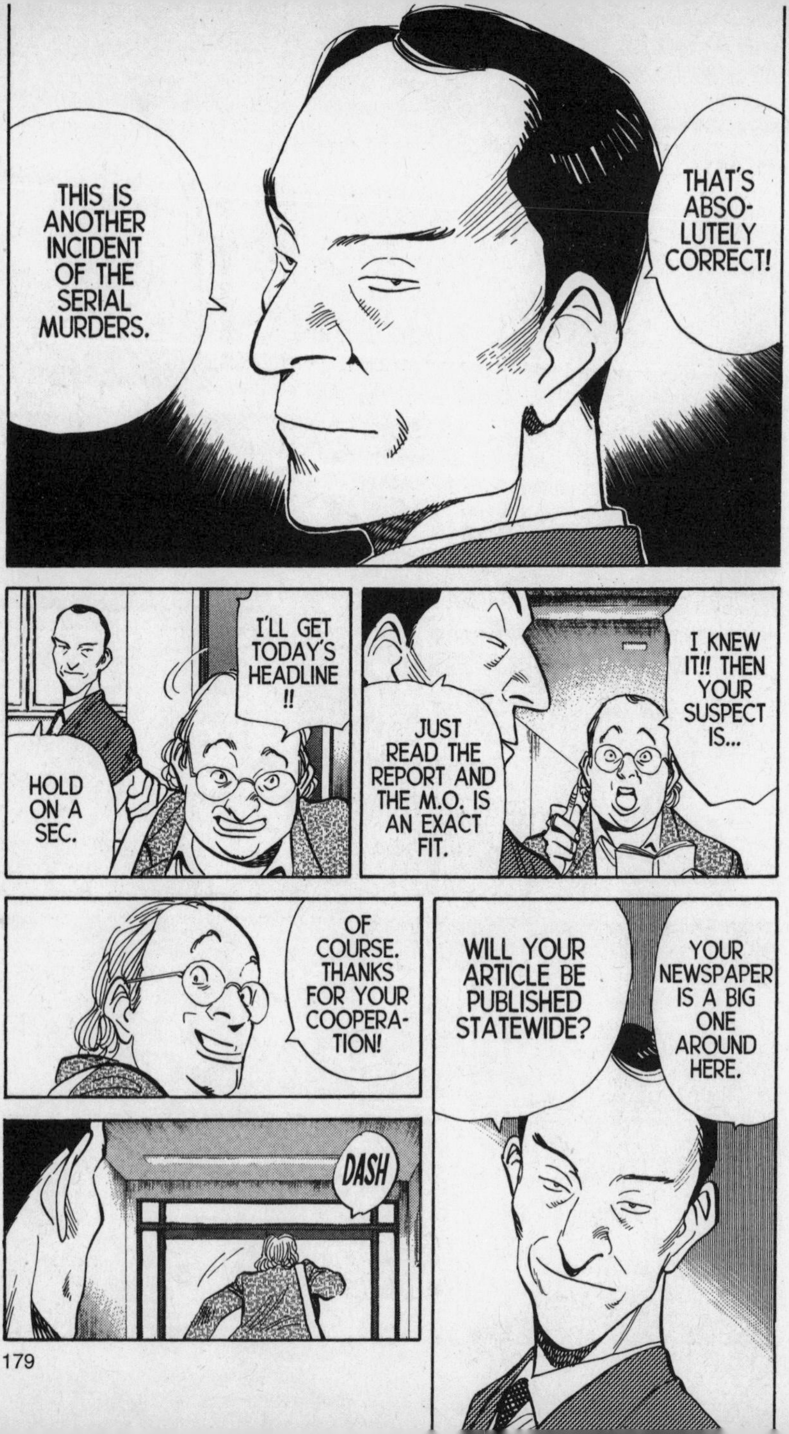
THAT'S ABSOLUTELY CORRECT!
THIS IS ANOTHER INCIDENT OF THE SERIAL MURDERS.
I KNEW IT!! THEN YOUR SUSPECT IS...
JUST READ THE REPORT AND THE M.O. IS AN EXACT FIT.
I'LL GET TODAY'S HEADLINE!!
HOLD ON A SEC.
YOUR NEWSPAPER IS A BIG ONE AROUND HERE.
WILL YOUR ARTICLE BE PUBLISHED STATEWIDE?
OF COURSE. THANKS FOR YOUR COOPERATION!
DASH

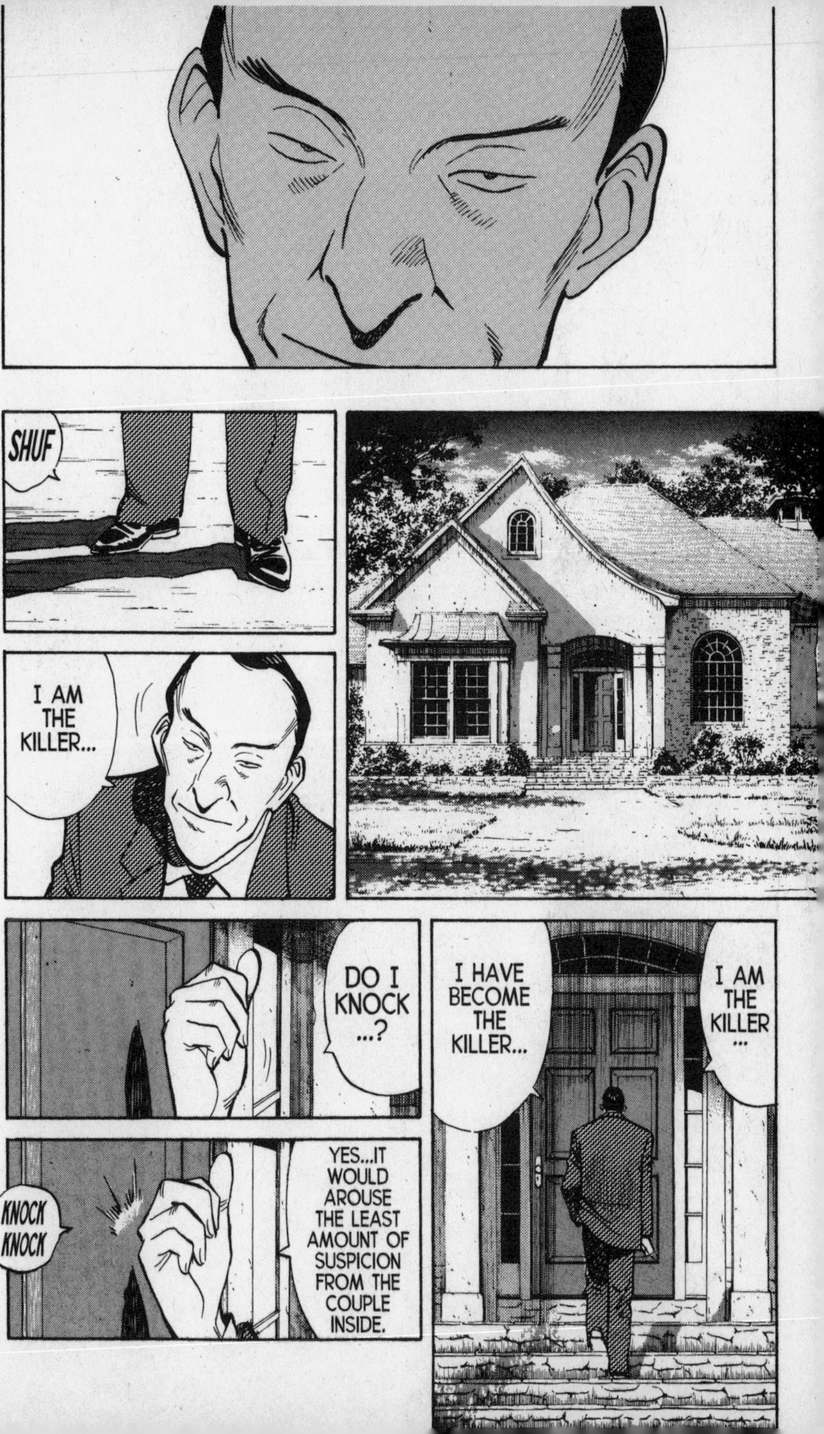
SHUF
I AM THE KILLER...
I AM THE KILLER...
I HAVE BECOME THE KILLER...
DO I KNOCK ...?
YES...IT WOULD AROUSE THE LEAST AMOUNT OF SUSPICION FROM THE COUPLE INSIDE.
KNOCK KNOCK

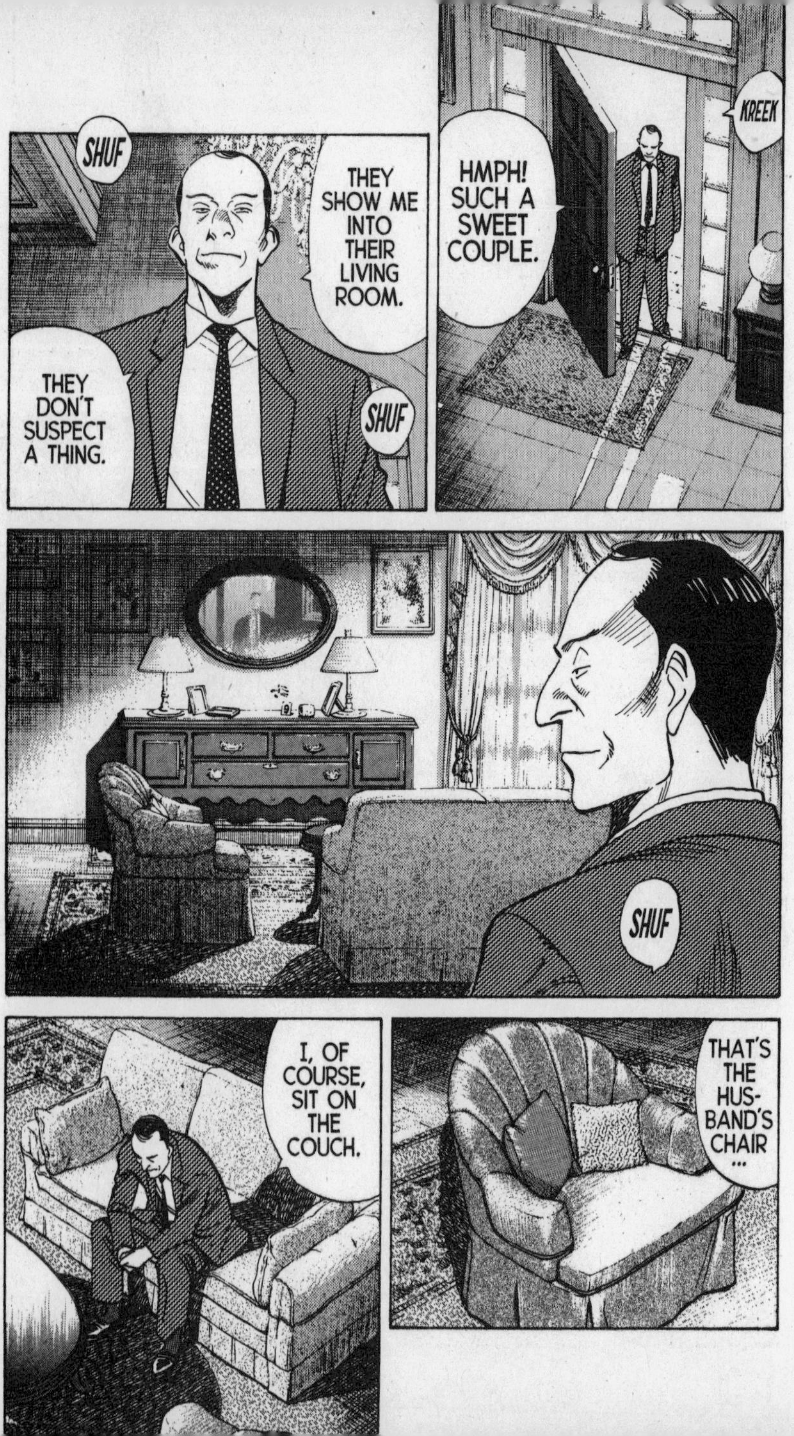
KREEK
HMPH! SUCH A SWEET COUPLE.
SHUF
THEY SHOW ME INTO THEIR LIVING ROOM.
SHUF
THEY DON'T SUSPECT A THING.
SHUF
THAT'S THE HUS-BAND'S CHAIR...
I, OF COURSE, SIT ON THE COUCH.

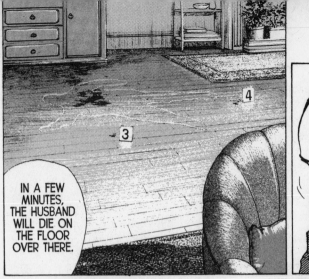

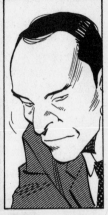

IN A FEW MINUTES, THE HUSBAND WILL DIE ON THE FLOOR OVER THERE.
BUT I STILL HAVEN'T DONE ANYTHING YET.
WHERE IS THE WIFE?
THAT'S RIGHT, SHE'S NOT IN THIS ROOM.
SHE'S IN THE KITCHEN MAKING TEA!
SHE IS STABBED IN THE BACK BEFORE SHE CAN SERVE IT...

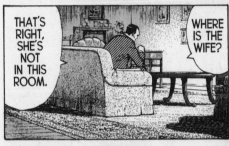

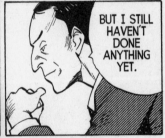

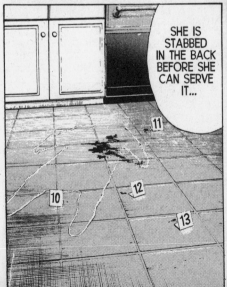

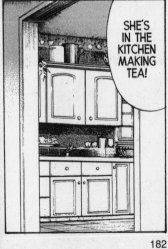

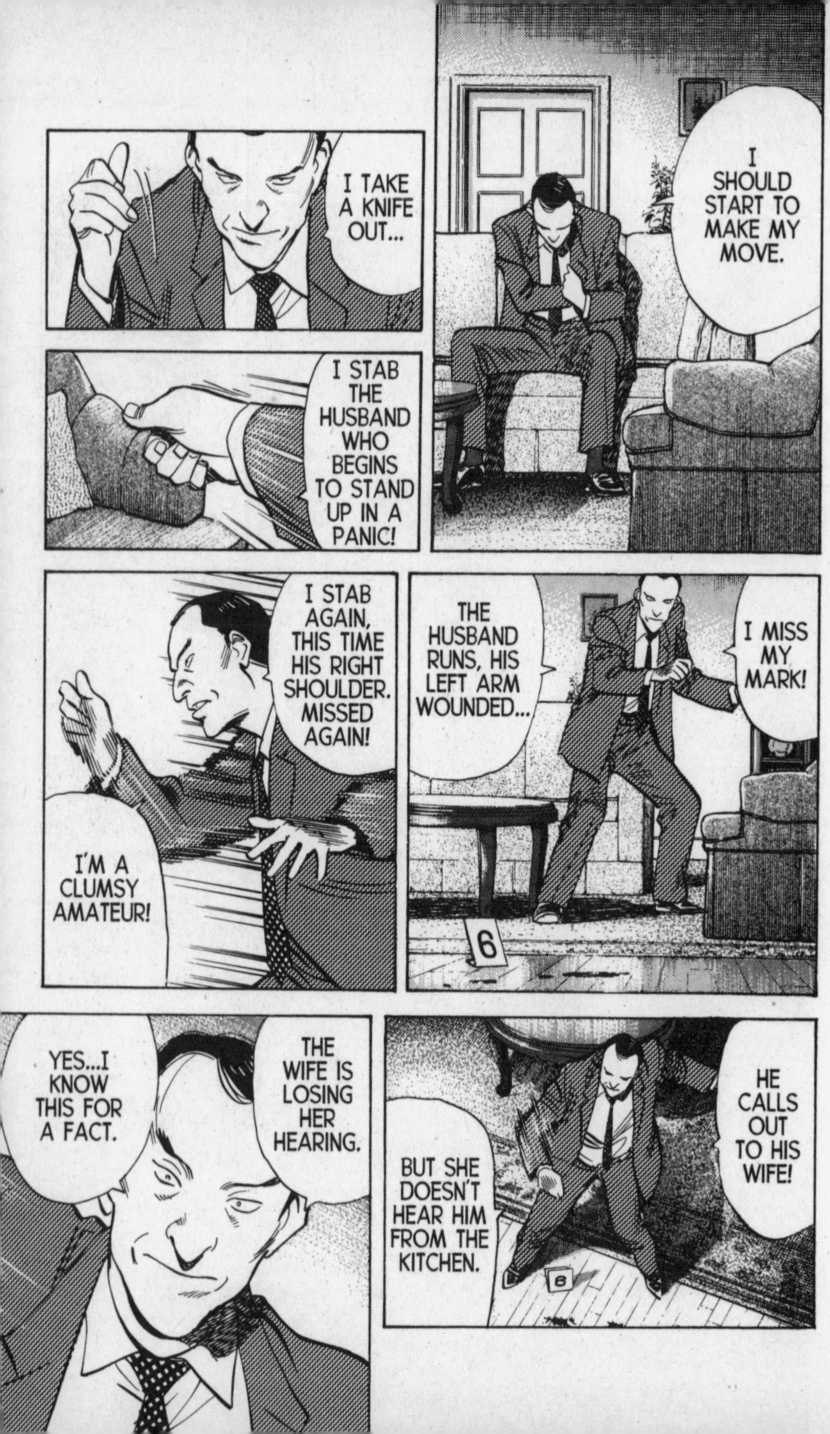
I SHOULD START TO MAKE MY MOVE.
I TAKE A KNIFE OUT...
I STAB THE HUSBAND WHO BEGINS TO STAND UP IN A PANIC!
I MISS MY MARK!
THE HUSBAND RUNS, HIS LEFT ARM WOUNDED...
6
I STAB AGAIN, THIS TIME HIS RIGHT SHOULDER. MISSED AGAIN!
I'M A CLUMSY AMATEUR!
HE CALLS OUT TO HIS WIFE!
BUT SHE DOESN'T HEAR HIM FROM THE KITCHEN.
6
THE WIFE IS LOSING HER HEARING.
YES...I KNOW THIS FOR A FACT.

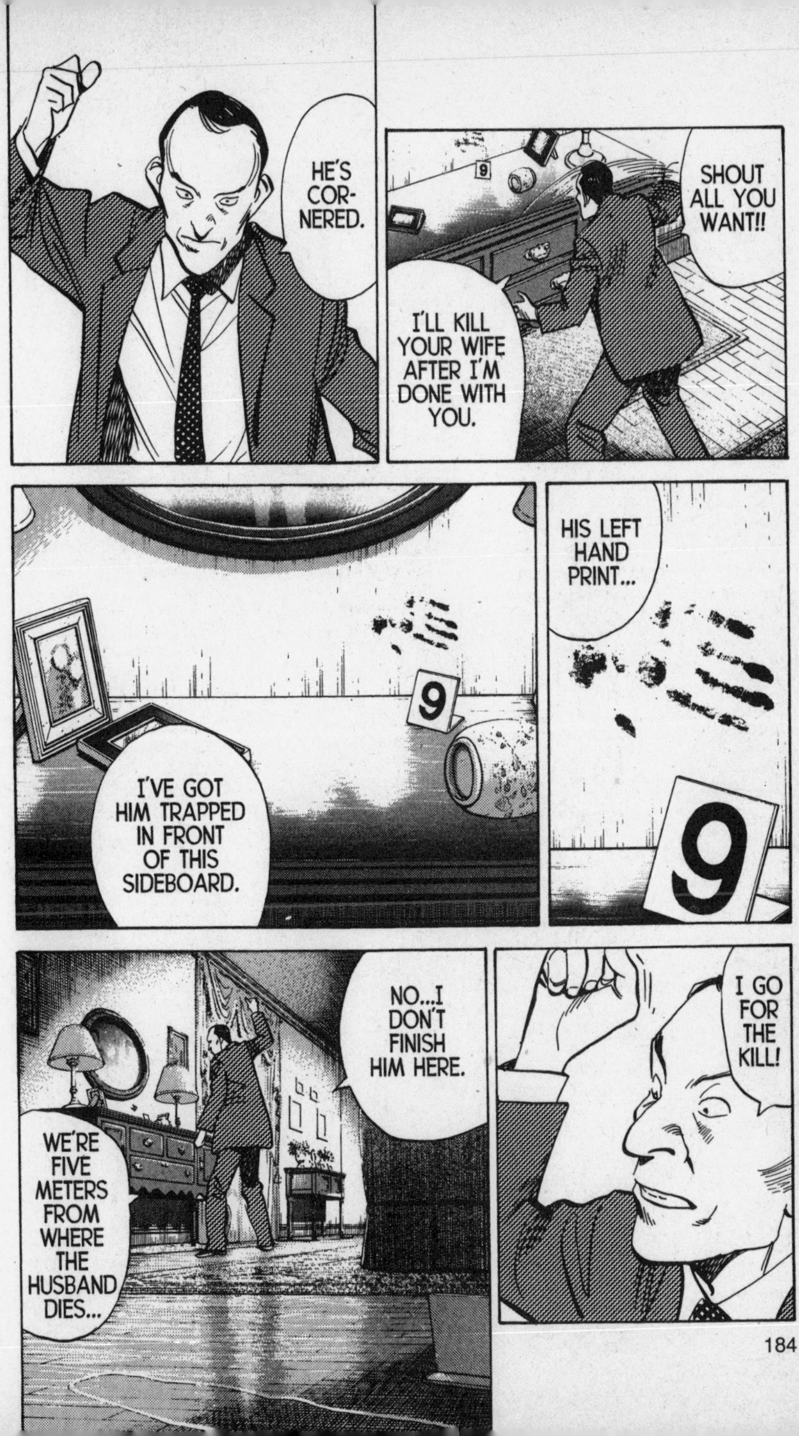
SHOUT ALL YOU WANT!!
I'LL KILL YOUR WIFE AFTER I'M DONE WITH YOU.
HE'S CORNERED.
HIS LEFT HAND PRINT...
I'VE GOT HIM TRAPPED IN FRONT OF THIS SIDEBOARD.
I GO FOR THE KILL!
NO...I DON'T FINISH HIM HERE.
WE'RE FIVE METERS FROM WHERE THE HUSBAND DIES...

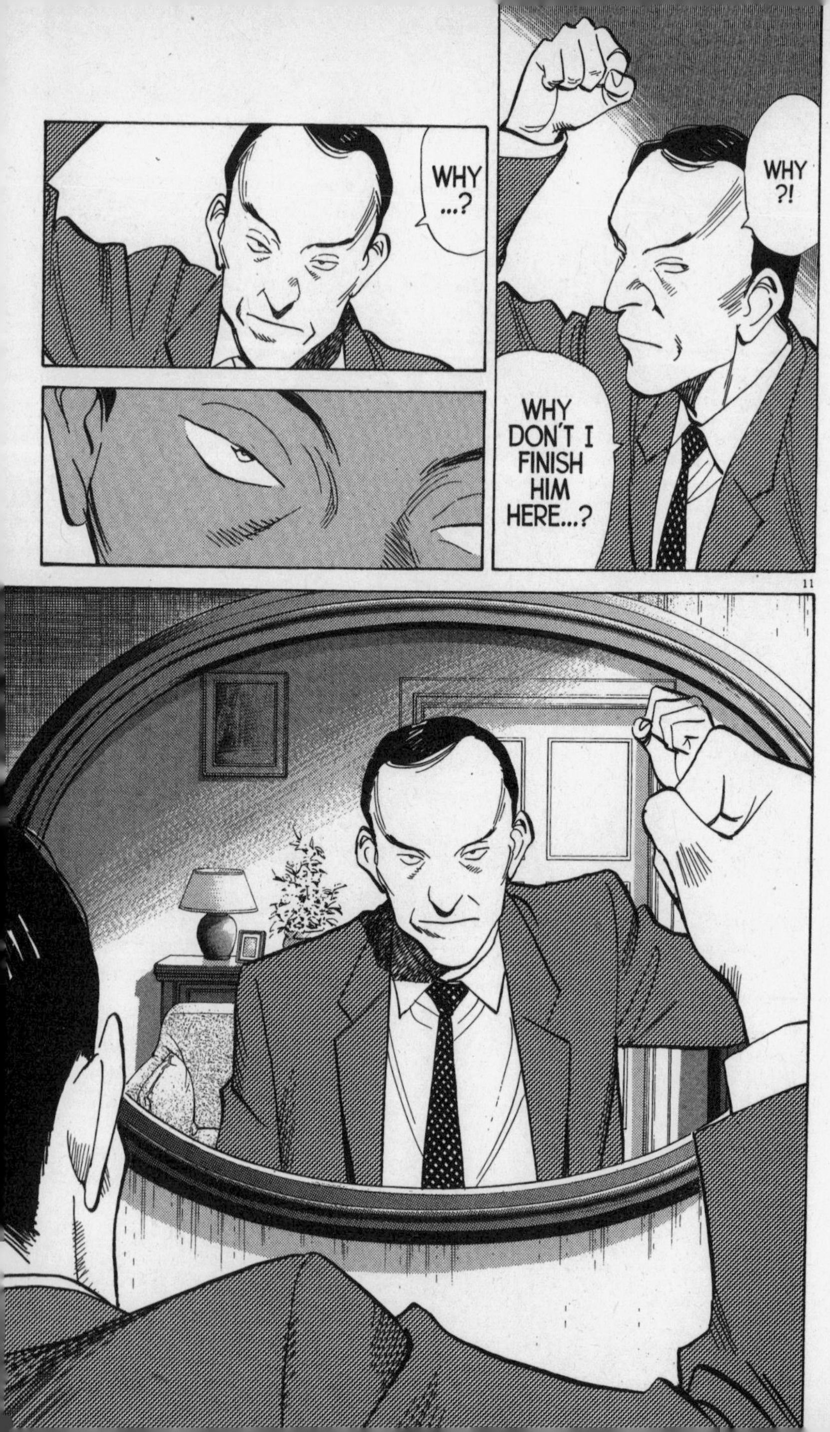
WHY ?!
WHY DON'T I FINISH HIM HERE...?
WHY ...?

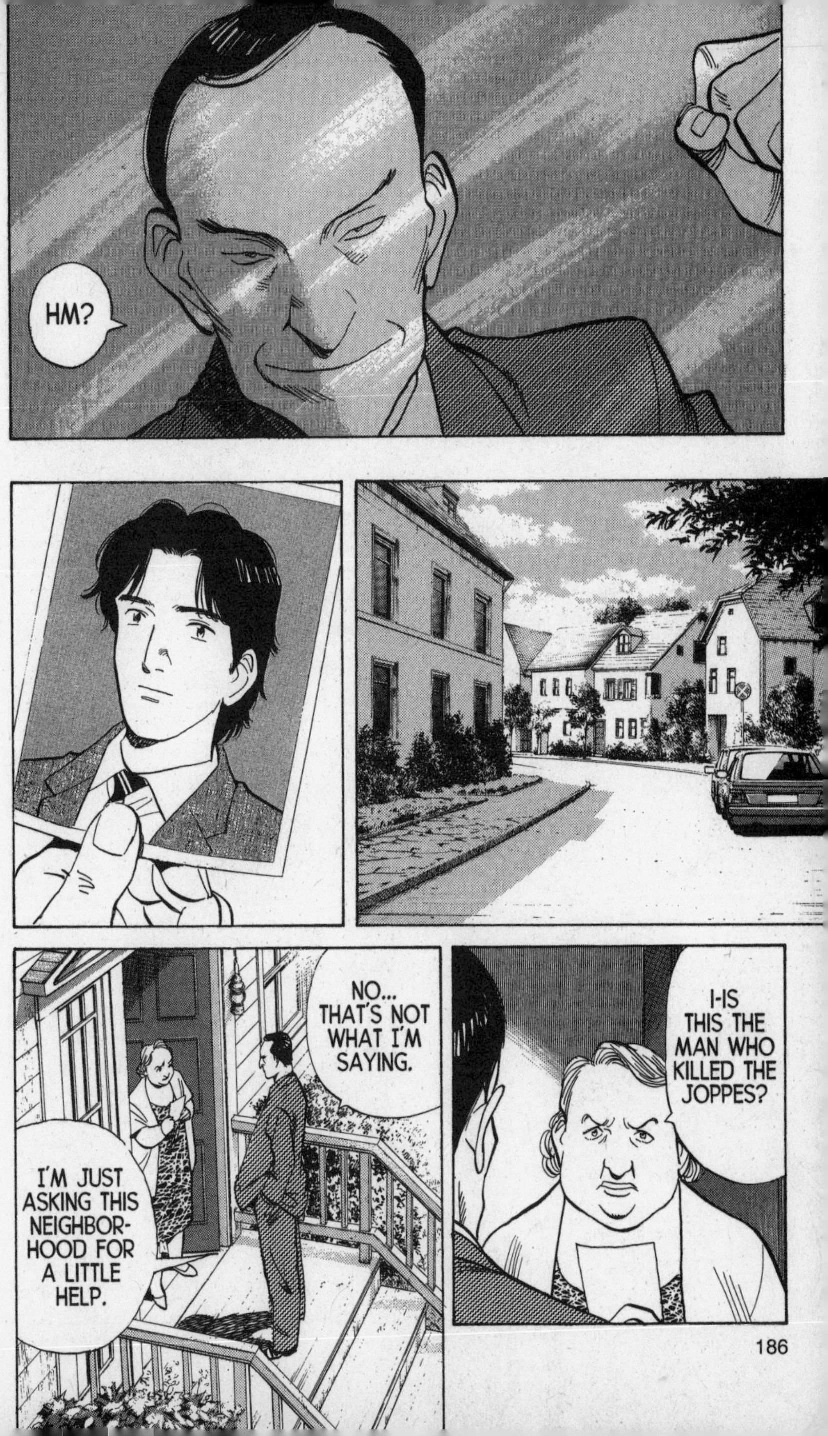
HM?
I-IS THIS THE MAN WHO KILLED THE JOPPES?
NO... THAT'S NOT WHAT I'M SAYING.
I'M JUST ASKING THIS NEIGHBOR-HOOD FOR A LITTLE HELP.

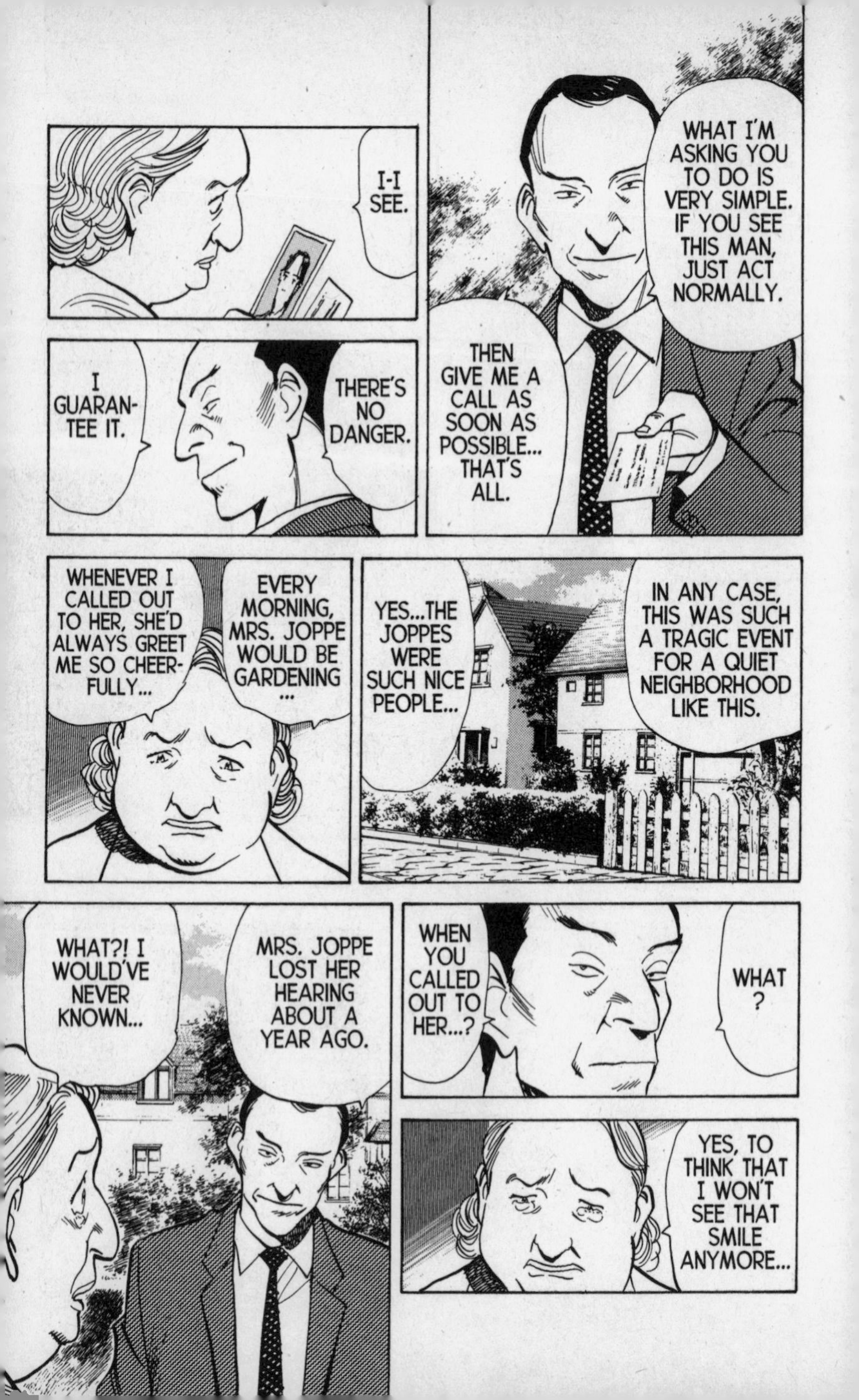
WHAT I'M ASKING YOU TO DO IS VERY SIMPLE. IF YOU SEE THIS MAN, JUST ACT NORMALLY.
THEN GIVE ME A CALL AS SOON AS POSSIBLE... THAT'S ALL.
I-I SEE.
THERE'S NO DANGER.
I GUARANTEE IT.
IN ANY CASE, THIS WAS SUCH A TRAGIC EVENT FOR A QUIET NEIGHBORHOOD LIKE THIS.
YES...THE JOPPES WERE SUCH NICE PEOPLE...
EVERY MORNING, MRS. JOPPE WOULD BE GARDENING ...
WHENEVER I CALLED OUT TO HER, SHE'D ALWAYS GREET ME SO CHEERFULLY...
WHAT ?
WHEN YOU CALLED OUT TO HER...?
YES, TO THINK THAT I WON'T SEE THAT SMILE ANYMORE...
MRS. JOPPE LOST HER HEARING ABOUT A YEAR AGO.
WHAT?! I WOULD'VE NEVER KNOWN...

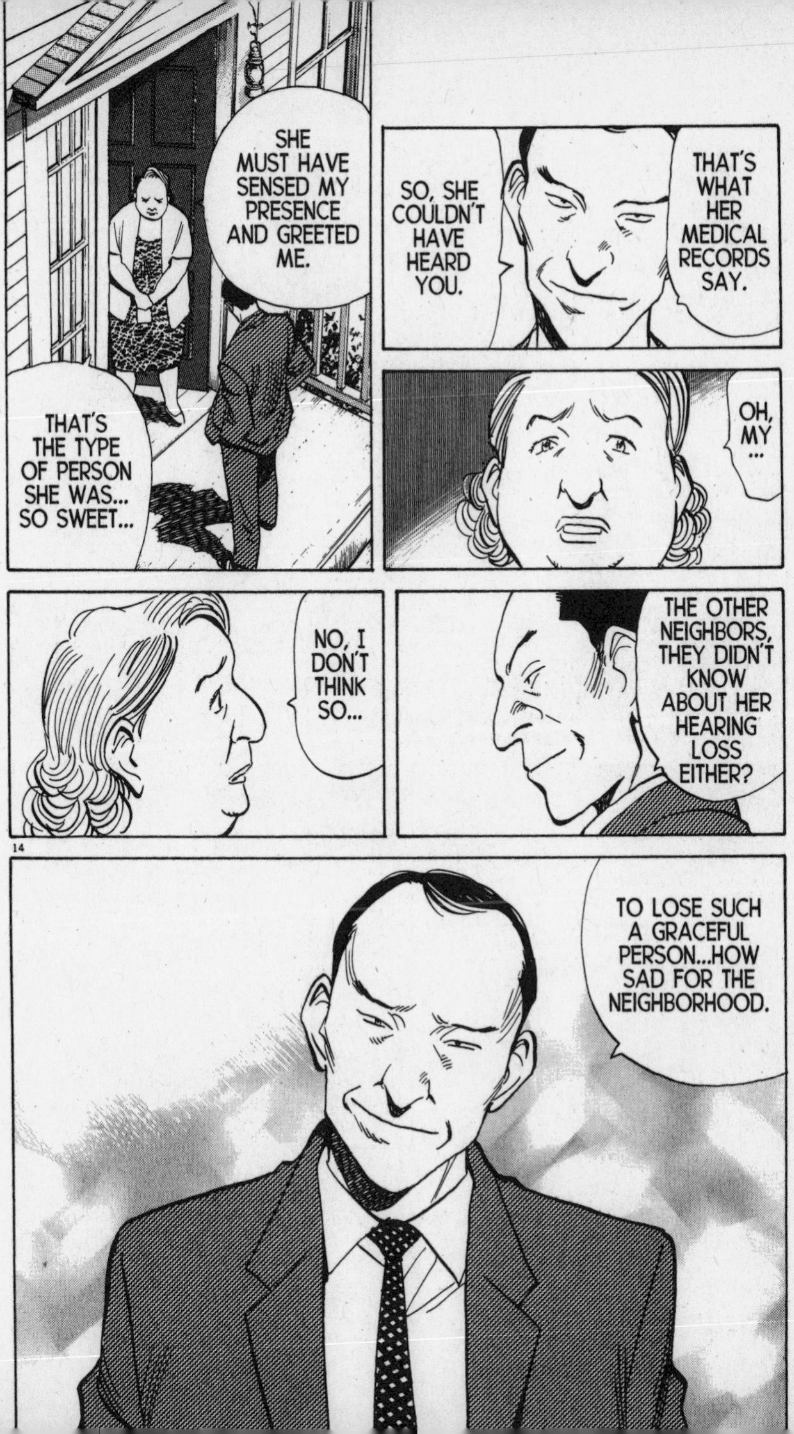
THAT'S WHAT HER MEDICAL RECORDS SAY.
SO, SHE COULDN'T HAVE HEARD YOU.
OH, MY...
SHE MUST HAVE SENSED MY PRESENCE AND GREETED ME.
THAT'S THE TYPE OF PERSON SHE WAS... SO SWEET...
THE OTHER NEIGHBORS, THEY DIDN'T KNOW ABOUT HER HEARING LOSS EITHER?
NO, I DON'T THINK SO...
TO LOSE SUCH A GRACEFUL PERSON...HOW SAD FOR THE NEIGHBORHOOD.

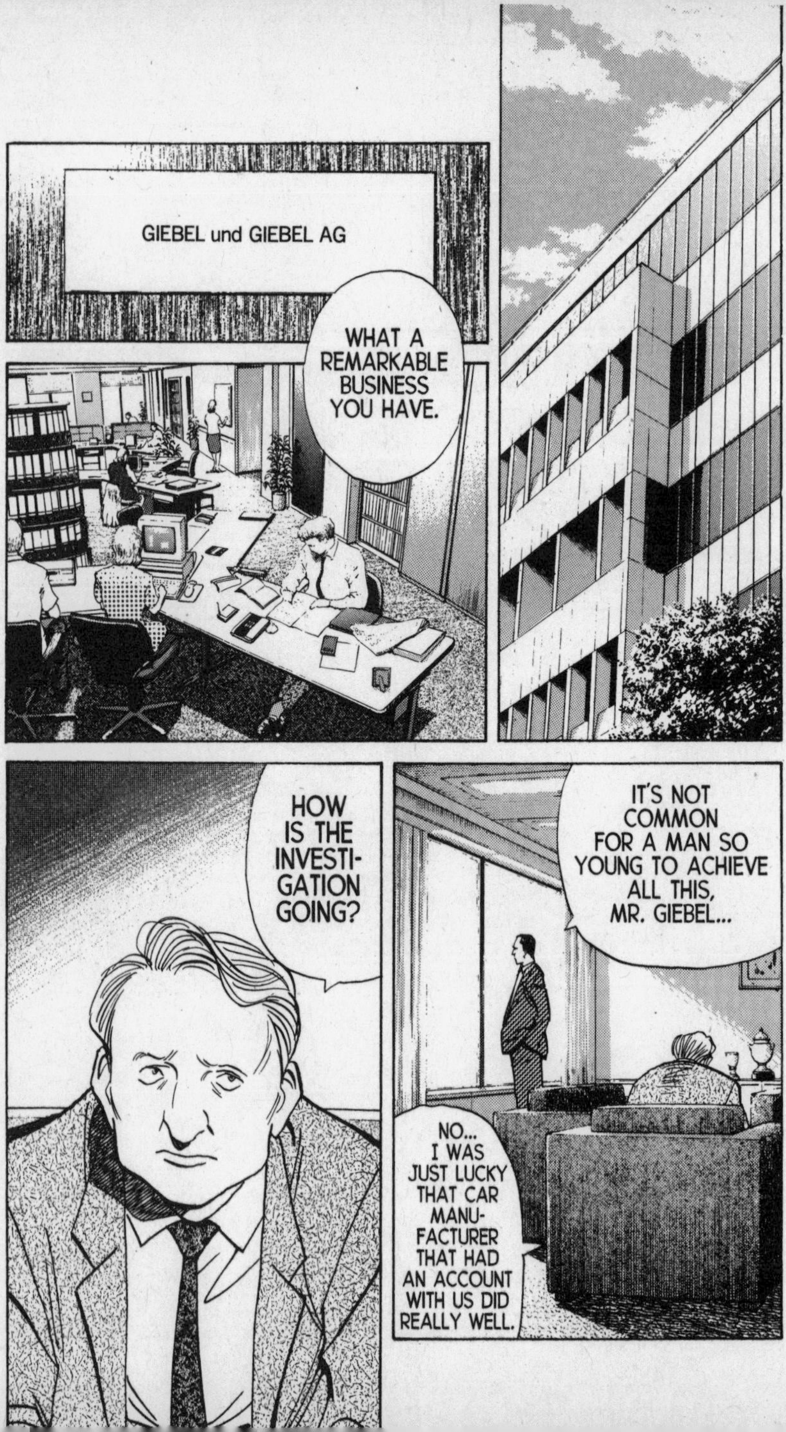
GIEBEL und GIEBEL AG
WHAT A REMARKABLE BUSINESS YOU HAVE.
IT'S NOT COMMON FOR A MAN SO YOUNG TO ACHIEVE ALL THIS, MR. GIEBEL...
NO... I WAS JUST LUCKY THAT CAR MANU-FACTURER THAT HAD AN ACCOUNT WITH US DID REALLY WELL.
HOW IS THE INVESTI-GATION GOING?

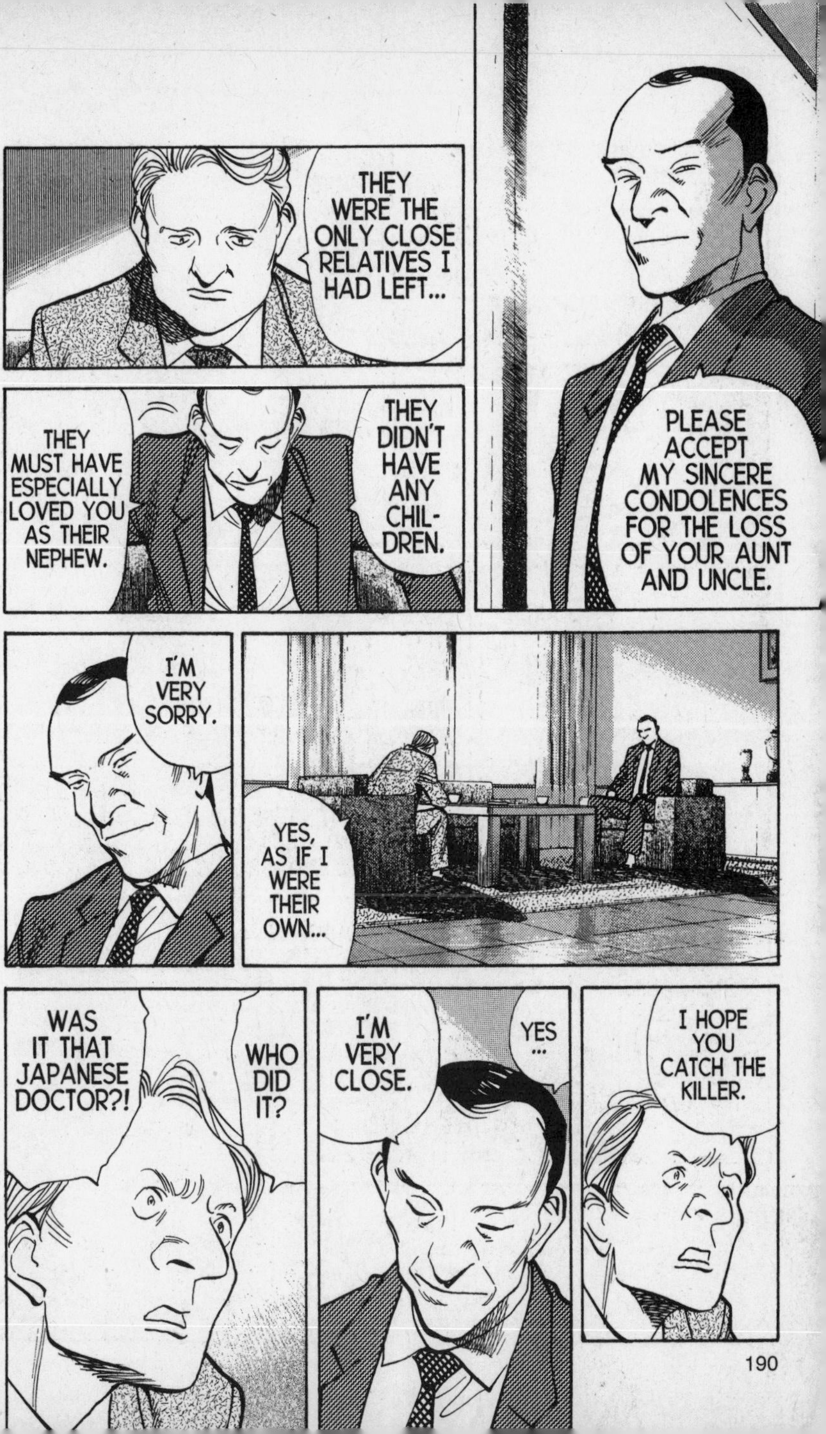
PLEASE ACCEPT MY SINCERE CONDOLENCES FOR THE LOSS OF YOUR AUNT AND UNCLE.
THEY WERE THE ONLY CLOSE RELATIVES I HAD LEFT...
THEY DIDN'T HAVE ANY CHIL-DREN.
THEY MUST HAVE ESPECIALLY LOVED YOU AS THEIR NEPHEW.
YES, AS IF I WERE THEIR OWN...
I'M VERY SORRY.
I HOPE YOU CATCH THE KILLER.
YES ...
I'M VERY CLOSE.
WHO DID IT?
WAS IT THAT JAPANESE DOCTOR?!

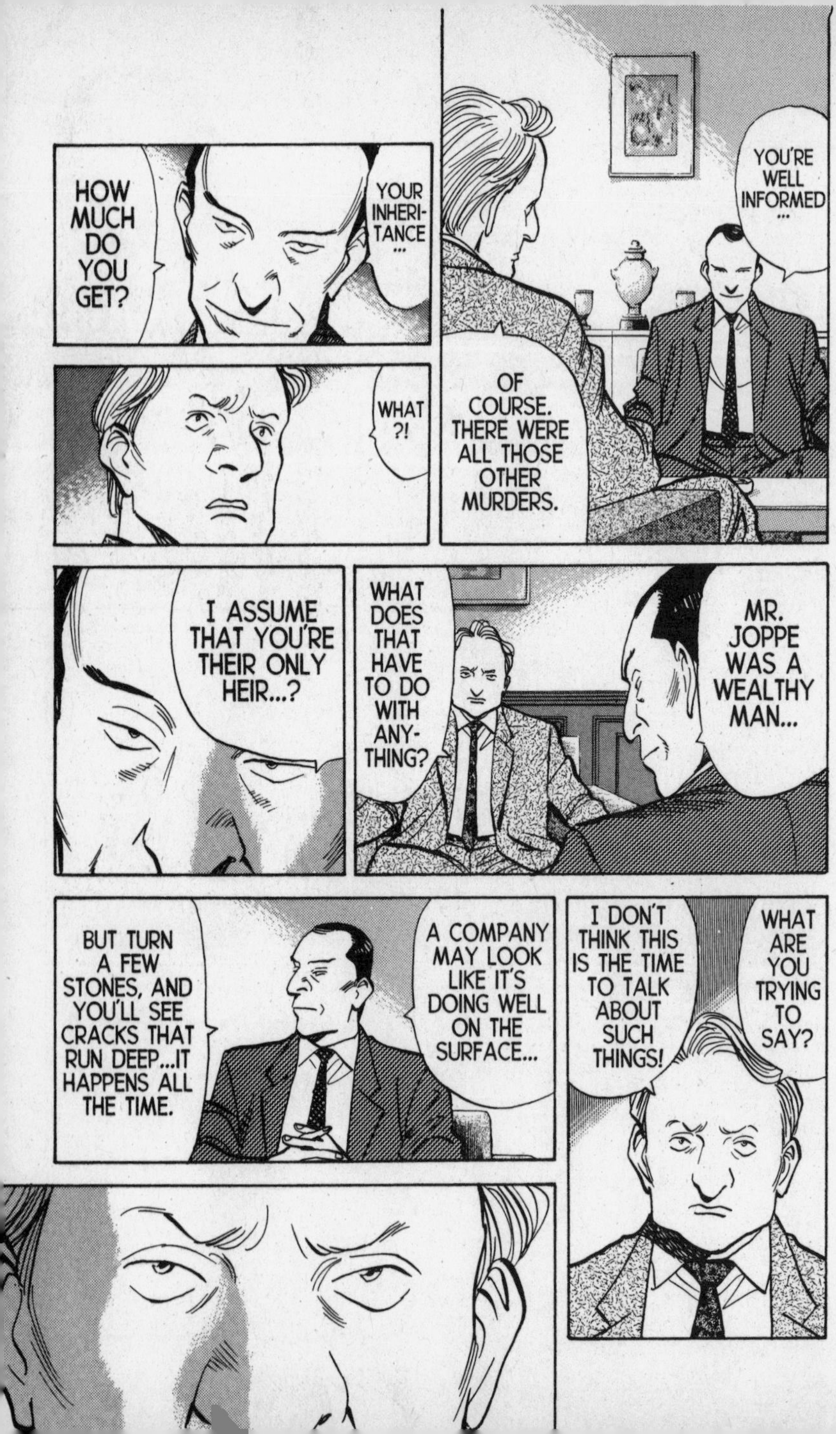
YOU'RE WELL INFORMED...
OF COURSE. THERE WERE ALL THOSE OTHER MURDERS.
YOUR INHERITANCE...
HOW MUCH DO YOU GET?
WHAT?!
MR. JOPPE WAS A WEALTHY MAN...
WHAT DOES THAT HAVE TO DO WITH ANYTHING?
I ASSUME THAT YOU'RE THEIR ONLY HEIR...?
WHAT ARE YOU TRYING TO SAY?
I DON'T THINK THIS IS THE TIME TO TALK ABOUT SUCH THINGS!
A COMPANY MAY LOOK LIKE IT'S DOING WELL ON THE SURFACE...
BUT TURN A FEW STONES, AND YOU'LL SEE CRACKS THAT RUN DEEP...IT HAPPENS ALL THE TIME.

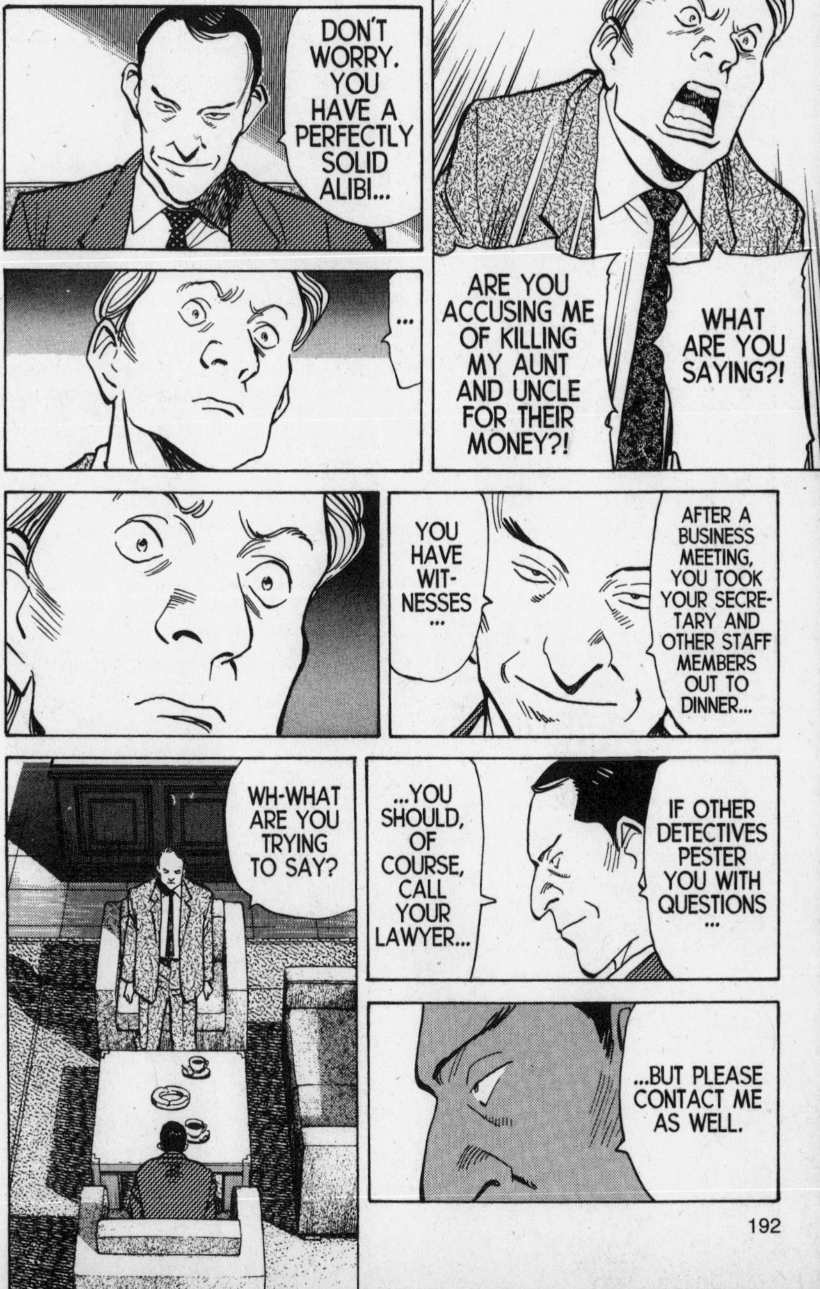
WHAT ARE YOU SAYING?!
ARE YOU ACCUSING ME OF KILLING MY AUNT AND UNCLE FOR THEIR MONEY?!
DON'T WORRY. YOU HAVE A PERFECTLY SOLID ALIBI...
...
AFTER A BUSINESS MEETING, YOU TOOK YOUR SECRETARY AND OTHER STAFF MEMBERS OUT TO DINNER...
YOU HAVE WITNESSES...
IF OTHER DETECTIVES PESTER YOU WITH QUESTIONS...
...YOU SHOULD, OF COURSE, CALL YOUR LAWYER...
...BUT PLEASE CONTACT ME AS WELL.
WH-WHAT ARE YOU TRYING TO SAY?

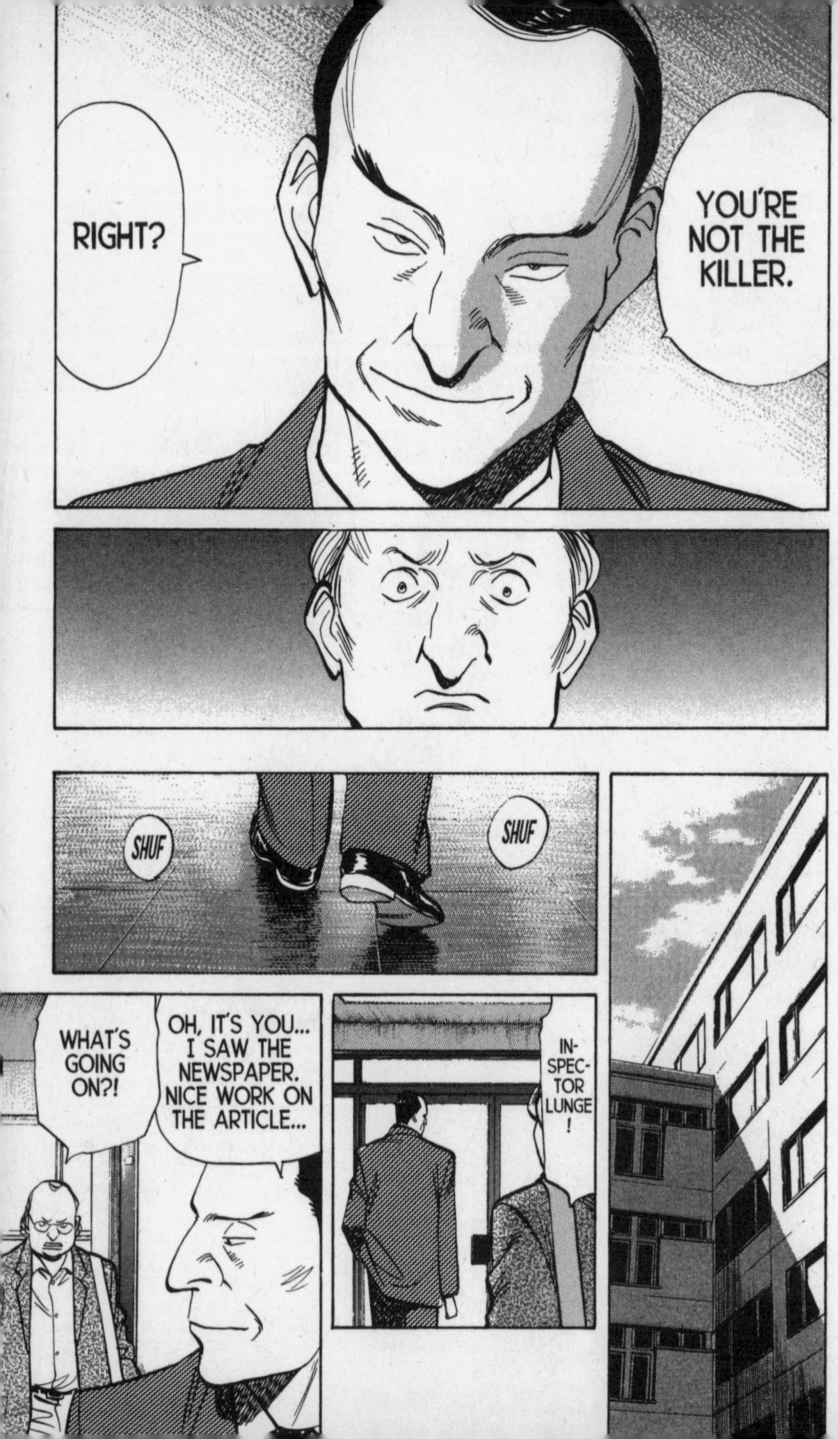
YOU'RE NOT THE KILLER.
RIGHT?
SHUF
SHUF
IN-SPEC-TOR LUNGE!
OH, IT'S YOU... I SAW THE NEWSPAPER. NICE WORK ON THE ARTICLE...
WHAT'S GOING ON?!

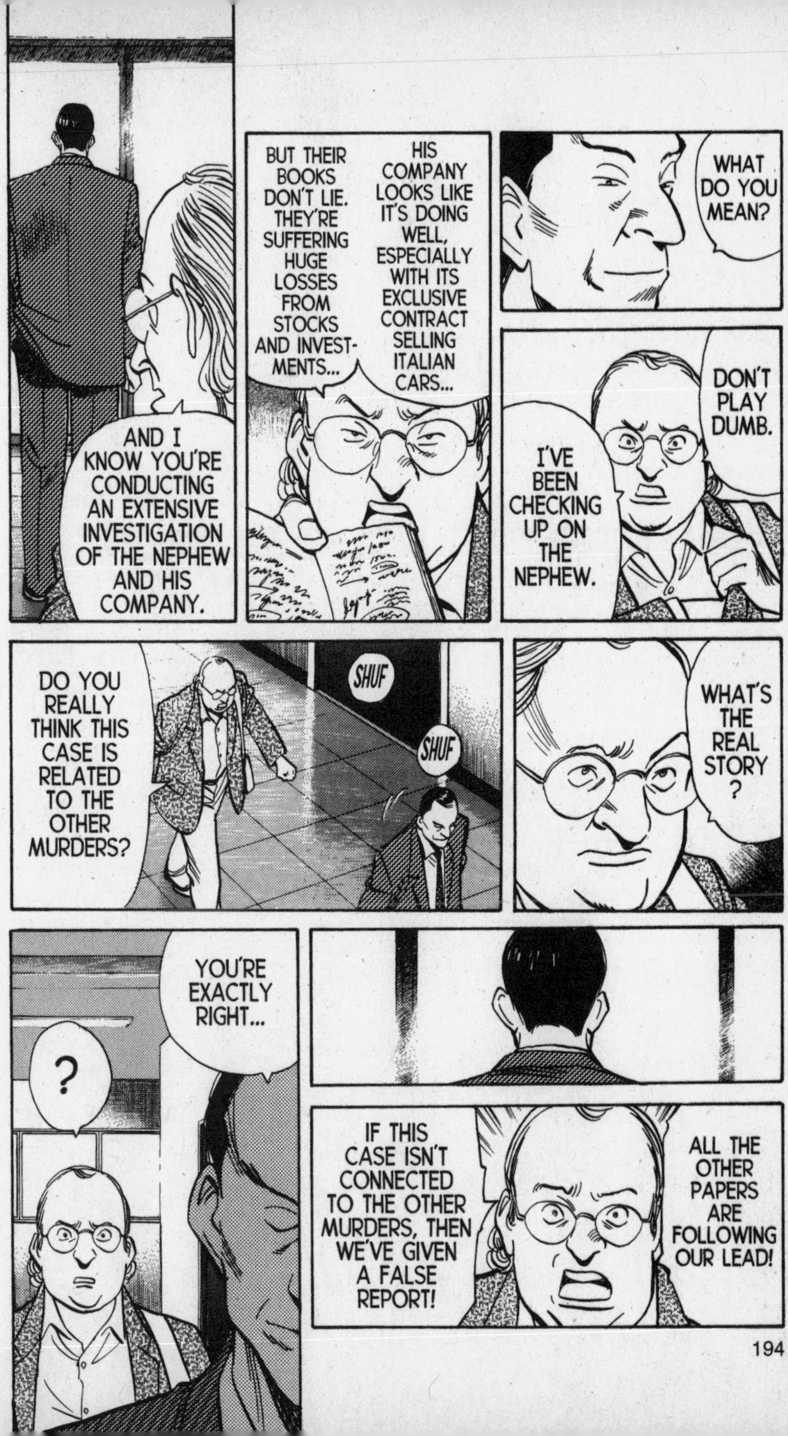
WHAT DO YOU MEAN?
DON'T PLAY DUMB.
I'VE BEEN CHECKING UP ON THE NEPHEW.
HIS COMPANY LOOKS LIKE IT'S DOING WELL, ESPECIALLY WITH ITS EXCLUSIVE CONTRACT SELLING ITALIAN CARS...
BUT THEIR BOOKS DON'T LIE. THEY'RE SUFFERING HUGE LOSSES FROM STOCKS AND INVEST-MENTS...
AND I KNOW YOU'RE CONDUCTING AN EXTENSIVE INVESTIGATION OF THE NEPHEW AND HIS COMPANY.
WHAT'S THE REAL STORY ?
SHUF
SHUF
DO YOU REALLY THINK THIS CASE IS RELATED TO THE OTHER MURDERS?
ALL THE OTHER PAPERS ARE FOLLOWING OUR LEAD!
IF THIS CASE ISN'T CONNECTED TO THE OTHER MURDERS, THEN WE'VE GIVEN A FALSE REPORT!
YOU'RE EXACTLY RIGHT...
?

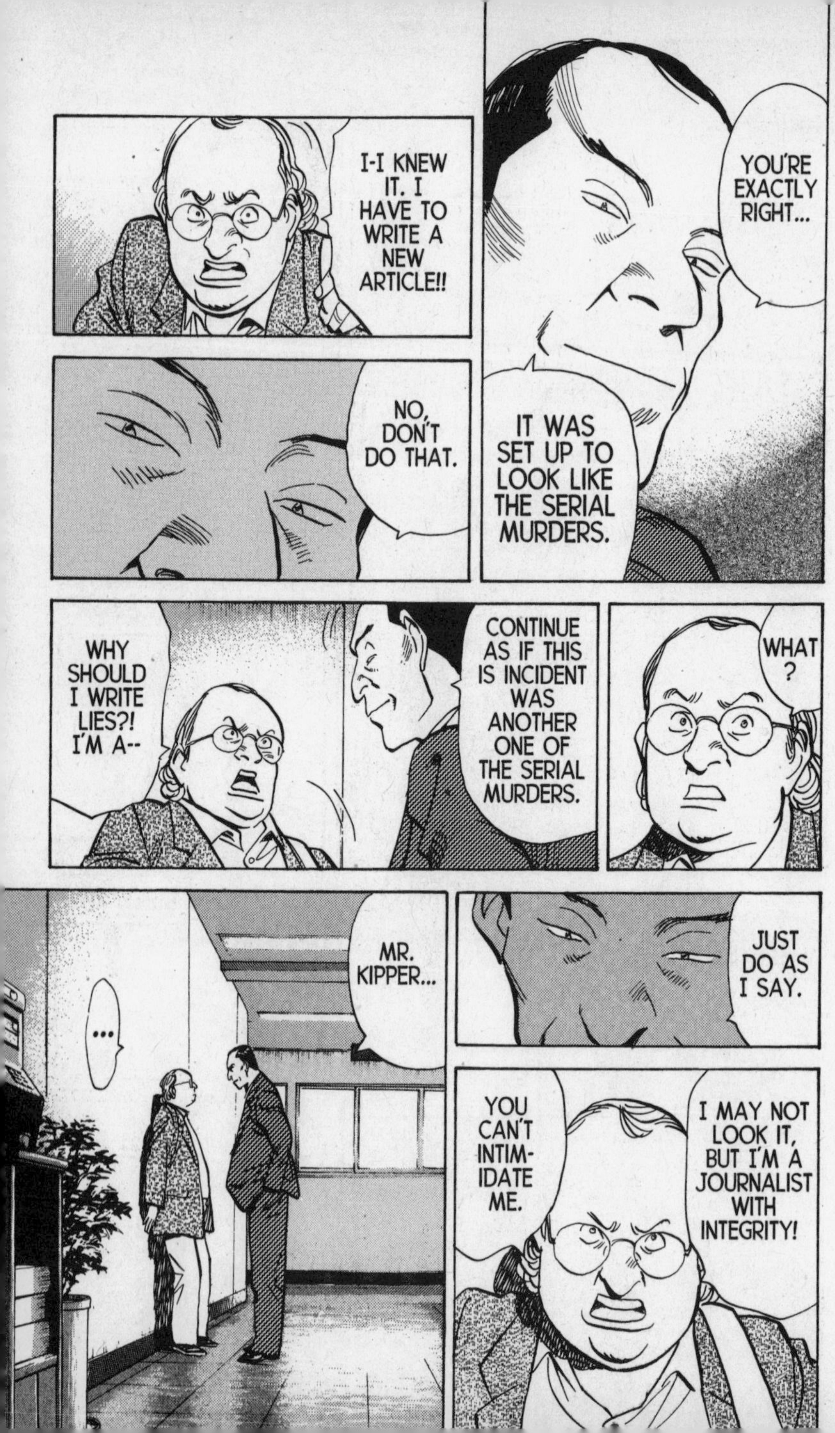
YOU'RE EXACTLY RIGHT...
IT WAS SET UP TO LOOK LIKE THE SERIAL MURDERS.
I-I KNEW IT. I HAVE TO WRITE A NEW ARTICLE!!
NO, DON'T DO THAT.
WHAT?
CONTINUE AS IF THIS IS INCIDENT WAS ANOTHER ONE OF THE SERIAL MURDERS.
WHY SHOULD I WRITE LIES?! I'M A--
JUST DO AS I SAY.
I MAY NOT LOOK IT, BUT I'M A JOURNALIST WITH INTEGRITY!
YOU CAN'T INTIMIDATE ME.
MR. KIPPER...
...

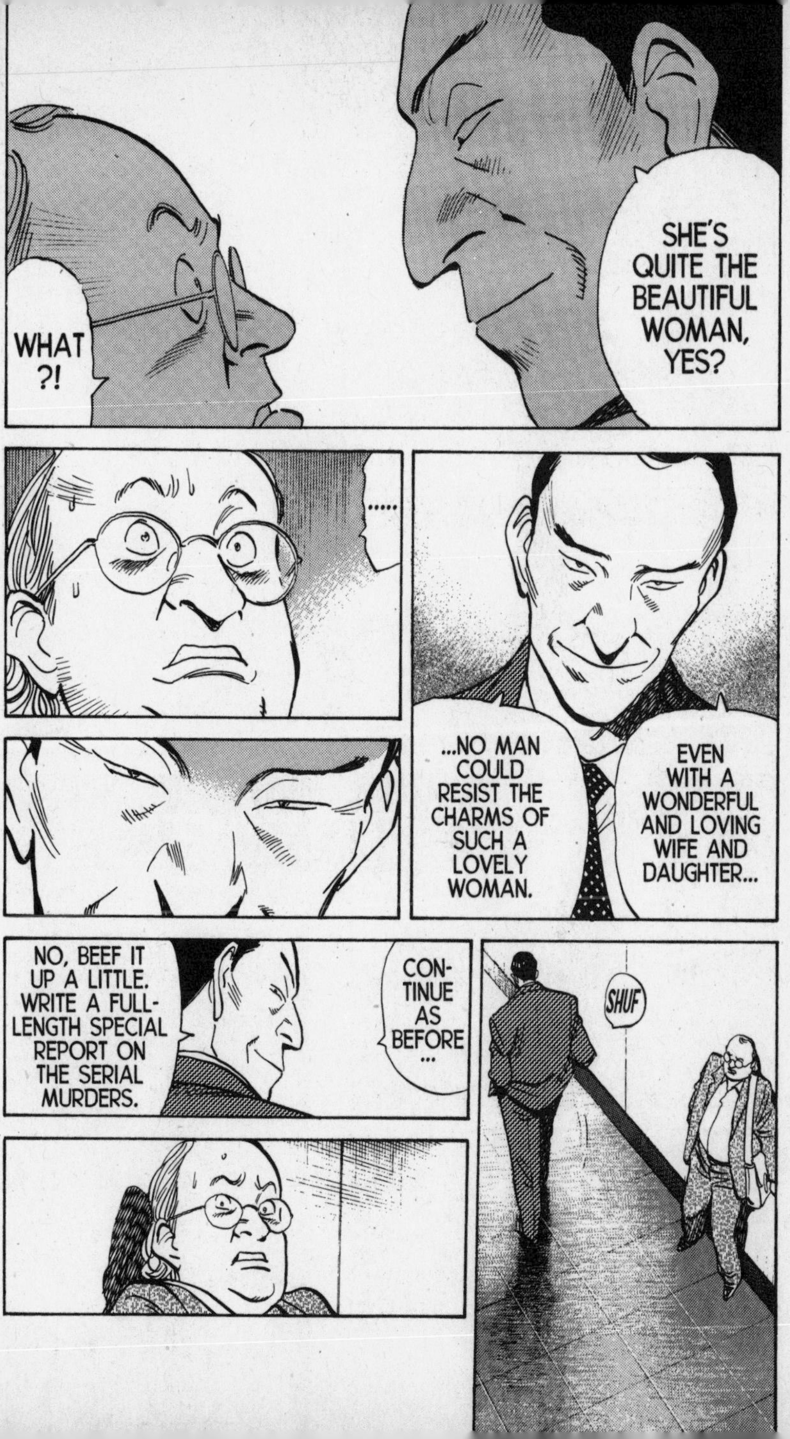
SHE'S QUITE THE BEAUTIFUL WOMAN, YES?
WHAT?!
EVEN WITH A WONDERFUL AND LOVING WIFE AND DAUGHTER...
...NO MAN COULD RESIST THE CHARMS OF SUCH A LOVELY WOMAN.
......
SHUF
CON-TINUE AS BEFORE ...
NO, BEEF IT UP A LITTLE. WRITE A FULL-LENGTH SPECIAL REPORT ON THE SERIAL MURDERS.

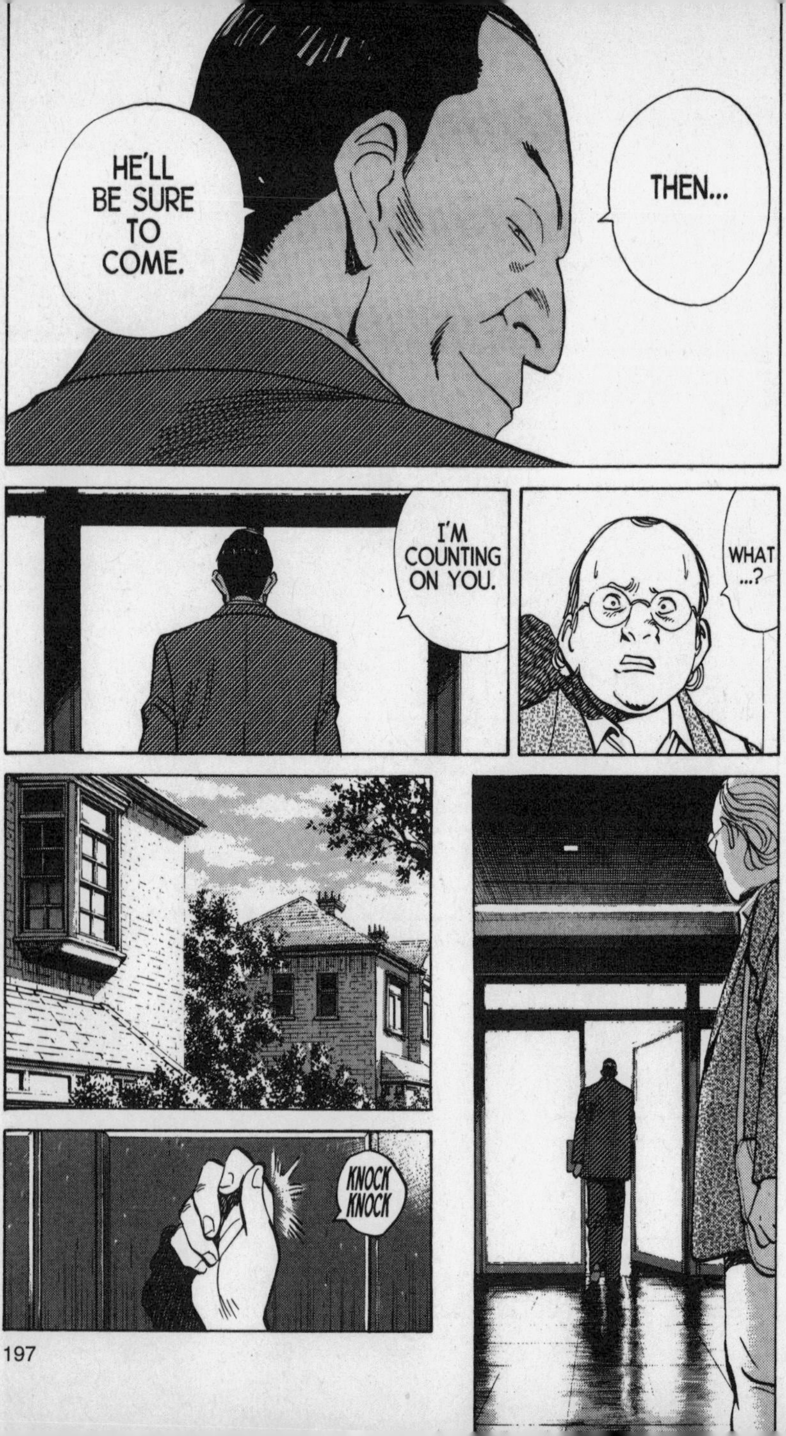
THEN...
HE'LL BE SURE TO COME.
WHAT ...?
I'M COUNTING ON YOU.
KNOCK KNOCK

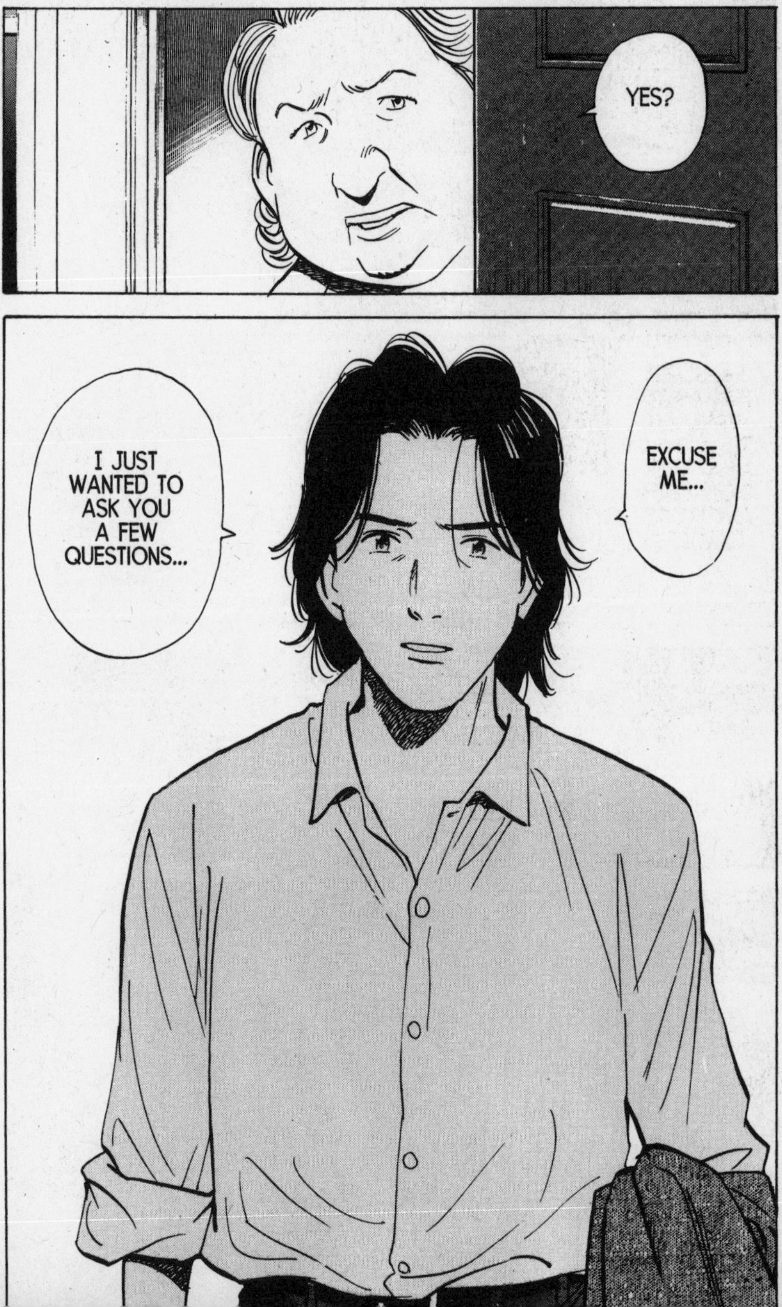
YES?
EXCUSE ME...
I JUST WANTED TO ASK YOU A FEW QUESTIONS...

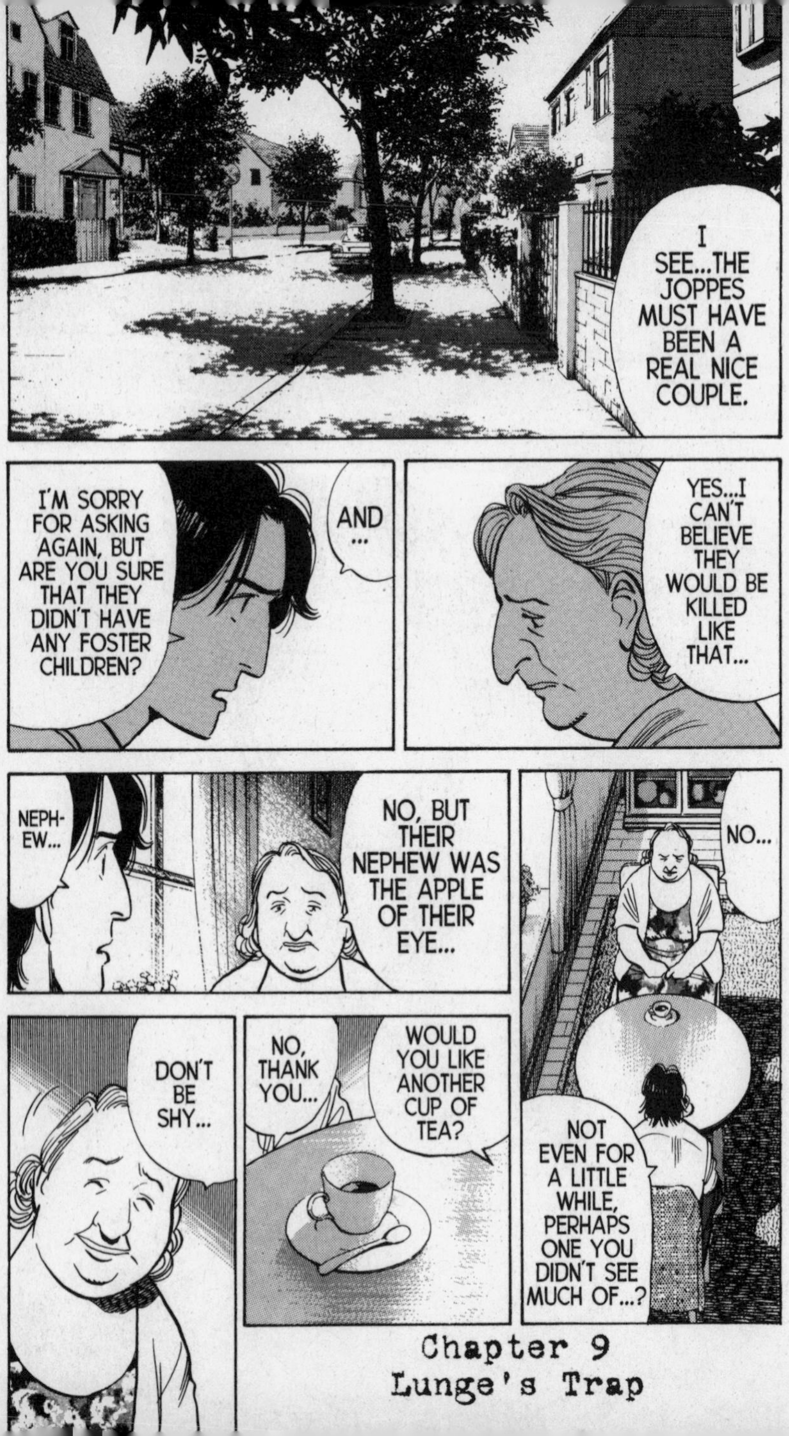
I SEE...THE JOPPES MUST HAVE BEEN A REAL NICE COUPLE.
YES...I CAN'T BELIEVE THEY WOULD BE KILLED LIKE THAT...
AND ...
I'M SORRY FOR ASKING AGAIN, BUT ARE YOU SURE THAT THEY DIDN'T HAVE ANY FOSTER CHILDREN?
NO...
NOT EVEN FOR A LITTLE WHILE, PERHAPS ONE YOU DIDN'T SEE MUCH OF...?
NO, BUT THEIR NEPHEW WAS THE APPLE OF THEIR EYE...
NEPH-EW...
WOULD YOU LIKE ANOTHER CUP OF TEA?
NO, THANK YOU...
DON'T BE SHY...

Chapter 9
Lunge's Trap

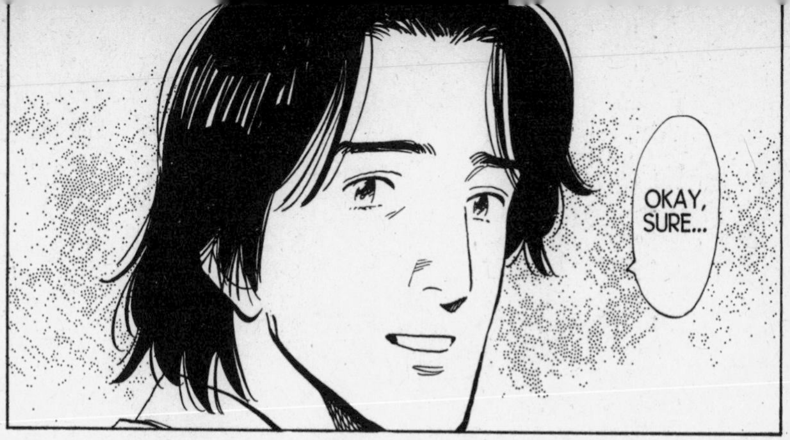
OKAY, SURE...

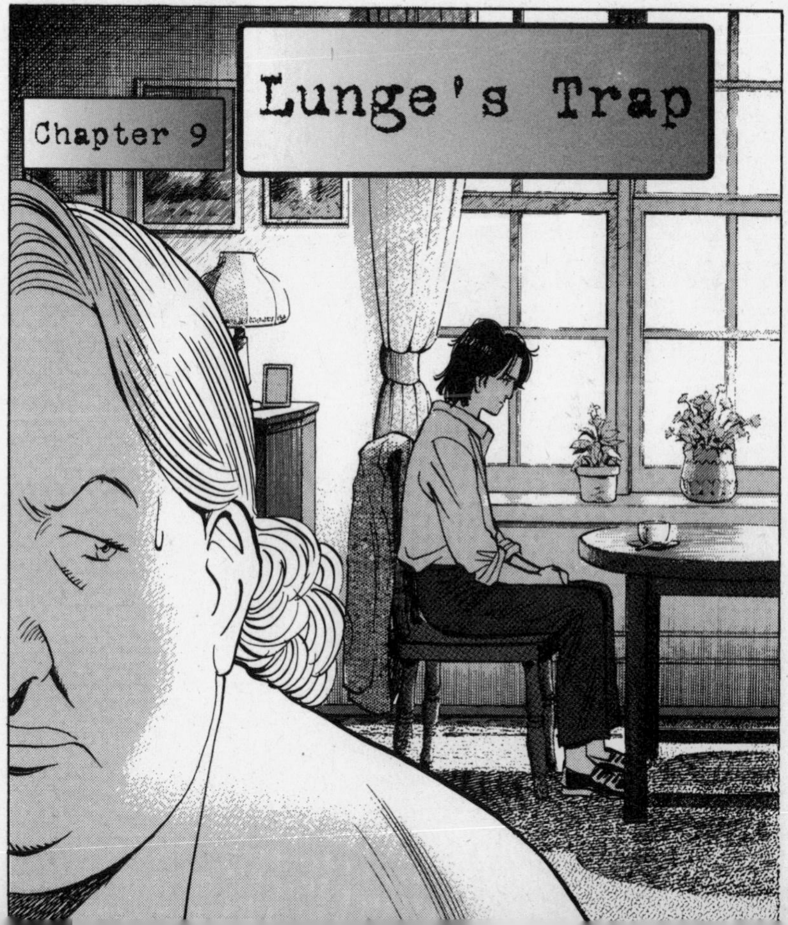
Chapter 9
Lunge's Trap

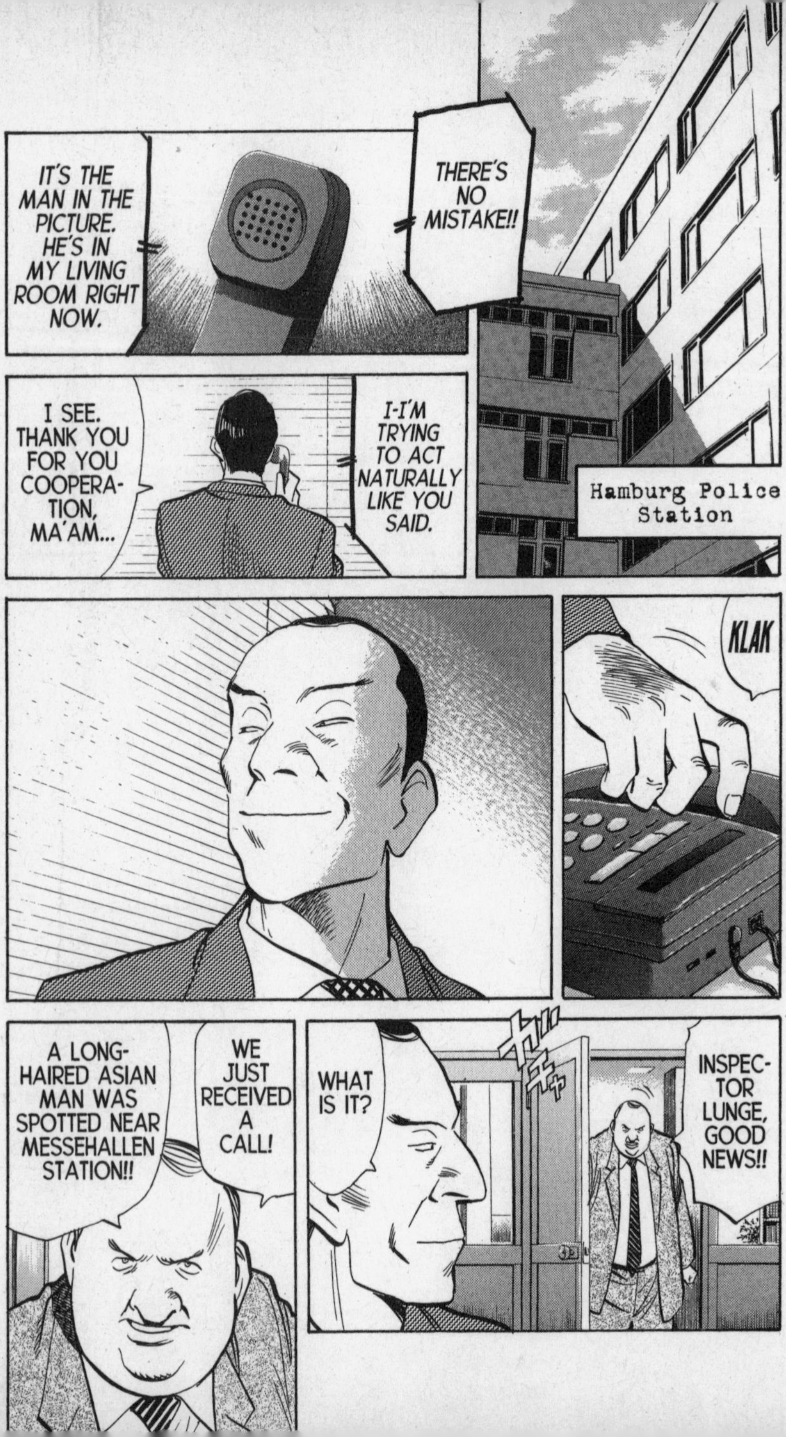
THERE'S NO MISTAKE!!
Hamburg Police Station
IT'S THE MAN IN THE PICTURE. HE'S IN MY LIVING ROOM RIGHT NOW.
I-I'M TRYING TO ACT NATURALLY LIKE YOU SAID.
I SEE. THANK YOU FOR YOU COOPERATION, MA'AM...
KLAK
INSPECTOR LUNGE, GOOD NEWS!!
ガチャ
WHAT IS IT?
WE JUST RECEIVED A CALL!
A LONG-HAIRED ASIAN MAN WAS SPOTTED NEAR MESSEHALLEN STATION!!

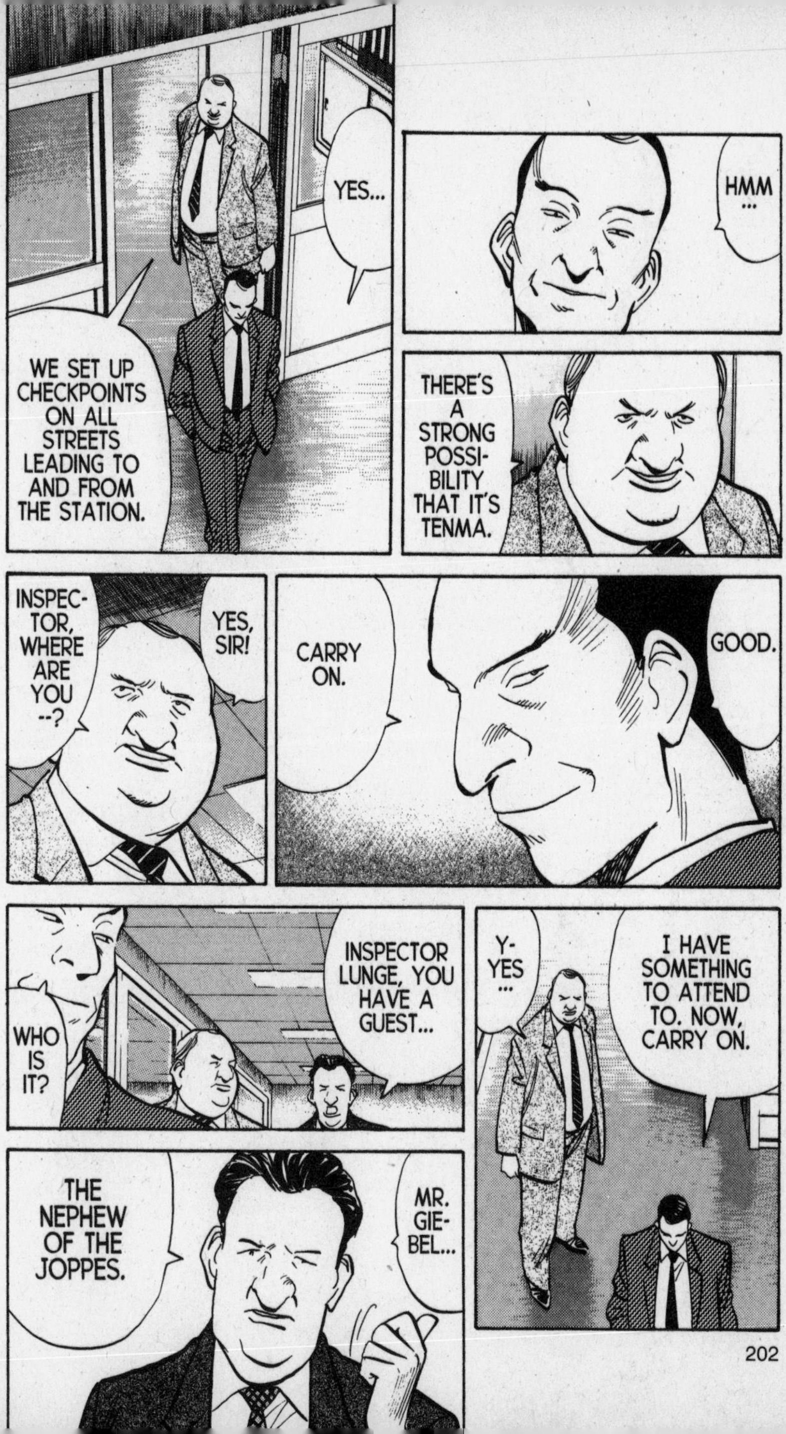
HMM...
THERE'S A STRONG POSSIBILITY THAT IT'S TENMA.
YES...
WE SET UP CHECKPOINTS ON ALL STREETS LEADING TO AND FROM THE STATION.
GOOD.
CARRY ON.
YES, SIR!
INSPECTOR, WHERE ARE YOU --?
I HAVE SOMETHING TO ATTEND TO. NOW, CARRY ON.
Y-YES...
INSPECTOR LUNGE, YOU HAVE A GUEST...
WHO IS IT?
MR. GIEBEL...
THE NEPHEW OF THE JOPPES.

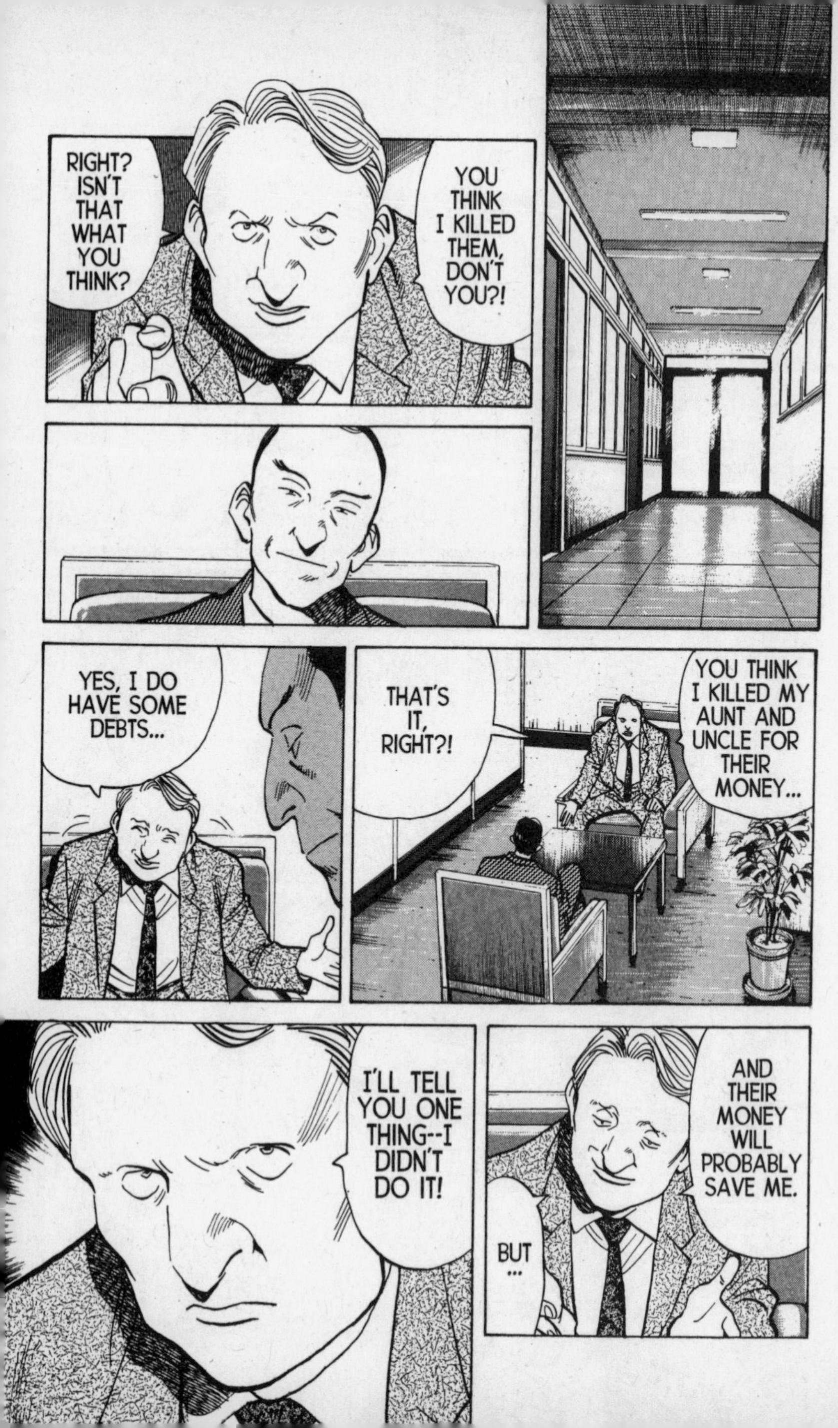
YOU THINK I KILLED THEM, DON'T YOU?!
RIGHT? ISN'T THAT WHAT YOU THINK?
YOU THINK I KILLED MY AUNT AND UNCLE FOR THEIR MONEY...
THAT'S IT, RIGHT?!
YES, I DO HAVE SOME DEBTS...
AND THEIR MONEY WILL PROBABLY SAVE ME.
BUT ...
I'LL TELL YOU ONE THING--I DIDN'T DO IT!

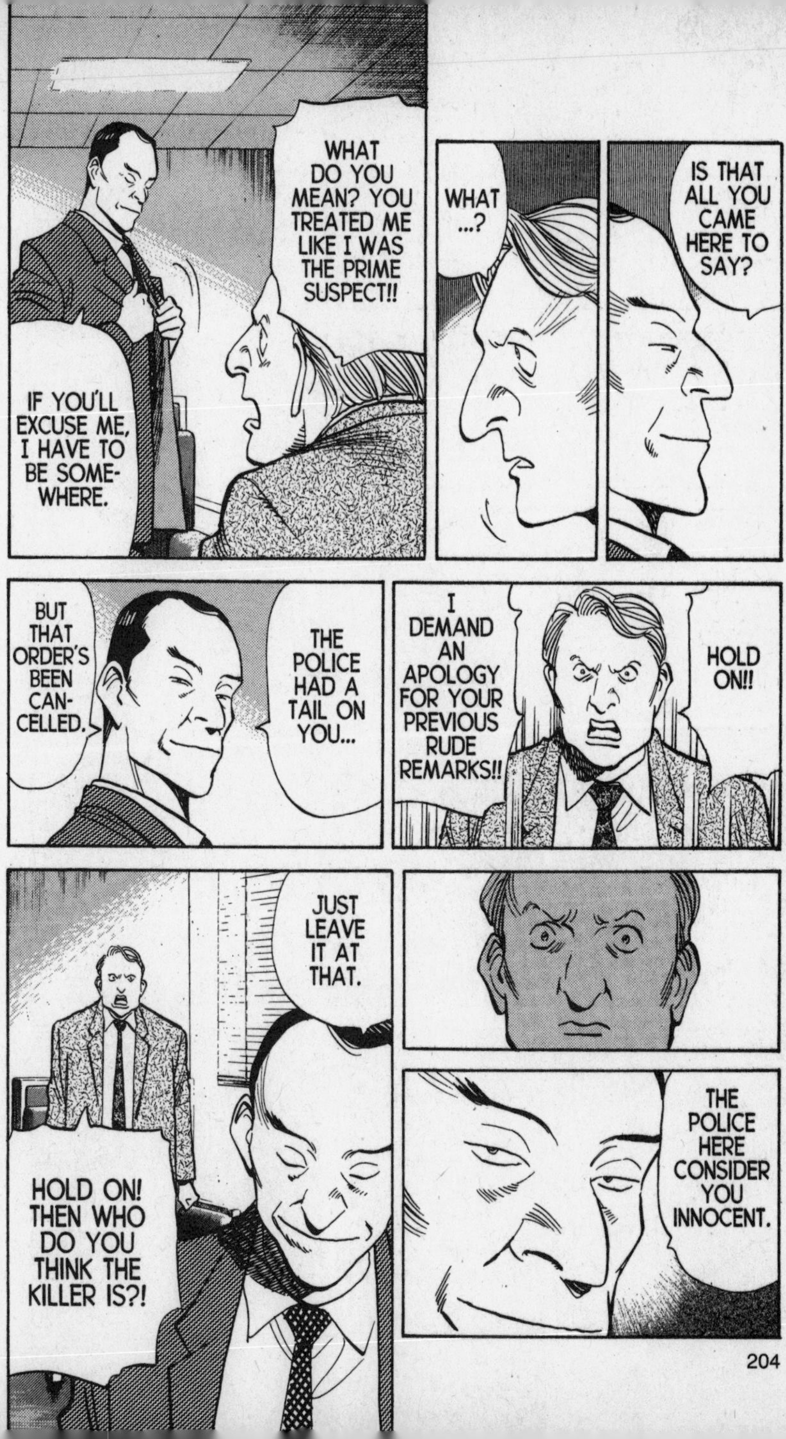
IS THAT ALL YOU CAME HERE TO SAY?
WHAT ...?
WHAT DO YOU MEAN? YOU TREATED ME LIKE I WAS THE PRIME SUSPECT!!
IF YOU'LL EXCUSE ME, I HAVE TO BE SOME-WHERE.
HOLD ON!!
I DEMAND AN APOLOGY FOR YOUR PREVIOUS RUDE REMARKS!!
THE POLICE HAD A TAIL ON YOU...
BUT THAT ORDER'S BEEN CAN-CELLED.
THE POLICE HERE CONSIDER YOU INNOCENT.
JUST LEAVE IT AT THAT.
HOLD ON! THEN WHO DO YOU THINK THE KILLER IS?!

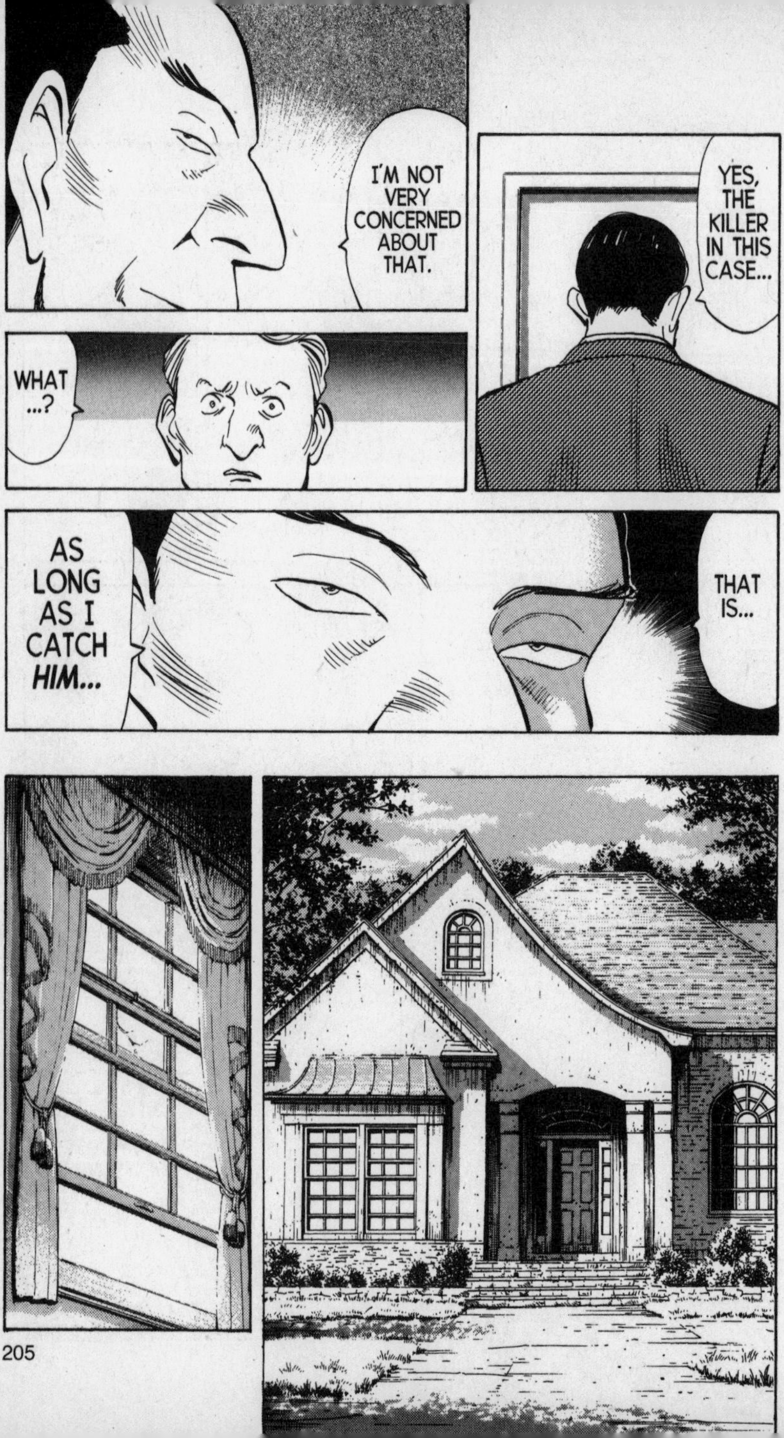
YES, THE KILLER IN THIS CASE...
I'M NOT VERY CONCERNED ABOUT THAT.
WHAT ...?
THAT IS...
AS LONG AS I CATCH *HIM*...

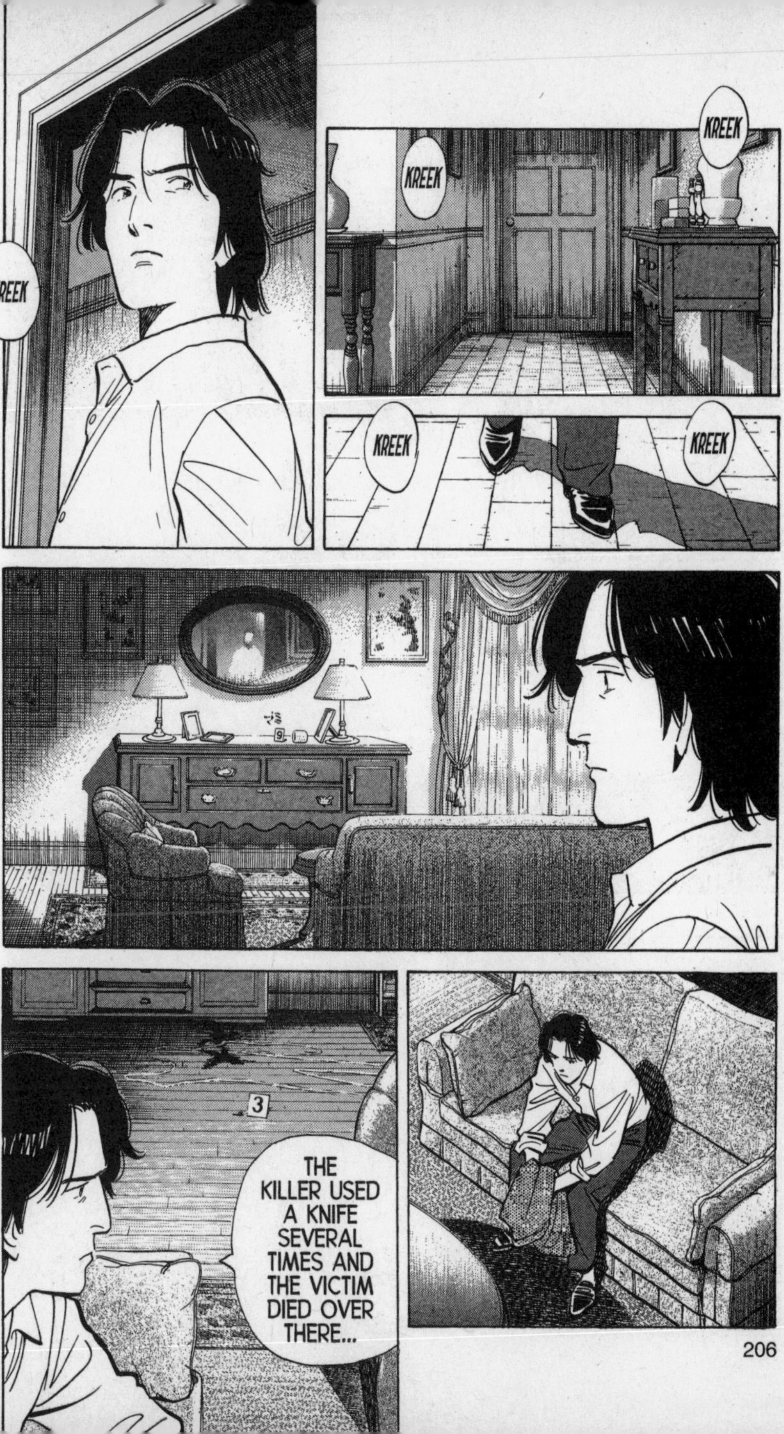
KREEK
KREEK
KREEK
KREEK
KREEK
THE KILLER USED A KNIFE SEVERAL TIMES AND THE VICTIM DIED OVER THERE...

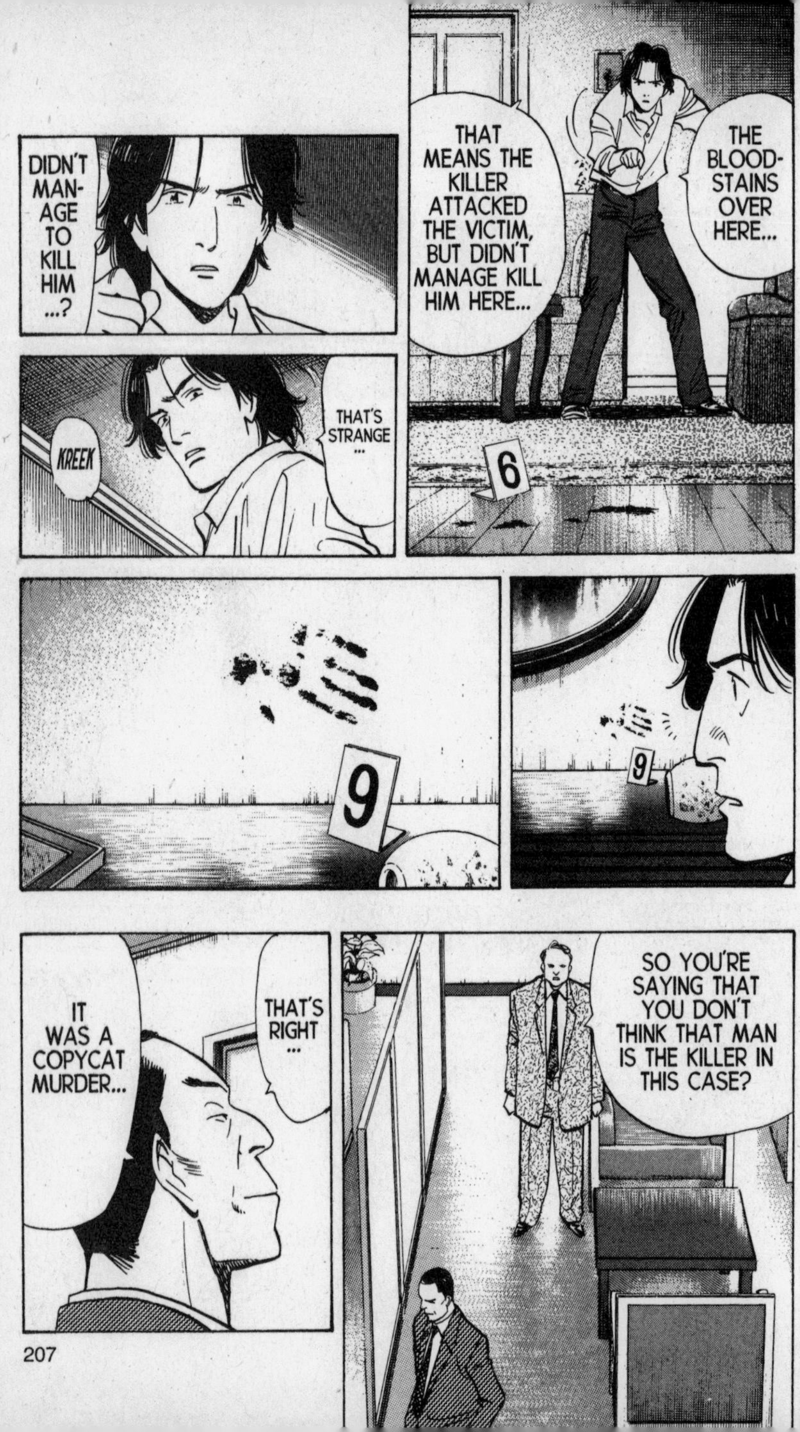
THE BLOOD-STAINS OVER HERE...
THAT MEANS THE KILLER ATTACKED THE VICTIM, BUT DIDN'T MANAGE KILL HIM HERE...
DIDN'T MAN-AGE TO KILL HIM ...?
THAT'S STRANGE ...
KREEK
6
9
9
SO YOU'RE SAYING THAT YOU DON'T THINK THAT MAN IS THE KILLER IN THIS CASE?
THAT'S RIGHT ...
IT WAS A COPYCAT MURDER...

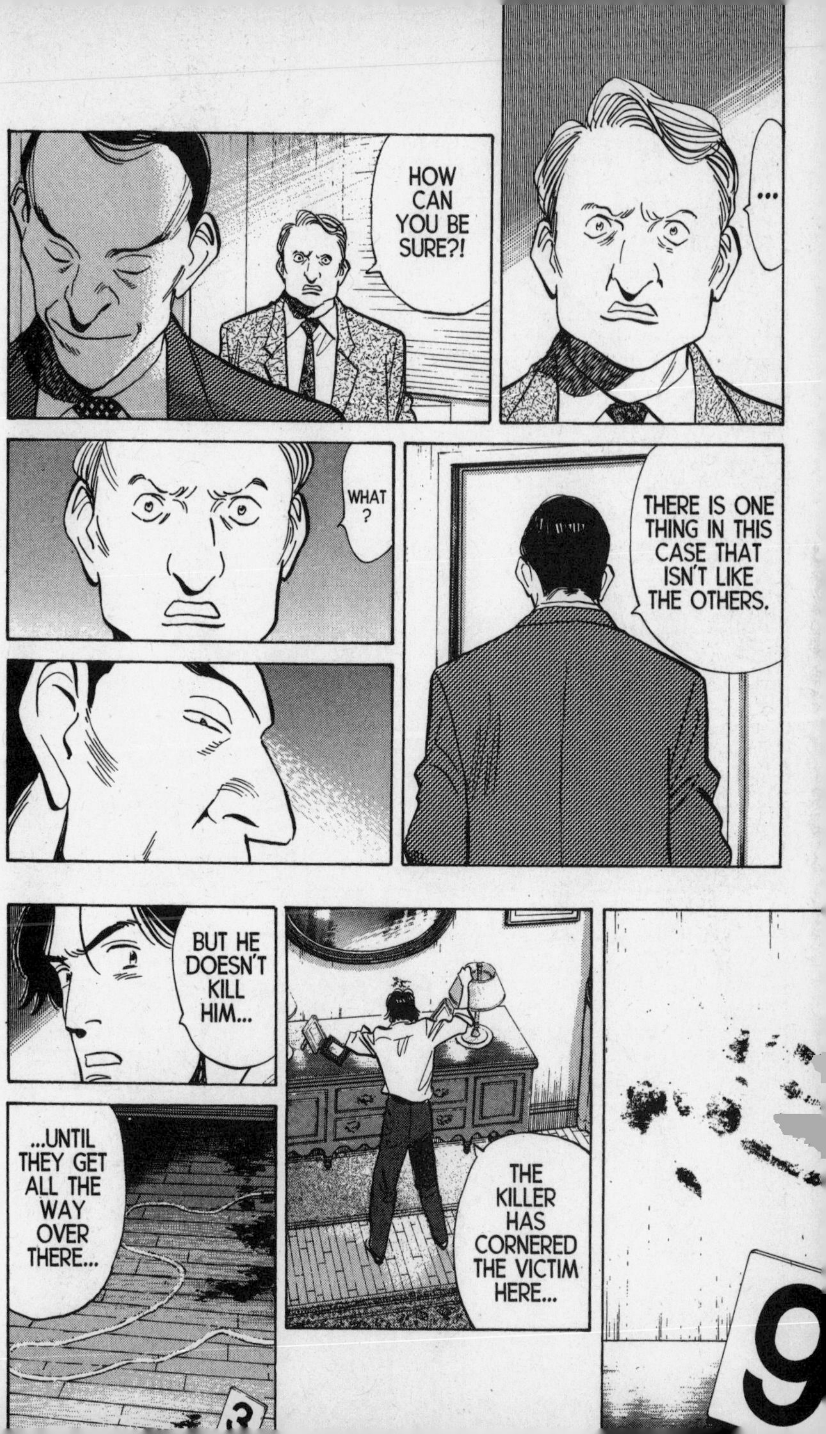
...
HOW CAN YOU BE SURE?!
THERE IS ONE THING IN THIS CASE THAT ISN'T LIKE THE OTHERS.
WHAT?
THE KILLER HAS CORNERED THE VICTIM HERE...
BUT HE DOESN'T KILL HIM...
...UNTIL THEY GET ALL THE WAY OVER THERE...

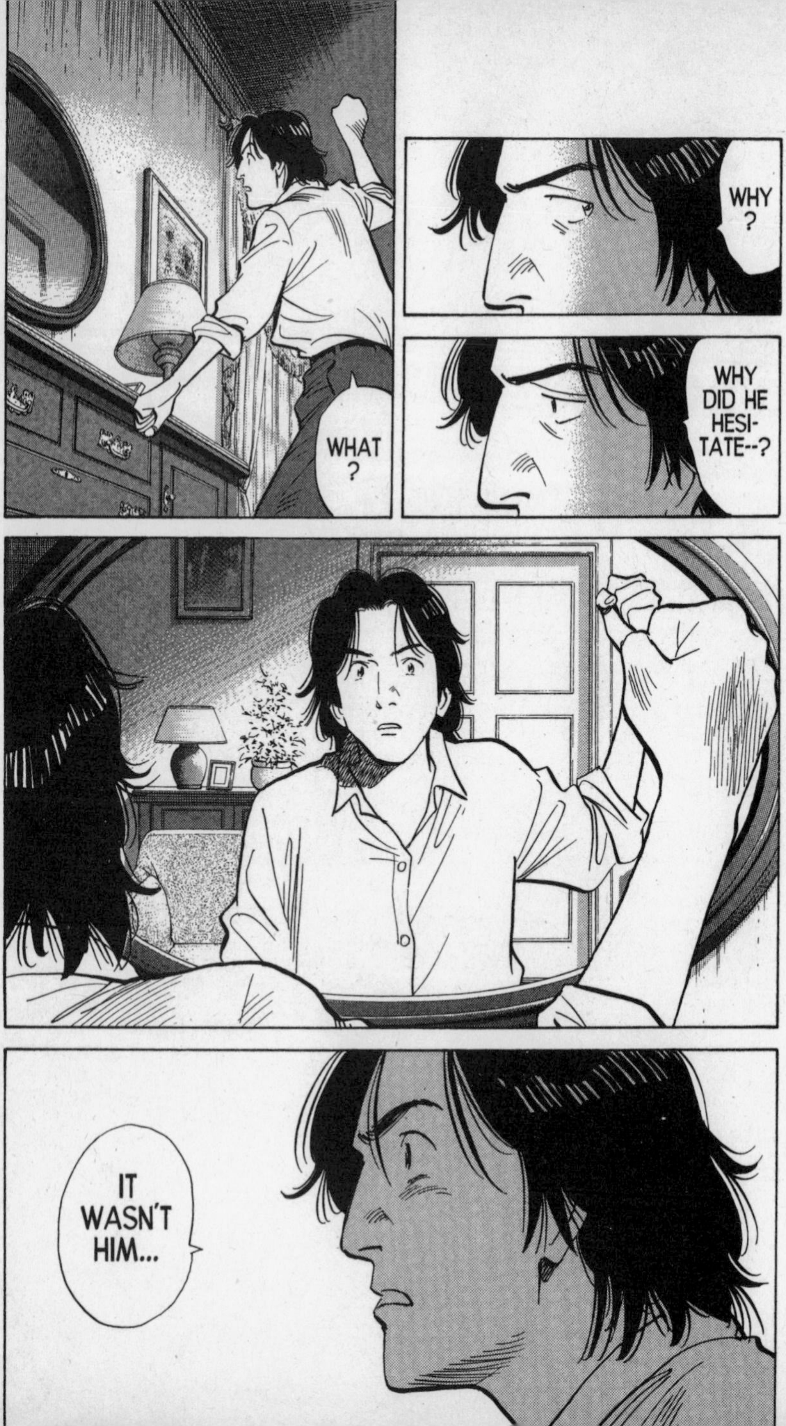
WHY ?
WHY DID HE HESI-TATE--?
WHAT ?
IT WASN'T HIM...

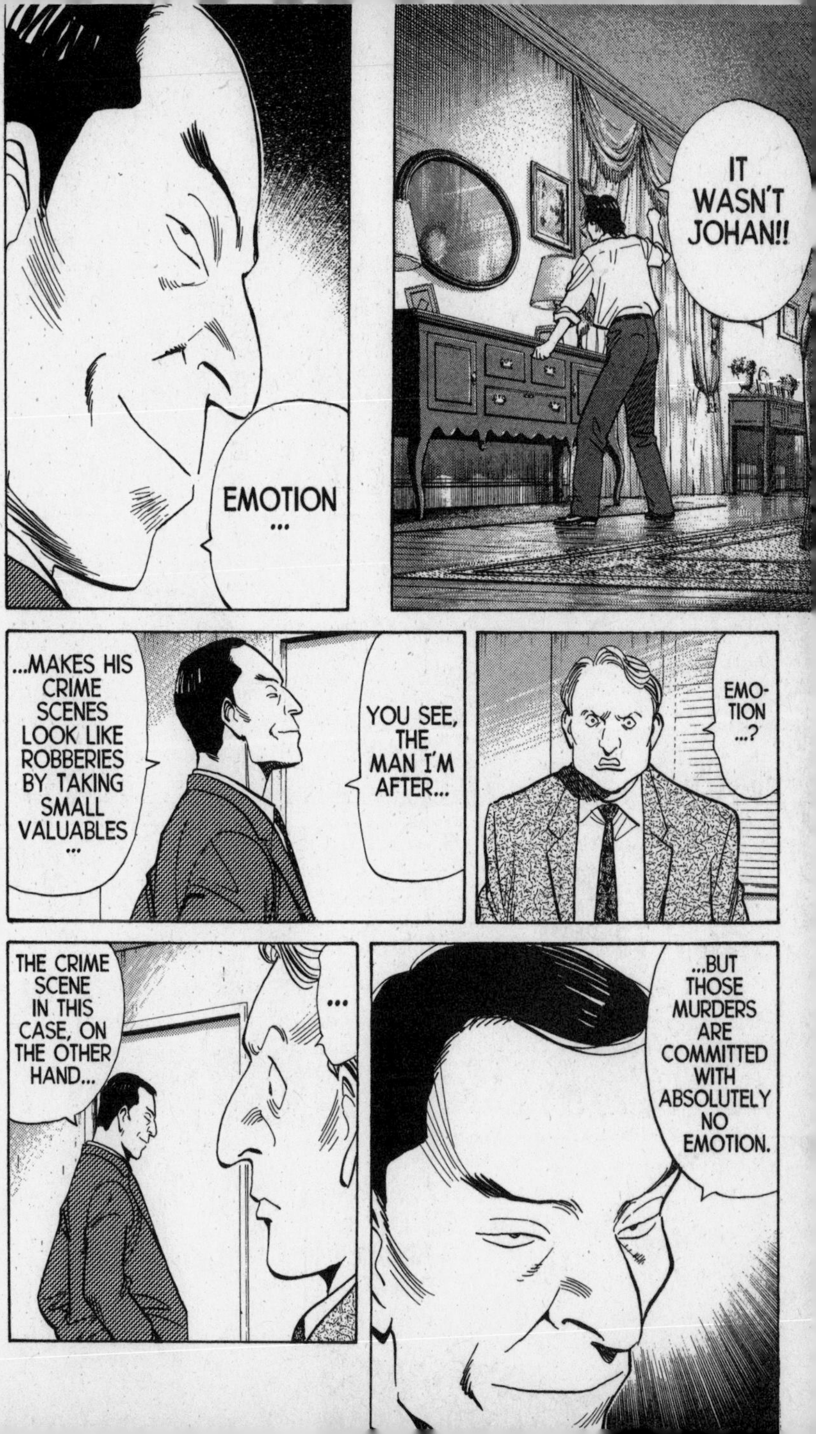
IT WASN'T JOHAN!!
EMOTION ...
EMO-TION ...?
YOU SEE, THE MAN I'M AFTER...
...MAKES HIS CRIME SCENES LOOK LIKE ROBBERIES BY TAKING SMALL VALUABLES ...
...BUT THOSE MURDERS ARE COMMITTED WITH ABSOLUTELY NO EMOTION.
...
THE CRIME SCENE IN THIS CASE, ON THE OTHER HAND...

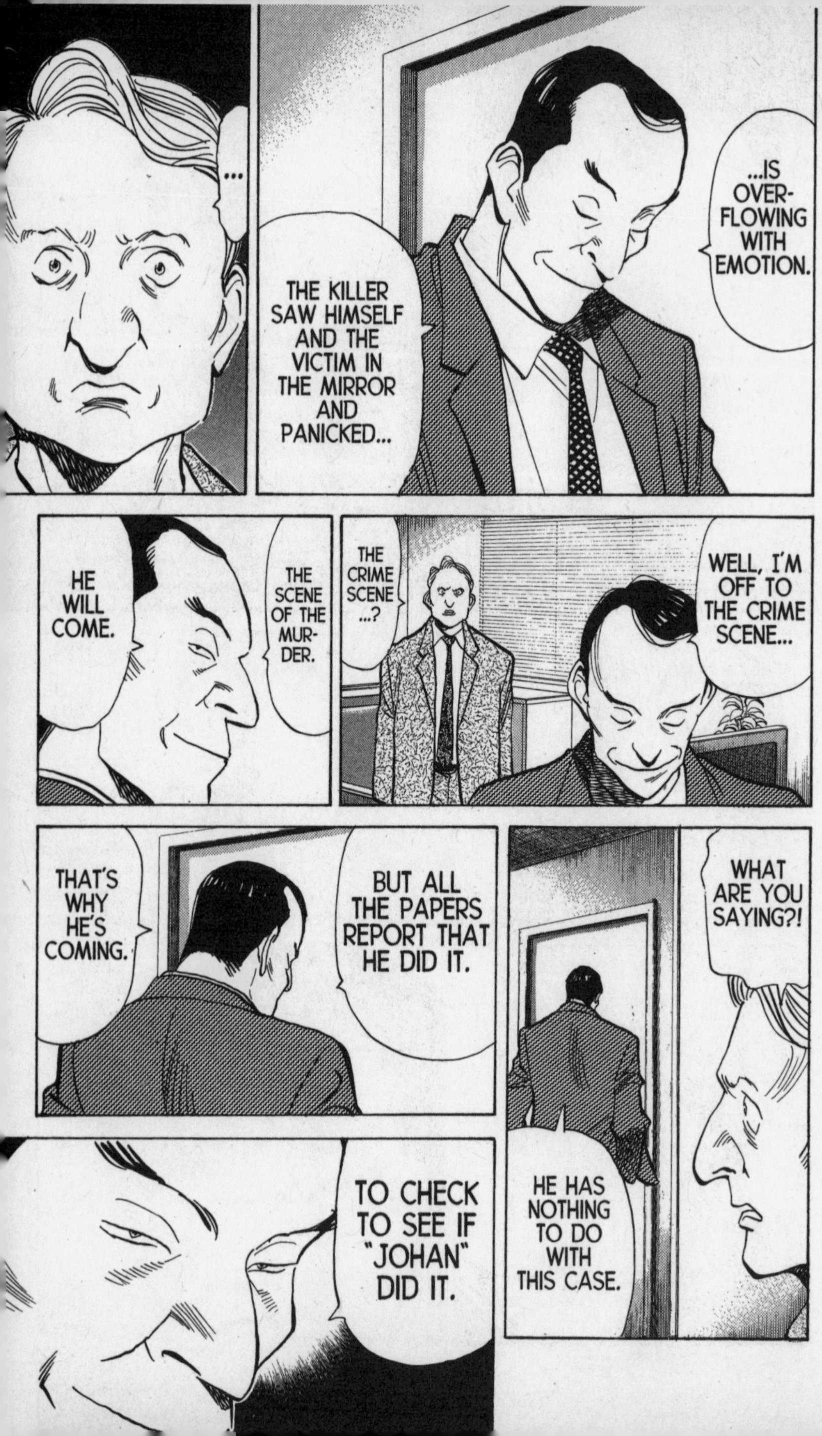
...IS OVER-FLOWING WITH EMOTION.
THE KILLER SAW HIMSELF AND THE VICTIM IN THE MIRROR AND PANICKED...
...
WELL, I'M OFF TO THE CRIME SCENE...
THE CRIME SCENE ...?
THE SCENE OF THE MUR-DER.
HE WILL COME.
WHAT ARE YOU SAYING?!
HE HAS NOTHING TO DO WITH THIS CASE.
BUT ALL THE PAPERS REPORT THAT HE DID IT.
THAT'S WHY HE'S COMING.
TO CHECK TO SEE IF "JOHAN" DID IT.

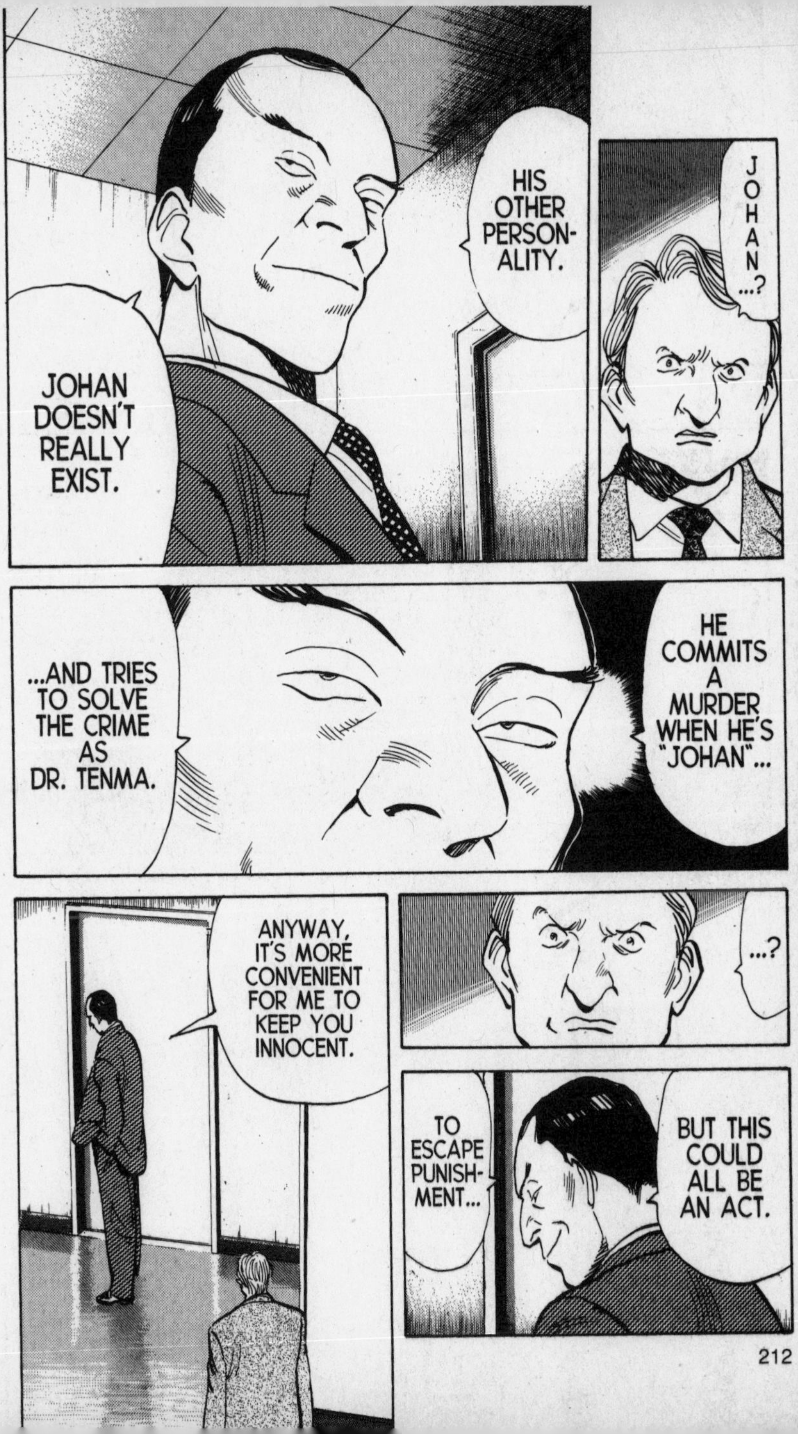
JOHAN ...?
HIS OTHER PERSONALITY.
JOHAN DOESN'T REALLY EXIST.
HE COMMITS A MURDER WHEN HE'S "JOHAN"...
...AND TRIES TO SOLVE THE CRIME AS DR. TENMA.
...?
BUT THIS COULD ALL BE AN ACT.
TO ESCAPE PUNISHMENT...
ANYWAY, IT'S MORE CONVENIENT FOR ME TO KEEP YOU INNOCENT.

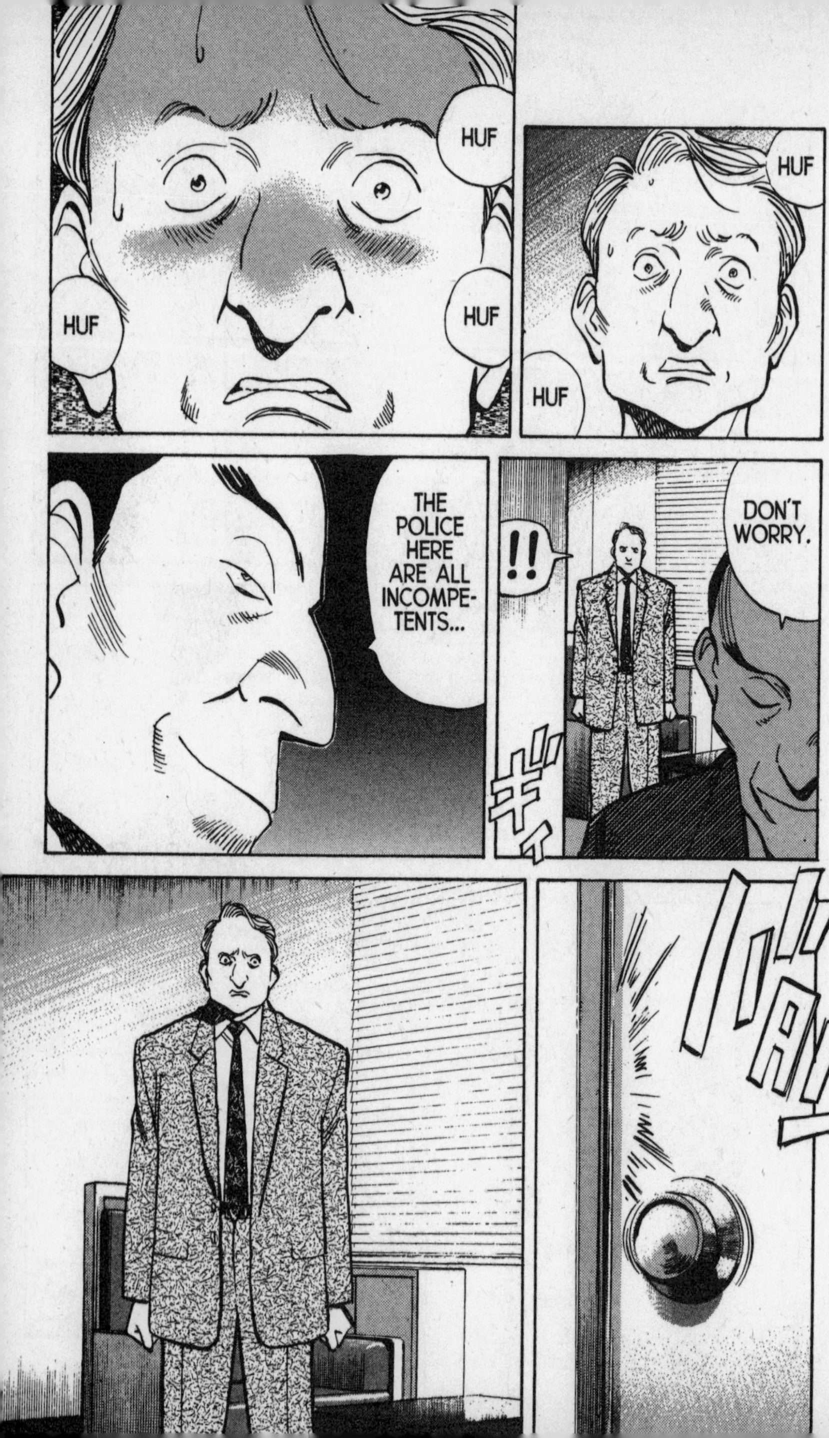
HUF
HUF
HUF
HUF
HUF
DON'T WORRY.
!!
ギィ
THE POLICE HERE ARE ALL INCOMPETENTS...
バン!

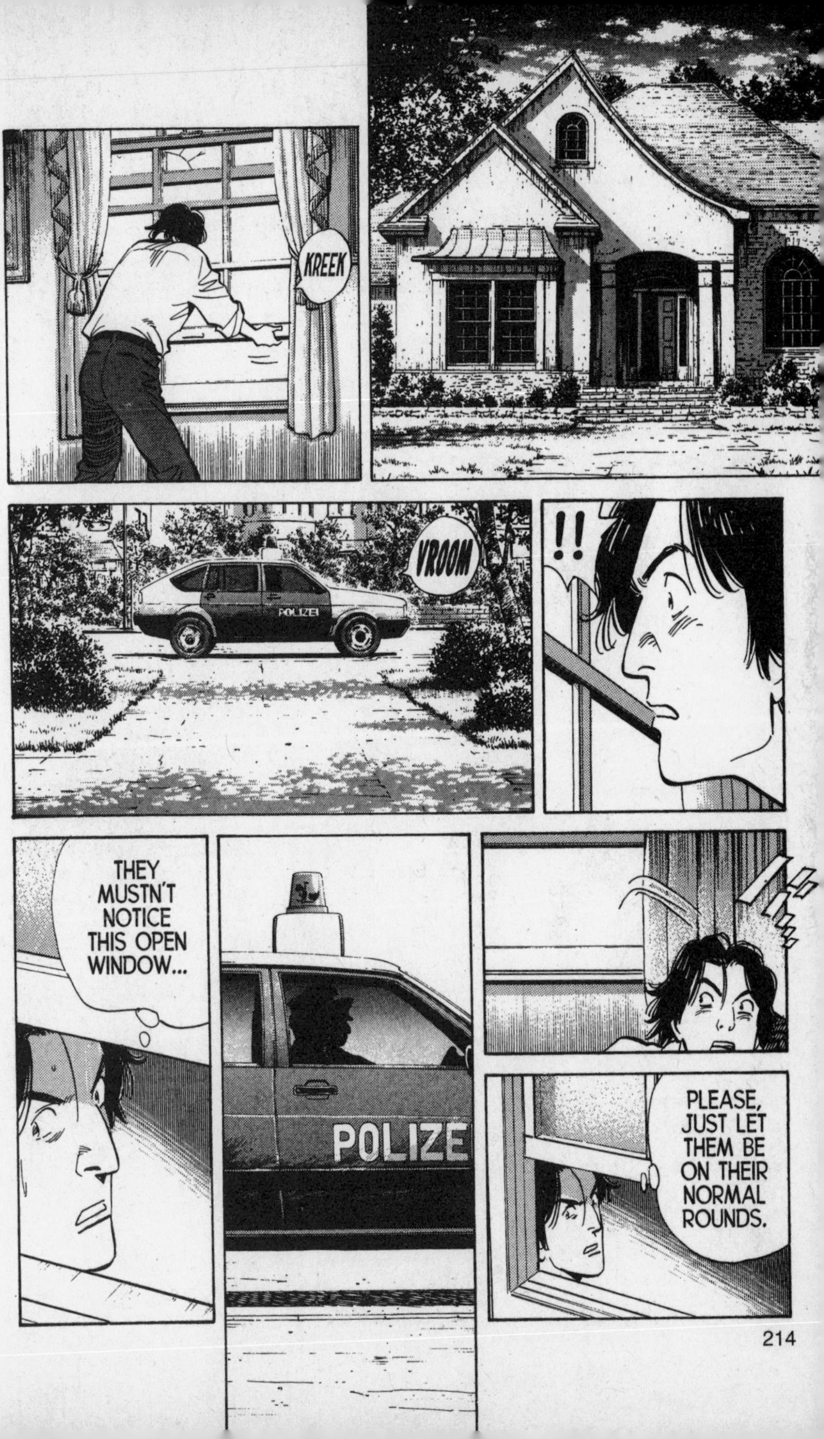
KREEK
!!
VROOM
POLIZEI
PLEASE, JUST LET THEM BE ON THEIR NORMAL ROUNDS.
POLIZE
THEY MUSTN'T NOTICE THIS OPEN WINDOW...

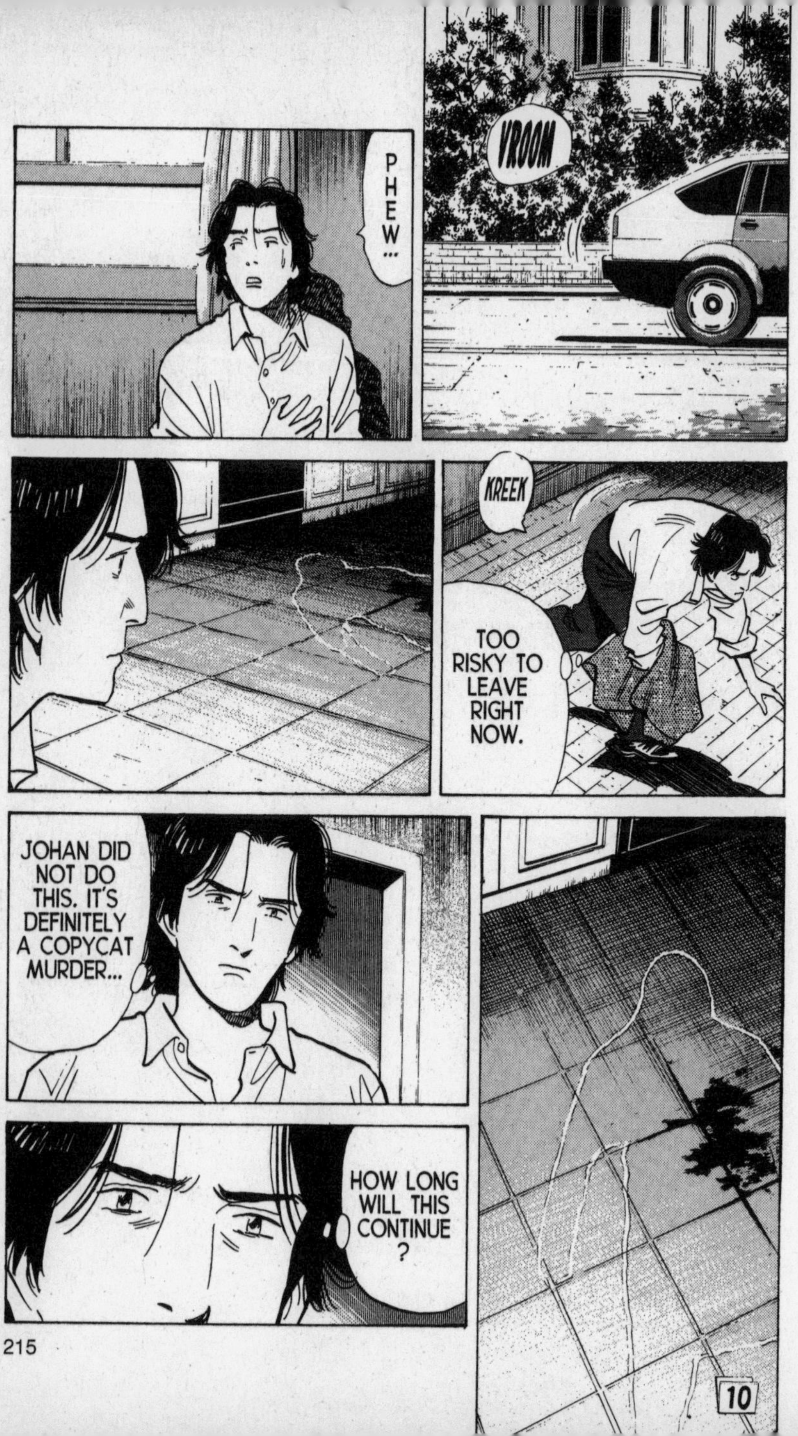
VROOM
PHEW...
KREEK
TOO RISKY TO LEAVE RIGHT NOW.
10
JOHAN DID NOT DO THIS. IT'S DEFINITELY A COPYCAT MURDER...
HOW LONG WILL THIS CONTINUE ?

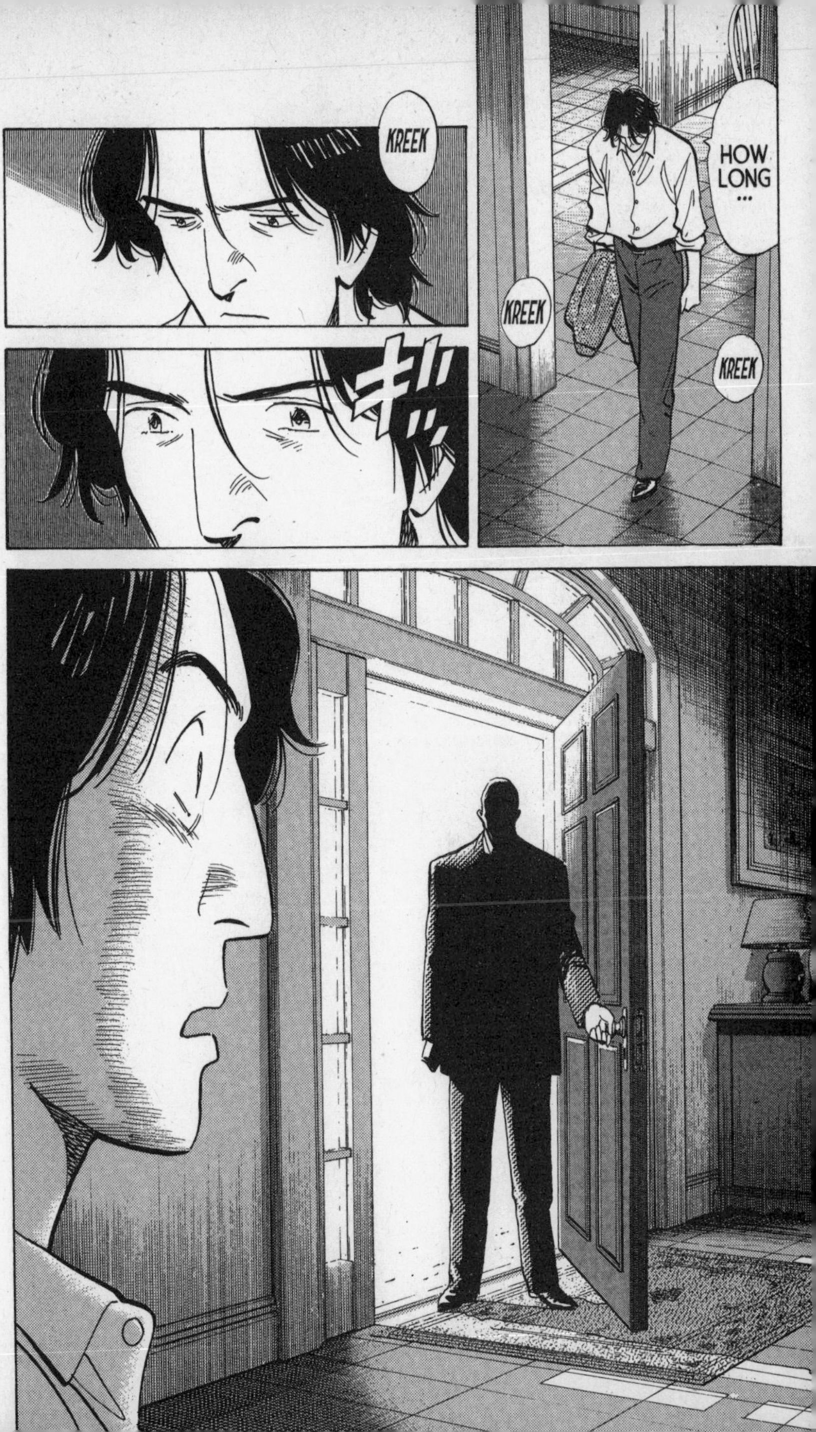
HOW LONG ...
KREEK
KREEK
KREEK
ギッ

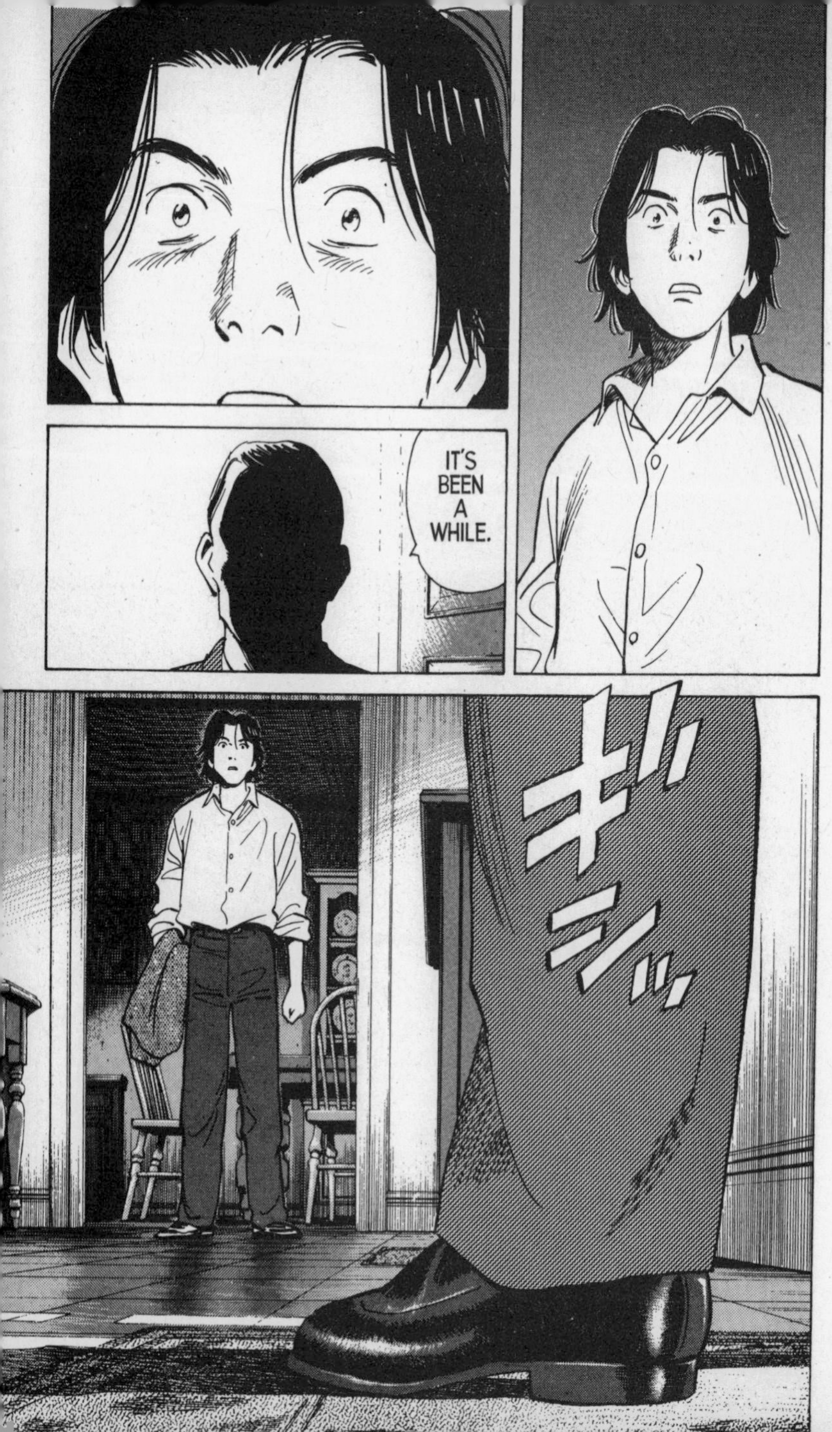
IT'S BEEN A WHILE.
ギシッ

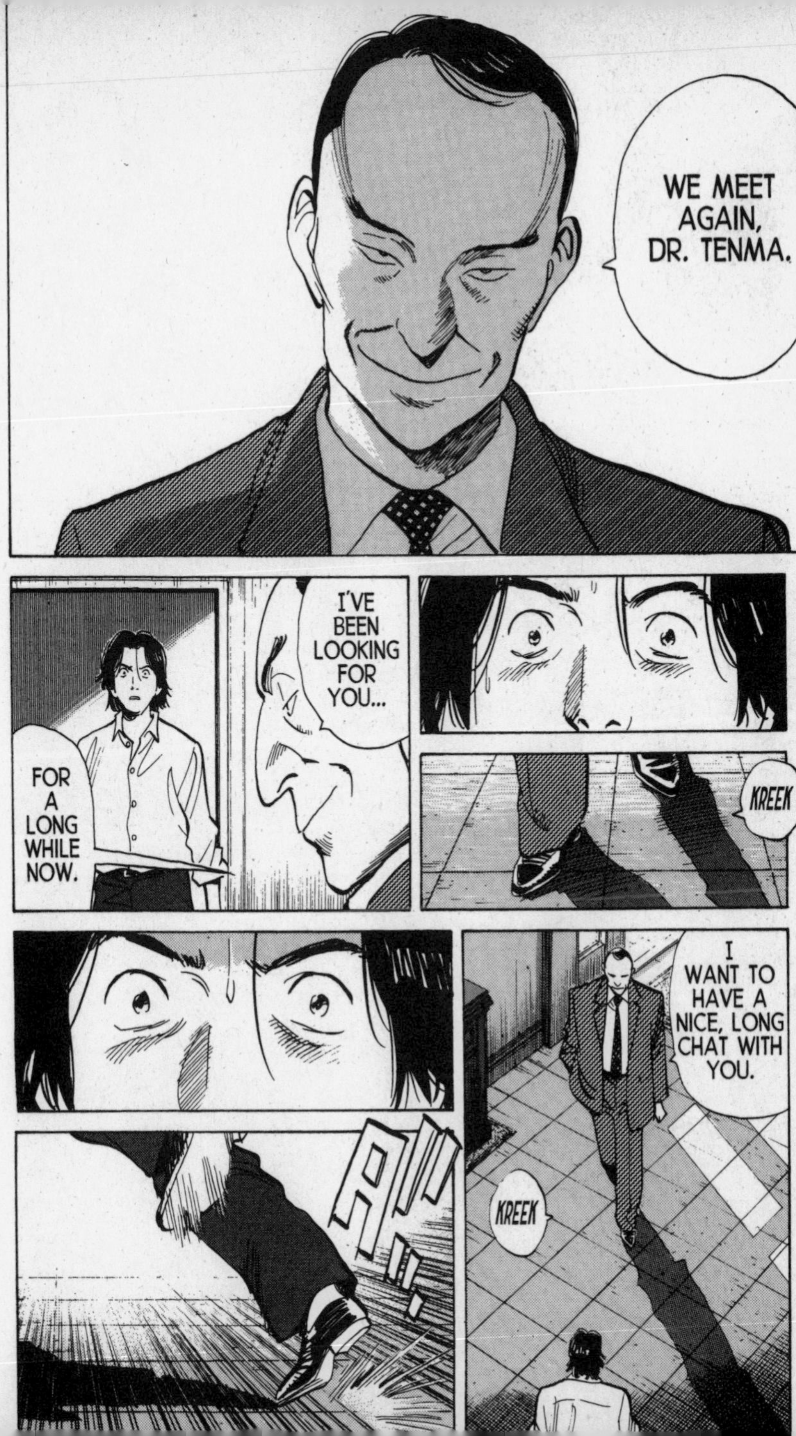
WE MEET AGAIN, DR. TENMA.
KREEK
I'VE BEEN LOOKING FOR YOU...
FOR A LONG WHILE NOW.
I WANT TO HAVE A NICE, LONG CHAT WITH YOU.
KREEK

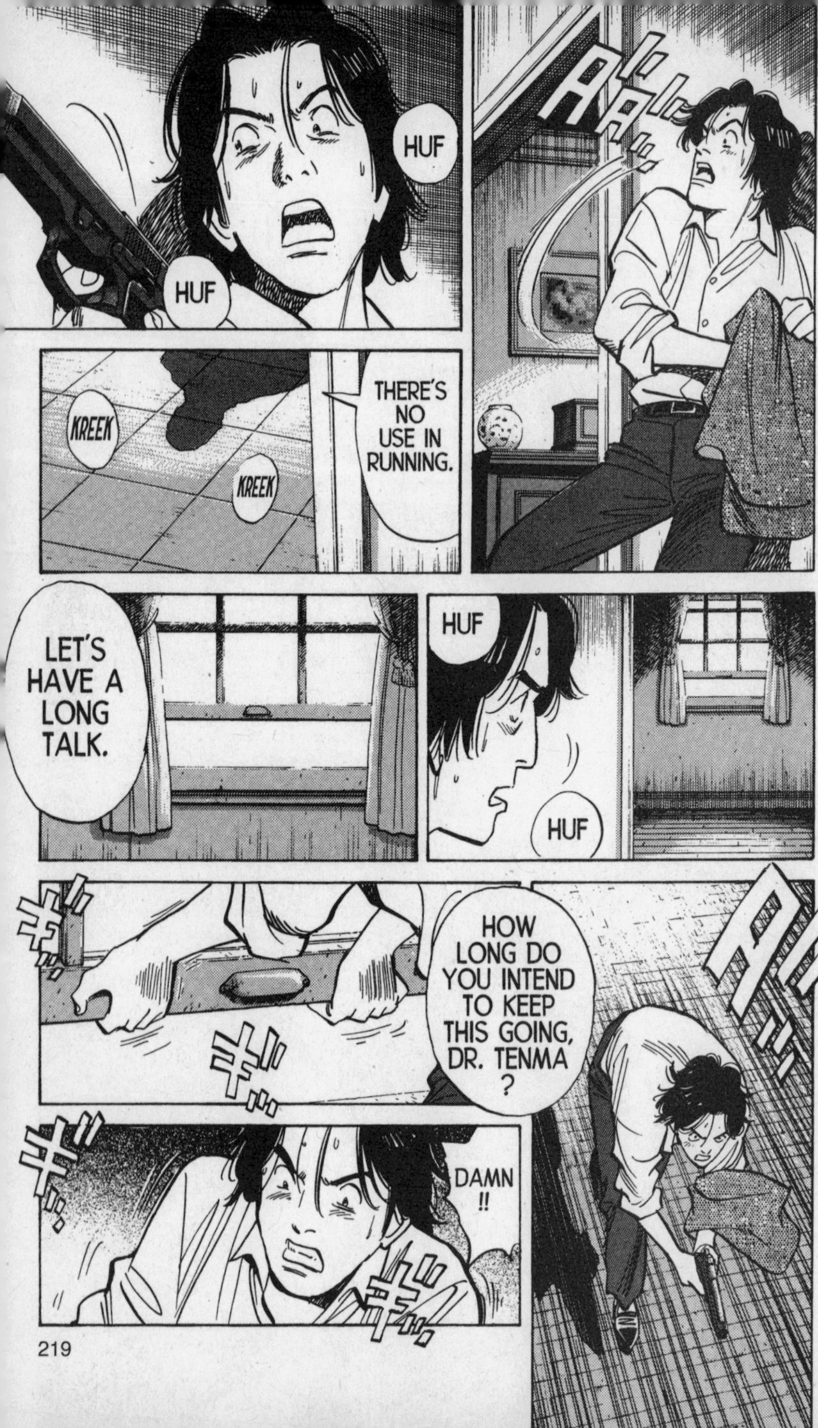
HUF
HUF
THERE'S NO USE IN RUNNING.
KREEK
KREEK
HUF
HUF
LET'S HAVE A LONG TALK.
HOW LONG DO YOU INTEND TO KEEP THIS GOING, DR. TENMA?
DAMN!!

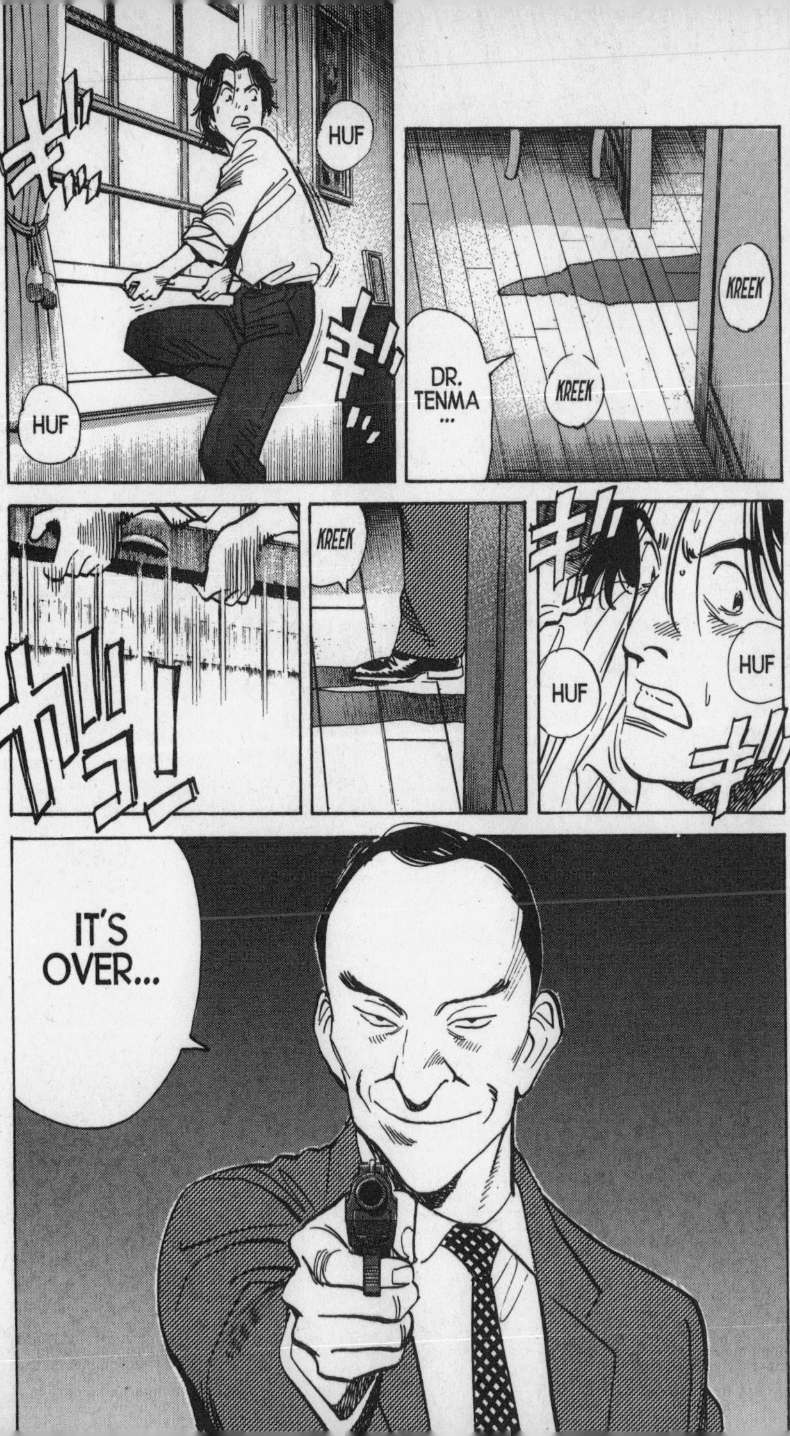
KREEK
DR. TENMA...
KREEK
HUF
HUF
HUF
HUF
KREEK
IT'S OVER...

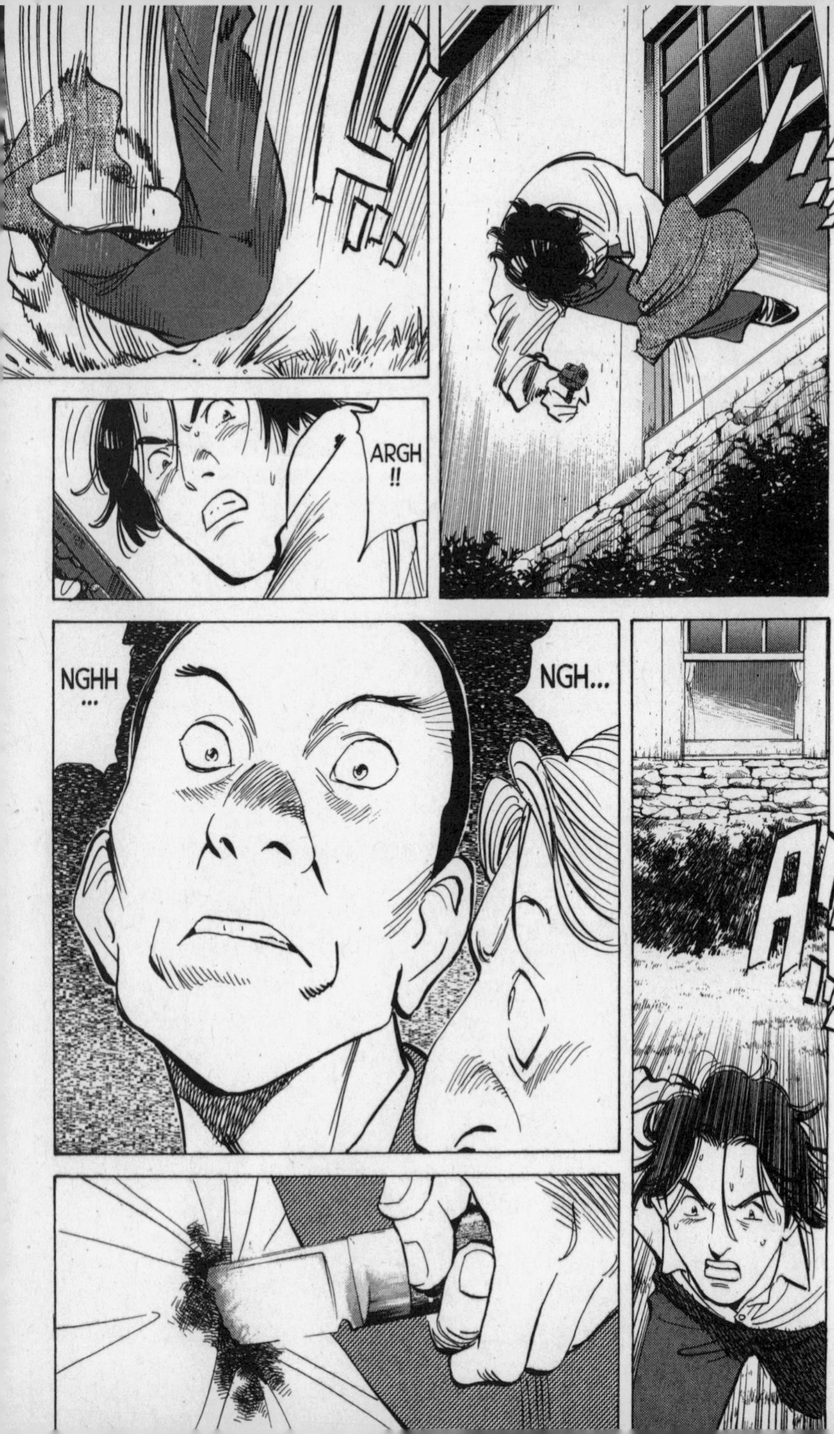
ARGH !!
A
NGH...
NGHH ...

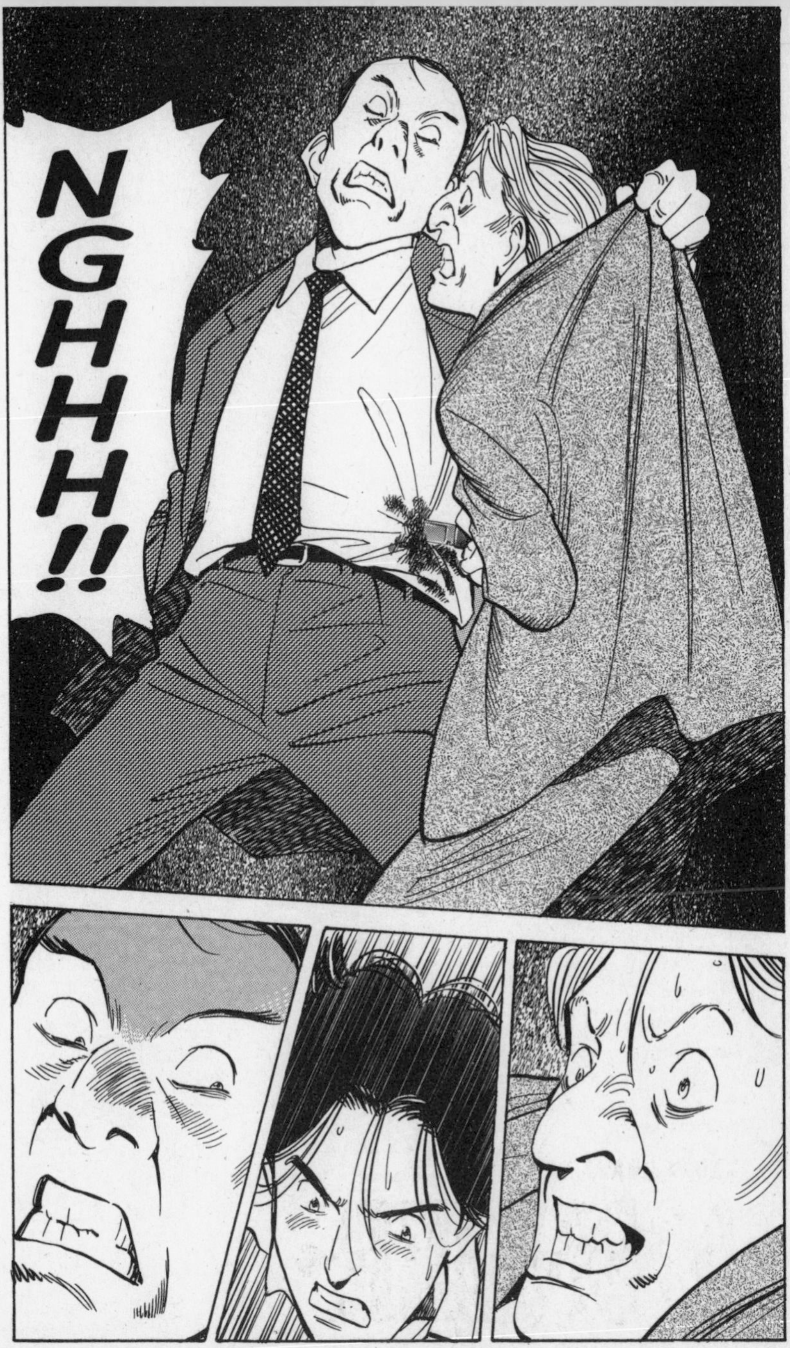
NGHHH!!

NAOKI URASAWA'S

MONSTER

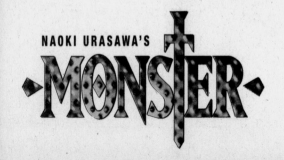

155.4—FX: Ta (dash)

155.5—FX: Ban (slam)

155.6—FX: Dada (dash)

155.7—FX: Da (dash)

157.2—FX: Ba (fwoosh)

159.1—FX: Za (shuf)

159.7—FX: Da (dash)

168.3—FX: Za (shuf)

169.5—FX: Bamu (slam)

169.6—FX: Buon (vroom)

170.1—FX: Oon (vroom)

173.1-2-FX: Dodon (babam)

Chapter 8

175.2—FX: Pasha pasha pasha (camera flashes)

Chapter 9

201.6—FX: Gacha (door opening)

213.3—FX: Gii (creak)

213.5—FX: Batan (slam)

214.5—FX: Ba (swip)

216.3—FX: Gi (creak)

217.4—FX: Gishi (shuf)

218.7—FX: Da (dash)

219.1—FX: Dada (swip)

219.6—FX: Da (dash)

219.7—FX: Gi gi (creak creak)

219.8—FX: Gi gi (creak creak)

220.2—FX: Gi gi (creak creak)

220.3—FX: Gi gi (creak creak)

220.5—FX: Gakon (rattle)

221.1—FX: Ba (fwoosh)

221.2—FX: Don (thud)

221.1—FX: Da (dash)

glossary

Chapter 1

26.1—FX: Ga (grab)

26.2—FX: Gi (squeeze)

26.5—FX: Ba (swoop)

Chapter 2

31.4—FX: Gi (creak)

36.2—FX: Gi (creak)

51.7—FX: Gishi Gishi (tp tp)

52.1—FX: Da (dash)

52.2—FX: Ba (fwap)

52.3—FX: Gata (clatter)

52.5—FX: Gata (clatter)

Chapter 3

61.2—FX: Ba (swish)

61.3—FX: wai wai wai (crowd noise)

69.3—FX: Wai wai wai (crowd noise)

69.6—FX: Zawa zawa (crowd noise)

69.6—FX: Wai wai (crowd noise)

71.3—FX: Wai wai (crowd noise)

72.1—FX: Wai wai (crowd noise)

77.2—FX: Burororo (bus engine)

77.3—FX: Burororo (bus engine)

78.1—FX: Buooo (vroom)

78.2—FX: oooo (vroom continued from previous panel)

Chapter 4

80.3—FX: kiki (brakes squeal)

81.1—FX: Buoon (vroom)

84.6—FX: Buoon (vroom)

84.8—FX: Gata goto (rattle)

88.7—FX: Basa (fwap)

92.2—FX: Bamu (slam)

93.6—FX: Bamu (slam)

93.7—FX: Buon (vroom)

93.8—FX: oon (vroom)

98.5—FX: Buon (vroom)

100.4—FX: Bamu (slam)

Chapter 5

118.1—FX: Gan (slam)

Chapter 6

130.1—FX: Ta (dash)

130.9—FX: Ka (footstep)

132.2—FX: Ka ka ka (footsteps)

132.4—FX: Ta (footstep)

133.3—FX: Gyagya (screech)

133.4—FX: Oon (vroom)

134.1—FX: Ba (vwoosh)

137.2—FX: Zaaan (roar of waves)

139.4—FX: Don (crash of wave)

140.8—FX: Basha basha (splash splash)

144.4—FX: Zaan (crash of waves)

146.5—FX: Zaan (crash of waves)

Chapter 7

153.5—FX: Ba (fwp)

153.6—FX: Ta (dash)

154.8—FX: Za (swp)

about the author

Naoki Urasawa, born in Tokyo in 1960, is Japan's manga master of the suspense thriller. Critically acclaimed and immensely popular, his award-winning works include *20th Century Boys*, *Master Keaton*, *Pineapple Army*, and *Yawara*.

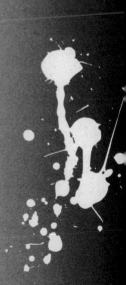

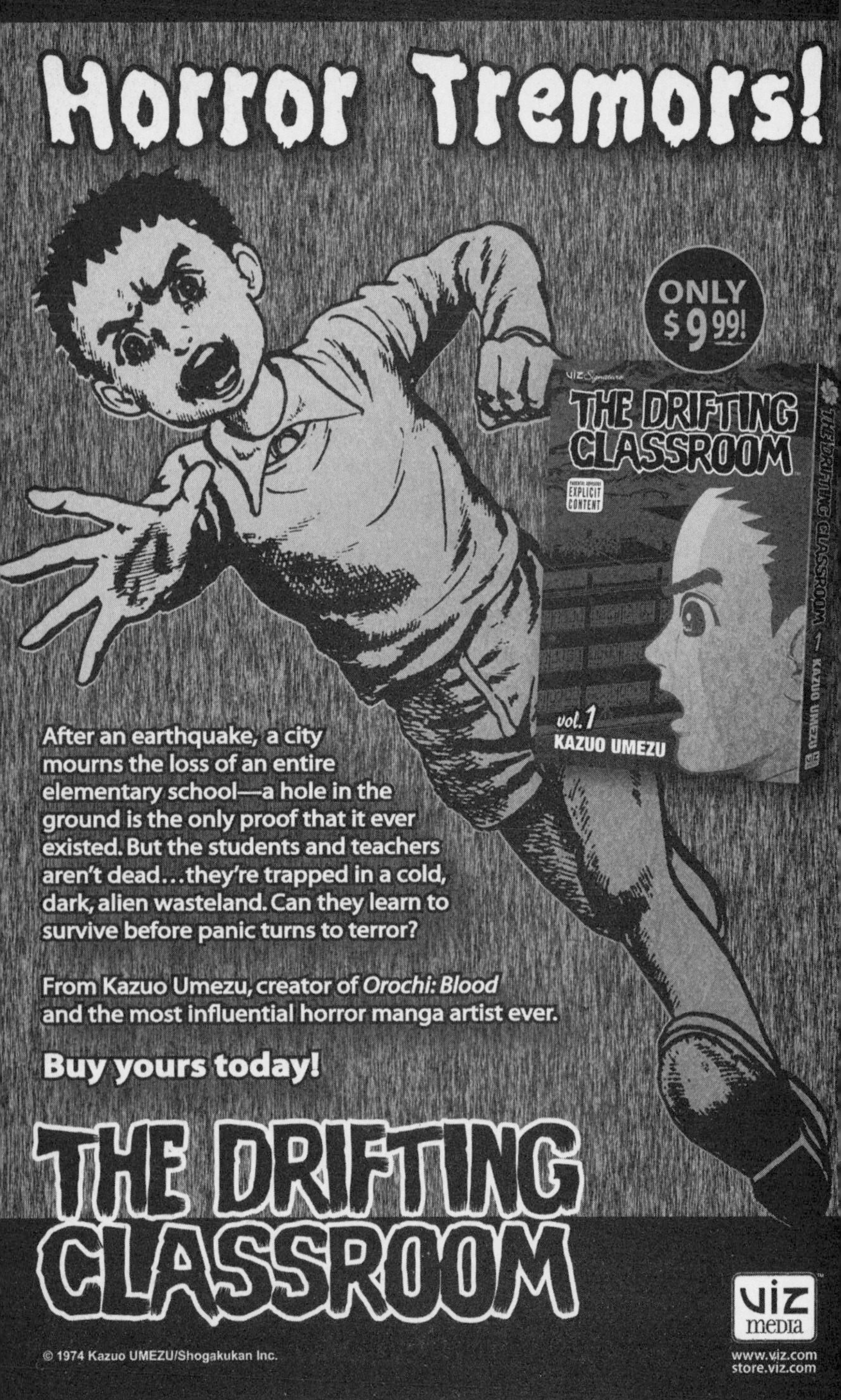

Horror Tremors!
ONLY $9.99!
VIZ Signature
THE DRIFTING CLASSROOM
PARENTAL ADVISORY EXPLICIT CONTENT
vol. 1
KAZUO UMEZU
THE DRIFTING CLASSROOM 1 KAZUO UMEZU
After an earthquake, a city mourns the loss of an entire elementary school—a hole in the ground is the only proof that it ever existed. But the students and teachers aren't dead…they're trapped in a cold, dark, alien wasteland. Can they learn to survive before panic turns to terror?
From Kazuo Umezu, creator of *Orochi: Blood* and the most influential horror manga artist ever.
Buy yours today!
THE DRIFTING CLASSROOM
viz media
© 1974 Kazuo UMEZU/Shogakukan Inc.
www.viz.com
store.viz.com

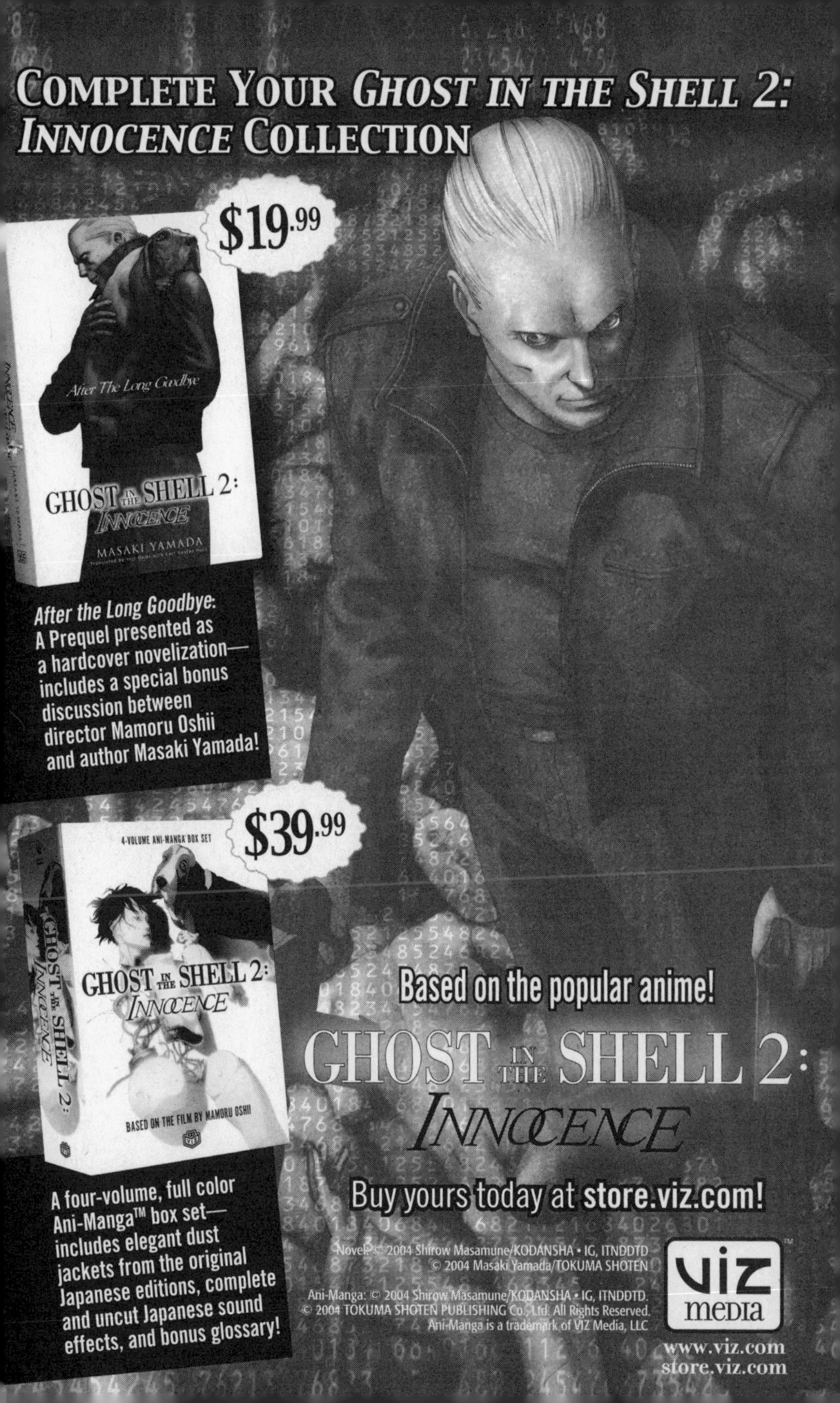
COMPLETE YOUR GHOST IN THE SHELL 2: INNOCENCE COLLECTION
$19.99
After The Long Goodbye
GHOST IN THE SHELL 2: INNOCENCE
MASAKI YAMADA
After the Long Goodbye: A Prequel presented as a hardcover novelization—includes a special bonus discussion between director Mamoru Oshii and author Masaki Yamada!
$39.99
4-VOLUME ANI-MANGA BOX SET
GHOST IN THE SHELL 2: INNOCENCE
BASED ON THE FILM BY MAMORU OSHII
A four-volume, full color Ani-Manga™ box set—includes elegant dust jackets from the original Japanese editions, complete and uncut Japanese sound effects, and bonus glossary!
Based on the popular anime!
GHOST IN THE SHELL 2: INNOCENCE
Buy yours today at store.viz.com!
Novel: © 2004 Shirow Masamune/KODANSHA • IG, ITNDDTD
© 2004 Masaki Yamada/TOKUMA SHOTEN
Ani-Manga: © 2004 Shirow Masamune/KODANSHA • IG, ITNDDTD.
© 2004 TOKUMA SHOTEN PUBLISHING Co., Ltd. All Rights Reserved.
Ani-Manga is a trademark of VIZ Media, LLC
viz media
www.viz.com
store.viz.com

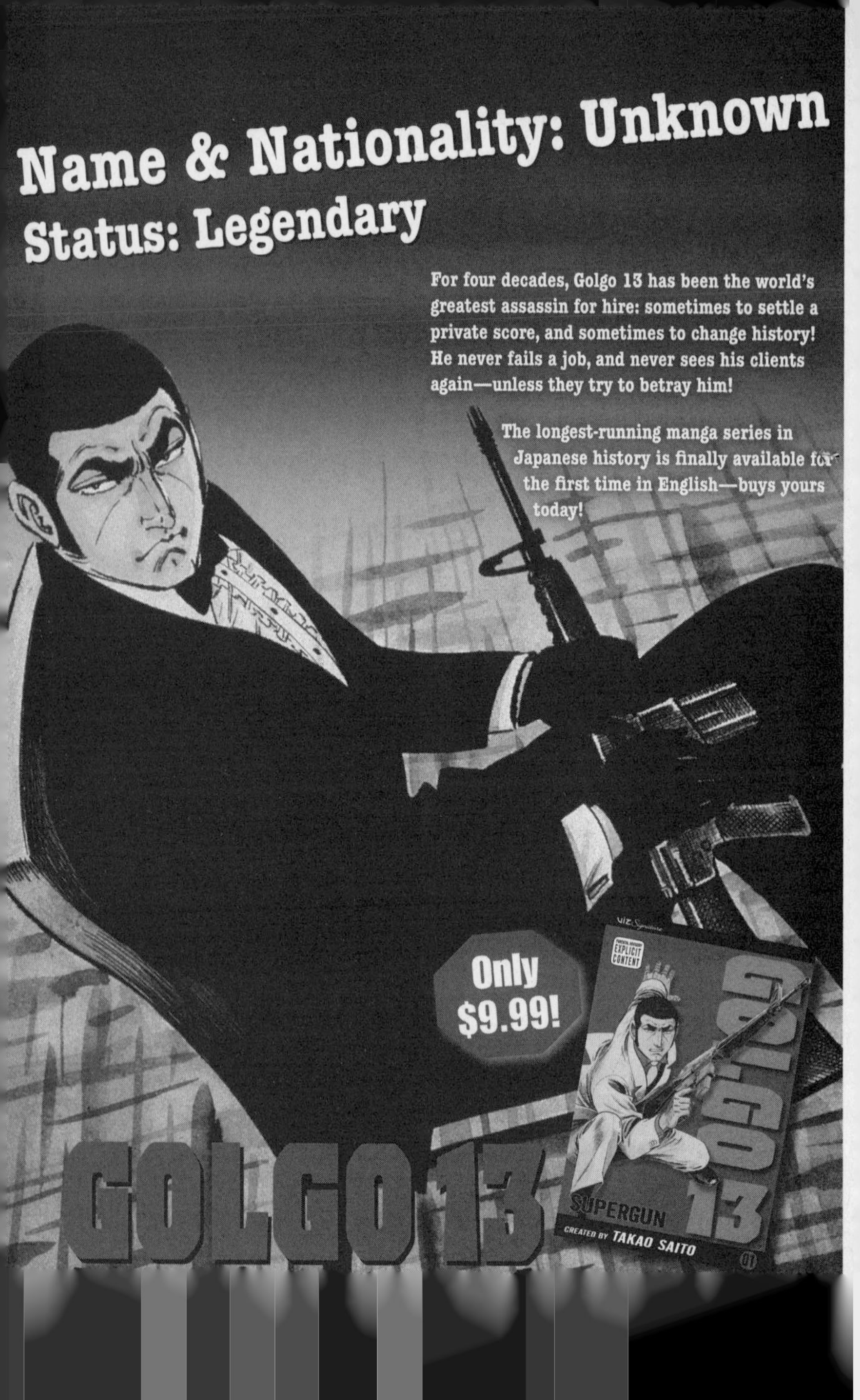
Name & Nationality: Unknown
Status: Legendary
For four decades, Golgo 13 has been the world's greatest assassin for hire: sometimes to settle a private score, and sometimes to change history! He never fails a job, and never sees his clients again—unless they try to betray him!
The longest-running manga series in Japanese history is finally available for the first time in English—buys yours today!
Only $9.99!
EXPLICIT CONTENT
GOLGO 13
SUPERGUN
CREATED BY TAKAO SAITO
01
GOLGO 13

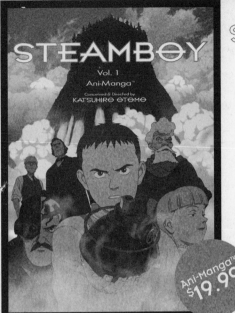
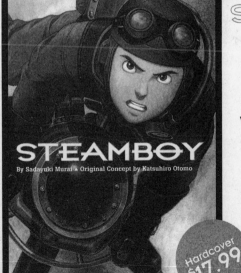

The Evolution of Science...
The Downfall of Man?

Based on the hit movie from Katsuhiro Otomo

STEAMBOY

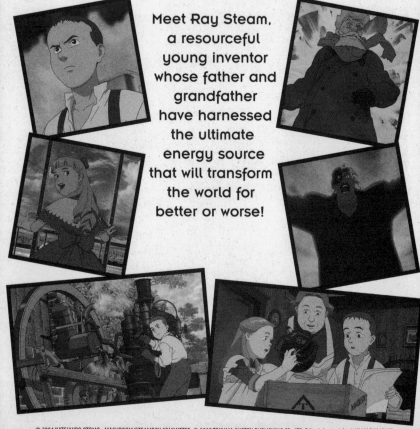

Meet Ray Steam, a resourceful young inventor whose father and grandfather have harnessed the ultimate energy source that will transform the world for better or worse!

LOVE MANGA?
LET US KNOW WHAT YOU THINK!

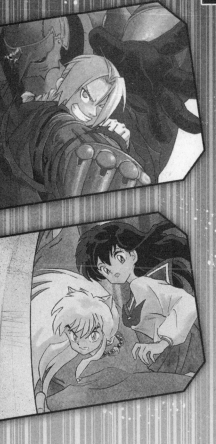

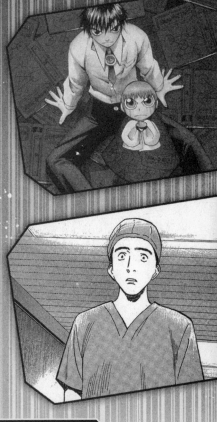

HELP US MAKE THE MANGA
YOU LOVE BETTER!

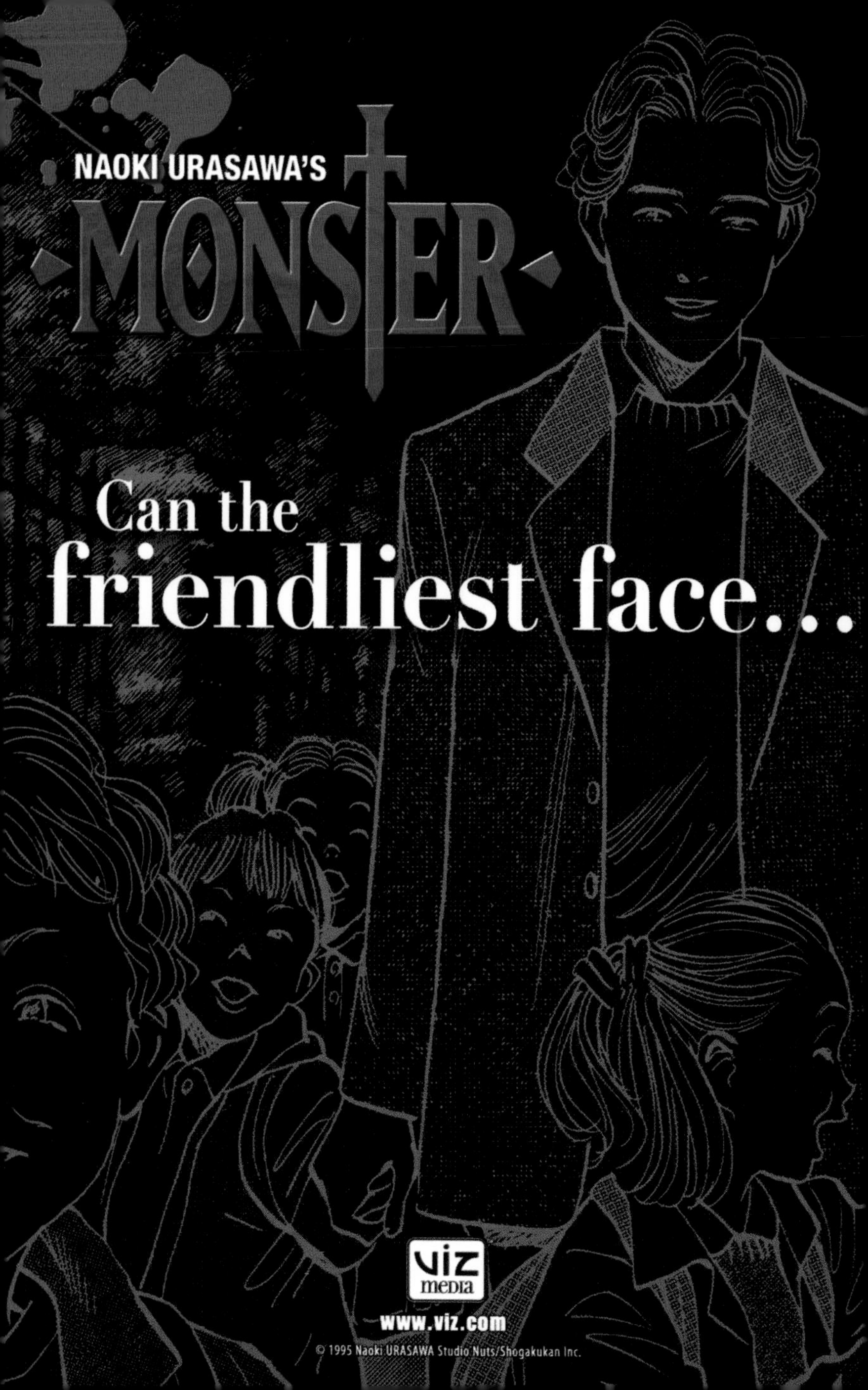
NAOKI URASAWA'S
MONSTER
Can the
friendliest face...
VIZ media
www.viz.com
© 1995 Naoki URASAWA Studio Nuts/Shogakukan Inc.

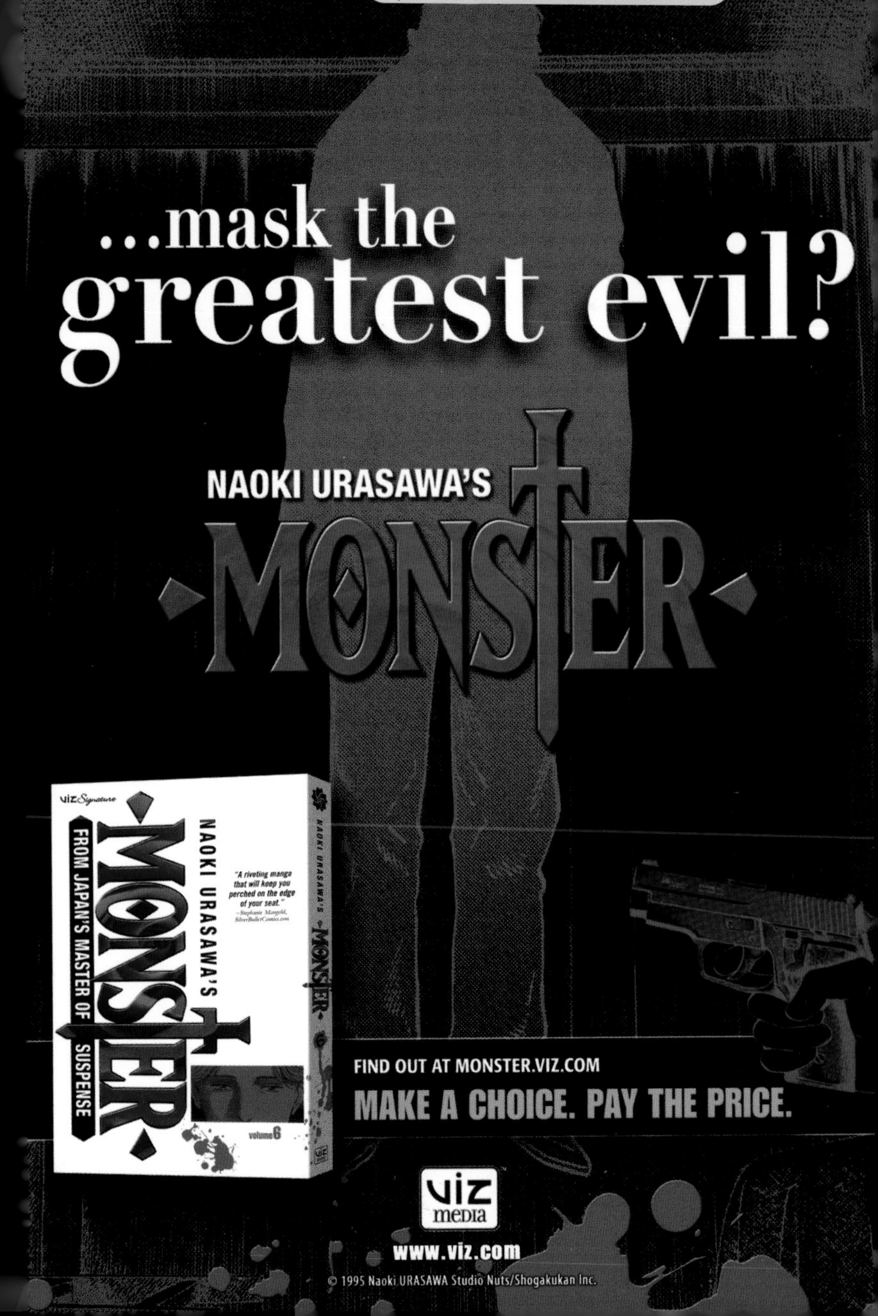
...mask the
greatest evil?
NAOKI URASAWA'S
MONSTER
viz Signature
NAOKI URASAWA'S
MONSTER
FROM JAPAN'S MASTER OF SUSPENSE
"A riveting manga that will keep you perched on the edge of your seat."
—Stephanie Mangold, SilverBulletComics.com
volume 6
FIND OUT AT MONSTER.VIZ.COM
MAKE A CHOICE. PAY THE PRICE.
viz media
www.viz.com
© 1995 Naoki URASAWA Studio Nuts/Shogakukan Inc.